RELIGION, FOOD, AND EATING IN NORTH AMERICA

D1270569

ARTS AND TRADITIONS OF THE TABLE
PERSPECTIVES ON CULINARY HISTORY

ARTS AND TRADITIONS OF THE TABLE
PERSPECTIVES ON CULINARY HISTORY

ALBERT SONNENFELD, SERIES EDITOR

For the list of titles in this series, see pages 337–338.

RELIGION, FOOD, AND EATING IN NORTH AMERICA

EDITED BY BENJAMIN E. ZELLER,
MARIE W. DALLAM, REID L. NEILSON,
AND NORA L. RUBEL

COLUMBIA UNIVERSITY PRESS
NEW YORK

Columbia University Press
Publishers Since 1893
New York   Chichester, West Sussex
cup.columbia.edu

Library of Congress Cataloging-in-Publication Data

Religion, food, and eating in North America / edited by Benjamin E. Zeller, Marie W. Dallam, Reid L. Neilson, and Nora L. Rubel.
    pages cm. — (Arts and traditions of the table: perspectives on culinary history)
    Papers presented over four years at the Religion, Food, and Eating Seminar at the American Academy of Religion.
    Includes bibliographical references and index.
    ISBN 978-0-231-16030-8 (cloth : alk. paper) — ISBN 978-0-231-16031-5 (pbk. : alk. paper) — ISBN 978-0-231-53731-5 (e-book)
    1. Food—Religious aspects—Congresses.   2. Food—North America—Congresses.   3. Food—Caribbean Area—Congresses.   4. Dinners and dining—Religious aspects—Congresses.   5. Dinners and dining—North America—Congresses.   6. Dinners and dining—Caribbean Area—Congresses.   7. Food habits—North America—Congresses.   8. Food habits—Caribbean Area—Congresses.   I. Zeller, Benjamin E., editor of compilation.   II. American Academy of Religion.

BL65.F65R45 2014
203—dc23

2013027854

Columbia University Press books are printed on permanent and durable acid-free paper.
This book is printed on paper with recycled content.
Printed in the United States of America
c 10 9 8 7 6 5 4 3 2 1
p 10 9 8 7 6 5 4 3 2 1

References to websites (URLs) were accurate at the time of writing. Neither the author nor Columbia University Press is responsible for URLs that may have expired or changed since the manuscript was prepared.

For our mentors

CONTENTS

PART 4: ACTIVIST FOODWAYS

FOREWORD

MARTHA L. FINCH

"FOOD FOR THE body is not enough. There must be food for the soul." So wrote the social activist Dorothy Day in 1940 to illustrate the aims and purposes of the Catholic Worker movement. In her formulation of the ideal society, Day explicitly correlated soul with body and heaven with earth, affirming that both spiritual and material human needs must be met in order to achieve a world in which justice prevailed. It's a given, of course, that food nourishes and sustains human existence; yet it is far more than simply a biological requirement. Indeed, *because* it is necessary for basic human survival, food is at the heart of religious life: not only does it provide physical nourishment and sustenance, but those who eat also invest what is (and is not) eaten with deep and compelling values. That is, food serves as both material element and sacred symbol; to refocus Day's formulation, food nourishes both body and soul. As this collection of essays reveals, sacred beliefs about food, on the one hand, and what people actually do with food—growing, harvesting, marketing, purchasing, preparing, offering, and consuming it—on the other, cannot be severed. Attempting to consider one without the other tells less than half the story; the whole is greater than the sum of its parts. Sacred meanings and values, however an individual or group defines "sacred," and everyday practices and experiences dynamically and continuously generate, reproduce, resist, and alter each other. This, *Religion, Food, and Eating in North America* lucidly and creatively demonstrates, is what makes "religious" food religious.

It doesn't take a great deal of reflection to recognize that food plays a critical role in all religious traditions and, within those traditions, in many doctrines and practices, both formal and informal. Throughout history and across religious communities in North America, individuals and groups have consumed or avoided particular foods and drinks to connect ritually with the divine, promote mystical experience, obey ethical principles, create and sustain distinct religious communities, achieve physical and spiritual health, celebrate religio-ethnic identities and traditions, reinforce or undermine religiously mandated gender roles, or improve society. The essays that follow investigate and disclose exactly what is religious about foodways among a variety of American groups, making this volume the first explicit effort to employ but then move beyond the customary themes in food studies analysis, such as identity, gender, ethnicity, boundaries, community, and commensality, to turn a clear eye on religion as another of these significant categories.

But the essays' authors see religion and its relationship to food in many different ways. Some consider the more familiar influences of theological or institutional directives on members' foodways, such as among Seventh-day Adventists and Unity adherents. Even in such cases, however, there were also larger social influences (e.g., Grahamism), confirming that religious institutions with their doctrinal mandates never exist in a cultural vacuum; they are continuously adopting and rejecting aspects of the societal norms in which they are embedded, as well as responding to the desires of their members. Other essays further confound neat understandings of religion; in attempting to untangle the complicated ways that sacred values and food practices intertwine, we discover a hybrid weaving together of ethnic and religious traditions, coupled with larger cultural forces, that together generate ongoing negotiation, adaptation, and innovation in food meanings and practices and personal and communal identities, whether in African American or Pacific Northwest Salish communities, in Jewish and Christian blended families, or among loosely affiliated "white Buddhists." Moreover, their intellectual ideals regarding food and efforts to materialize those ideals afford some religious (and quasi-religious) Americans a venue both for personal transformation and for social engagement and activism: feeding the poor, saving the environment, treating animals humanely.

Attending to religion, food, and eating exposes the complex, heterogeneous, mutable, on-the-ground ways that food works as a primary creative force melding religion with all other facets of human (and non-human) life. Considering religious foodways—that is, how people invest seemingly mundane foods (gumbo, wine, salmon, raw kale, bagels, sugar, pork chops) and their production and consumption with sacred meanings and how they put, or avoid putting, those meanings and values into practice by eating and not eating alone and with others in particular times and particular settings—illuminates the exceedingly concrete, visceral ways that human beings go about being religious.

Food for the body and soul, indeed.

ACKNOWLEDGMENTS

THIS BOOK IS a direct outgrowth of the Religion, Food, and Eating in North America seminar, which convened at the Annual Meeting of the American Academy of Religion (AAR) from 2008 to 2012. In the seminar, contributors shared papers about religion and foodways, and a wide range of interested parties discussed the projects. Although seminars are formally limited to twenty members, over the years much larger numbers of active participants attended the meetings and provided thoughtful feedback on the papers under discussion. As a result, the genuine contributor list for this book should be much lengthier than the short list of essay authors actually published here. The volume editors profoundly thank the dozens and dozens of people who attended the AAR sessions and offered feedback on these essays (and others) as the project took shape. We also thank the program committee and annual meeting directors at the AAR, who guided us through the process of creating the seminar. This anthology is a demonstration of what works best in the academy: the product of many eyes, ears, and hands that have crafted, reflected on, responded to, and collaborated within an extended conversation on an exciting new topic in the study of religion.

The editors wish to thank our families for their support throughout the process. Benjamin E. Zeller thanks his colleagues at Lake Forest College and Brevard College for their encouragement and conversations, and especially his students at Brevard and Lake Forest in his Religion and Food classes. He greatly thanks Emily R. Mace, without whose support this project would never have gotten off the ground. Marie W. Dallam thanks her colleagues at the Honors College of the University of Oklahoma for their support and encouragement and is especially grateful for input from Julia Ehrhardt. She also thanks Jean Longo for her perennial enthusiasm. Nora L. Rubel thanks her colleagues at the University of Rochester for their encouragement, as well as her students over the years from UNC-Chapel Hill, Connecticut College, and the University of Rochester. It is for them that she wanted to make this book. She also thanks Rob Nipe, who reads everything she writes. Reid L. Neilson wishes to thanks his friends at the Church History Department of the Church of Jesus Christ of Latter-day Saints for their support of his scholarship and writing. He is delighted to have participated in a project that married two of his great loves: religion and eating. The editors also thank the copyright owners of the illustrations used in this book for their permission to do so.

INTRODUCTION

RELIGION, FOOD, AND EATING

MARIE W. DALLAM

RELIGIOUS FOODWAYS

Eating and drinking are physical needs, required to maintain bodily health and give us energy on a daily basis. But most of us do not eat just *anything*: we have a range of foods with which we are familiar, and within that are subsets of foods that we enjoy in greater and lesser degrees. Social factors also influence our eating and drinking habits. For example, economics, geography, ethnicity, health, and age are likely to play strong roles in which foods and beverages we choose to consume or eschew at any given time. Entire cultural groups have explicit rules about foods, and these may include ideas about what foods are encouraged and what foods are taboo, what materials count as food, what specific foods are consumed during rituals and holidays, what kinds of food combinations are acceptable and forbidden, how foods must be prepared, and how foods must be eaten. When we further add a religious filter to any examination of a people's food practices, the reasons for what and how we eat become even more complex.

The study of how humans relate to food, appropriately called "food studies," is a broad, interdisciplinary field. Although food studies is not new, having existed since the mid-twentieth century, until the 1990s it was a relatively quiet area. In recent decades the field has experienced explosive growth, with many scholarly publications, new academic associations and graduate programs, and a wide range of scholars staking out territory in the world of food studies. They approach the study of food from all possible perspectives, using tools from history, life sciences, cultural anthropology, biochemistry, sociology, psychology, and many other disciplines. The study of *foodways*, a subfield, specifically examines cultural communities and group behavior in relation to food and eating. The essays in this book take as their subject religious foodways.

The term "foodway" refers to a set of beliefs and practices that govern consumption.[1] In other words, a foodway is an expression of our "ways" around food: how we grow or acquire it, how we prepare it, how we display or use it, and how and when we consume it. To talk about the foodways of a group, then, is to talk about what people consider food, what they do with food, what they think about the food and the eating, and their ideas about what the food means to them. The goal of this volume is to consider religious foodways and how they are distinctly meaningful in relation to concepts of the sacred.

On first thought one might think of myriad ways that religion, food, and eating cross paths. Many religions have sacred rituals involving both special foods and acts of consumption. For example, in Hinduism consecrated foods called *prasad* are placed on an altar as an offering to the gods; subsequently the participants eat the food together and share in the blessings. In Christianity members engage in a ritual of remembrance in which they communally eat bread and drink wine or water. There are many variations on this ritual: Catholics, for example, ingest a wafer and wine and may perform the ritual as often as once a day, whereas Seventh-day Adventists prefer unleavened bread and nonalcoholic grape juice in a communion ritual that occurs four times a year. Another way that religion, food, and eating readily intersect is through religiously formulated rules about food preparation. In Islam, meat is unacceptable for eating unless it has been ritually slaughtered in accordance with Qur'anic law. Jewish law, which includes similar rules for preparation, additionally forbids any combination of dairy and meat products in food preparation and consumption. All these examples of religiously defined food practices are relatively straightforward; most questions about what people do and why they do it are explained in standard textbooks on religion. What this book seeks to do is move beyond basic descriptions of rituals and rules to examine questions of *how*: How do foodways connect with religious ideas to support a religious culture? How do foodways teach adherents religious expectations? How are food practices used to express religious legitimacy? How do people of mixed faith navigate competing religious foodways? And what does it all mean? These questions are not simple to answer. The essays in this book seek to engage with this religio-cultural complexity, examining individual religious practices and traditions to decipher and articulate the substance of religious foodways.

Complicating this project is the fact that foodways are not uniformly mandated or followed across religious boundaries. Just as the role of deities varies from one religion to another, and just as the role of texts and other sacred discourse varies from one religion to another, there is no universal standard for how foodways relate to religious understanding. In fact, even within individual religious traditions there can be multiple (even conflicting) practices and approaches to food and eating. Thus it would not make sense to investigate a single aspect of food in several different religions as though this would reveal consistent principles of religious foodways. Rather, to understand how food practices function within different religions, we must examine a wide variety of texts, rituals, interactions, personal and community practices, historical circumstances, and overt discussions. We must examine how religion directly and deliberately speaks to foodways just as we must examine how foodways sometimes act as abstract or passive expressions of religious ideas. We must examine not only practices of consumption but acts of *not* eating, for these too may contain religious significance.

In recent decades scholars have embraced the fact that a real understanding of American religious phenomena cannot focus only on doctrines, leaders, and institutions but must also include the vernacular beliefs and practices of members. In other words, the study of religion now includes studying *lived* practices in addition to the ideals put forth as official teachings and official behaviors. The study of religious foodways is a clear example of this new approach to comprehending history and culture. In modern society it can be difficult to identify food practices that are specifically religious, since so many nonreligious food practices are promoted and followed. Likewise, making distinctions between food practices that are primarily religious rather than primarily motivated by something else can be a complicated process. Through specific examples and case studies, the essays in this volume help to explain the religious nature of food practices by examining them in rich detail and carefully unpacking the deeper meanings to which they speak. Whether a foodway appears to have been constructed carefully and deliberately, such as the design of a macrobiotic diet, or randomly and haphazardly, such as the eating habits of a child left to his or her own devices, analysis of any given food practice usually reveals some sort of inner logic. Religious foodways not only contain inner logic but also express core values stemming either from formal theology or from the practitioners of religions themselves. Rarely do religious foodways stand alone: they are tied inherently, often dialectically, to concepts of identity and salvation and the nature of the divine. The essays in this volume acknowledge the ultimate significance that food and eating hold for many faith communities and that they are important markers of religio-cultural history.

RELATED LITERATURE

Just as food studies is a relatively new field, the connections among religion, food, and eating in America have not yet been studied widely and systematically. Nonetheless, many studies of food and eating have involved religion in peripheral ways without making it the center of interpretation. Among these foundational works are several from the 1980s that explore the historical development of religious food practices around the globe, and these volumes provide the groundwork for the construction of this area of study.[2] In *Good to Eat*, Marvin Harris provocatively argues that rather than being expressions of belief, most current religious food practices began as practical measures that were relevant in their original time and place. For example, he claims that the Hindu aversion to beef stems from issues of population control and the cost of cattle production in India, rather than from an expression of the cow's sacred place in Hindu cosmology. In *Holy Feast and Holy Fast*, historian Caroline Walker Bynum explores the social and cultural context of medieval Europe to discuss how food functioned in Christian practice, such as via feasts and the communion ritual. By focusing on asceticism and food production, Bynum reveals that food and food practices played a particularly significant role in the spiritual lives of medieval women. On a similar theme, Rudolph M.

Bell's *Holy Anorexia* considers the psychological role of extreme fasting among religious women of the Middle Ages.[3]

In the ensuing decades, several excellent cultural histories have been published that focus on food and also touch on religion; however, these typically seek to elucidate a subject other than religious belief, religious practice, or religious history. Examples include Hasia Diner's *Hungering for America*, which explores the culinary lives constructed by Italian, Irish, and eastern European Jewish immigrants to North America, and Robert C. Fuller's *Religion and Wine*, which explores how religious politics has affected wine production and consumption in the United States.[4] Similarly, in the context of examining a particular community, works in the religious studies field, including Robert Orsi's *The Madonna of 115th Street* and Karen McCarthy Brown's *Mama Lola*, discuss food and consumption in some detail in order to clarify larger points about the faith group under consideration.[5]

Numerous recent publications exploring religious food and eating demonstrate burgeoning interest in the area of food and religious history.[6] The anthology *Food & Judaism*, for example, includes essays relating to foodways in both Jewish religion and Jewish culture, and it covers a wide range of time and geographic locales. The collection *Food & Faith in Christian Culture*, which spans eight centuries of history, examines worldwide patterns of Christian eating in relation to changing social and political contexts. And *Foreigners and Their Food* examines how notions of food and eating are constructed within texts of the Abrahamic faiths.[7] Not to be overlooked is a related group of theologically oriented texts that consider food and drink within Christianity and strive to speak to believers about the nature of faith and practice.[8] These stand in a different category from the present volume, which intentionally avoids theological reflection and does not assume any specific religious truths.

For many of the authors in this volume, three particular texts have been of monumental importance because they pioneered new paths in the area of religion and food and because they focus on the North American context. Daniel Sack's *Whitebread Protestants: Food and Religion in American Culture* examines the countless roles that food has taken in mainline Protestant churches of the past century, from communion rituals to potluck dinners, and from creating new social ministries to awakening political consciousness. He uses specific examples to consider how stances on food have influenced the thinking, behavior, and socialization of middle-class white Protestants, and he looks at food as both a literal form of material culture and a powerful symbol of ideas. Also focused primarily on American Protestants, R. Marie Griffith's *Born Again Bodies: Flesh and Spirit in American Christianity* considers the long history of health reform and fitness cultures, especially those related to diet, in conjunction with Christianity. Her analysis also includes a consideration of links between dietary control and other kinds of body-oriented controls that have played key roles in American history, such as sexual and racial controls. Last, Madden and Finch's anthology *Eating in Eden: Food and American Utopias* focuses on communities, both literal and figurative, whose foodways express an orientation toward utopian ideals and whose stories reveal the challenges inherent in trying to live out those ideals. Unlike the present collection, only some of the communities included in that anthology are explicitly religious, such as Puritans and Shakers, yet many issues in the present volume resonate with those first raised in *Eating in Eden*.[9] In part this collection furthers the theoretical work begun by *Eating in Eden*, especially in the areas of identity formation and boundary maintenance, but it widens the subject focus beyond utopian communities. Likewise, the works by Sack and Griffith have provided the intellectual launching-point for studies initiated by many of the authors in this volume. Certainly one of the goals with *Religion, Food, and Eating in North America* has been to pick up where all three of these earlier texts left off, not duplicating the ground they have covered but rather moving forward and expanding the analytical domain of food and religion.

The authors of this volume employ a wide range of theorists, and while it would not be prudent to provide introductions to all of them, a few are worth noting at the forefront. One thinker employed repeatedly is Mary Douglas, an anthropologist who studied food practices in numerous social contexts. Douglas asserted that fear of spiritual pollution often guides food practices, and as people pursue common goals related to seeking purity, those actions also foster community. By studying what and how people eat, Douglas suggests, we can learn who they are, what they believe, and how they relate to each other.[10] Likewise, theorists who delve into the essence of a person's worldview are relevant for thinking about how material objects and practices are structured in relation to the sacred, and comparative theorists Mircea Eliade and Thomas A. Tweed are both significant in this regard. Eliade's concept of the *axis mundi* (center of the world) and, similarly, Thomas Tweed's concept of *dwelling* are both helpful for discerning ways that people understand their physical and spiritual world(s) and position themselves within it/them. By extension, these concepts help us conceive of foodways as expressions of identity within a constructed sacred cosmos.[11]

No volume can possibly examine every food custom from all around the world, all across time. For this reason the editors have sought to limit this volume's focus in several ways: geographically, we are looking at practices in the North American milieu; culturally, we are considering foodways related to specific religious groups and beliefs; temporally, we are primarily interested in the twentieth and twenty-first centuries, though several of the essays touch briefly on examples from earlier times. The essays are multidisciplinary and interdisciplinary, which should enable readers to think about different ways that a researcher can observe and understand the food-eating-religion nexus. We have gathered essays on a variety of religions as well as a variety of religiously framed relationships of people to food. Ideally an edited collection such as this would have a perfect religious balance, including at least one essay about every major faith tradition. However in the course of several years of soliciting essays for this project, it became clear that there is genuine imbalance in what is being studied. While we received many submissions about food practices in North American Christianity and Judaism from all ranges of time, we had difficulty obtaining essays that combined lenses of ethnicity and religion, essays that looked at Canada or the Caribbean, and essays on non-Western faiths, particularly Asian traditions in America. All this work is important and needs to be done.[12] The imperfect balance of the present volume reflects the current state of scholarship. As it stands, this is the first volume to look across traditions to find commonalities in the expression of the relationship of both food to religion and eating to religion. We seek to articulate what common relational threads exist between religion and foodways in the North American cultural context, and we consistently use religion as the central axis of interpretation.

GENERAL THEMES

The book is subdivided into four thematic sections, described in detail below, yet their boundaries are permeable. The themes employed here have been chosen to assist readers rather than to isolate subjects. Many of the essays could be at home in more than one thematic section depending on which part of its content is highlighted. In fact, grouping and classifying these essays was one of the greatest challenges we faced as editors. To that end, we wish to point out several recurrent themes that readers may want to consider, all of which are present among the essays but not delineated by the categories we have constructed. These themes are foodlore, distinction, abundance, conversion, and politics.

It has long been recognized that both material and performative culture have the ability to express the ethos of a community. Microstudies of a culture can reveal deep things about the beliefs and history of the people who create and express it, whether the bit of culture being studied is hip-hop dance, Amish quilts, Pueblo vessels, or a pot of gumbo. *Foodlore* is another example of this type of expression. The term "foodlore" refers to the guiding narratives about food—especially how and why particular items are or are not eaten—that communities construct and participate in.[13] Sometimes foodlore can only be extrapolated from actions and behaviors because it is not expressed as a cogent narrative, though at other times there are clear stories about the hows and whys of eating and foods. Foodlore is not necessarily historically and scientifically accurate, but it has meaning and resonance in peoples' lives, and it guides their behavior. Although it is typically a secondary theme, many of the authors in this volume examine versions of foodlore that are tied to ideas of the sacred, especially in essays by Crawford O'Brien, Hicks, Gross, Perez, Mehta, and Blazer.

Many of the essays raise the concept of *distinction*, which often has a negative subtext. That is to say, there are instances in which a foodway's primary role is to distinguish members of the group from nonmembers by giving the members a way to feel superior, both spiritually and behaviorally, and thus deeming themselves distinct among the religious. Such boundary setting allows them to designate as *other* any people who do not follow the same gastro-religious path and to justify maintaining a social separation. We see this boundary-work theme raised in essays by Grumett, Hicks, Holbrook, Blazer, and Rapport, all of whom point to instances of food playing a central role in religious distinction.

Various responses to *abundance* arise in this volume, as they inevitably will in any examination of American cultural history and ideology.[14] Certainly, around the world Americans tend to be associated with an abundance of food and gluttony. Many of the essays in this volume touch on the theme of rejecting abundance, and the pursuit of foodways that are more deliberately restrained if not altogether ascetic. Authors whose work overtly relates to this theme include Grumett, Primiano, Rapport, LeVasseur, Rubel, Wilson, and Zeller. Others, though, more subtly speak to the concept of restraint, such as Holbrook's examination of nutritional tweaks in Nation of Islam recipes, and Crawford O'Brien's notes on changes in Coast Salish First Salmon ceremonies and overall fishing practices in relation to environmental changes and salmon decline.

Conversion is another theme that arises across essays in the volume. Conversion typically describes a person making a comprehensive change in behavior or identity; for instance, we call it conversion when one changes their religion from Catholicism to Islam, or we might say that someone has converted from being a Democrat to a Republican. In these essays we see several instances of people converting to a new foodway. Zeller addresses this question explicitly, applying conversion theories to case studies of vegetarians and locavores, but other essays address the issue more implicitly, such as those by Blazer, Mehta, Primiano, and Wilson, who are thinking about the dynamics around smaller-scale kinds of conversion within religious traditions.

Just as "the personal is political," so too can eating, and even food itself, be *political*. Struggles of a political nature can happen through foodways, where foods and food practices express social disagreements and plays of power. Because food is both a commodity and a necessity for living, it can potentially be used as a tool by either side in a disagreement, regardless of whether the tension is in any way related to food itself. Food-related political dynamics and uses of food to exert individual and local power are clearly evident in essays by Perez, LeVasseur, Robinson, and Crawford O'Brien but are also expressed more subtly within issues examined by Holbrook, Hicks, Primiano, and Rubel.

Finally, we should note that many of the essays have a simple parallel applicability in that they raise questions that are relevant for other faith contexts. For example, the core issues about authority and ethics in Robinson's study of halal slaughter in Chicago are also relevant for Jews, as well as for Christians who follow Levitical Law. In Gross's engaging study of values conveyed through Jewish children's cookbooks, she mentions similar cookbooks published by the Evangelical Moody Bible Institute, which certainly prompts us to think about the various ways that children of all different faiths learn about religious identity. Rubel encourages us to think broadly about the ongoing development of North American religion, especially the ways that sacred practice often transforms in response to social and cultural pressures as much as it responds to divine call. Readers will find many other, similarly useful, parallels in the essays of this volume.

THEOLOGICAL FOODWAYS

For the reader's ease, the volume is divided into four thematic sections. The first section, theological foodways, gathers together essays about religious mandates for the physical practices of eating and drinking. Divinely inspired instructions about food are often believed to result not only in physical health but in a kind of heightened spiritual purity. In other words, believers follow careful food rules not just to demonstrate correct behavior but because they seek personal spiritual results. These four essays also examine how theological foodways can change, and what that can mean for devout believers. By coincidence, rather than design, each of the food practices examined in this section is a variation on Christian vegetarianism; this emphasis mirrors the present trend of surging academic interest in this subject area.

David Grumett argues against the Christian tendency to consider food rules as "other." By examining both theology and history, he reveals a vegetarian imperative in Christianity, a point that is often elided in modern scholarship. Grumett further demonstrates vegetarianism's longstanding place in Christian belief and practice by providing examples from early Christianity up through the twentieth century.

Jeremy Rapport explores two alternative American religious groups that have espoused vegetarianism since the nineteenth century: the Seventh-day Adventists and the Unity School of Christianity. Both groups, especially in their formative period, considered it one part of a healthy diet, though the specific religious reasons for their vegetarian mandates were quite different. Both groups show that profound ideas about the connection of people to God can be expressed through foodways.

Leonard Norman Primiano focuses on the Peace Mission Movement, whose central ritual of worship is an extensive communion banquet. Primiano is concerned with changes to eating instigated by the second leader, Mother Divine, some of which were drastic transformations of principles articulated by her late husband, Father Divine. Her incorporation of a macrobiotic vegetarian diet into Peace Mission theology is interesting not only because of its impact on member thinking and behavior but also because it represents a clear shift in spiritual power.

Annie Blazer examines the Hallelujah Diet, a vegan raw foods regimen promoted by a contemporary Evangelical health ministry called Hallelujah Acres and used as both a curative and a preventative. Hallelujah Diet adherents extol the divine nature of a foodway that they believe transcends the conventional boundaries of "religion," as they assert that the diet itself is a religious practice that has the power to align all persons with God.

IDENTITY FOODWAYS

The second thematic section focuses on personal and group identity. The preparation and consumption of food can function as rituals that connect practitioners to a religio-cultural heritage, sometimes intentionally and other times inadvertently. Communal food practices can reinscribe a religious identity from which people may feel disconnected or in some cases can teach key elements of that religious identity anew. Four essays in the second section highlight how foodways can serve as methods of religious identification, both individual and communal.

Rachel Gross examines the enculturation of religious identity in baby boomer children through the vehicle of the cookbook. Jewish children's cookbooks, by teaching a range of particular food practices, were a passive but effective tool for resisting the general trend of assimilation in mid-twentieth-century America. Gross shows that anxiety about children losing their Jewish identity was diminished as parents saw their children engaging in recreational learning through culturally focused cookbooks.

Suzanne Crawford O'Brien studies the First Salmon ceremony practiced by Native American Coast Salish in the Pacific Northwest. This annual rite involves members of the community catching, welcoming, celebrating, preparing and eating a special fish, acts that reify the spiritual connection between the people and their salmon ancestors. The ceremony also provides an opportunity to retell the salmon legends and reinvigorate community values through a blending of past and present.

Derek S. Hicks uses the example of gumbo to show how foodways connect African Americans to a religio-cultural heritage. On a deeper level he also uses gumbo as an analogy for understanding black religious identity in the United States. He asks: Is gumbo a regional food? Is it an ethnic food? Is it a religious food? By exploring the ways in which gumbo is all these things, Hicks also demonstrates the complexity of black religious identity in the United States.

Samira K. Mehta's essay shows that food and foodways are a medium through which interfaith anxieties are expressed and ultimately resolved. Mining examples from American popular culture, Mehta considers how people of mixed Jewish and Christian heritage use food to forge new ways to observe and preserve both religio-cultural paths. She also raises the engaging and complicated question of how to distinguish *religious* foods from *ethnic* foods.

NEGOTIATED FOODWAYS

Scholars regularly distinguish ideal religion from lived religion. While authorities in every tradition promulgate a tight list of correct beliefs and practices, practitioners make adjustments to fit with their actual experiences as living humans. Thus lived religion is what people really believe and do within the framework of what religion dictates. Religious foodways are in sync with this, in that there may be a gap between the ideal and the lived practices. In the third section essays specifically address negotiated foodways and cases in which lived religious foodways are distinct from the ideal religious foodways we might expect to see.

Elizabeth Perez examines the history of sugar offerings made to deities in the Afro-Cuban Yoruba tradition. She shows that Cuban cultural history, particularly discriminatory socioeconomics, has directly affected and altered religious understandings, including dictating the types of sugar products preferred by various orishas (gods). In this case religion "on the ground" has provided the impetus for ritual transformation.

Kate Holbrook interrogates value messages encoded in the foodways of two groups, the Nation of Islam and the Church of Jesus Christ of Latter-day Saints. In both cases she finds that in food practices, especially recipe construction, secondary religious values have trumped the primary, or more expected, religious values normally articulated by these groups.

Jeff Wilson examines Buddhism-based food practices in North America, specifically the practice of "mindful eating." Many modern teachers now use the Buddhist concept of *mindfulness* to encourage pleasurable yet controlled eating practices in efforts toward improving the health of mind, body, and spirit. However, mindful eating, Wilson argues, is a significant alteration to the traditional concept of mindfulness because it emphasizes tangible worldly benefits rather than renunciation and indifference to the body.

Focusing on the issue of holiday modification, Nora L. Rubel examines practices of fasting and feasting during the Jewish holidays Yom Kippur and Sukkot. Rubel argues that a deemphasis on the traditional Sukkot feast has concomitantly caused the cultural addition of a feast to mark the end of Yom Kippur, just prior to Sukkot. Furthermore, she finds that this modification is likely caused by American cultural preferences for Yom Kippur over Sukkot.

ACTIVIST FOODWAYS

In the fourth and final section, we see the subjects of study trying to change the world through divinely ordained foodways. Leaders and members believe their practices stand as an exemplar of right thinking and right ways of existing, and these ideas are rooted in what God has ordained as ethical. In a sense, they are all working to combat injustice, especially forms of social inequity and exploitation, through revolutionary foodways. They do not all see themselves as activists, but rather as people trying to obey a higher calling, yet it is easy to see that they share much in common with other forms of progressive activism rooted in religious traditions.[15]

Todd LeVasseur examines what he calls the "Ecological Reformation": the modern-day religious drive to engage in socially just food practices. In recent years, as environmental concerns have come into vogue and captured popular attention, variations of this Ecological Reformation have become evident among religions all around the world. By examining a Christian community in rural Georgia that has been focused on social justice and foodway justice since the 1940s, LeVasseur provides a window into some of the long-term challenges of sustaining this kind of commitment.

Sarah E. Robinson focuses on the Taqwa-Eco Food Cooperative, a post-9/11 group that encouraged Chicago-area Muslims to embrace local, sustainable, socially just foodways. Taqwa did not achieve great success in Chicago's Muslim community because its criticisms of American agricultural practices stood in contrast with the goal of Muslim assimilation. In the ensuing years, green initiatives have become much more popular and now represent a bona fide "American" stance; ironically, this means that since Taqwa's demise it has become more socially acceptable for Muslims to embrace and promote sustainable foodways.

In the concluding chapter, Benjamin E. Zeller pulls out the lens more broadly to raise metaquestions. By applying frameworks from the social science of religion to the rhetoric and practices of activist-oriented vegetarians and locavores, Zeller demonstrates that there are many possible insights to be gained from the ideological combination of food studies and religious studies. Furthermore, he leaves no doubt that in today's society, a foodway can truly function as a religion.

NOTES

1. This use of the term "foodway" first emerged from manuscripts of New Deal writers as they collected information about American life in the late 1930s. The term gained currency during the 1960s and 1970s through the teaching and publications of both Don Yoder, a University of Pennsylvania folklorist who also worked in Religious Studies, and Warren Roberts, a folklorist at Indiana University in Bloomington.

2. The food studies books discussed in this section are all relevant to religion in some way. There are many excellent works on food history, food culture, and food identity that have been influential on the present text and its authors, including several groundbreaking articles from the 1970s. A comprehensive bibliography of such books and essays is beyond the scope of this introduction. Compilation works include Carole Counihan and Penny Van Esterik, eds., *Food and Culture: A Reader*, 2nd ed. (New York: Routledge, 2008); Carole M. Counihan, ed., *Food in the USA: A Reader* (New York: Routledge, 2002); and Jacqueline S. Thursby, *Foodways and Folklore: A Handbook* (Westport, Conn.: Greenwood Press, 2008).

3. Marvin Harris, *Good to Eat: Riddles of Food and Culture* (New York: Simon and Schuster, 1985); Caroline Walker Bynum, *Holy Feast and Holy Fast: The Reli-*

gious *Significance of Food to Medieval Women* (Berkeley: University of California Press, 1987); Rudolph M. Bell, *Holy Anorexia* (Chicago: University of Chicago Press, 1985).

4. Hasia R. Diner, *Hungering for America: Italian, Irish, and Jewish Foodways in the Age of Migration* (Cambridge: Harvard University Press, 2001); Robert C. Fuller, *Religion and Wine: A Cultural History of Wine Drinking in the United States* (Knoxville: University of Tennessee Press, 1996).

5. Robert A. Orsi, *The Madonna of 115th Street: Faith and Community in Italian Harlem, 1880–1950* (New Haven: Yale University Press, 1985); Karen McCarthy Brown, *Mama Lola: A Vodou Priestess in Brooklyn* (Berkeley: University of California Press, 1991).

6. Also important to note is *Journal of the American Academy of Religion* 63.3 (Fall 1995). The articles in this special issue on religion and food primarily examined religion and eating/not eating, rather than religious food and foodways, but they serve as a moment of intellectual development between the early and more recent works in this area.

7. Leonard J. Greenspoon, Ronald A. Simkins, and Gerald Shapiro, eds., *Food & Judaism* (Omaha: Creighton University Press, 2005); Kenneth Albala and Trudy Eden, eds., *Food & Faith in Christian Culture* (New York: Columbia University Press, 2011); David M. Freidenreich, *Foreigners and Their Food: Constructing Otherness in Jewish, Christian, and Islamic Law* (Berkeley: University of California Press, 2011).

8. Examples include David Grumett and Rachel Muers, *Theology on the Menu: Asceticism, Meat, and the Christian Diet* (London: Routledge, 2010); and Norman Wirzba, *Food and Faith: A Theology of Eating* (New York: Cambridge University Press, 2011).

9. Daniel Sack, *Whitebread Protestants: Food and Religion in American Culture* (New York: St. Martin's, 2000); R. Marie Griffith, *Born Again Bodies: Flesh and Spirit in American Christianity* (Berkeley: University of California Press, 2004); Etta M. Madden and Martha L. Finch, eds., *Eating in Eden: Food and American Utopias* (Lincoln: University of Nebraska Press, 2006).

10. Mary Douglas, *Purity and Danger: An Analysis of Concepts of Pollution and Taboo* (New York: Praeger, 1966); also see related ideas in Mary Douglas, ed., *Food in the Social Order: Studies of Food and Festivities in Three American Communities* (New York: Russell Sage Foundation, 1984); and Emile Durkheim, *Elementary Forms of the Religious Life*, trans. Karen E. Fields (1915; repr. New York: Free Press, 1995).

11. Mircea Eliade, *The Sacred and the Profane: The Nature of Religion*, trans. Willard R. Trask (New York: Harcourt Brace, 1959); Thomas A. Tweed, *Crossing and Dwelling: A Theory of Religion* (Cambridge: Harvard University Press, 2006). Also relevant are Eliade, *Patterns in Comparative Religion*, trans. Rosemary Sheed (1958; repr. Lincoln: University of Nebraska Press, 1996); and Mary Douglas, "Deciphering a Meal," *Daedelus* 101, no. 1 (Winter 1972): 61–81.

12. We hope that this book will serve as an invitation to, and inspiration for, more scholars to dig into these subjects and bring forth that new work.

13. As with "foodways," the term "foodlore" originates in manuscripts of New Deal writers. Charles Camp explains: "Like folklore, it is a canon of shared beliefs or 'lore' that is widely held but limited to a certain culture or situation." *Encyclopedia of Food and Culture*, ed. Solomon H. Katz (New York: Scribner's, 2003), s.v. "Foodways."

14. The theme of abundance is deftly examined in several essays in Madden and Finch, *Eating in Eden.*

15. See, for example, Helene Slessarev-Jamir, *Prophetic Activism: Progressive Religious Justice Movements in Contemporary America* (New York: New York University Press, 2011).

RELIGION, FOOD, AND EATING
IN NORTH AMERICA

Part One

THEOLOGICAL
FOODWAYS

One

DYNAMICS OF CHRISTIAN DIETARY ABSTINENCE

DAVID GRUMETT

W HAT MAKES A dietary practice "religious"? Dietary practice
can be a key means by which religious groups identify themselves and develop cohesion, but a particular set of practices
cannot be classified as religious purely on the grounds that a specified
group of people who are religious happen to observe them. The set of
practices might extend beyond group boundaries to encompass people
who are not adherents of the religion in question. Furthermore, members
of a particular religious group might observe specific practices on a whim,
or see in them no religious significance. In this case, even if the practices were distinctive to that group and their observance distinguished
them from other religious groups, they could not strictly be classed as
religious.

To establish whether specific dietary practices are religious in the tru-
est sense, those practices need to be related to the theological discourse
of the particular religious community that observes them. They also need
to be located within the wider logic of practice with which that community, both consciously and unconsciously, identifies. In the first section I
examine a range of Christian communities in the United States in which

distinctive dietary practices have been observed and promoted and situate those practices within the wider history of Christian diet.

In so doing I might be seen to be setting myself a challenging task. In Christian and post-Christian societies, solid food rules (in contrast with those surrounding alcohol) have often been associated with "other" religions. In our current religiously pluralistic age, this perception has, if anything, grown. As the discussion proceeds, it will therefore be important to understand the underlying doctrinal reasons why Christians have sometimes regarded dietary practice as unimportant, and why those reasons for not taking diet seriously are ultimately difficult to support.

Christians interact with members of other religions and might share table hospitality with them. These interactions present Christians with different images of what it means to be religious. In particular, they make proper appraisal of the place of food in Christian life a pressing matter. The Christian dietary practice analyzed in this chapter should not, however, be seen as simply an attempt to cash in on an interesting feature of non-Christian religions. From the perspective of the Christians being studied here, the doctrine of the incarnation affirms that, in taking physical human form, God in Christ brought the whole of material reality into his presence. This makes the whole of material reality, including food and diet, an intrinsically relevant sphere of Christian concern.

The view of the relationship between dietary practice and tradition, cosmology, scripture, and theology here presented is therefore structurally specific to Christianity. Sources of authority and interpretive methods function differently in different religions, and the same explanatory framework cannot be applied to all. Nevertheless, by developing a framework appropriate to Christianity, I also wish to offer a starting point for considering the specifically religious character of dietary practices in religion generally. Dietary practices are increasingly prominent as secular spiritual disciplines, being an area of everyday life in which practitioners seek to recover order, meaning, and purpose without making any personal commitment to Christianity or any other institutional religion.[1] These developments make it increasingly difficult to distinguish dietary disciplines pursued for specifically religious ends from those embraced for reasons of self-help (e.g., to address health problems) or self-improvement (e.g., to cultivate a discipline of mindfulness). If diet is to continue to be a significant and meaningful identifier for religious believers, however, it is important that such distinctions continue to be made.

CONSTRUCTING BODILY BOUNDARIES

Food has performed a significant role in defining and preserving the boundaries between different church bodies and different human bodies. By requiring abstention from specific foods, especially meat, particular Christian churches and groups have established markers of inclusion in their corporate body and of exclusion from that body. Moreover, by associating immoderate eating with promiscuity and seeking to prevent both, Christian groups have sought to impose moral and spiritual discipline on their members' physical bodies.[2]

The ideological power of this sexual symbolism of food links the two activities that reveal most potently the permeability of bodily boundaries. In Christian dietary discourse, abstinence has frequently been associated with the regulation of sexual desire. Early Christian ascetics realized that reducing their overall food intake and avoiding some foods altogether reduced that desire. They might well have learned about the severe adverse effects of extreme fasting on the reproductive system from contemporary famines, seeking to endure these effects voluntarily for spiritual ends.[3] The key principle believed to govern this causal relationship between diet and sexuality was that both foods and human bodies exhibited the four properties of heating, cooling, drying, and moistening. Ascetics confined themselves to very small quantities of foods classified as "cold" and "dry" and avoided "hot" and "moist" foods, believing that these fanned the flames of sexual passion. Meat was viewed as the paradigmatic "hot" food, and therefore to be avoided completely.[4]

In the United States several Christian communities have embraced vegetarianism. The earliest was the Ephrata cloister of Seventh Day Baptists in Lancaster County, Pennsylvania. The cloister was founded in 1732 by Johann Conrad Beissel, who had emigrated from Germany to escape religious persecution. Beissel recommended a diet of bread and grains and proscribed fatty and meaty dishes, and archaeological evidence suggests that this was followed at least during the community's early decades.[5] A related aspect of the community's asceticism was the celibacy of its higher-ranking members, which they believed left them free to serve God. This associates them closely with the dietary discipline of the desert fathers just described.

Another Christian vegetarian group, the Dorrellites, became established in Leyden, Vermont. Their founder William Dorrell was born in

Yorkshire, England, in 1752. His vegetarianism was based on the belief that humans should not kill any living creature, and it extended to a complete prohibition on the use of leather or animal skins.[6] The community around him differed radically from the Ephrata cloister, however, in a key aspect of moral teaching: members could be married and moreover need not marry before entering into sexual relations.

These two eighteenth-century groups were well defined and self-contained, with a vegetarian diet part of their distinctive identities. They had mainly local appeal, were centered on the direct leadership of their founders, and did not endure much beyond their death, at least in their vegetarian forms. A third community, which also had European origins and developed in the early nineteenth century, was the Bible Christian Church. It promoted what would become the Christian vegetarian norm of sexual continence, or restraint, within the context of marriage and family life. In 1817 forty of its numbers had arrived in Philadelphia from Salford, near Manchester in England, with their minister William Metcalfe to found a new congregation. The church was small, like its eighteenth-century predecessors, never growing larger than about one hundred people.

Yet during the 1830s interest in vegetarianism spread in wider society as part of a nexus of concerns that included health reform, teetotalism (complete abstention from alcohol), and sexual morality. A key figure in this development was Presbyterian minister and temperance lecturer Sylvester Graham, whose interest in vegetarianism was sparked by contact with Bible Christians and sustained by correspondence with Metcalfe.[7] Graham was particularly well-known for developing graham flour as part of his program of opposition to white bread, which he regarded as insufficiently nutritious. He also created the graham cracker. Made with the same flour, the graham cracker had a taste and consistency similar to a digestive biscuit, with its dryness intended to curb sexual urges.[8]

This wider social interest in vegetarianism inevitably spread into the churches. For example, vegetarian experiments occurred in some Shaker communities during the 1840s, partly in response to health concerns about meat.[9] Vegetarianism was, by this time, mostly aligned neither with the free love of the Dorrellites nor the celibacy of Ephrata but with continence in the context of married family life. Continence was regarded as a moral virtue commended by scripture. Its promotion also had the practical effect of strengthening the boundaries of those Christian communities that had a strong sense of their own distinctive identity by discouraging a plurality of sexual relationships and nurturing the bonds of marriage and family within the community.

The extent to which the Bible Christians and other Christian groups shaped the 1830s health reform movement is contested. Historian Jayme Sokolow acknowledges Graham's work as a minister but discounts Metcalfe's possible influence on him, arguing that Graham advocated vegetarianism on physiological grounds whereas Metcalfe's case was biblical.[10] Similarly, Stephen Nissenbaum suggests that Graham's work as a temperance lecturer signaled the end of his active ministry and also dismisses his links with Metcalfe as unimportant.[11] But such assessments rely too heavily on assumptions about the nature of ministry and the sources on which Christian theology draws. The growing interest from the 1830s in dietary reform, in which Christian ministers, laypeople, and communities played a prominent role, should instead be seen as part of the Christian traditions of dietary abstinence as a medicine for the soul and of bodily health as linked inextricably with spiritual well-being, both signifying and facilitating a disciplined spiritual life.

WITNESSING SCRIPTURE

Stories of feasting and fasting are prominent in scripture. Indeed, the epic history of fall and redemption that scripture unfolds is precipitated by Adam and Eve's simple act of eating from the tree of the knowledge of good and evil (Gen. 3.6). From this dietary transgression follows their loss of sexual innocence and expulsion from Eden. This narrative suggested to various Christian writers—such as Evagrius of Pontus, John Cassian, and Gregory the Great—that gluttony was the cardinal sin, which engendered all others.[12] In turn, Christ as the second Adam was seen as redeeming the world by offering on the cross his body, which is represented in the Eucharist as bread. The centrality of food to this history of fall and redemption is beautifully illustrated in Lucas Cranach the Elder's "Virgin and Child Under an Apple Tree," in which Jesus stands in the lap of his mother Mary under the tree, holding an apple in his left hand and offering a broken piece of bread in his right.

By means of fasting, Christians have identified themselves with key figures from scripture, such as Moses, Hannah, David, Elijah, Ahab, Hezekiah, Anna, and Paul, whose fasts scripture records.[13] Yet the undoubted hero of early Christian hermits was John the Baptist. A voice crying in the wilderness announcing the coming of the Messiah, John offered in his ascetic life, dress, and diet of locusts and wild honey (Mt. 3.4; Mk. 1.6) the most striking ascetic role model in Christian scripture.[14]

In some cases scriptural interpretation has provided the principal foundation for Christian vegetarianism. A notable example is William Metcalfe and the Bible Christian Church, already discussed. Some of Metcalfe's ideas were quixotic. He argued that the Genesis 9.3 description of God giving to humans for food all moving things referred, more precisely, to all creeping things, which he identified with the vines of Noah's vineyard and their grapes. When an animal was described as "permitted," this meant that its milk was permitted, not its flesh. Metcalfe also maintained that the sheep and oxen offered by Solomon at the consecration of the Temple (1 Kings 8.63) were pieces of money whose value equaled that of the animal after which they were named and with whose image they were imprinted. Furthermore, he believed that the Jerusalem Council's prohibition of all things strangled (Acts 15.29) had been intended to proscribe all things that had suffered a violent death, that is, all animals. His vegetarianism extended to fish, and he contended that the references to Jesus eating fish (Lk. 24.42; Jn. 21.9–13) were in fact to water plants or other tasty vegetarian foods.[15]

Other points that Metcalfe raises are harder to dismiss. He saw the vegetarian Golden Age depicted in the opening of Genesis as representing a condition to which humanity should aspire, and the commandment to humans not to kill as prohibiting animal slaughter. In the wilderness God fed his people not with flesh but with manna (Ex. 16) and did not represent the land of promise as a place where flesh would be eaten. Paul states that it is good not to eat flesh (Rom. 14.21). The meaning of the vision of Peter's sheet (Acts 10.9–22) is that no person is to be regarded as unclean, not that meat eating is permissible. Metcalfe asserts, in terms more common in present-day theology than in the theology of his own day, that Christ did not come into the world to abrogate or destroy the Jewish law, in which dietary rules were central, but to fulfill it.[16]

The fasting figure in scripture with whom modern Christians are most likely to identify is Jesus Christ himself. After baptism by John, Jesus retreated into the wilderness to be tempted by Satan for forty days and nights (Mt. 4.1–11; Lk. 4.1–13). Accounts state that, through this whole period, he ate nothing. Significantly, abstinence during the season of Lent—

from meat and, in the premodern era, from dairy products too—has often been identified with this time of fasting by Christ, an association that has grown stronger in modern times as a means by which churches have promoted Lenten abstinence.[17] By abstinence, it is suggested, Christians may emulate the discipline of Christ, show solidarity with Christ, and grow closer to Christ.

In a few cases links between scripture and diet are made explicit, such as in Food for Life's emblazoning of the biblical references Ezekiel 4.9 and Genesis 1.29 across the packaging of its sprouted grain bakery products.[18] More typically, however, forms of Christian life have been followed that, while inspired by scripture, do not make continual reference back to it. It is to these that I now turn.

INHABITING SUSTAINABLE COMMUNITIES

Collective life is widely recognized as a key feature of Christian identity. Most Christians accept that it is not possible to be Christian in total isolation from other people. In some cases Christians have affirmed this truth by forming a distinctive geographical community characterized by a rule of life. The vegetarian Ephrata cloister and Dorrellites have already been discussed, but communities with similarly distinctive dietary identities that have persisted into the present day include the Hutterites and the Amish. The nonvegetarian food of these communities, especially the Amish, is well-known for its simplicity, as well as its production by sustainable and often nonmechanized agricultural methods.

Such communities have, in their own diverse ways, continued the ancient Christian tradition of monasticism. This enables groups of Christians to live together in a community of mutual support in order to pursue, in varying proportions, a life of prayer, study, and manual labor. In the ancient context, however, communal living could potentially undermine ascetic discipline. When obtaining provisions, a community could benefit from economies of scale unavailable to individual households, being able to obtain exotic foods or foods of a higher quality from further afield. The dietary practices of large numbers of people gathered together in one place could thereby affect the local and regional economy significantly.

It is instructive to examine how monastic communities have sought to avoid this pitfall. In the early period of monastic history, monks living in community enjoyed a dietary standard no more than equal to that of the surrounding populace, as a result of their strict discipline. Matters of food and dining were regulated closely in monastic rules in order to prevent abuses. These rules encouraged monks to live in practice-based solidarity with their locality and region, experiencing a greater degree of abstention than that naturally imposed by their material conditions as a large community. A key virtue was moderation in all things, including food.

The principles were similar in the different monastic rules. The relationship among food choices, economic activity, and nature is expressed with particular clarity by the fourth-century monastic founder Basil of Caesarea. He relates simplicity of diet to the place where the community is located, stating:

> We ought to choose for our own use whatever is more easily and cheaply obtained in each locality and available for common use and bring in from a distance only those things which are more necessary for life, such as oil and the like or if something is appropriate for the necessary relief of the sick—yet even this only if it can be obtained without fuss and disturbance and distraction.[19]

Similarly, in nineteenth-century Shaker communities menus were determined largely by what was available locally and by regional preferences.[20] Yet the importance of locality probably explains why most Shaker communities did not adopt vegetarianism, even though many experimented with it: a completely vegetarian diet might well involve more labor and greater expense than one including some meat, by excluding foods that are sometimes naturally and conveniently available.

In recent years theological awareness of the impact of human diet on ecology has increased greatly, especially in response to global warming.[21] Renewed interest in simplicity and the local sourcing of foods echoes monastic traditions, which, as living traditions, continue to inspire Christians today.[22] Their practices are sustainable both in the ecological sense of not consuming more of the earth's resources than is needed to sustain a healthy life and in the economic sense of not permitting human life to be driven by a succession of wants and desires, which continually surpass what has previously been obtained and impel a fruitless quest for satisfaction by consuming material goods.

PRODUCTION, CONSUMPTION, AND SALVATION

In Europe until well into the seventeenth century, all citizens were legally required to observe church fasts. In England Lent was enforced by an annual royal proclamation. Seasonal fasting was promoted for a range of social, economic, and political reasons, including the preservation of food stocks for the poor. Such public fasting was also a feature of life in colonial New England.[23] Another contrasting tradition, originating in the Reformation and developed by John Wesley, saw dietary abstinence as a matter of personal choice rather than state or church regulation.

In the United States the ideal of personal choice, and ultimately free consumer choice, became the main principle governing diet. The spread of modern consumer capitalism meant that, if Christians were to influence the dietary practices of society, they needed to appeal directly to people's appetites by mass marketing. Among the first examples of such appeals were graham flour and graham crackers, which have already been discussed, but a far more important product to emerge on the market in the late nineteenth century was breakfast cereal. At the beginning of their development, the Christian context of breakfast cereals was proclaimed by their names, which included Food of Eden, Golden Manna, and even Elijah's Manna. Quaker Oats, although not invented nor ever produced by the Society of Friends, presented an image of simplicity and integrity. Association with this Christian context of breakfast foods could only reap commercial benefits. Popular vegetarian writers such as Dio Lewis alluded to the continuing Christian basis of vegetarianism, quoting classic Christian vegetarian sources like Luigi Cornaro, George Cheyne, and John Wesley.[24] Dietary discipline was portrayed as a sign and even a means of personal and societal redemption.

The figures dominating early twentieth-century breakfast cereals were the Kellogg brothers. John Harvey Kellogg had worked as superintendent of the vast Seventh-day Adventist headquarters, the Battle Creek Sanatorium, which welcomed thousands of guests each year for health treatments and rehabilitation. With his business-minded younger brother Will Keith, he founded the Battle Creek Toasted Corn Flake Company to market his invention. The company also pioneered other meat substitutes, such as peanut butter. Adventism gave Christian impetus to the development of these products. The movement's key foundational teachings were established by the visions of Sister Ellen White, received in 1863 during the Civil War. These included the importance of eating no more than two meals a day and abstaining from meat, lard, cake, and spices. Positively, White's visions commended fruits, vegetables, and graham bread.[25]

The Kelloggs' relationship with White soured, however, owing to rivalry and their challenging of key Adventist tenets such as sabbatarianism and White's infallibility. The result was that, in 1907, Will Keith was expelled from the Adventist Church.[26] Thus was severed an important concrete Christian link with twentieth-century mass food production, with the theological basis of dietary discipline being superseded in mainstream culture by modern scientific justifications. Nevertheless, the Adventist Church continued to own health food companies like Madison, Loma Linda, and Worthington, which pioneered soya and wheat gluten meat- and dairy-substitute products such as soybean meat, soymilk, and vegetarian sausages. Moreover, based at Loma Linda University, Adventists have from the late 1950s conducted pioneering research on the health benefits of a vegetarian diet, such as much lower rates of heart disease, cancer, diabetes, strokes, and other major degenerative diseases. William Shurtleff and Akiko Aoyagi describe this research as the "single most important development in the field of vegetarianism since World War II," and as having "played a leading role in changing the attitudes of health care professionals."[27]

Evidently much changed during the century separating the modest abstinence of small rural communities like the Dorrellites and the publicity fanfare surrounding the Kelloggs' delivery of the largest batch of cereal ever to a business customer, transported on a long railroad train.[28] Theirs was, in the memorable phrase of Gerald Carson, a "cornflake crusade." This crusade undoubtedly promoted Christian virtues and improved health. Yet by entering mainstream culture, products that had been given their initial impetus by a Christian ascetic ethic progressively lost their Christian associations. Moreover, whereas breakfast cereals had originally been developed to encourage abstinence from the standard breakfast fare of pork, beans, and pie, they became consumer products of choice produced and marketed by an industry at least as powerful as the Chicago stockyards, which they had been founded to displace. Tellingly, the Kellogg brothers, like the stockyards, based their national production and distribution network on the railroads.

FOOD, CONTEMPLATION, AND PRACTICE

The preceding examination has shown that diet has long been a key concern of Christian writers, ministers, theologians, and entrepreneurs, having been promoted by a range of scriptural texts, role models, church traditions, rules of life, and actual food products. Yet despite these numerous precedents and inspiring sources, issues surrounding food and eating seem to remain more marginal to present-day Christian theology and spirituality than in most of the other major world religions.[29]

Contrary trends should not, of course, be overlooked. The most notable among these is the continuation of abstinence and fasting disciplines in many Orthodox churches and recent efforts within the Roman Catholic Church to strengthen these disciplines.[30] By interrupting consumption, these disciplines have the potential to inform a wider theology of food and diet. Yet, at least in the West, their occasional performance acquires meaning against a largely unchallenged background norm of undifferentiated consumption.

It could be said that the reason for the greater prominence of dietary discipline in daily life in non-Christian religions than within Christianity is that Christians do not observe food taboos nor have rules about how animals should be slaughtered. Yet from a historical viewpoint, neither of these statements is true, as shown by the speculations of various patristic writers about animals such as the hare, and the Armenian *matal* sacrifice, which has continued into the present day.[31] More important, however, the statements assume that taboos and slaughter rules are implanted in religions at their inception and continue forever unchanged. The reality is that taboos and related practices surrounding foods have evolved and been received into the religions that they have come to characterize for a range of symbolic, doctrinal, ecological, practical, and economic reasons.[32] Just one example, already discussed, is Lenten abstention from meat and dairy products. This does not, of course, make a particular evolved practice any less truly or properly part of either a specific religious tradition or of religion in general. On the contrary, because religious traditions provide guidance and rules for daily living, it would be remarkable if they did not offer a practical wisdom emerging from deep, ongoing engagement with the concrete realities of material life.

As already affirmed, central to Christianity is the incarnation, in which God becomes a fully human person with a fully human, physical body. In principle this insight provides excellent foundations for a theology of food and eating. Moreover, dietary disciplines feature prominently in the Christian Old Testament and some are reaffirmed in the New Testament (Acts 15.29). Yet in practice such disciplines have become increasingly marginalized in Christianity. Where they have existed, they have too often been established on shaky grounds, such as the belief of the Bible Christians that Jesus was vegetarian, rather than by drawing on core Christian theology.[33]

In the next section I outline three structural reasons for Christianity's ambivalence to food disciplines. These reasons are selected not because they have arisen as direct challenges to alternative views that food is important, but because they have helped shape a theological mindset in which food is assumed to be insignificant. The first reason is based on Christian views of the body and its relation with the soul. The second concerns the relationship Christians have typically seen between Eucharistic eating and everyday eating. The third addresses Christian attitudes toward rules and material practice generally.

FOOD, THE BODY, AND THE SOUL

Ideas about the quantity and quality of food required by humans depend on theories about how the body is constituted and the nature of embodiment in the wider material world. The current mainstream Christian view of the relationship between food and the body recognizes, in principle, the importance of food to human bodily flourishing. Yet historically this recognition has sometimes imperiled a full understanding of the embodied character of human identity in current life and at the resurrection.

During the twelfth century many theologians saw bodily identity as constituted by a physical seminal core into which food was not absorbed, citing biblical texts in their support. Matthew 15.17 states that whatever is taken into the mouth descends into the stomach and then leaves the body. The same idea is put slightly differently in Mark 7.19: food enters not the heart of a person but the stomach, from where it is ejected from the body. According to this view, known as anti-assimilationism, it was impossible for food to become part of the core of the true physical body, which persisted through time, or of the resurrected body, which would exist in heaven.[34] This anti-assimilationist anthropology, which regarded food as superfluous to the body's genuine needs, helps to explain why a figure such as Johann Conrad Beissel, the founder of the Ephrata cloister discussed earlier, could regard food as necessary for humans only following Adam and Eve's expulsion from Eden.[35] In his view, as well as in that of the desert fathers earlier discussed, the functions that food sustained were necessarily sinful.

In the thirteenth century a change in ideas occurred. As a result of the influence of Aristotle on theologians such as Thomas Aquinas, the anti-assimilationist model was largely superseded by one in which food was fully assimilated into the physical core of the human body. This might have been expected to have led to greater appreciation of the spiritual importance of food, but it did not. Christian theologians wished to identify human nature with something that persisted unchanged through time, not with ordinary mutable matter. The physical human body, now seen as subject to change through time in all its parts, could no longer be regarded as immutable. In consequence, a revised concept of the soul as detachable from the physical body developed. This was key to Thomas Aquinas's doctrine of purgatory and thereby exerted particular influence on Roman Catholicism.[36] But the new concept was also important in promoting ideals of religious virtue as concerned primarily with interior prayer and dispositions rather than with concrete, physical life.

This view of the soul continues to influence attitudes toward the importance, or rather unimportance, of dietary discipline in Christian life. But it is in tension with the Pauline view that human life is sown as a physical body and resurrected as a spiritual body (1 Cor. 15.44). The idea of the spiritual soul, if understood with sufficient theological nuance, can certainly be reconciled with this idea of bodily continuity through and beyond earthly life. Nevertheless the practical effect of the concept of the spiritual soul has been the neglect of actual bodily practices such as eating.

DINING AND THE EUCHARIST

The Eucharist, which commemorates Jesus's Last Supper with his disciples and his body and blood offered on the cross, is central to the identity of most Christian groups. It is a meal in which bread and wine are shared. This could, in theory, place food and eating at the center of Christian spirituality. But by being understood primarily as liturgy, the Eucharist has paradoxically more often had the effect of diverting theological attention away from everyday acts of eating. In the United States and other Western nations, modern theologians who discuss food and eating typically do so to metaphorize these everyday acts such that their concrete significance is lost. For example, feasting becomes an image of the artistic celebration of God's grace rather than an activity linked with the seasonal provision of the earth and the preparation, consumption, and symbolism of real foods.[37]

In Catholic Eucharistic theology, the elements of bread and wine offered at the altar become the body and blood of Christ, which communicants consume when they taste the elements. Ordinary food and drink thereby gain significance by becoming something else. Similar analyses of the Eucharist could be offered in other Christian traditions. The classic Anglican (Episcopalian) formula that the bread and wine are outward and visible signs of inward, spiritual graces can be seen as producing a similar outcome, displacing real eating and drinking with a spiritual experience such that the Eucharist is seen as having no direct implications for those everyday activities.

Yet the use of bread and wine in the Eucharist is theologically apposite. In their manufacture, both elements undergo a material transformation that mirrors the theological transformation their recipients experience in the Eucharist. In the rising of dough and the fermentation of grape juice, one product becomes another as a result of a process that was, prior to modern times, not fully understood.[38] Because of this correspondence between the elements and the transformative theology they convey, they function analogically. The theological significance of the Eucharist therefore emerges from food and drink, which are offered with thanksgiving, from understanding and maybe participating in processes of manufacture, and from actually consuming the products themselves, which sustain and inebriate the human body. Far from justifying the sidelining of everyday food and diet as serious theological concerns, Eucharistic theology depends on these and draws attention back to them.

CHRISTIANITY AND RELIGION

Christian dietary discipline, especially fasting, has been shaped by Christians reflecting on their own traditions. This has been largely a process of acquiring greater self-understanding. Yet Christian food practices have also evolved through external engagements with other religious groups. Christians' desire to differentiate themselves from these groups has led them to adopt distinctive dietary practices.

The notion that dietary disciplines are marginal or irrelevant to Christianity has developed in modern times as a corollary of the view that Christianity is, as a religion, fundamentally different from any other. This may be seen clearly in the attempts of many omnivorous Christian missionaries to make converts eat meats that were previously forbidden to them.[39] Needless to say, such missionaries had little conception of the role that food rules had played in previous eras in forming Christian identity, whether the prohibition of blood, strangled animals and carrion at the Jerusalem Council (Acts 15.29), the observance of Mosaic food rules by Irish monks, the prohibition of quadruped flesh in medieval monasteries, or many others.[40]

The tendency to regard food rules as non-Christian, or the absence of such rules as a necessary marker of Christian identity, has been lent considerable support by readings of the New Testament that have assumed that the nascent Christian church effected a complete break with Judaism. Many crude supersessionist oppositions have been constructed between a dying legalistic, ritualistic, and superstitious religion based on exclusivist tribalism and justification by works—which, according to this presentation, Christ came to abolish—and a free, universal, spiritual revelation founded on inclusivist faith. But in the aftermath of the Holocaust, Christian biblical scholars, church historians, and theologians have fundamentally rethought these suppositions. In particular, New Testament scholars such as E. P. Sanders have presented early Christianity as having far greater continuity with Judaism than previous generations of scholars would have accepted.[41]

This interpretive shift reveals that arguments about the place of law, ritual, and material practice in spiritual life are rarely just theological. They are impelled by a range of pretheological theories—or, as Bourdieu would have it, logics of practice—which typically go unacknowledged.[42] Mary Douglas highlighted this wider theoretical context in her preface to the new edition of *Purity and Danger*, in which she discussed how her concerns in that work with boundaries and social order were motivated by a determination to refute the fashionable 1960s antistructuralist view that these were epiphenomena of bureaucratic late modernity.[43] In fact, she argues, boundaries and social order are widespread and necessary features of the everyday material life of human societies.

What is unusual about modern secular society in the United States and elsewhere is not the absence of rules governing daily life but the separation that has occurred between those rules and everyday life as embodied in religious codes. Such codes allow rules about food and eating to be internalized, and to be informed by a cosmology that invests food with spiritual and doctrinal significance. They locate its production and consumption within a liturgical and often seasonal context. These historical, theoretical, and theological perspectives provide important background to understanding the place of dietary practices in modern Christian theology, and in Christian encounters with members of other faiths and followers of secular spiritualities. They call Christians more generally to reassess the importance of food and other material practices in an age of scarce resources, which are often distributed inequitably. In particular, they call Christians to refrain from neosupersessionist discourses, which instrumentalize other religions and their practices in order to construct Christianity as unique and superior to them.

CHRISTIAN ABSTINENCE, RELIGIOUS ABSTINENCE, SUSTAINABLE ABSTINENCE

Awareness of the tremendous importance that Christian communities in the United States have historically attached to dietary abstinence opens possibilities for new comparative engagements with other faiths and spiritualities based around food practices. This task is especially pressing in an age in which a range of problems linked to diet—food miles, climate change, heart disease, obesity, anorexia—pose major social and political challenges. Christians might recognize with humility that, as a result of their religion's close links with modern industrialized consumer society, their own recent mainstream tradition might not provide the resources needed to respond to the problems this society has spawned. Engagements with other religions have the potential to bring Christians to recover key elements of their own tradition, such as an awareness that the world is a gift to humankind within limits.

How then might Christian dietary abstinence be distinctive? In the United States Christians live not in a diaspora context in which particular food practices preserve their identity but as a dominant religious group, and indeed as the historically privileged religion. This gives them unrivaled freedom to develop dietary practices in their modern context that draw wisely and flexibly on a rich and diverse tradition of dietary abstinence as part of a constructive theological response to the real problems the world currently faces. This might include reducing meat consumption through moderation or fasting, or even eliminating meat altogether in appropriate circumstances. Moreover, producing and consuming food as part of a concrete local community will cut food miles. Such disciplines have the potential to positively influence other areas of moral and social life, and production and trade. Current pressing global issues, as well as a deepened spirituality, might help the world's first global religion take a backward glance and recover some of the historic identity and material context it has lost.

DISCUSSION QUESTIONS

1. Can religious food abstinence be distinguished from nonreligious food abstinence, and if so, how?
2. How does Christian dietary discipline differ from the dietary disciplines of other religions?
3. Why have Christians sometimes had an ambivalent attitude to dietary discipline?

NOTES

1. Examples include Carol J. Adams, *The Inner Art of Vegetarianism: Spiritual Practices for Body and Soul* (New York: Lantern, 2000); and Donald Altman, *Art of the Inner Meal: Eating as a Spiritual Path* (New York: Harper, 1999).
2. Martha L. Finch, *Dissenting Bodies: Corporealities in Early New England* (New York: Columbia University Press, 2010), 169–75.

3. Aline Rousselle, *Porneia: On Desire and the Body in Antiquity* (Oxford: Blackwell, 1988), 160–64.

4. For systematic use of the humoral motif, see Trudy Eden, *The Early American Table: Food and Society in the New World* (DeKalb: Northern Illinois University Press, 2008).

5. Jeff Bach, *Voices of the Turtledoves: The Sacred World of Ephrata* (University Park: Pennsylvania State University Press, 2003), 87–88.

6. Karen Iacobbo and Michael Iacobbo, *Vegetarian America: A History* (Westport, Conn.: Praeger, 2004), 4.

7. Anon, *History of the Philadelphia Bible-Christian Church for the First Century of Its Existence from 1817 to 1917* (Philadelphia: Lippincott, 1922), 40.

8. Daniel Sack, *Whitebread Protestants: Food and Religion in American Culture* (New York: St. Martin's, 2000), 188–89.

9. Margaret Puskar-Pasewicz, "Kitchen Sisters and Disagreeable Boys: Debates Over Meatless Diets in Nineteenth-Century Shaker Communities," in *Eating in Eden: Food and American Utopias*, ed. Etta M. Madden and Martha L. Finch, 109–24 (Lincoln: University of Nebraska Press, 2006).

10. Jayme A. Sokolow, *Eros and Modernization: Sylvester Graham, Health Reform and the Origins of Victorian Sexuality in America* (Rutherford, N.J.: Fairleigh Dickinson University Press, 1983), 58, 102.

11. Stephen Nissenbaum, *Sex, Diet, and Debility in Jacksonian America: Sylvester Graham and Health Reform* (Westport, Conn.: Greenwood, 1980), 13, 39.

12. William Ian Miller, "Gluttony," *Representations* 60 (1997): 92–112.

13. Ex. 34.28, Dt. 9.9, 9.18 (Moses); 1 Sam. 14.24 (Hannah); 1 Sam. 23.14, Ps. 63.1b (David); 1 Kings 17.6 (Elijah); 1 Kings 21.27–29 (Ahab); 2 Kings 19.1 (Hezekiah); Lk. 2.36 (Anna); 2 Cor. 11.27 (Paul).

14. James A. Kelhoffer, *The Diet of John the Baptist: "Locusts and Wild Honey" in Synoptic and Patristic Interpretation* (Tübingen: Mohr Siebeck, 2005).

15. William Metcalfe, "Bible Testimony on Abstinence from the Flesh of Animals as Food," in *Out of the Clouds: Into the Light*, 161–80 (Philadelphia: Lippincott, 1872).

16. Ibid., 155–79.

17. John Henry Newman, *Parochial and Plain Sermons*, 8 vols. (London: Rivingtons, 1870–79), 6:1.

18. www.foodforlife.com. The references are: "And you, take wheat and barley, beans and lentils, millet and spelt; put them into one vessel, and make bread for yourself" (Ez. 4.9); "God said: 'See, I have given you every plant yielding seed that is upon all the earth, and every tree with seed in its fruit; you shall have them for food'" (Gen. 1.29).

19. Basil of Caesarea, *The Asketikon of St Basil the Great*, ed. Anna Silvas (Oxford: Oxford University Press, 2005), 215.

20. Stephen J. Stein, *The Shaker Experience in America: A History of the United Society of Believers* (New Haven: Yale University Press, 1992), 156.

21. E.g., Matthew Halteman, *Compassionate Eating as Care of Creation* (Washington, D.C.: Humane Society of the United States, 2008); and Michael S. Northcott, *A Moral Climate: The Ethics of Global Warming* (London: Darton, Longman and Todd, 2007), 232–66.

22. Tito Colliander, *Way of the Ascetics* (Crestwood, N.Y.: St. Vladimir's, 2003); and Adalbert de Vogüé, *To Love Fasting: The Monastic Experience* (Petersham, Mass.: Saint Bede's, 1989).

23. R. Marie Griffith, *Born Again Bodies: Flesh and Spirit in American Christianity* (Berkeley: University of California Press, 2004), 30–33.

24. Ibid., 40–47; R. Marie Griffith, "Fasting, Dieting and the Body in American Christianity," in *Perspectives on American Religion and Culture*, ed. Peter W. Williams, 216–27 (Oxford: Blackwell, 1999), 220.

25. Gerald Carson, *Cornflake Crusade* (London: Gollancz, 1959), 71–72.

26. Ibid., 142–44.

27. William Shurtleff and Akiko Aoyagi, *Bibliography and Sourcebook on Seventh-Day Adventists' Work with Soyfoods, Vegetarianism, and Wheat Gluten, 1866–1992* (Lafayette, Ca.: Soyfoods Centre, 1992), 8.

28. Horace B. Powell, *The Original Has This Signature—W. K. Kellogg* (Englewood Cliffs, N.J.: Prentice Hall, 1956), 127.

29. Ryan Berry, *Food for the Gods: Vegetarianism and the World's Religions* (New York: Pythagorean, 1998).

30. Kallistos Ware, introduction to *The Lenten Triodion* (London: Faber & Faber, 1978), 35–37); and Pope Paul VI, *Paenitemini* (London: Catholic Truth Society, 1973 [1966]).

31. David Grumett and Rachel Muers, *Theology on the Menu: Asceticism, Meat and Christian Diet* (London: Routledge, 2010), 72–88, 107–27. The hare was sometimes regarded as unclean because of its purported sexual practices. The Armenian *matal* sacrifice, which continues into the present day, includes a codified liturgy and a communal feast.

32. Frederick J. Simoons, *Eat Not This Flesh: Food Avoidances from Prehistory to the Present* (Madison: University of Wisconsin Press, 1994).

33. Analyzed in David Horrell, "Biblical Vegetarianism? A Critical and Constructive Assessment," in *Eating and Believing: Interdisciplinary Perspectives on Vegetarianism and Theology*, ed. Rachel Muers and David Grumett, 44–59 (Lon-

don: T & T Clark, 2008); and Stephen H. Webb, *Good Eating: The Bible, Diet, and the Proper Love of Animals* (Grand Rapids, Mich.: Brazos, 2001), 102–40.

34. Philip Lyndon Reynolds, *Food and the Body: Some Peculiar Questions in High Medieval Theology* (Leiden: Brill, 1999), 40–41.

35. Bach, *Voices*, 87.

36. Thomas Aquinas, *Summa Theologica*, 22 vols. (London: Burns, Oates and Washburn, 1920–24), 20:3.

37. E.g., David Ford, *Self and Salvation: Being Transformed* (Cambridge: Cambridge University Press, 1998), 266–81.

38. David Brown, *God of Grace and Body: Sacrament in Ordinary* (Oxford: Oxford University Press, 2007), 138–40, 169–70.

39. Tristram Stuart, *The Bloodless Revolution: Radical Vegetarians and the Discovery of India* (London: HarperPress 2006).

40. *The Rule of St. Benedict* 46, ed. Timothy Fry (Collegeville, Minn.: Liturgical, 1981); and David Grumett, "Mosaic Food Rules in Celtic Spirituality in Ireland," in *Eating and Believing: Interdisciplinary Perspectives on Vegetarianism and Theology*, ed. Rachel Muers and David Grumett, 31–43 (London: T & T Clark, 2008).

41. E. P. Sanders, *Jewish Law from Jesus to the Mishnah* (London: SCM, 1990).

42. Pierre Bourdieu, *The Logic of Practice*, trans. Richard Nice (Cambridge: Polity, 1992).

43. Mary Douglas, *Purity and Danger: An Analysis of Concepts of Pollution and Taboo*, rev. ed. (London: Routledge, 2002), x–xxi.

RECOMMENDED READING

Albala, Ken, and Trudy Eden, eds. *Food and Faith in Christian Culture.* New York: Columbia University Press, 2011.

Griffith, R. Marie. "Fasting, Dieting, and the Body in American Christianity." In *Perspectives on American Religion and Culture.* Edited by Peter W. Williams, 216–27. Oxford: Blackwell, 1999.

Grumett, David, and Rachel Muers. *Theology on the Menu: Asceticism, Meat and Christian Diet.* London: Routledge, 2010.

Sack, Daniel. *Whitebread Protestants: Food and Religion in American Culture.* New York: St. Martin's, 2000.

Wirzba, Norman. *Food and Faith: A Theology of Eating.* New York: Cambridge University Press, 2011.

Two

"JOIN US! COME, EAT!"

VEGETARIANISM IN THE FORMATIVE PERIOD OF THE SEVENTH-DAY ADVENTISTS AND THE UNITY SCHOOL OF CHRISTIANITY

JEREMY RAPPORT

THE SEVENTH-DAY ADVENTISTS and the Unity School of Christianity, two important alternative religious communities that emerged in the second half of the nineteenth century, both advocated vegetarian diets during their formative periods. The groups are at opposite ends of a Protestant theological spectrum. Seventh-day Adventists teach that redemption and salvation require faith in Jesus understood as the Son of God along with strict adherence to biblical laws. The Unity School of Christianity teaches that God is an omnibenevolent force pervading the universe and that Jesus exemplified the possibilities that all humans could develop. Humans can achieve redemption and salvation by thinking the right way about the God principle. Yet both these groups espoused basically the same vegetarian diet early in their development. Both groups used a vegetarian diet to create and maintain religious boundaries and as part of their religious visions. Adhering to a vegetarian diet indicated that one belonged to the community since it provided a way for new converts to unify around a practice that was central to life, a way of eating. In other ways, though, vegetarianism functioned quite differently between the groups. The two communities' origins, although sharing a context of health concerns on the part of the founders, were also quite different. This curious combination of a similar practical approach to a human problem of salvation understood in vastly different terms makes the study of vegetarianism in these two movements particularly revealing.

Because both Seventh-day Adventists and Unity used a similar form of vegetarianism to enact their religious beliefs, the practice is a highly useful anchor point with which to structure a study of the creation of these religious communities. Moreover, an examination and comparison of vegetarianism in the two movements reveals how each community made and maintained boundaries and negotiated the community's relationship with the larger culture. Thus this most mundane of issues—how a person is to eat—reveals the ways in which two communities espousing very similar diets came to very different conclusions about how that diet influenced the path to redemption and salvation.

The larger movement out of which Seventh-day Adventism emerged had become fractious in the aftermath of the failure of its major prophecy, which stated that Jesus would return to Earth on October 22, 1844. Ellen G. White (1827–1915), the charismatic figure of the young Seventh-day Adventist movement, made her claims amid a chorus of competing explanations for the failure of that prophecy. Because White mandated vegetarianism as a biblical requirement for the chosen people, practicing it meant accepting the authority of White as prophet. Vegetarianism functioned as a way to declare one's assent to White's authority; it therefore helped solidify Seventh-day Adventists as a movement.

For early Unity adherents, vegetarianism as a marker of community membership was less clear-cut. Charles (1854–1948) and Myrtle Fillmore (1845–1931), the founders of the Unity movement, taught that vegetarianism was a practice that aided in regenerating the physical body, which they understood as a central part of the larger process of redemption and salvation. However, they wrote in several places that vegetarianism was not required for membership, although their "Statements of Faith" would seem to contradict that position. In any case, the Fillmores did consistently maintain that vegetarianism was not required to regenerate the body. Rather it made the process easier and more efficient. They supported this claim with citations of various scientific studies that seemed to support their position, as well as with numerous testimonies to the salutary effects of vegetarianism. The Fillmores used vegetarianism, in part, to rhetorically tie Unity to larger discourses in American culture about the authority of science and the authority of personal experience. Thus Unity members who became vegetarians did so in part because they accepted the argument that the practice was rational and capable of being proved efficacious by personal experience. Unity vegetarians were marking themselves as members of the modern world and marking themselves as part of a new religion.

Unity also made clear efforts to fit vegetarianism into the larger culture's food practices by creating vegetarian Thanksgiving and Christmas menus and publishing numerous recipes that purported to show how easy and how satisfying a vegetarian diet could be. The Fillmores were trying to show that being a vegetarian would not single one out from the surrounding culture. Because it demonstrated the ways in which the movement tied itself to discourse such as science, which the culture understood as authoritative, and tied itself to the ritual calendar, Unity's practice of vegetarianism revealed one way that the movement integrated into American culture even while engaging in practices that were unusual in that culture.

THE CONTEXT OF VEGETARIANISM IN SEVENTH-DAY ADVENTIST AND UNITY PRACTICES

As part of a larger dialogue on health, vegetarianism was an issue in American discourse on diet since the early nineteenth century. Reformers such as Sylvester Graham (1794–1851) advocated a nonmeat diet both as salutary in and of itself and as an aid in the effort to prevent various types of perceived vice, such as excessive consumption of alcohol, masturbation, and overly vigorous sexual drives. Many reformers focused on diet in conjunction with new forms of disease treatment such as hydropathy, the attempt to regain health through the use of water in various forms.

Graham, a Presbyterian minister, temperance lecturer, and self-styled doctor, was perhaps the most influential thinker on diet during this era. Based on theories about the connection between the stimulating effects of certain kinds of food, notably meat, and the effect of blood on behavior, he advocated a mild, vegetarian diet, which Graham believed would prevent overstimulation of the blood and therefore help prevent such evils. Graham also believed that commercially produced bread was one of the major reasons for the overall poor health of Americans. According to Graham, bread should always be made at home by the family's wife and mother out of unbolted, or unrefined, flour. It should be eaten cold and should be a staple of the diet.[1] Graham's teachings on diet were adopted and adapted by both the Seventh-day Adventists and Unity as part of their religious messages and practices.

The people who would start the Seventh-day Adventist Church began their work in the wake of events on October 22, 1844. Across the Northeastern United States, Millerites—followers of William Miller (1782–1849), a Baptist lay preacher from Low Hampton, New York—were stopping to evaluate what had happened; or, more precisely, what had not happened. Miller's predicted second coming of Jesus had not occurred, and people who had invested their spiritual lives in his predictions now had a harsh reality to face: was Miller's date wrong? Were they somehow at fault for the nonevent? Was the entire prediction the hopeful fantasy of a sincerely devout yet deluded man? While Jesus had clearly not returned to Earth, many Millerites were not ready to give up on the hope of a second coming. After all, many of these people had literally staked their lives on the prediction, dispensing their estates, selling their farms, and letting crops die in the fields.[2] Many had also dedicated their lives to spreading the message to their friends and neighbors and therefore had an interest in a plausible explanation for the embarrassing nonevent.

One explanation was that the date had not been wrong, but the event the date signified had been misunderstood. October 22 signified, rather than Jesus's return to Earth, the return of Jesus to the heavenly sanctuary to begin its cleansing. Once that was accomplished, Jesus would in fact return to Earth. Those who would become known as Seventh-day Adventists took this view. Adventists now set no precise date for Jesus's return except to say that it would happen when the required heavenly events are accomplished and when the faithful have sufficiently aligned themselves with biblical law. Adventists developed a system of practice and belief that negotiated the complex boundaries of a religious movement centered on the culmination of history that was, at the same time, concerned about life in the mundane world. Vegetarianism was a central tenet of that system.

By contrast, Unity was born at the end of the nineteenth century when Myrtle Fillmore, wife of Kansas City, Missouri, real estate man Charles Fillmore, experienced a bodily healing that she attributed to having learned the common New Thought prayer technique known as affirmation.[3] Beginning with Myrtle Fillmore's healing using the affirmation "I am a child of God and do not inherit sickness" and her healing of friends and neighbors using similar New Thought techniques, early Unity adherents clearly placed issues such as the health and well-being of the body at the heart of their religious ideals. Vegetarianism evidently developed, at least in part, as a corollary of those ideals. So in April 1921, when the Fillmores issued a second version of Unity's Statement of the Faith, it included a prohibition on meat eating: "We believe that all life is sacred and that man should not kill nor be a party to the killing of animals for food; also that cruelty, war, and wanton destruction of human life will continue as long as men kill animals for food."[4]

While April 1921 marked the first Unity doctrinal statement regarding dietary teachings, vegetarianism certainly was not a new development for Charles and Myrtle Fillmore. They had abstained from meat eating since the last decade of the nineteenth century. Vegetarianism was also a topic of interest in Unity's magazine as early as 1903. It continued to be a well-covered topic in Unity's publications, with several pieces on vegetarianism, a column called "The Vegetarian" in the weekly paper, and at least one address at the Unity Auditorium on the topic. Unity also operated the Unity Inn, a vegetarian cafeteria in Kansas City.

According to Unity author Thomas Witherspoon, Myrtle Fillmore adopted vegetarianism in 1895 largely because of her relationship with Harry Church, Unity's printer. Witherspoon claims that Fillmore explained her decision as a natural and easy process: "The appetite left me without my even thinking about it and I am sure I outgrew the demand for murdered things."[5] However, working in a small office with the entire Unity staff, she probably had ample opportunity to discuss ideas such as vegetarianism with Church, whom James Dillet Freeman describes as having "a long brown beard" and being "a Seventh Day [sic] Adventist and a vegetarian."[6] The Fillmores had a link with a Seventh-day Adventist who practiced the Adventist diet, and Unity publications on vegetarianism show that they absorbed at least some of Sylvester Graham's teachings. Both the Adventist and the Unity diets were heavily influenced by the practices advocated by Graham, including abstention from meat, tobacco, caffeine, and alcohol and the regular consumption of graham bread. Also, the Adventists and the Unity movement enacted the lived realities of their religious lives using a similar dietary system to create and maintain group boundaries and to express their relationships with the divine entities they each wanted to engage.

However, important differences also existed between how vegetarianism was adopted by members and the way it influenced each group's relationship with its divine forces. Seventh-day Adventist vegetarianism was a religious obligation that encountered resistance from adherents and was at times the source of internal community conflict as well as continuity. Ellen G. White seemed conflicted about it, and on occasion she even admitted to lapsing from the practice. On the other hand, Unity treated vegetarianism as a beneficial practice that any rational person would want to adopt. It was part of a ritualized healing system and was encouraged for religious and salutary reasons. Hence it was not necessarily religiously problematic for Unity members to eat meat, and Charles Fillmore resumed eating fish at the end of his life. Looking at how vegetarianism mediated the relationship between the faithful and the divine reveals important differences in how Adventists and Unity members understood the divine and their obligations as humans seeking divine aid on the path to salvation.

RELIGIOUS ASPECTS OF VEGETARIANISM

Ellen G. White began having visions on health reform as early as 1848. In the fall of that year she had a vision in which she was told that Adventists must avoid tobacco, coffee, and tea. White's second health vision occurred in February 1854. This vision contains the first prescriptions dealing with food: "In words that echoed Sylvester Graham she told of seeing that Sabbath-keepers were making 'a god of their bellies,' that instead of eating so many rich dishes they should take 'more coarse food with little grease.'"[7]

Although clear directives about diet did not appear in the earliest Seventh-day Adventist Statements of Beliefs, White had been teaching vegetarianism to her followers since the early 1860s. The original diet reform was strict: "To the typical Seventh-day Adventist in the 1860s, health reform meant essentially a twice-a-day diet of fruits, vegetables, grains, and nuts. Since Ellen White's vision on June 5, 1863, meat, eggs, butter, and cheese had joined alcohol, tobacco, tea, and coffee on her index of proscribed items." Ideally the Whites would take two meals a day, one at 7:00 a.m. and one at 1:00 p.m., consisting only of fruits, grains, vegetables, nuts, and milk.[8]

Those proscriptions eventually formed the tenets of Ellen G. White's comprehensive health vision, the one most associated with Seventh-day Adventist health and diet reform. The vision itself occurred after an extensive stay at the Dansville hydropathy center where White's husband, James, was attempting to regain his health. During a visit to Otsego, Michigan, White had further visions on health and diet that contained messages to avoid drugs and stimulants. Adventists were to exercise extreme caution in meat eating and were to take pure air, sunshine, and water treatments to maintain health.[9] Adventist dietary and health reform therefore developed in conjunction with White's prophetic authority, and White clearly understood these various health practices as part of submitting to God's commands.

The Adventist dietary system was eventually compiled in a collection of White's writing titled *Counsels on Diet and Foods.* White portrayed vegetarianism as part of a quest for perfection: "God desires us to reach the standard of perfection made possible for us by the gift of Christ. . . . He has revealed the principles of life. It is our work to obtain a knowledge of these principles, and by obedience to cooperate with Him in restoring health to the body as well to the soul." Seventh-day Adventists were required to understand the basis of good health and to put those ideas into practice. Because White taught that this was God's will, not just a recommendation for a happier life, it was therefore considered a sin to break the laws of health: "It is as truly a sin to violate the laws of our being as it is to break the ten commandments."[10]

White taught that intemperance of all kinds was sinful and an obstacle to cultivating spirituality: "Let none who profess godliness regard with indifference the health of the body, and flatter themselves that intemperance is no sin, and will not affect their spirituality. A close sympathy exists between the physical and the moral nature." She also connected temperance to the fall of and restoration to Eden: "With our first parents, intemperate desire resulted in the loss of Eden. Temperance in all things has more to do with our restoration to Eden than men realize." She thus understood control of appetite as one of the keys to becoming a godly people. Because she believed the human body was a gift from God, she taught that humans should not treat their bodies any way they please. Humans owed a duty "to render to God perfect service [because] . . . we are absolutely dependent upon God."[11]

White integrated her dietary teachings with her teachings on preparing for Jesus's return. She claimed, "I was again shown that the health reform is one branch of the great work which is to fit a people for the coming of the Lord. It is as closely connected with the third angel's message as the hand is with the body."[12] Health and diet reform were just as important as observation of the Saturday Sabbath or acceptance of the October 22 message that said that Jesus had inaugurated God's plan for the culmination of history. Dietary reform prepared people for the second coming by aiding them to align themselves with God's will for humanity. Since one condition for Jesus's return was that the faithful observe God's laws, in White's teachings salvation depended on overcoming the appetites that caused the original downfall of humans.

White advocated a diet she considered to be both humanity's original diet and the best one for human health. "In order to know what are the best foods, we must study God's original plan for man's diet. He who created man and who understands his needs appointed Adam his food." White argued that humanity's original diet contained no meat of any sort: "It was contrary to his plan to have the life of any creature taken. There was to be no death in Eden." So from White's perspective, humans must return to this diet, "The Lord intends to bring His people back to live upon simple fruits, vegetables, and grains."[13] Because going back to original biblical principles was a key part of the second coming, vegetarianism, which White read as part of the description of human life in Genesis, was also a logical part of preparing for Jesus's second coming.

The last four-fifths of *Counsels on Diet and Foods* is an elaboration of the dietary system. White discussed everything from the necessity of eating slowly and thoroughly chewing all food to the dangers of coffee and tea. She gave recipes and cooking tips along with meal plans and advice on permissible variations in the diet. Because food and diet played such an important part on the path to salvation, Seventh-day Adventist adherents had to completely and properly understand their use and practice.

Like White's understanding of the practice, for the Fillmores vegetarianism played a central role in larger issue of bodily health and control in salvation.[14] Health was an outward sign of one's relationship with God for the Fillmores, and worldly concerns such as diet played an important role in salvation. Unlike White and the Adventists, for Unity adherents vegetarianism was not primarily about submitting to God's will. Rather, it was portrayed as a logical practice for those who understood God's design of the world and plan for humanity.

Myrtle Fillmore summed up her view of this issue in a short passage that appears in *Myrtle Fillmore's Healing Letters*: "When we make health, wholeness, holiness the dominant thought of our minds, re-educating our physical senses to their true purpose, our body temples will be sure to manifest their God-given perfection, because our bodies are the fruit of our minds."[15] She believed that the condition of the body was determined by the reality the mind creates, so a person's manifestation of reality can be understood as a function of the mind and its thoughts. One prime function of the human mind is as a link to God. Among the many attributes Fillmore ascribed to God's nature is the "all-powerful Spirit of restoration." Tuning into this spirit through correct use of the mind is the basic requirement for the individual to manifest health.

However, the process of attaining perfect health as described by Fillmore also involved facilitating the body's cooperation. Fillmore described a partnership between the mind and the body this way: "There is a divine law of mind action that we may conform to, and that will always bring satisfactory results. There is also a physical side to the operation of this divine law. The body and its needs must have our consideration."[16] The mind and the body must work together to return the self to its natural state of health. Fillmore developed her complete notion of this mind-body interaction as a process of learning the truth, investigating the situation, and taking appropriate action. Describing a person who understood mind-body interaction correctly, she wrote:

He holds to the truth that his body is pure and alive and perfect in every part, because he wishes to use this perfect mental pattern to direct him in his treatment. He then looks into his thought habits to see that they are prompted by faith and divine love and wisdom and life and joy and freedom. He looks into his living habits to see that he is taking good care of the body and meeting the requirements of its many departments and functions. He acquaints himself with the different parts of the body, and learns what it is they are truly built for. He learns what each needs and supplies them.[17]

A person interested in healing the body must first learn the proper ideas, assimilate those ideas into the mind, and then take the appropriate actions with the body. One of the most important of these appropriate actions is a proper diet, which is one centered on the vegetarian principles that Fillmore learned from the Seventh-day Adventist Harry Church in those early days in the Unity offices.

The first public statement on vegetarianism in Unity was Charles Fillmore's October 1903 article entitled "As to Meat Eating," published in *Unity*, the second iteration of the magazine of their emerging movement. In the article Fillmore used traditional religious arguments such as the citation of biblical passages (Gen. 1:29, in which God gives humans every "herb yielding seed") to support vegetarianism. He also discussed the morality of diet and traced the perceived scientific rationale behind vegetarianism to justify vegetarianism as the proper diet for Unity practitioners.

Fillmore argued that Christians once believed diet to be of no real concern because of the New Testament "injunction to take no thought about food." But he discovered that diet did make a difference in one's spiritual progress: "It is found that food does have a part in body structure, and that the metaphysician must take it into account if he would reach the higher substance demonstrations." He argued instead that because sustaining life is the object of eating, life itself is the object of eating. An energizing force Fillmore described as "the life idea" infused all forms in existence, and if that life idea is withdrawn, the form collapses and dies. This meant, according to Fillmore, that what people ate was not simply food but a means to create the life force. Therefore in order to be pure, food must be free from any semblance of death or decay: "If we are eating aggregations of life ideas hid within the material forms, we should use discrimination in choosing those forms. Our food should be full of life in its purity and vigor. There should be no idea of death and decay connected with it in any degree."[18] In Unity's developing New Thought theology, an idea had real power and consequence in the material world, so if a person was physically consuming ideas contained in the flesh of slaughtered animals, that had a marked effect on the person's material well-being.

Poor diet did not nourish the human form, which Fillmore discovered for himself. When he first began studying "Truth," he took no heed of his diet, but as his learning progressed he came to a realization:

But gradually a new phase set in. I found I was having vibrations in the sympathetic nerve centers—the subconscious mind was being quickened, and I was becoming a conscious vital battery. The vital currents gradually grew stronger and stronger until I could hardly control them. Appetite, passion, emotion, etc., were greatly increased. Then my prayers for guidance were answered and a system of communication set up with the higher realms of consciousness. I was shown that the food that entered the organism had to pass through a process of regeneration every day before it was in condition to be built into the new body in Christ. Just how to carry on this regenerative process in the various subconscious centres was also shown, and here is where I discerned the effect of foods in body building.[19]

Through Charles Fillmore's process of spiritual exploration he discovered that what people ate affected who they were. A Unity adherent could help the processes the body goes through to incorporate the new life it absorbs via its food by consuming the proper type of food.

Charles Fillmore also related, in biological and scientific language, what he understood to be the workings of this system. Individual living cells contained a "vitalizing element" that dead cells had lost. The new cells that individuals appropriated in the form of food would become part of the individual's consciousness. The effect these appropriated cells had depended on the individual's ability to regenerate them. While people who did not consciously regenerate the cells they consumed did derive some benefit simply from the way bodies absorb food, individuals who consciously regenerated the cells they consumed obtained the best benefits of the food. Fillmore described the regeneration process as putting the individual's mark on the nature of the food he or she consumed: "The stamp of individual identity is put upon it [cells in the food consumed] through a concerted effort of the I AM, in spiritual mediation and affirmation."[20]

Fillmore next claimed that the process of regeneration of cells was best carried out when the individual consciously cooperated with the regenerative process by consuming food of the "highest and purest" character. If an individual consumed decaying cells, such as those from a dead animal, then that individual was consuming "corruption and decay." Consuming corruption and decay caused real problems, though most people did not realize it: "Yet ignorant man loads his system with these elements of discord and decay and expects to get life out of them. No wonder his body dies."[21] Eating meat was introducing chaos into an ordered system that should be regenerated with plant foods. Plant foods were easier on the body because they required less energy and effort to transform into a usable life force for the individual consuming them. Meat, in contrast, required a concerted effort by the individual, including the effort at overcoming another animal's life force, in order to transform chaotic, dead matter into something the body could use to sustain its own life force. Fillmore claimed that the chaos introduced by meat consumption eventually caused the body to break down and die. By avoiding the chaos, decay, and corruption introduced into the body by the consumption of meat, humans made the process of regenerating the body easier.

Like Ellen G. White, Fillmore also attributed the negative consequences of meat eating to violating biblical law. When they ate meat, Fillmore wrote, humans also disobeyed a divine law: "Man is today suffering in his body and mind the results of this transgressed law, and he will continue to suffer until he observes in the fullest degree the command, 'Thou shalt not kill.' "[22] Fillmore understood biblical law and New Thought tenets to be mutually reinforcing. Unlike White, who understood compliance with biblical law to be a mandate for the faithful preparing for Jesus's return, Fillmore saw the purpose of adhering to biblical law to be related to creating a personal transformation that allowed bodily healing in this world and served as a mark of a renewed relationship with the divine.

ENACTING BELIEF, MAINTAINING BOUNDARIES, AND ESTABLISHING RELATIONSHIPS

The everyday consumption of food became an important part of Seventh-day Adventist and Unity belief and practice. By helping each group to enact its beliefs, vegetarianism helped each group to create and maintain behavioral boundaries that allowed adherents to better understand their religious lives and their relationships with the outside world.[23] Examining vegetarianism reveals several important facets of practicing these alternative religious lives.

For Seventh-day Adventists, as time progressed with no second coming, believers were forced to deal with everyday issues such as marriage, family, disease, and diet and those issues' relationship to ultimate claims about God's will for the faithful. In part, then, it is logical that a church concerned mainly with big issues such as the end of time and Jesus's return would also concern itself with more mundane issues such as diet as the end of time receded further and further into the future.

Since the sense of urgency associated with the end of time faded as that end kept moving away from the believers, the Seventh-day Adventists had to deal with everyday issues in order to remain vital to their faithful. The date of Jesus's return has not been revealed; therefore believers must be ready for it to occur at any time. Because of this uncertainty, now built into the Adventist belief system, it is particularly important for the saved to be identified and ready. They must be following God's requirements when the second coming occurs or their chance at salvation is gone. Because White considered the diet described in Genesis to be identical to the diet she advocated, diet reform restored biblical laws that White believed to be an important part of the preparatory work required to escape God's wrath and be counted among the saved when Jesus did return. Practicing vegetarianism allowed the Adventists to maintain distinctions between clean and unclean and to restore the original diet of humans, as identified in Genesis, while at the same time creating a behavioral boundary with the non-Adventist world.

That boundary helped White and the Adventists fight intemperance and the consumption of food for pleasure, which they considered to be an integral part of the first sin. Because of this, humans who reformed their diet in the manner she prescribed would also be working to restore a state of perfection—a state like the one that existed before humans violated the commandment of God and were ejected from paradise. Reform of the diet was therefore a necessary first step toward regaining the perfection of Eden, which would become available to those who were among the saved after Jesus's return and final judgment.

For early Unity adherents, vegetarianism can also be understood as a gauge of the movement's development and its efforts to differentiate itself from the rest of the New Thought world. The Fillmores originally intended Unity to be an extraecclesiastical, educational organization. They wanted their teachings to supplement the lessons people received in more orthodox churches. Thus they would schedule meetings so that they did not conflict with common service times for local churches and encourage people to attend their regular churches.

However, as the organization grew it became more like a traditional denomination. The Fillmores began to make a concerted effort to solidify the movement's religious identity as it became clear that more people were attending Unity meetings in place of Sunday church services. For example, in response to numerous requests for a clear list of Unity teachings, the Fillmores began issuing their Statement of the Faith in 1921. During the early twentieth century they also moved away from explicit associations with other New Thought movements, notably the International New Thought Alliance, an umbrella organization that tried to promote New Thought.[24] Vegetarianism functioned to help Unity define its religious identity and demonstrate its newly established principles to the growing number of people interested in its teachings. Because Unity was the only major New Thought movement to advocate vegetarianism, the practice also provided a way to mark Unity adherents off from other New Thought practitioners.

The anthropologist Mary Douglas has argued that food laws are associated with purity laws. Part of purity is controlling and ordering the world that surrounds a person, and since food is an everyday part of life, in order for it to be pure it must be controlled. Also, on a basic level, groups maintain purity standards in part to help identify members of the group. Those within the group follow the group's laws and therefore are identified as members. This was clearly an issue for Ellen G. White in her writing on diet reform: "The people whom God is leading will be peculiar. They will not be like the world."[25] If the world eats meat and drinks liquor and smokes tobacco, then God's people will do none of these things. In this way, a people waiting on the return of Jesus could be identified. Since salvation depended on identification of those who both thought the right way and acted the right way, establishing who was among the saved group entailed knowing, among other things, who was following the dietary laws.[26] Dietary laws allow those living in the world and waiting on Jesus's return to identify those who are following God's laws. This process of identifying the faithful through vegetarianism also provided Adventists with a form of special knowledge that helped them to identify with their vision of God's plan for the world.

Mary Douglas wrote of impurity or pollution as that which is judged to violate patterns and that which follows no particular conception of order.[27] Much of the Unity literature on vegetarianism used language that portrayed meat as the opposite of an ordered whole and as impure, chaotic, and decaying matter. Therefore, according to Douglas's interpretation of impurity and pollution, meat is impure because it violates the pattern of life. The divine, as Charles and Myrtle Fillmore perceived it, intended humanity to be free from both physical suffering and death. Therefore in Unity the pattern of the ideal human life is disease- and death-free. Meat, as a dead and partial part of a whole, living organism, represented the polar opposite of Unity's interpretation of the divine's intention for life. For Unity, meat was a violation of the pattern of life. When an animal was killed and butchered, it was, both symbolically and literally, no longer whole and so was also impure. According to Unity's vegetarian teachings, consuming impure food impeded the power necessary to complete the regeneration process required to sustain an individual's life. Vegetarianism as a practice in the early Unity movement can therefore also be understood as a way to cultivate the power necessary for an individual Unity practitioner to connect with the divine and to renew her or his bodily health.

For Charles and Myrtle Fillmore, practicing vegetarianism as part of regeneration leading to an immortal being with a spiritual body was all part of a logical process. The mind must first know and understand an important truth—that humans are not merely flesh-and-blood creatures that walk the Earth but are part of a greater reality, known by numerous names, one of which is God. Because God is perfect and disease- and death-free, disease and death are not natural to the human condition but mere maladies that can be overcome using the correct thought and the correct practices of health and purity. Thinking and eating correctly allow the body to regenerate and to reach its spiritual being in which eternal life and permanent well-being are realized.

⁂

Examining the lived reality of any religious group helps to make clear the relationship between important tenets and practices within the group. In the case of vegetarianism in the Seventh-day Adventist and Unity movements, the practice functioned in similar ways to mark off group membership and to help members better understand their faith. However, examining vegetarianism reveals a number of very different stances between the two groups about living the religious life.

One important general issue is control. A precise, elaborate system for a person's diet suggests that the group prescribing the diet is concerned with ordering and controlling life. In a group that was born out of a chaotic, disordering event such as the Great Disappointment, it is perhaps not surprising to see such a concern for control and order in an individual's life. But control in the Adventist sense is also clearly tied to aligning oneself with practices understood to be God's will. For Unity, controlling one's diet was an important way to control one's place in this world, which in turn would allow the Unity adherent to realize the availability of God's blessing to all humans. Thus control for the Adventists was about obedience, while control for Unity adherents was about power to act in this world.

Beyond concerns about the religious meaning of vegetarianism or the general themes that the study of vegetarianism reveals, examining vegetarianism reveals important information about the relationship between gender roles and religious authority. It is significant that for both of these groups in which women played vital leadership roles, food was a central method of establishing behavioral boundary markers and defining an adherent's relationship with the divine. By claiming authority over diet using religious justifications, Ellen G. White and Myrtle and Charles Fillmore were marking out new religious territory using a realm traditionally controlled by women. Both White and the Fillmores reinforced their authority to make alternative religious claims by legitimating those claims with food practices. The legitimacy of the women in leadership roles in these two movements was thus reinforced by linking their claims to religious authority with a central domestic practice, the preparation and serving of food. Vegetarianism may have been a dietary alternative in late nineteenth-century America, but by having women claim its central role in redemption and salvation, the Seventh-day Adventists and Unity effectively used the practice to justify their alternative religious claims.

DISCUSSION QUESTIONS

1. Why is purity associated with vegetarianism in both of these movements?
2. How is drawing religious boundaries using food practices different from drawing religious boundaries in other ways?

3. In what ways might the practice of vegetarianism have allowed the leaders of these two movements to exert control over their followers?

4. Vegetarianism in both of these movements is relatively uncommon today. What factors do you think explain the decline of vegetarianism as a religious practice for the Seventh-day Adventists and the Unity School of Christianity?

5. What does the use of vegetarianism to create religious boundaries help us to understand about women's roles in alternative religions?

NOTES

1. For a more complete account of Sylvester Graham, see Stephen Nissenbaum, *Sex, Diet, and Debility in Jacksonian America: Sylvester Graham and Health Reform* (Westport, Conn.: Greenwood, 1980).

2. Stephen D. O'Leary, *Arguing the Apocalypse: A Theory of Millennial Rhetoric* (New York: Oxford University Press, 1994), 108.

3. Still the most comprehensive history of New Thought is Charles S. Braden, *Spirits in Rebellion: The Rise and Development of New Thought* (Dallas: Southern Methodist University Press, 1963). For a useful overview of the style of religiosity that New Thought represents and the movement's relationship with the larger American religious culture, see Catherine Albanese, *A Republic of Mind and Spirit: A Cultural History of American Metaphysical Religion* (New Haven: Yale University Press, 2007), 1–18, 394–495.

4. "Unity's Statement of the Faith," *Weekly Unity*, April 16, 1921, 3.

5. Thomas Witherspoon, *Myrtle Fillmore: Mother of Unity* (Unity Village, Mo.: Unity Books, 1977), 206.

6. James Dillet Freeman, *The Story of Unity* (Unity Village, Mo.: Unity Books, 2007), 65.

7. Ronald L. Numbers, *Prophetess of Health: Ellen G. White and the Origins of Seventh-Day Adventist Health Reform* (Knoxville: University of Tennessee Press, 1992), 39–40.

8. Ibid., 160–61.

9. Ibid., 86.

10. Ellen G. White, *Counsels on Diet and Foods* (Washington, D.C.: Review and Herald Publishing Association, 1976), 16, 17.

11. Ibid., 43, 56.

12. Ibid., 69.
13. Ibid., 81.
14. For a more complete account of vegetarianism in Unity, see Jeremy Rapport, "Eating for Unity: Vegetarianism in the Early Unity School of Christianity," *Gastronomica: The Journal of Food and Culture* 9, no. 2 (Spring 2009): 35–44.
15. Myrtle Fillmore, *Myrtle Fillmore's Healing Letters* (Unity Village, Mo.: Unity School of Christianity, n.d.), 84.
16. Ibid., 38.
17. Ibid., 83.
18. Charles Fillmore, "As To Meat Eating," *Unity* 19, no. 4 (October 1903): 195.
19. Ibid., 196.
20. Ibid., 197. The I AM in early Unity thought is that which is in the individual that links the individual to the larger divine presence.
21. Ibid.
22. Ibid.
23. To be sure, not all early Seventh-day Adventists or Unity adherents practiced vegetarianism. Anecdotal evidence about Adventists arguing over eating meat at camp meetings, or Charles Fillmore, seemingly in jest, nailing sandwiches with ham in them to trees at Unity picnics, points to diverse levels of adherence to such top-down dictates. Nevertheless, given the theological importance of vegetarianism, the amount of publishing resources spent on its promotion by the two movements, and Unity's operation of a successful vegetarian café in Kansas City, it is reasonable to assume that both movements widely embraced vegetarianism.
24. For an overview of Unity's problematic and fractious relationship with the International New Thought Alliance, see Neal Vahle, *The Unity Movement: Its Evolution and Spiritual Teachings* (Philadelphia: Templeton Foundation Press, 2002), 383–97.
25. White, *Counsels on Diet and Food*, 72.
26. Mary Douglas, *Purity and Danger: An Analysis of the Concepts of Pollution and Taboo* (London: Routledge, 1966).
27. Ibid., 41.

RECOMMENDED READING

Douglas, Mary. *Purity and Danger: An Analysis of the Concepts of Pollution and Taboo.* London: Routledge, 1966.

Griffith, R. Marie. *Born Again Bodies: Flesh and Spirit in American Christianity.* Berkeley: University of California Press, 2004.

Numbers, Ronald L. *Prophetess of Health: Ellen G. White and the Origins and Seventh-day Adventist Health Reform.* Knoxville: University of Tennessee Press, 1992.

Vahle, Neal. *The Unity Movement: Its Evolution and Spiritual Teachings.* Philadelphia: Templeton Foundation Press, 2002.

White, Ellen G. *Counsels on Diet and Foods.* Washington, D.C.: Review and Herald Publishing Association, 1976.

Three

"AND AS WE DINE, WE SING AND PRAISE GOD"

FATHER AND MOTHER DIVINE'S THEOLOGIES OF FOOD

LEONARD NORMAN PRIMIANO

T HE STORY OF religion in America is more than the narrative of those individual traditions that consciously migrated to the United States from various parts of the globe, be they Roman Catholic, Eastern Orthodox Christian, many varieties of Protestant, Jewish, Muslim, Hindu, Buddhist, and so forth. Equally significant is the existence of indigenous American religions that evolved on the mainland both before and after its colonization by Europeans. Such resident systems of belief and practice naturally embrace Native American religions but also include the multitude of hybridized movements that emerged out of the interaction of allochthonous religions with inhabitants of the United States, as well as with the country's physical-cultural space, from the Church of Jesus Christ of Latter-day Saints to Christian Science, and from Seventh-day Adventists to Scientology. This essay discusses such a movement: an indigenous religion that was one of the best-known traditions emerging from the first decades of twentieth-century urban America. Identifying itself as the International Peace Mission Movement and founded by African American minister Reverend M. J. Divine, better known as Father Divine (1879–1965), the Peace Mission is a communal, intentional, celibate community that continues—though with a greatly reduced membership—into the twenty-first century.

Strikingly relevant to the theme of this book, Father Divine's International Peace Mission Movement is one of the most colorful exemplars of the practice of faith through religious cookery in the United States. The Movement's religious food culture began in the early 1900s in Sayville, Long Island, when Father Divine first devised a ritualized Eucharistic celebration in the form of an actual dinner, in fact, a multicourse banquet. Religion scholars Jualynne E. Dodson and Cheryl Townsend Gilkes cite Father Divine's movement as a tradition "where communion invokes a 'real meal' that includes all of the courses normally associated with a Thanksgiving or Christmas dinner."[1] This American religious love-feast paired the ritualistic eating of food with the spiritual nourishment of its followers. Woven amid the abundance of courses were homiletic texts—in the form of songs, testimonials, ecstatic dancing, and energetic preaching by God himself—testifying to the positive nature of Father Divine, his formula for the practice of a "radical" religion, and the sacred destiny of the United States. Indeed, followers revered and continue to revere "THE REVEREND M. J. DIVINE, MS. D., D. D., FOUNDER, BISHOP AND PASTOR OF THE PEACE MISSION MOVEMENT" as the incarnation of God in the body of a human being.[2]

This chapter serves to familiarize readers with one of the best-known "Black Gods of the Metropolis," a significant figure in the history of American religion.[3] Clearly illustrating how "food and religion are inevitably intertwined in American culture," the Father Divine story is a necessary foundation for the appreciation of another notable, yet unstudied, individual in the life of the Movement, Father's second wife, Mrs. Sweet Angel Divine (1925–).[4] Better known as "Mother Divine" (or, in the Movement's understanding of the action of reincarnation, "Mother Divine in the Second Body"), she assumed leadership of the Peace Mission after Father died in 1965 and has shouldered the responsibilities of caretaking and perpetuating Father's reputation and religious vision for nearly fifty years (fig. 3.1).

Guarding the use of Father's spoken and written words, as well as his photographic image, Mother Divine has also worked to sustain the Movement's ritual traditions, spirituality, and sense of creativity and order. In the late 1970s, however, Mother Divine made her own distinctive and

FIGURE 3.1 Images of Father and Mother Divine on a laminated "International Peace Card" used to shield a water glass at Father's place at the head of the Holy Communion Banquet Service table. Circle Mission Church, Philadelphia, May 1, 2011. Photograph by Leonard Norman Primiano, used with permission.

bold contribution to the everyday lives of the followers who lived around her, as well as to the history of the Peace Mission. Impressed with the ideas she gleaned from the food system known as macrobiotics, she radically changed members' eating habits. Moving the communitarian Peace Mission away from the carbohydrate-rich starches, fried foods, vegetables, and meats reminiscent of the southern food traditions of its original adherents—including those of Father Divine himself—she adopted a macrobiotic-based vegetarian diet for her spiritual children. These dietary reformations, which included the use of organic ingredients, also transformed the types and preparation of foods served in the Keyflower, the Movement's last public dining room in Philadelphia.

To understand the alteration of Peace Mission eating habits, it is important to appreciate that the study of food , while ostensibly mundane, is quite complex. In this case, it requires that considerable attention be paid to the personal feelings of followers and to the complex theological assumptions underpinning their religious community. The individuals who have inhabited the Peace Mission have consistently taken offense at what scholars and the popular press have written in the past concerning their founder and their own lives as members of a spiritual utopia. Therefore they do not like to give interviews, disclose traceable background information, or reveal personal data about themselves, a feeling increased by their spiritual outlook of "impersonalism," the deemphasis of self in favor of appropriate concentration on the works of their God.

Using methods of historical ethnography and contemporary folkloristic ethnography, this analysis elaborates on the food innovations of Mother Divine—her own theology of food—examining how her dietary hierophany challenges general scholarly assumptions about homogeneity within sectarian communities, as well as previously drawn and inadequately informed conclusions about the foodways of the Peace Movement specifically. Such analysis speaks to the significance of this North American religious leader who used dietary changes as a catalyst for transforming the members' understanding both of the meaning of their bodies and of the connection of food to religion, health, and longevity. Mother Divine's theology of food could be understood as a rather benign means of routinizing charisma, as a second-generation religious leader's attempt to reengage and energize her aging and declining flock with a fresh sensibility about the benefits of healthy food and balanced eating. I will argue, however, that Mother Divine's innovations represent a far more potent instance of feminine power simultaneously engaging food to create beauty and to sustain control. Mother Divine is the portrait of a leader using a distinctive religious aesthetic of food—its growing, selecting, purchasing, cleaning, slicing, preparing, spicing, cooking, decorating, serving, blessing, as well as dining and testifying—to maintain authority over her band of spiritually elite followers and to continue to order the world around her.[5] This argument underscores the expressive significance of Mother Divine's innovations, foregrounding them as examples of the creative quality of religious belief (or what I have termed elsewhere as "vernacular" belief and practice) notably present within sectarian movements and their leaders.[6]

"IT'S GOOD TO BE AROUND THE BODY OF GOD!": FATHER DIVINE AND HIS PEACE MISSION

To appreciate the evolution of Mother Divine's ideas about food, one must review the history, beliefs, and practices of the Peace Mission.[7] Organized around the central figure of Father Divine in the early decades of the twentieth century, Peace Mission members, who were for the most part African Americans, particularly women, believed this charismatic "dark-complected" minister (to use their term for racial differentiation) to be their deity of deliverance out of the "depressions, lacks, wants, and limitations" of everyday life.[8] Given the racism and discrimination faced by black people in America during the Jim Crow era and beyond, these "lacks" were countless: limited civil rights, poor housing, undignified employment, racial segregation, lack of access to goods and services, nonexistent luxuries. Peace Mission beliefs, as uniquely formulated by Father Divine, were a response to these conditions and included aspects of several religious ideologies influential in late nineteenth- and early twentieth-century America: Adventist, Holiness, Roman Catholic, black church, storefront Christianity, and especially ideas from the New Thought Movement, including Christian Science and the Unity School of Christianity.[9] Catherine Albanese summarizes what she understands as the roots of his thinking and his early activities:

> Whatever his early years were like, Father Divine must have been a traveling preacher for some time when, according to reports, he appeared in

Americus, Georgia, in 1912 and Valdosta, Georgia, in 1914. Here he taught a blend of mysticism and practicality in which, if a person were truly identified with the Spirit of God, health and plenty would result. Most probably, he drew this idea partially from the perfectionism of holiness religion and partially from the mind-cure teachings that . . . were part of New Thought. Yet Father Divine made the idea his own and it became the basis of a lifetime of religious leadership.[10]

Beginning in Long Island in 1919, in Harlem from 1932, and in Philadelphia from 1942 to 1965, Father Divine created a "practical religion" of personal fulfillment through the merging of consciousness and resources *with him* as fiscal shepherd and God-incarnate. Through his communal economic plan, Father advised followers to commit their individual savings to a larger accumulative purchasing force. With his spiritual children, he assembled an entrepreneurial portfolio of income-producing real estate and businesses in cities such as New York, Los Angeles, and Philadelphia, as well as in rural communities in the Hudson River Valley, which were known as "The Promised Land."[11] These properties were acquired with no mortgages, with full payment strictly in cash, and often with white followers negotiating the purchases, thus nullifying the grip of racism that might otherwise have hindered the accrual of property in white communities. The Peace Mission also employed its members as "coworkers" in its own collectively administered and staffed hotels, shops, garages, farms, grocery stores, and cafeterias. These businesses served members of all races and religions without question, with the lodging offering African Americans, in particular, quality accommodations and services several decades before the changes brought about through the American Civil Rights Movement. Benjamin Kahan has referred to these entrepreneurial activities as Divine's system of self-sufficient "celibate economics," not President Franklin Roosevelt's New Deal, but a "Divine Deal."[12]

"THE ABUNDANCE OF THE FULLNESS": HOLY COMMUNION BANQUET SERVICES

In addition to serving as rural centers of quiet repast for followers outside of the intensity of New York City, the Promised Land was formed to grow and supply food for the series of Peace Mission cafeterias, grocery stores, and Holy Communion Banquet Services running inside the metropolis and feeding both followers and nonfollowers. This ministry of food distribution at affordable prices was a notable result of Divine economics and a key dimension of the Peace Mission's social justice program from the 1920s through the Depression era of the 1930s and up until the closing of the final public cafeteria, the Keyflower in the Divine Tracy Hotel in Philadelphia, in the early 1990s. During interactions at Peace Mission restaurants and businesses, patrons were exposed to Father Divine's message through the staff, his portraits and religious mottos hung prominently on walls, and stacks of the movement's newspaper, *The New Day* (published as a weekly until 1989). It was during the daily or weekly Holy Communion Banquet Services, however, that spectacular opportunities arose for the more direct experience of Father's messages whether they were read aloud, played as recordings, or offered by the magnetic pastor himself. Throughout his ministry, Father Divine's followers felt transformed by the presence of their mystical leader and energized by his preaching style. Father's sermons could be experienced in a variety of other contexts within Peace Mission life: prayer and praise services, "Righteous Government" meetings, and annual business meetings. The banquet services in particular, however, tied his "words of spirit and life" to ritual feasting, an expression of spiritual and material abundance offered to all worthy communicants.[13]

The banquet service was not an elaborate church supper or an occasion for socializing and conversing with like-minded believers and visitors at a table while eating. In fact, while the testifying and singing were robustly communicated to all who could hear, mundane conversation or even comments about the ritual to the person occupying an adjacent seat were discouraged. This time was rather an opportunity to commune with God, whether Father Divine was personally present or not. One communed with God through the choral and congregational singing; the emotional testimonies of health renewed, lives restored, even objects found; and the occasion's dramatic expression of "the abundance of the fullness," the actualization of plenty for those who had done without.[14]

A report from a nonmember provides useful details of early banquet services. Under pressure from the highly prejudiced Sayville community, the district attorney of Suffolk County in New York hired "the services of a good-looking and rather intelligent young colored woman" from Harlem in 1930 to enter the community to inform him about the activities inside the Movement's Sayville home. The report offered the following account of the food served in this era of the Peace Mission.

> They gave me a seat at the foot of the table, facing Father and Mother Divine. The meal served that night was hot tea, milk and postum, rice, macaroni, white potatoes, green peas, baked beans, mashed turnips, corn, baked tomatoes, turkey, ham chops, corn meal bread, biscuits, graham bread, cake, pie, peaches, and a salad and they served such meals everyday. When they have company they serve a few other things to complete the meal, by adding veal stew and fried eggs. But they have the same every day. Turkey was served every day I was there, except Tuesday, they served fried chicken in the place of turkey. [15]

It is important to view the report of such meals in the context of those who read it in the predominantly white Sayville community: in the midst of the world economic crisis known as the Great Depression, this bounty was being served in the household of an African American man who ostensibly did no work except for ministry. A full meal in an era of intense economic hardship, the banquet service escalated as the years progressed, from full to sumptuous on special occasions. Assuring readers that "all of Father Divine's menus are lavish," *The New Day* noted in detail "a typical holiday menu" from September 13, 1962, the anniversary of the dedication of Woodmont, Father Divine's suburban Philadelphia estate:[16]

MENU
Apricot Nectar
HORS D'OEUVRES
Hot:
Miniature Frankfurters
Gherkins Wrapped in Bacon
Miniature Fish Sticks
Crabettes
Cold:
Smoked Oysters
Cocktail Shrimps
Red Rose Caviar
Black Caviar

Norwegian Smoked Sild

Artichoke Hearts Antipasto

Smoked Fish Plate

VEGETABLES:

Creamery Whipped Potatoes

Wild Rice

Buttered Corn on the Cob

Sliced Fresh Buttered Carrots

Tiny Rosebud Beets

French String Beans with Mushrooms

Fresh Asparagus Spears with Hollandaise Pimento Sauce

SEA FOOD:

Ocean Fresh Fried Deep Sea Scallops

Imported Sauteed Frog Legs with Tartar Sauce

MEATS:

Small Baked Squabs with Tasty Fillings

Rare Roast Sirloin of Beef with Yorkshire Pudding

Baked Virginia Ham with Pineapple Garnish

Roast Capon with Chestnut Dressing and Cranberry Sauce

SALADS:

Lettuce Wedges and Sliced Tomatoes

Avocado Mandarin Plate

Waldorf Gelatin Mold

Pineapple Cottage Cheese Mold

Assorted Relish Plate with Olives and Celery

CHEESES:

Roquefort

Cheddar

Swiss

American Cheese

BREADS:

Crescent Butter Rolls

Fancy Danish Pastries

Ritz

Butter Baskets

Woodmont Blackberry Preserves

BEVERAGES:

Assorted Iced and Hot Beverages

FRUIT BOWL:
Fresh Assorted Fruit Bowl
DESSERT:
Fruit Medly [*sic*] Mold
Ice Cream Mold
Delectable Velvet Chocolate Pie
Blueberry Tarts
Fruit Cake

The road from cornmeal biscuits and ham chops to Red Rose caviar and rare roast sirloin with Yorkshire pudding represents a fascinating thirty-year food transformation, blessed and distributed by Father Divine at the head of the long Banquet Table. Significantly, the diversity of dishes offered at these banquet services did not complete its evolution at Father's death. As explored below, Father's second wife would formulate and advance her own vision about how food relates spiritually to abundance, good health, old age, and happiness. Insight into who Mother Divine is and her contributions to the Peace Mission's food culture are essential to anyone seeking a richer appreciation both of this community and the complexities of intentional religious communities in America.

"I KNOW YOU ARE GOD!": THE SECOND MOTHER DIVINE

While an advocate of celibacy, Father Divine had two nonphysical "spiritual" marriages, the first to an African American woman named Penninah, the first "Mother Divine."[17] In 1946, four years after Penninah's unacknowledged death, he again legally wed. The marriage of the more than sixty-year-old Father Divine to a twenty-one-year-old white Canadian woman was a source of tremendous public criticism in the United States for a religious group that was already a source of national conversation and controversy. As he had done many times in the past, Father Divine used the public commotion over his interracial marriage as a way to spread his messages. The marriage, he said, was the ultimate example of God's approval of racial integration, international peace, and the "life of Christ."[18]

The second Mother Divine was born Edna Rose Ritchings in Vancouver, British Columbia, in 1925.[19] In 1940 she encountered the teachings of Father Divine in Vancouver. She became convinced of his godhood and of the belief that ultimate peace was attainable only by living a daily life inspired by Jesus Christ and Father Divine. In 1945 she moved to Philadelphia, took the name "Sweet Angel," and became one of Father's secretaries. In 1946 she declared to Father that she wanted to marry him for the sole reason that "I know you are God." They were legally wed on April 29 in Washington, D.C., where interracial unions were permitted. Their marriage was proclaimed by Father Divine to be interracial, spiritual, and celibate, exemplifying the true harmony of the nations of the world.

If the marriage was publicly controversial in postwar racist America, within the Peace Mission itself it was also a matter of concern for those members who did not understand Father's need for another marriage. While some individuals responded by leaving the movement, for those who remained the wedding heralded an important event in the history of the Peace Mission by introducing a new, young, vigorous leader-in-waiting. In the minds of such followers, the Divine marriage marked a transition between two distinct eras or "Dispensations" in the evolution of the Peace Mission Movement. The first era was one of struggle both within and outside its community of followers. Within the community, the struggle was to lift its many black members out of poverty to economic independence. Outside the community, the struggle was primarily with racial prejudice. Father Divine fed and housed his "children," built businesses, acquired property, and fought political battles. Beginning with the 1946 marriage, the second "Dispensation" is seen by followers as "the realization of Heaven on Earth."[20] With greater economic stability and racial equality secured, the Peace Mission under its second Mother has focused increasingly on educating the public about Father's teachings and on the pursuit of mental and physical purity in support of spiritual health.

Since Father Divine's physical passing in 1965, Mother Divine has presided over the Peace Mission, and the Movement has developed a matriarchal quality. Mother maintains her husband's moral and religious standards as she looks after the spiritual and temporal needs of their "children" or followers. With a current membership of about fifty elderly men and women, Mother Divine leads the Peace Mission from her Woodmont estate in Gladwyne, Pennsylvania.[21] What keeps followers spiritually, mentally, and materially connected to God and his "Spotless Virgin Bride" are the three "Holy Communions"—the formal and informal meals—that they share together in faith each day.

"REAL, REAL, REAL": THE BANQUET SERVICE AS EUCHARIST

Father Divine often referred to the formal Holy Communion Banquet Service as a ritual: "our Private Banquet is the place where we take our Daily Communion. That is our system of our [sic] religious ritual."[22] Scholars would certainly see the banquet service as constituting a ritual, for it is "a repeated socio-religious behavior: a chain of actions, rites, or ritual movements following a standard protocol."[23] The second Mother Divine's book describes Holy Communion as "the only sacrament observed by the followers and is performed daily as a ritual in the Churches and private homes."[24] The banquet service is an intense demonstration of reverence and devotion. For visitors who come to dine without proper initiation, such unabashed expressions of belief can prompt surprise, even embarrassment.

Indeed, the Peace Mission has maintained one of the most sensual Eucharists of all such rituals emerging out of the Christian tradition. Andrew McGowan acknowledges that "it takes some effort to perceive the Eucharist of later Christian tradition as food, let alone as a meal. . . . Yet Christian liturgical tradition has eating and drinking at its origin, not merely as incidental actions in religious ritual, but as actual food."[25] The Peace Mission Eucharist effectively involves *all* the human senses as one touches the plates, vocalizes a testimony, hears the songs and sermon, tastes the foods, smells the aromas, and sees a dazzling assortment of sights—from women known as Father's "Rosebuds" dressed in red, white, and blue uniforms, to thoughtfully designed flower arrangements and sculpted foods, such as butter lilies and lamb-shaped ice cream (fig. 3.2).

The members, even as twenty-first-century octogenarians, still proclaim that their God is "real, real, real," and that the banquet service is the generator of this nexus of the material and the spiritual.[26] Transitional and transformative in nature, the banquet literally fills one physically while making everyone at the table, from adherents to harmonizers to visiting strangers, a participant observer in what followers believe is the celebration and generation of positive consciousness and "atONEment"

FIGURE 3.2   Molded butter star topped with an American flag, Holy Communion Banquet Service, Father Divine Day, Woodmont, Gladwyne, Pennsylvania, September 10, 2011. Photograph by Leonard Norman Primiano, used with permission.

with the spirit of God, Father Divine.[27] Simply being present forces one to engage with regulated behaviors guided by Father's enacted tradition. Peace Mission rituals are powerful public display events centered on food, but also religious performances featuring an artistic outpouring and amalgamation of timing, precision, personal behavior, manner, etiquette, appearance, posture, and expressions of speech and song.

"IT WAS TIME FOR THEM TO LEARN HOW TO EAT": FROM TRADITIONAL TO NUTRITIONAL

In the 1984 edition of his well-regarded study of Father Divine, historian Robert Weisbrot's concluding chapter discusses the final years and achievements of Father Divine's ministry. Mother Divine in the 1960s, he writes, had taken on "the daily administration of the Peace Mission working closely with Father Divine's able secretarial staff." Assessing her leadership, he offers:

> Although not an innovator or social crusader as Father Divine has been in his prime, Mother Divine had proven herself well suited to lead the Peace Mission in its search for spiritual purity and organizational stability. She made an impressive, intelligent, demure presence at Peace Mission banquets, and a graciously effective diplomat to guests from all walks of life. It was clear that Father Divine's earlier social radicalism was to be merely revered, not revived, but within the Peace Mission's own centers the Father's vision of a chaste, integrated communal society would go on as before.[28]

While Mother Divine may have appeared a "demure presence" at the banquets, she was actually studying these rituals and planning on a series of changes to her followers' foodways, transformations that she would also offer, in the spirit of her husband, to the public at large. At the same time that Weisbrot was preparing his epilogue, Mother Divine was setting into motion a personal plan to invigorate the spiritual and physical purity of her community.

Emulating Father's economic and spiritual entrepreneurism, Mother conceptualized in the early 1980s a new business enterprise, an approach to the last Peace Mission restaurant controlled by her followers. The restaurant would serve a new type of healthy food she and her followers could also eat for their own well-being. At the Keyflower Dining Room, Mother Divine combined the business of retail food preparation with the necessities of sustaining her followers by synthesizing the ideas of Father Divine with macrobiotics, an approach to food and eating born in Japan and nurtured in late-twentieth-century America.

Using her influence over her followers, Mother Divine literally took control of their bodies and decided what they would eat. What Mother carried out was the radical transformation of her followers into macrobiotic vegetarians, a unique and distinctive approach to food selection, preparation, presentation, and consumption based on whole cereal grains, beans, and fresh, locally grown produce consumed in season, with no meat, dairy products, night-shade vegetables, white sugar, or white flour permitted. In Philadelphia informational lectures and cooking courses about the macrobiotic system were already available by the late 1970s. The transformation of the foods served at Mother Divine's hotel cafeteria and banquet tables can be traced to the early 1980s when she began attending such lectures in Center City, Philadelphia. Mother was especially drawn to the lectures of Stanley Walker, an African American macrobiotic counselor and follower of the well-known macrobiotic teacher Michio Kushi. Walker could not help but notice a well-dressed, middle-aged woman often seated in the back row of the room where he lectured. When she finally approached him to introduce herself, he was amazed to learn that this woman was none other than Mrs. Sweet Angel Divine. Mother Divine expressed to Stan Walker her interest in macrobiotics and her desire to spread its practice to the followers of her husband's religious movement. Mr. Walker was well aware of Father Divine and his work because of the meals he ate at Peace Mission cafeterias in the 1960s for very reasonable prices or for free. Mother Divine asked if Walker would consider being hired as a teacher of macrobiotics to the followers responsible for food preparation at the Keyflower as well as in her own household. He enthusiastically agreed, bringing his wife, Geraldine, into the process. So began Mother's unique experiment, her bold reordering of the ways her followers would eat and think about food.

Geraldine Walker recounts her early experiences working with Peace Mission followers:

> [Mother] invited us to come to the Keyflower and there were nine cooks and they were all observing and we did a level one cooking class. It was Spring 1985. . . . It did not catch on right away. [It was a] hard time [for] them. . . . [Mother Divine] wanted me to do whatever I knew. She was the one [who put her foot down] doing that behind the scenes. Mother took the leadership and said this lady and her husband are coming to show you a healthier way of eating. And that was it. All she wanted me to do was teach them what I knew and they took notes, and they were standing and observing. And next week, I went and started cutting [in a macrobiotic manner] and prepping. First, they watched and then they started to participate and that's how it went like that. . . . At one point, they went completely macrobiotic, and they really didn't like it. They really rebelled. . . . So because of that she brought back the meat and slowly some more things have come, and she justifies it as a vast improvement to their meals.[29]

The appeal of macrobiotics as a system that connects eating to health had both positive and negative elements for Mother Divine. As the leader of one alternative belief system, she may well have been attracted to the holistic macrobiotic philosophy simply because it was "alternative"; coming herself from a belief system that held unconventional views of the relationship of spirit and body and their connection to eating and health, she likely felt comfortable with the personal and societal challenges macrobiotics represented and the language and concepts its educators used. That macrobiotics emerged from Japan and not America posed a bit of a problem as it went against the grain of the Peace Mission's nationalistic propensities, but any such misgivings would have been outweighed by the thrust of the macrobiotic "holistic approach to life, the integration of spirituality with physical health and wellness."[30]

An additional problem that Mother Divine faced in advocating macrobiotic adherence was Father Divine himself. Her husband had in the past directly castigated both diners who admired the physical benefits of the banquet services alone ("The Kingdom of God is not meat and drink") and those who asked to abstain from certain foods at his table.[31] Father Divine consistently portrayed such requests as an excessive reliance on the material over the spiritual, an ambiguity he could not abide. Responding in 1933 to the complaint of a California visitor who expected that "there would be no taking of life in Heaven" but saw meat being served at the banquet table, he preached:

GOD through the mouth of Paul, by the inspiration of the Spirit . . . said, "Eat what is set before you and ask no questions." . . . The next point of view for your consideration, to those that are of the dietarians and metaphysicians, I would like to say I AM not taking thought of what I will eat today for tomorrow, and neither AM I taking consideration what I shall wear. . . . I would not be free indeed if I were bound as to what I should eat, drink or wear. I do not take thought! . . . I AM not bound not to eat it, I AM not bound to eat it.[32]

As Father's congregants grew older, he grew more conciliatory. Twenty years later, at the Circle Mission Church, he honored the request by some diners for unsalted food but punctuated the point that such dietary precautions remain unnecessary:

I would like to say that I have requested and asked the cooks and others who are preparing the food to prepare food suitable for the dietetians [sic] and for all those who do not care for seasoned food; although, if you have been awakened in the Light of Truth, you may be able to eat anything and it will not hurt nor harm you.[33]

Early in his ministry and years before Mother encountered his teachings in British Columbia, Father Divine preached to his followers a very specific gospel of eternal health and physical resilience: "Father Divine has come to save the body. The mind and the spirit are already saved. But the body has been dying. I have come in order that your bodies might live forever."[34]

In Father's opinion, there was nothing wrong with the meals served from Peace Mission kitchens for decades; they energized his followers' physical forms and revitalized their spiritual relations with him. As Jill Watts remarks, "He linked health to appetite and encouraged his followers to eat large well-balanced meals."[35] R. Marie Griffith adds, "Emphatically targeted on health, nonplussed by illness, Divine refused even to speak of those who died in his midst—asserting only in the abstract that those who allowed themselves to expire had not believed fully in him."[36]

Father may himself have preached about the human body being physically sustained by spiritual connectivity to him, but Mother Divine, representing the second generation of believers, was forced to deal with troubling evidence to the contrary. She associated the traditional Peace Mission diet of heavy, fatty, salty, sugary foods with the fact that loyal followers were becoming ill and dying, even if they were living to advanced ages. Even more jolting, Mother witnessed Father's declining health including complications from diabetes throughout the late 1950s and into the 1960s.[37] Father's physical death—or the "voluntary passing" of his body, as the followers term it—in 1965 was no doubt an incredible blow. She and the members attempted to blunt the incongruity of God dying of illnesses brought on by old age by creatively reinterpreting his departure from the scene as totally voluntary, a supreme sacrifice. Mother erected an art-filled tomb at their Woodmont estate that she paradoxically identified as a "Shrine to Life," borrowing a theme from the Christian theology of the Resurrection.

Whatever reversals back to meat eating occurred among followers, macrobiotic food choices remained part of the daily dishes offered at the Keyflower until its closing. Such fare reflected a vernacular macrobiotics, a hybrid of macro ideals and Peace Mission needs. Such dishes included miso soup; brown rice and other grains; nondairy vegetable entrees; use of tofu, tempeh, seitan, organic fruit and produce; and bancha tea. The same menu could be found at the Holy Communion Banquets served upstairs in the Divine Tracy Hotel dining room and, of course, in the Chapel Dining Room at Woodmont (fig. 3.3).

Banquets prepared by the hotel and Woodmont staff included such entrees as soy-sage balls with shitake mushrooms in a ginger-miso sauce; tofu with mustard topping; tempeh sautéed with root vegetables; dairy-free mushroom stroganoff; tofu sautéed over whole-wheat fettuccini; and seitan sautéed with red and green peppers. Salads were accompanied by freshly picked watercress, basil, mint, or edible flowers. Grains such as short-grain brown rice accompanied by the sesame seed and salt condiment called *gomashio* were a matter of course, as were organic juices and desserts sweetened with brown rice syrup.[38] Such banquets stood in stark contrast to those served in the past in Brooklyn, Sayville, Harlem, Newark, Jersey City, or wherever Father Divine's community established an outpost. These feasts were marked by collard greens cooked with fatback, macaroni and cheese, corn pudding, white rice with brown gravy, mashed and baked sweet potatoes topped with marshmallows, fried pork chops, roasted chicken with corn-bread dressing, and roasted duck with baked apples.

In a rare 1996 interview, Mother Divine explained her rationale for originally making the changes in what food was served. Noting that in the late 1960s the Peace Mission was asked by the Philadelphia Redevelopment Authority to renovate the Divine Tracy Hotel or sell it, Mother Divine decided to upgrade it because of its location in the section of Philadelphia known as University City, home to the University of Pennsylvania and Drexel University.

We felt that there [in that area], that we could contact a different type of person, so they could learn to know Father Divine and what he advocated more than just thinking of him as a minister of the Gospel that was interested in feeding the people material food because they were in want. And I felt too that the Peace Mission had been feeding families for three generations and that it was time for them to learn how to eat. So we decided to change the menu at the Divine Tracy from the traditional type of food— which was a lot of meat, potatoes, gravy, and vegetables—to a more nutritional diet advocating what Father advocated [which] was prevention. He

FIGURE 3.3 Mother Divine seated and waiting for guests to enter, Holy Communion Banquet Service table with extension, Chapel Dining Room, Woodmont, Gladwyne, Pennsylvania, July 24, 2011. Photograph by Leonard Norman Primiano, used with permission.

really believed in preventative health. We decided to do away with white sugar and white flour and all additives and preservatives and serve chicken and turkey and tofu and tempeh and that sort of thing. And we served desserts, and when we first started, there were not so many healthy desserts on the market, but we made our own and we made them with rice syrup, different types of sweeteners that were more healthy and people were very happy to change. . . . Also, people who lived in the Peace Mission had special diets and Father wanted to accommodate them. Father was trying to accommodate them so they could stick to their diet and live in the Peace Mission.[39]

This valuable statement shows Mother drawing statements from her husband's sermons that support her position while dismissing others. Here Mother is theologizing certain ideas of Father Divine, and like the second generation of believers in the early Christian Church, she is picking the ideas that promote her own agenda. Her decisions exemplify how she, as a religious leader, used her own vernacular theological logic to develop a unique understanding of what was consistent Peace Mission ideology and what was advantageous to the survival of a declining community. While there is no direct evidence that she, unlike Father, was familiar with the New Thought ideas of Charles and Myrtle Fillmore's Unity Society of Christianity, her actions evoked that metaphysical movement's similar contradictory advocacy of vegetarianism in the face of their foundational belief that "the mind could correct all."[40] Her statement also illustrates her decision to depart from Father's purpose of working to assist the poor directly, especially black Americans, in cities with a cuisine that they normally recognized. She was instead reaching out to a larger, more diverse audience—reminiscent of past Peace Mission communities in Australia, Panama, Switzerland, Germany, and England—especially the multiracial and multiethnic international community surrounding the universities. She wanted to feed their stomachs affordably, but also to educate their minds about natural whole foods. Such an approach would ideally awaken in them an interest in Father and in higher spiritual transformation. From the comfort of her Main Line estate, she could commune with nature on its seventy-two acres, disengaging with the city and its population, while connecting with the macrobiotic call "to abandon self-destructive habits and bring [one's] way of eating and living into greater harmony with nature."[41] Living a life infused with "Woodmount consciousness," as the special atmosphere of the estate was defined, Mother could meld Father Divine's principles of higher spiritual consciousness with the macrobiotic call to honor nature through the cleansing of body and mind.

MOTHER DIVINE'S THEOLOGY OF FOOD

What then is Mother Divine's theology of food and of the body? It is the idea that whole food—healthfully prepared, very reasonably priced, and eaten in a spotlessly clean environment—has a spiritual impact. For her, that is a religious principle. If for Father Divine nourishment was a necessary physical means for a spiritual renewal, for Mother nutrition plays a different role, more directly and more avowedly theological. Father "rejoiced" in abundance, as the Bible says; it was a sign of one's spirituality that one had abundance. Mother Divine envisioned a different form of abundance as the reward of righteous eating, the direct connection to longevity—immortality. Indeed, the way people achieve eternal life in the physical heaven Father identifies as the United States is by being inwardly clean and whole, a state of purity achieved partly through healthful eating. Proper food not only feeds one but cleanses one internally in the same manner one should keep the body externally clean. Goodness is therefore a matter not only of behavior but of one's actual physical makeup. Mother Divine's theology of food acknowledges that righteousness equals longevity and that internal righteousness has to do with what is consumed. Mother Divine's theology of the body emphasizes health, exercise, and the path to Divine consciousness through eating well. Fascinatingly, these changes have clearly had an impact on the membership, for their longevity since the 1980s has been astounding, with some members living beyond one hundred years.

The ninth edition (2011) of the anthology *Extraordinary Groups: An Examination of Unconventional Lifestyles*, a text used in a variety of undergraduate courses on American religious movements, concludes in its updated report on the Peace Mission that Father Divine's utopia "is in trouble. . . . But the movement has not changed."[42] Whether it is the place of scholars to declare a particular religion "in trouble" is a matter for debate within the discipline or, perhaps, the classroom. This exploration of Mother Divine's

Peace Mission, however, specifically challenges any perceptions that readers might have about the static nature of sectarian movements, or for that matter any system of religious belief and practice. This chapter hinges on the observation and argument that the lived expressions of everyday religious life are in creative and constant flux.[43] The expressive culture of food is one of the keys to unlocking the intricacies and nuances of the vernacular religion of both everyday believers and religious leaders. In the case of Mother Divine, the energies emerging from the banquets as transitional, transformative, and sustaining ritual public display events served as markers for her contributions to the movement—from transitional figure to leader, from concerned leader to transformative food innovator, and from vernacular theologian of food to sustainer of a tradition in decline—but, like Father Divine's spirit, ever continuing.

DISCUSSION QUESTIONS

1. What does it mean to have a "theology of food"?
2. How do Father and Mother Divine's theologies of food differ?
3. How can a knowledge of foodways and eating assist the understanding of an individual or a community's "vernacular religion"?

NOTES

I wish to thank Deborah Ann Bailey, Ben Danner, John Di Mucci, Will Luers, Kathleen Malone O'Connor, Kathy McCrea, Nicholas Rademacher, Lisa Ratmansky, and Geraldine Walker, as well as Anne Schwelm of Cabrini College's Holy Spirit Library, for their assistance. I am especially grateful to Rudy V. Busto and Ben Zeller for their unfailing support, and to my colleagues Laura Sauer Palmer, Matt Slutz, and Nancy Watterson, who read multiple drafts of this essay. Of course, this research would not be possible without the assistance of Mother Divine and the brothers and sisters of Father Divine's International Peace Mission Movement in Philadelphia. Their kindness and cooperation have been extraordinary. The title of this essay is taken from the words of Mother Divine; field notes, Holy Communion Banquet Service, Woodmont, January 10, 2010.

1. Jualynne E. Dodson and Cheryl Townsend Gilkes, "'There's Nothing Like Church Food': Food and the U.S. Afro-Christian Tradition: Re-Membering

Community and Feeding the Embodied S/spirit(s)," *Journal of the American Academy of Religion* 63, no. 3 (1995): 529.

2. Father Divine is so described in an interior wall of his tomb called the "Shrine to Life." Capitalization in the original.

3. The phrase is from Authur Huff Fauset, *Black Gods of the Metropolis: Negro Cults of the Urban North* (Philadelphia: University of Pennsylvania Press, 1971, 2002). See also Leonard Norman Primiano, "'The Consciousness of God's Presence Will Keep You Well, Healthy, Happy, and Singing': The Tradition of Innovation in the Music of Father Divine's Peace Mission Movement," in *The New Black Gods: Arthur Huff Fauset and the Study of African American Religions*, ed. Edward E. Curtis IV and Danielle Brune Sigler (Bloomington: Indiana University Press, 2009).

4. Daniel Sack, "Food and Eating in American Religious Cultures," in *Perspectives on American Religion and Culture*, ed. Peter W. Williams (Malden, Mass.: Blackwell, 1999), 203.

5. It is beyond the scope of this essay to consider fully the gendered aspects of this argument, but future research will address that dimension, as well as the politics of race in a sectarian movement that has ostensibly erased race. See Beryl Satter, "Marcus Garvey, Father Divine and the Gender Politics of Race Difference and Race Neutrality," *American Quarterly* 48 (1996): 43–76; and Leonard Norman Primiano, "'Bringing Perfection in These Different Places': Father Divine's Vernacular Architecture of Intention," *Folklore* 115 (2004): 24, n. 14.

6. Leonard Norman Primiano, "Vernacular Religion and the Search for Method in Religious Folklife," *Western Folklore* 54 (January 1995): 37–56; and Primiano, "Manifestations of the Religious Vernacular: Ambiguity, Power, and Creativity," in *Vernacular Religion in Everyday Life: Expressions of Belief*, ed. Marion Bowman and Ülo Valk, 382–94 (Sheffield, UK: Equinox, 2012).

7. "It's Good to Be Around the Body of God" is a Peace Mission song frequently offered during Holy Communion Banquet Services.

8. "If We Divide Against Ourselves How Can We Expect to Have Victory Over Depressions, Lacks, Wants and Limitations?" *Liberty Net*, http://www .libertynet.org/fdipmm/worddrtv/38112100.html.

9. Jill Watts, *God, Harlem U.S.A.: The Father Divine Story* (Berkeley: University of California Press, 1992), 1–71; Catherine Albanese, *A Republic of Mind and Spirit: A Cultural History of American Metaphysical Religion* (New Haven: Yale University Press, 2007), 476–78; and Albanese, *America, Religions and Religion*, 5th ed. (Boston: Wadsworth, 2013), 149–50.

10. Albanese, *America, Religions and Religion*, 2nd ed. (Belmont, Calif.: Wadsworth, 1992), 209.

11. Carleton Mabee, *Promised Land: Father Divine's Interracial Communities in Ulster County, New York* (Fleischmanns, N.Y.: Purple Mountain Press, 2008).

12. Benjamin Kahan, "The Other Harlem Renaissance: Father Divine, Celibate Economics, and the Making of Black Sexuality," *Arizona Quarterly* 65, no. 4 (2009): 48–49.

13. "The Ground Breaking Ceremony for Father Divine's Library," *Liberty Net*, http://www.libertynet.org/fdipmm/newsletr/2008aug.html.

14. "The Deliverer Has Truly Come," *Liberty Net*, http://www.libertynet.org/fdipmm/wrddrtv2/56050721.html.

15. "Sayville's Colored Messiah Investigated by Dist. Atty.," *Suffolk County News*, April 25, 1930, 7.

16. *The New Day*, February 14, 1976, 7.

17. Watts, *God, Harlem U.S.A.*, 45–47.

18. "Since the First Use of Atomic Energy in 1945," *Liberty Net*, http://www.libertynet.org/fdipmm/mdbook/dispentx.html.

19. Primiano, "Mother Divine," in *Encyclopedia of Women and World Religion*, ed. Serinity Young, 2:678–79 (New York: Macmillan, 1998).

20. Quote from field notes, Holy Communion Banquet Service, Woodmont, May 8, 2011.

21. Primiano, "'Bringing Perfection,'" 14–18.

22. May 28, 1941, message printed in *The New Day*, February 4, 1978, 11.

23. Juha Pentikäinen, "Ritual," in *Folklore: An Encyclopedia of Beliefs, Customs, Tales, Music, and Art*, 2nd ed., ed. Charlie T. McCormick and Kim Kennedy White (Santa Barbara: ABC-CLIO, 2011), 1110.

24. Mother Divine, *The Peace Mission Movement* (Philadelphia: Imperial Press, 1982), 27–28.

25. Andrew McGowan, "Food, Ritual, and Power," in *Late Ancient Christianity, A People's History of Christianity*, ed. Virginia Burrus, 2:145 (Minneapolis: Fortress Press, 2010).

26. Father Divine frequently punctuated his sermons with the reminder to his followers of the ever presence and reality of God in the midst of his Church, a point often referenced and reiterated at contemporary Holy Communion Banquet Services.

27. Quote from field notes, Holy Communion Banquet Service, Unity Mission Bible Institute, February 6, 2011.

28. Robert Weisbrot, *Father Divine and the Struggle for Racial Equality* (Urbana: University of Illinois Press, 1984), 220. See also Weisbrot, "Father Divine's Peace Mission Movement," in *America's Alternative Religions*, ed. Timothy Miller (Albany: State University Press of New York, 1995), 289.

29. Walker, interview with the author, June 20, 2011.

30. Kimberly J. Lau, *New Age Capitalism: Making Money East of Eden* (Philadelphia: University of Pennsylvania Press, 2000), 62. See also Albanese, *A Republic of Mind and Spirit*, 484–88.

31. November 13–14, 1951, message printed in *The New Day*, February 7, 1976, 6.

32. November 17, 1933, message printed in *The New Day*, February 26, 1977, 11.

33. March 10, 1950, message printed in *The New Day*, March 13, 1976, 19.

34. From an unpublished edition of Fauset's *Black Gods of the Metropolis* in Fauset Collection, box 5, folder 98, p. 87, cited in Clarence E. Hardy III, " 'No Mystery God': Black Religions of the Flesh in Pre-War Urban America," *Church History* 77, no. 1 (2008): 144.

35. Watts, *God, Harlem U.S.A.*, 67. R. Marie Griffith, using Watts as a source, notes the influence on Father Divine of New Thought, most especially the Unity School ideas of Charles Fillmore. Particularly important for Griffith is Father Divine's development of the conviction that the human body is an important materialized reflection of a developed, spiritualized consciousness. My own work on the expressive culture of the Peace Mission seen through use of space, the built environment, photography, song, foodways, etc. bears out the sacrilization of the material, as well as its indication of powerful spiritual advancement and social liberation for followers. Griffith's analysis is a valuable reading of the history of the Peace Mission; however, according to my ethnographic research on the contemporary movement, her perspective does not speak to the diverse ways that Father Divine addressed issues about the body or the way that the mission has developed since 1965. R. Marie Griffith, "Body Salvation: New Thought, Father Divine, and the Feast of Material Pleasures," *Religion and American Culture* 11 (2001): 119–53; Griffith, *Born Again Bodies: Flesh and Spirit in American Christianity* (Berkeley: University of California Press, 2004).

36. Griffith, *Born Again Bodies*, 153.

37. Weisbrot, *Father Divine and the Struggle for Racial Equality*, 219–20.

38. In a religious community mindful of its traditions, Mother Divine enacted further changes that were quite dramatic within the community. Father Divine, for example made it a point always to punctuate the table with starched linen napkins rolled and positioned in a glass at each place. Mother

Divine changed this practice at Woodmont, having the nonlinen napkins folded and placed on the table itself. Also, at Father's banquets the salads were always served after the entrees, yet Mother decided that they should be served first. These changes were tantamount to a decision to change the order of a Eucharistic service, or the formal ordinance concerning the decoration of an altar or Communion table in a church. See Wood, "Divine Liturgy," *Gastronomica* 4, no. 1 (2004): 19–24, for a description of a Divine Tracy Hotel banquet service circa 2001–2002.

39. Mother Divine, interviews with the author, filmed by Will Luers, May 25 and June 18, 1996.

40. Trudy Eden, "Metaphysics and Meatless Meals: Why Food Mattered When the Mind Was Everything," in *Food and Faith in Christian Culture*, ed. Ken Albala and Trudy Eden (New York: Columbia University Press, 2011), 172; see also Satter, *Each Mind a Kingdom: American Women, Sexual Purity, and the New Thought Movement, 1875–1920* (Berkeley: University of California Press, 1999), 105–10, 251.

41. Lau, *New Age Capitalism*, 65.

42. Richard T. Schaefer and William W. Zellner, *Extraordinary Groups: An Examination of Unconventional Lifestyles*, 9th ed. (New York: Worth, 2011), 275–76.

43. Primiano, "Vernacular Religion"; Primiano, "Manifestations of the Religious Vernacular: Ambiguity, Power, and Creativity," in Bowman and Valk, *Vernacular Religion in Everyday Life*, 382–94.

RECOMMENDED READING

Primiano, Leonard Norman. " 'Bringing Perfection in these Different Places': Father Divine's Vernacular Architecture of Intention." *Folklore* 115 (2004): 3–26.

——. "Vernacular Religion and the Search for Method in Religious Folklife." *Western Folklore* 54 (January 1995): 37–56.

Watts, Jill. *God, Harlem U.S.A.: The Father Divine Story*. Berkeley: University of California Press, 1992.

Weisbrot, Robert. *Father Divine and the Struggle for Racial Equality*. Urbana: University of Illinois Press, 1984.

Four

HALLELUJAH ACRES

CHRISTIAN RAW FOODS AND
THE QUEST FOR HEALTH

ANNIE BLAZER

HALLELUJAH ACRES IS a health ministry aimed at Evangelical Christians in the United States.[1] The organization encourages an alternative to conventional medicine and to the standard American diet (which they call "SAD"). Hallelujah Acres advocates a vegan, raw foods diet (food is not heated above 115°F) as God's plan for perfect eating and as a curative treatment for most illnesses and diseases. At lifestyle centers, experts on the Hallelujah Diet demonstrate and instruct guests on how to eat and live accordingly. In the summer of 2011 I conducted participant observation fieldwork at a lifestyle center in Lake Lure, North Carolina, near the organization's headquarters in Shelby. I spent five days with the center's leaders, staff, and guests, conducted interviews with Hallelujah Acres administrators and educators, and acquired print and media resources from the organization on Bible-based raw foods eating.

Spending a week at the lifestyle center is an investment. Participants pay $1,200 for the educational experience, and many invest far more in appliances, supplements, and additional resources available for purchase at the center. In general, people seek out Hallelujah Acres's lifestyle centers for two reasons: curative health treatments or preventative health practices. The vast majority turn to Hallelujah Acres for curative means; of the eleven guests at the lifestyle center I attended, three had advanced cancer, one had early stage cancer, one experienced significant pain from arthritis, and one experienced many health problems that doctors had failed to diagnose. Two guests were present as spouses of these ailing individuals and adopted the diet to be supportive but would not have sought out Hallelujah Acres on their own, and three guests enrolled in the program for preventative reasons. According to the center's leaders, this combination of majority cancer patients, some other ailments, spouses, and a small number of people interested in the preventative aspects of the diet was fairly representative of the groups that pass through the lifestyle center.

My research shows that, for the most part, believers turn to Hallelujah Acres when conventional medicine fails to cure their ailments. For those who experience healing through changing their diet, belonging to the Hallelujah Acres community affirms a sense of distinction and moral superiority that resembles Evangelical ideology generally.[2] This is evident in three ways. First, the group advocates a diet that sets it apart from the majority of Americans and believes that a biblically based raw foods diet is more special and powerful than similar, nontheistic raw foods or health foods diets.[3] Second, the group criticizes food practices taken for granted in many Christian church communities and decries the ignorance of church friends and leaders, setting themselves above and apart from fellow Christians. And third, the group demonizes and criminalizes conventional medicine, presenting the Hallelujah Diet as medically and scientifically superior. As such, Hallelujah Acres is an example of a subset of Evangelical Christians who use the ideology of distinction to further set themselves above and apart from "the world" and the Christian mainstream.

HALLELUJAH ACRES

Hallelujah Acres has been headquartered in Shelby, North Carolina, since 1992. Founder Rev. George Malkmus was diagnosed with colon cancer in 1976. At that time he pastored a church of six hundred in upstate New York, broadcasted a weekly radio program called *America Needs Christ*, and oversaw the church's private school comprising grades K–12 and an adult

FIGURE 4.1   Reverend George Malkmus, founder of Hallelujah Acres, was diagnosed with colon cancer in 1976. He found changing his diet to be an effective means of cancer treatment and wrote *Why Christians Get Sick* in 1989, encouraging other Christians to change their diet as a means to improve their health. Reverend Malkmus is currently seventy-eight years old. Photo courtesy of Hallelujah Acres Lifestyle Center, Lake Lure, North Carolina, 2012.

Bible institute. The diagnosis came as a shock to Malkmus, who wrote: "I didn't understand. How could God bless the ministry so abundantly and allow something like this to happen? I searched my life to see if there was something I had done or failed to do for which God was punishing me. But to the best of my knowledge I was serving the Lord with a pure heart and a clean life."[4]

Having recently lost his mother to colon cancer, Malkmus decided to explore alternative treatment options. On the advice of Texas evangelist and self-proclaimed "health nut" Lester Roloff, Malkmus completely changed his diet. Using the Bible verse Genesis 1:29, which reads, "Then God said, 'I give you every seed-bearing plant on the face of the whole earth and every tree that has fruit with seed in it. They will be yours for food'" (NIV), Roloff convinced Malkmus that his cancer could be cured with a raw foods diet of fruits, nuts, and vegetables. After one year on the diet and with no conventional cancer treatments, Malkmus saw his tumor disappear. According to Malkmus, since adopting a predominantly raw foods diet he has experienced no significant health problems, and he is now in his seventies.

Based on his successful experience with this biblically based raw foods diet, Malkmus felt compelled to share his story with other Christians and published *Why Christians Get Sick* in 1989.[5] The short book presents Malkmus's main idea that Christians get sick because they eat the same diet as non-Christians. In the late 1980s he began conducting Christian health seminars, and in 1992 he and his wife founded Hallelujah Acres. Malkmus developed a vegan diet of 85 percent raw foods for three meals a day, fresh vegetable juice three times a day, and a flax seed supplement. His nutritional recommendations have changed very little since he developed this diet, but Hallelujah Acres has created a modified version of the diet for persons with significant health problems. This is called the Recovery Diet, and it increases the vegetable juice dosage to 8 ounces every hour and recommends other supplements like a probiotic, a digestive enzyme, iodine, B12, and curcumin. In the twenty years since its founding, Hallelujah Acres has grown from a small-time, family-run operation to a national network of over five thousand "health ministers" promoting the Hallelujah Diet through seminars at churches nationwide, an Internet TV station, monthly magazines and weekly e-mail newsletters, weekend educational retreats, and lifestyle centers offering weeklong in-home training on the Hallelujah Diet.[6]

Hallelujah Acres currently has four lifestyle centers across the United States. The center in Lake Lure is the oldest, founded in 2002, and is the model for the other three centers. Activities at the lifestyle center include daily Bible study, classes on aspects of raw foods living (including kitchen setup, medical justifications for a raw foods diet, and tips for how to maintain the diet after leaving the center), juice and food preparation, group exercise, and viewings of DVDs that feature doctors and scientists promoting vegan and raw foods diets. Ed, one of the health ministers in charge of the lifestyle center I attended, told our group that "doctors don't know anything about nutrition" and promised a reeducation on dietary concerns like protein (you can get all the protein you need from vegetables) and calcium (dairy-based calcium sources are harmful and plant-based calcium sources are beneficial).[7] This reeducation was to occur through DVDs featuring "real science." Over the five-day period that I and eleven other guests spent at the lifestyle center, run by Ed and his wife Karen, we watched seven DVDs and listened to a two-part audio recording, all propounding the benefits of a plant-based diet.[8] Very few of these DVDs were made from a Christian perspective, and all featured doctors, scientists, and researchers.

This use of secular materials demonstrates a central tension within Hallelujah Acres's reeducation: Hallelujah Acres presents doctors in general as ignorant or blatantly evil yet relies on credentialed experts to support its dietary recommendations. The organization integrates science that supports its diet with Bible verses and religious testimonies of healing. Evangelicals are adept at juggling distinction and engagement, and this double presentation of medical expertise as sometimes willfully ignorant/evil and sometimes trustworthy falls in line with the way Evangelicals perceive larger American culture: most of it is out of sync with God's plan, but by using the Bible and one's sense of God's plan, one can discern the parts of the world that are appropriate or necessary for correct Christian living.[9]

DISTINCTION FROM THE MAJORITY OF AMERICANS

Raw foods advocates in the United States have been promoting raw foods as a means to health and happiness since at least the early-twentieth century. The Nature Boys of the 1920s, for example, explored spiritual aspects of raw foods and saw consuming only uncooked fruits, vegetables, and nuts as a way to connect closely with nature. Some Christian groups like the Seventh-day Adventists have advocated a meatless diet as biblically appropriate. Hallelujah Acres comes out of this history of understanding diet, and particularly a vegetable-based diet, as physically curative and spiritually significant. However, what separates Hallelujah Acres from its predecessors is the desire to frame the Hallelujah Diet as a distinctively Evangelical Christian practice that enacts God's will. For those at the lifestyle center, beginning the Hallelujah Diet was a lifestyle change comparable to the choice to dedicate one's life to Jesus Christ; and as the following conversations show, following the Hallelujah Diet was a way to reexperience conversion and security in salvation.

On the second evening of our stay at the lifestyle center, the group expressed some anxiety about the challenges of staying on the diet after leaving Hallelujah Acres. Ed, the leader, responded, "You have to want this for you, not for anyone else. Not for your husband, or your mom or anyone. It has to be for you. I tried it just as an experiment on my own body, and it felt so good, I knew it was for me. And I have not let anything get in my way—not coffee, not burgers, nothing. I didn't want to be broken down and sick anymore. You have to latch onto it for you."

When one of the guests, June, asked about peer pressure from family and friends, Ed told her, "It doesn't matter. My family teased us but I didn't care. It's such a blessing to be healthy. You'll go home and that cheesecake will be staring you in the face, but you'll just think, is it worth it?"

"So, when family comes, you make them what?" June pressed him.

"Okay, let's say I'm all Hallelujah Acres and Karen isn't," Ed responded. "I would just make my food on the side and then sit at the table with the family and talk with them and laugh with them and not treat it like a big deal at all."

June brought up an important difference between Ed's situation and hers. "But, for us, we're the mothers. We have to cook for the family and they still eat the old way."

"You have to fend for your kids just like you always have. You just say, I don't want to be sick, and be a model for them," Ed told her.

"But I don't want to make that food for them anymore," June protested.

"Well, you have to," Ed told her. "You have to make them what will make them happy. But you can show them how good your food is." Ed and June both implicitly recognized an Evangelical mainstay of family dynamics—gendered hierarchy and responsibility. According to many contemporary Evangelical teachings on family and marriage, wives and husbands are meant to serve each other, but the husband fulfills God's plan by acting as the head of the household. Therefore if the husband is not on the Hallelujah Diet, the wife can model a different choice but will still be expected to provide meals that the husband will enjoy.[10]

Joshua, a middle-aged man from Australia suffering from undiagnosed health problems, voiced a concern. "I understand, but I have a wife and a family who won't eat like that. It's easy here because we're in this sheltered environment. Also, I run a business and—I know what you're gonna say: plan ahead and juice ahead and freeze it, huh?"

"You just answered your own question," said Ed. "Look, before Karen and I moved here [to the lifestyle center], we both worked full time. We split up the cooking duties and we made it work. You have to think ahead. Make extra and freeze it. We're training you to think ahead. I'm not saying the real world isn't work, and you may not be sick enough to stick to it. You might have to break down more and get more sick before you're ready to stick to it. I hope not. You have to make a decision. Are you in or are you out? Because you can't do both."

In this moment, perhaps unwittingly, Ed mirrored the rhetoric of Evangelical conversion. Evangelicals claim that one cannot live as a Christian and as a worldly person at the same time—you cannot do both. While Evangelicals promote cultural engagement as a way to spread a Christian message, they are clear that the way one engages with the world must always preserve the distinctiveness and moral superiority of Evangelical Christianity. One way to practice this is to be present in worldly situations and model Evangelical distinction.[11] Sitting at the dinner table and eating something different is a means to demonstrate that one is "in," that is, that one is firmly committed to the Hallelujah Diet and by extension to Evangelical Christianity.

Ed seemed unsure whether the group was convinced about why the Hallelujah Diet matters. "Look," he said, "those other foods are full of excito-toxins. They get into your brain and they make you excited. Those fast food burgers are designed in a laboratory to make you want them again. It works just like the tobacco companies. They don't want you wandering off and getting healthy. They want you for a repeat customer. Why do you think they're so popular? Especially with kids? That is not food, it's poison."

"Why would the government allow that?" asked Joshua.

"Profits. Money," said Ed matter-of-factly. "You have to take responsibility for your health. And it's not easy. For me, I was just wrung out. I was done. I would be praying, saying, Lord, there is something missing. What is missing? This is it. Nutrition. Nutrition was missing. That's what's missing in the church—nutrition. Nutrition is the missing link."

The rhetoric of "something missing" is common in conservative Christianity. Evangelicals often posit that before their conversion to Christianity, they felt there was something missing in their lives. They then narrate turning to Jesus Christ as a method for filling that void in their lives.[12] Ed's words are interesting because he uses language of "something missing" that would be familiar to the guests at the lifestyle center to position nutrition and the Hallelujah Diet as having the same power as Jesus to complete the lives of believers.

"What did we read this morning [at Bible study]?" Ed continued. "God promises long life and blessing. Look, this is how I think about it. God is not a micro-manager. For example, George [Malkmus] was out there growing his church and doing great work for the Lord and he gets colon cancer. It's like God is saying, hey, I can't protect you from every meal you eat. The church says, why do you have to go and make food a religion? We're not making food a religion. We're just saying, think about it. Look into the science. What was God's intention for humans? Where did he put humans originally?"

"In the garden," someone responded.

"So, it's okay to be a Christian vegetarian, but the church looks at [the Hallelujah Diet] like it's a cult, but that's ridiculous," Ed said.[13]

Evangelicals are invested in a faith perspective that positions them as separate and morally superior to "the world." Hallelujah Acres supports this and creates layers of distinction by positioning its diet as unique and important in comparison with the rest of the world, with Christianity at large, and with secular health food advocates. These layers of distinction reinforce a sense of moral superiority over the world, the church, and the health food movement. Those who attend lifestyle center training are spending a week withdrawn from their jobs, their church, and their day-to-day routine. This experience of a break with daily life can serve to reinforce a sense of distinction.

Hallelujah Acres pursues this experience of concrete distinction by constructing a community that is literally set apart: a complex of houses,

FIGURE 4.2 Staff and guests at the Hallelujah Acres Lifestyle Center in Lake Lure, North Carolina, prepare salad greens and a raw cauliflower dish with a vegan cheese-substitute sauce in the center's kitchen. Food preparation was a major portion of the daily activities at the center. Photo courtesy of Hallelujah Acres Lifestyle Center, Lake Lure, North Carolina, 2011.

condominiums, and commercial spaces for those adhering to the Hallelujah Diet and lifestyle. The organization has plans under way for "The Villages of Hallelujah Acres . . . the nation's first and one-of-a-kind master-planned healthy lifestyle community." A letter from George Malkmus in the promotional materials for The Villages reads:

> The number one amenity at The Villages is the community itself, the people who are choosing to call this wonderful place "home." Living with like-minded neighbors who are truly interested in a healthy lifestyle and supporting one another is truly a rare opportunity. Can you imagine having neighbors who actually respect your choice to adopt The Hallelujah Diet? Please consider this your invitation to live in a community like none other, to enjoy the assurance and comfort of a brand new estate home, garden

home or condominium, and to live in harmony with others who appreciate their God-given gift of health and vitality.[14]

This letter implies that one's current neighbors do not approve of or respect the Hallelujah Diet. While those who follow the Hallelujah Diet are encouraged to cultivate a sense of distinction and moral superiority, there is also a recognition that maintaining that distinction can be socially isolating.

The Villages provides a solution—one can cultivate a sense of distinction while also experiencing a sense of community with one's neighbors. For those who have committed to this diet and lifestyle, maintaining their choices relies heavily on a support network. When I conducted follow-up research, I found that of the people who attended the lifestyle center at the same time as I did, those who had attended with others (either spouses or friends) were better able to maintain their lifestyle change upon leaving the center. A sense of distinction and moral superiority can be highly motivating, but it can also be isolating and lonely. There is an ongoing recognition in Hallelujah Acres promotional materials that maintaining the Hallelujah Diet is difficult when one lives one's life surrounded by neighbors who don't respect or understand one's diet choice. Whether these neighbors are actually those that live in your neighborhood and invite you to a backyard cookout, or your church friends who invite you to a potluck, or your work friends who invite you to holiday parties, all these events are sure to be teeming with meat, dairy, and cooked foods. The Villages is a recognition of the struggle to remain distinct and the desire for a like-minded community.

DISTINCTION FROM OTHER CHRISTIANS

Hallelujah Acres challenges food practices that are prevalent in the larger Evangelical community. According to Ed, "You can't pray a spiritual prayer over a physical meal and expect it to make a difference. God wants us to use common sense. You're gonna reap what you sow."[15] To Ed and to others on the Hallelujah Diet, praying over one's food cannot affect the nutritional value of what one eats. For Ed, it was just "common sense" to eat foods in line with God's intentions for human eating as modeled by the Garden of Eden. This idea sets those on the Hallelujah Diet apart not only from the majority of Americans but also from the majority of Evangelicals, including many church leaders.

On one morning walk I spoke with June and Lena, two women who had come to the lifestyle center with a third friend, Ginny. The three of them worked together at a large church in Virginia. They consistently brought up the health of their pastor. June told me on our walk:

> You know, the church we go to in Virginia, it's a real megachuch. Like over 3,000 people. And Ginny is like, well, people joke and call her Mother Superior there. She has been the pastor's secretary for over 20 years. She knows everybody. You would never know it from her humble way, but she is well regarded in our church. And our pastor got colon cancer and Ginny—now, Ginny is already getting up at 7 a.m., working full time, always having lunch and dinner with people from the church, 72 years old—and she would get up at 5 a.m. and make him carrot juice, then go to his house and put the carrot juice in his fridge before he got up to go to work. Sometimes he would drink it, but if she missed a day, he would ask, "Where's my carrot juice?" So, he asked where we were going this week and when we told him, he just turned up his nose at it.[16]

That same day at lunch, Ginny told us that she had bought the DVD *Healing Cancer from the Inside Out* for her pastor earlier that year. This presentation is a secular medical approach to vegan dieting and was not produced by Hallelujah Acres. The film presented an ominous view of the "cancer industry," claiming that the American Cancer Society's goal is to convert people into longtime patients for profit. Because the American Cancer Society emphasizes early detection, not prevention, the film argued that the American Cancer Society is business driven, not health driven. It went so far as to claim that the medical establishment uses "rubber numbers" and distorts statistics to justify maintaining the status quo of the cancer industry. The filmmakers contended that if the medical establishment recognized diet as curative, this would injure the profits of hospitals, pharmaceuticals, and the medical profession generally. Therefore it is in the medical community's best interest to treat, but not cure, cancer.[17]

Ginny had bought this DVD for her pastor when he was diagnosed with colon cancer. She said, "I gave it to him and he said he would watch it but . . . [shakes her head]. Then I talked to his wife and said, it would mean so much to me if he would take a look at it, and she said that she wants him to watch it too."

Karen asked if her pastor currently had cancer. Ginny responded, "Well, he's been given a full bill of health, but we know what that means—nothing." According to *Healing Cancer from the Inside Out*, cancer is likely to return unless patients radically change their lifestyle choices.

"I don't understand why he won't watch it," said Ed. "What harm can it do to watch a video? He's afraid he will feel convicted." Again, Ed invoked language of religious transformation. For a believer, to feel convicted means that the believer senses God dictating a new course for his or her life, and the believer must resolve this feeling of conviction by realigning his or her life with God's will.

June added, "It's also that there are a lot of doctors in the congregation, and they love him. And this is what they told him to do."

"[They told him to do] the conventional treatment," said Ginny. "He asked his doctor, does this have anything to do with diet? And the doctor said, no, it's stress. It's all the stress in your life. And he does have a lot of stress."

"That's ridiculous," said Ed indignantly. "I mean, stress can cause cancer, don't get me wrong. But that's just ignorance on the part of the doctor to say that food has nothing to do with it. It's ignorance."[18]

Throughout these conversations, Ed and others described the Hallelujah Diet in similar terms to Evangelical Christianity—you convert to the diet, adhering to it is hard work but incredibly important, and adhering to the diet sets you apart from the world at large.

What also became clear was that the diet sets one apart from the larger Evangelical community. June, Lena, and Ginny differed from their pastor on this issue; they were certain that the Hallelujah Diet was an important religious choice. Mirroring contemporary witnessing strategies, they tried to model the diet and educate others about the benefits of this choice without being overly pushy. This example reveals that within church communities, Hallelujah Diet adherents may be seen as radical. Perhaps because veganism and raw foods are most often seen culturally in liberal populations, the majority of Evangelicals may be suspicious of veganism and raw foods diets as practices that indicate liberal political beliefs and New Age spirituality. June, Lena, and Ginny turned to medical expertise (the DVD) and their own knowledge of Evangelical modeling (witnessing through demonstrable behavior, not verbal argument) to frame their vegan, raw foods diet as accommodating, not challenging, Evangelical beliefs. But clearly they were troubled by their pastor's reluctance to learn about and try the Hallelujah Diet.

DISTINCTION FROM CONVENTIONAL MEDICAL SCIENCE

Hallelujah Acres demonstrates a conflicted relationship with medical science. The leaders of the organization reject traditional medical treatments but use doctors and scientific experts to justify this rejection.[19] Because Evangelicals already rely on a distinction between "the saved" and "the world," it is easy to map this distinction onto scientific experts. Those who recommend conventional treatments are of the world and, at best, unaware of the error of their ways or, at worst, part of a financial conspiracy to exploit the sick. Scientists and doctors who recommend dietary changes that resemble Hallelujah Acres's recommendations are lauded as the enlightened few in a sea of ignorant or malicious counterparts. However, the religious perspective of the doctor is not taken into account. Rev. George Malkmus serves as the religious expert promoting the diet as God's will, but he cannot convince people or does not try to convince people with religion alone. He mobilizes scholars, experts, and medical professionals to support his dietary recommendations. Hallelujah Acres seems to see health as the realm of medicine and to see religion and medicine as separate spheres. Therefore the desire to infuse health practices with religious meaning still relies on the scientific expertise of medical professionals far more than on the religious testimonies of believers.

My roommate during my week at the lifestyle center was Cynthia, a middle-aged woman suffering from stage IV cancer. Cynthia had completed chemotherapy six weeks earlier, and her doctors had told her there was nothing else that could be done for her cancer. We talked about our health problems—I had developed tendinitis in my wrists from computer overuse. Cynthia told me, "I hope you find something here. I know I'm hoping for it for me." Cynthia had explored another raw foods cancer treatment center but thought it was too full of "new age junk," and she suspected the women running it were lesbians. "Well, the first person I saw there was this woman who looked like a man. She had short hair—I mean, my hair is short, but this is my hair grown out from the chemo—her hair was shorter than mine and she had it slicked back. She was built like a man and she wore a man's shirt. And the lady that started it, she had left this other lady in charge and they were real close, never married." She left this implication hanging in the air, then continued, "I don't care what people say about the world changing and accepting others. I don't accept it. It's wrong."

This conversation illuminates a central tension within Hallelujah Acres: raw and vegan diets are culturally affiliated with liberal politics, including open stances on homosexuality. Hallelujah Acres does not explicitly deal with this tension, but the institution's ongoing emphasis on the Hallelujah Diet as biblically sound resonates with the Evangelical political style of relying on Bible verses to support conservative stances, particularly regarding homosexuality. Though the diet instruction that Cynthia would have received had she stayed at what she surmised was a lesbian-run facility would most probably have been very similar to the Hallelujah Diet, Hallelujah Acres's biblical framing of diet instruction did not threaten her deeply held conservative beliefs on homosexuality.

I changed the subject and asked about her daughter who had dropped her off at the lifestyle center that afternoon. I asked if she was going to college. "No, she went last year, but this year—just a lot of things came up. [pause] Yep, I found out my husband was cheating on me with my best friend. You never think that sort of thing is gonna happen to you. And I got a hysterectomy and was home alone recovering because he was never there because he is a jerk. Then I got the cancer diagnosis." Cynthia's daughter called on her cell phone just then, ending our conversation.[20]

Over the course of the week, I paid particular attention to Cynthia. I don't think she told anyone else about her marital problems or about her experience with the other raw foods community. She was clearly in a lot of pain—I would hear her sighing and whimpering at night, and whenever we had a break she would lie down for a restless nap. She was not a very vocal participant in the center's activities, but at night she would talk to me about her intentions to adhere to the Hallelujah Diet. "There is so much cancer in me, I'm just in pain all the time. I told my kids they have to help me. I said, I'm not ready to die. They said, well, Ma, we don't want you to die either. So I'm going to stick to it."[21]

For Cynthia and for many of the people in advanced stages of illness who attend Hallelujah Acres lifestyle centers, the diet is a source of hope for healing. As scholar R. Marie Griffith has noted, New Thought has greatly influenced religious health practices in America.[22] New Thought was a late nineteenth-century set of religious ideas that emphasized the power of the mind to affect human reality. It greatly influenced mid-century New Age and health movements, perhaps most famously articulated in Norman Vincent Peale's *The Power of Positive Thinking*, published in 1952.[23] Though there is no indication of a direct connection between New Thought and Hallelujah Acres, Christian dieting precedents that developed in the 1960s and 1970s reflected New Thought logic and promoted the idea that prayer was an effective method of controlling food urges.

At Hallelujah Acres, this was also the case. Each morning at the lifestyle center began with a glass of carrot juice, a shot of BarleyMax (barley juice made from a dehydrated powder), and group Bible study examining Bible verses that Ed and Karen described as "God's promises." The twelve guests, Joe (a staff member), Ed, and Karen would gather around the dining room table and take turns looking up verses from a list provided. Throughout Bible study, Ed emphasized positive thinking as a curative part of the Hallelujah Diet. For example, during the second Bible study of our stay at the lifestyle center, we were going around the table reading verses aloud and Emily, a middle-aged woman recently diagnosed with breast cancer, read Romans 15:13 to the group: "May the God of hope fill you with all joy and peace as you trust in him, so that you may overflow with hope by the power of the Holy Spirit" (NIV).

Emily reflected on this verse, saying, "I'm not worried. I'm following the Lord. God got me on this other track, and He's taking care of it. And my sisters say, you are an inspiration. I may have a breast problem or a tumor, but I feel great. I don't feel sick."

"Put cancer in your back pocket," Ed told the group. "It doesn't have to consume you every day. Don't tell everyone you meet about your tumor markers. That just keeps it in your mind. We've got to get our minds off of our self."[24]

In this conversation Ed and Emily's emphasis was on hope as a healing practice in itself. One effect of this emphasis, however, was that people who adhered to the diet but did not get better questioned whether they lacked the faith to be fully healed. Later that same day, I had a conversation with Joshua, the Australian man with undiagnosed health problems. Joshua told me that he suffered from digestion issues. "I'll wake up in the night with belching and my tummy rumbling like a volcano." He had undergone five colonoscopies in the past three years. The doctors told him that everything was normal, "but I don't feel normal." This was Joshua's second week at the lifestyle center, and while his digestion issues had quieted over the previous week, his discomfort had returned this week. When I listened to Joshua talk about his life in Australia, I could hear in his voice his hesitation to embrace the raw foods vegan diet of Hallelujah Acres:

> Before coming here, my diet was somewhat erratic, but healthy. I got this guy that brings me fish the day he catches them. They're so good. They melt in your mouth. My wife loves to cook. She already does stuff like this—big salads with lots of ingredients—lettuce, tomato, carrots, radishes, etc. If she makes a pumpkin soup, we use fresh pumpkin, carrots, and sweet potato in there. I go to the farmer's market and she experiments. It's somewhat erratic, I'll admit. I drink alcohol sometimes, the odd dairy. I'll have cheese every few weeks.

Joshua's description made it seem like he was not planning to change his diet upon leaving the lifestyle center. He told me, "It's costing me quite a bit to be here. . . . I wasn't sure if I should come here, but my wife encouraged me. I prayed about it, maybe my faith isn't as strong as it should be, I don't know."[25]

For Joshua and for others at the center, faith was a means of committing to the diet. Faith, and particularly the conviction that God wants Christians to be healthy, informed the diet practices at the center. Joshua remained skeptical about the necessity of committing to the diet and, through Hallelujah Acres headquarters, scheduled an appointment for a medical scan that revealed a lingering infection in an old root canal. After receiving this diagnosis, he seemed much happier.

Despite Ed and Karen's insistence that the Hallelujah Diet is entirely curative, most of the lifestyle center attendees continued to seek conventional medical advice. Even Emily, a few months after leaving the center and staying on the diet, e-mailed the group saying, "I am still fighting my cancer. The tumor has slowly gotten bigger over time and I am now seeking mainstream methods to try to recover from it. I am still doing the diet and lifestyle although I haven't been able to do much exercise lately because I don't have the energy. I would appreciate your prayers. I will keep you posted on how I am doing."[26] My roommate, Cynthia, did not recover from her cancer and died a few months after leaving the center. Her daughter returned my phone call to let me know. Cynthia had been bedridden for weeks before her death and her daughter said, "I'm just relieved she's not in pain anymore."[27] For some the Hallelujah Diet was an effective treatment. Brian, a middle-aged man suffering from painful arthritis, and his wife, Marsha, reported much improved health after several months on the diet. Marsha told me that Brian lost over fifty pounds and cut down from seven prescription medications to one.[28]

This range of experiences demonstrates a wider complexity than allowed by Ed and Karen's presentation of the diet as entirely curative. When I told Karen of Cynthia's death, she said, "Oh, Cynthia. She was very sick. She had cancer when she came. I think she may have had stage IV when she came. And she had already had all of that chemo and treatments that lower your immune system. No, I didn't know that she had died. No, I didn't know that. Thank you for telling me. I would've liked to have sent something. We keep getting people coming here sicker and sicker, and by the time they get here, it's difficult."[29] In her response, Karen did not fault Cynthia's faith or question whether she had adhered to the diet. She pointed instead to Cynthia's medical history and faulted the chemotherapy for impeding Cynthia's recovery.

Hallelujah Acres sees itself as set apart from the secular world, the larger Christian community, and conventional medicine. Using the Evangelical notion of distinction, it promotes its lifestyle as morally superior. According to founder George Malkmus:

Christians get sick because they have conformed to the diet and lifestyle of this world. Christians eat in the same fast food restaurants and consume the same junk food as the world community. Compare the diet of the average Christian with that of the average non-Christian and you will find absolutely no difference in what they eat. Each group eats the same diet, thus creating the same physical problems. Do you realize that the percentage of Christians experiencing cancer, heart attacks and strokes, diabetes, as well as all other physical problems is the same in both the Christian and non-Christian communities?[30]

Malkmus founded Hallelujah Acres because he believed that Christians should not be the same as non-Christians and that by using the Bible, a Christian could discern God's intended diet for humans and avoid sickness and disease. However, as this chapter has shown, to justify the vegan raw foods diet that Malkmus found in Genesis, Hallelujah Acres relies on expertise of medical professionals. This creates an uneasy relationship with medical science, and my research shows that lifestyle center attendees were unlikely to fully reject conventional medicine. Adhering to the Hallelujah Diet can enable a sense of distinction and moral superiority. However, this distinction rests on a shaky foundation as those on the diet may continue to suffer from health problems and may choose to pursue conventional treatment, undermining their distinctiveness and moral superiority. As such, Hallelujah Acres reveals how food practices can reinforce a religious group's ideology, like Evangelical distinction, but can also challenge that ideology.

DISCUSSION QUESTIONS

1. How do Hallelujah Acres's diet practices reflect Evangelical notions of distinction and moral superiority?
2. Ambivalence is the state of having simultaneous, conflicting feelings. What examples of ambivalence did you see in this chapter? How do those on the Hallelujah Diet deal with these experiences of ambivalence?
3. What do you make of Emily's decision to pursue conventional treatment for her cancer? How might Ed react to this decision? Why?
4. How does Hallelujah Acres balance distinction and moral superiority with community and belonging? What role does food play in this balance?

NOTES

1. Much scholarship on American Evangelicalism argues that Evangelicalism is not as homogenous as Evangelical spokespeople present. This important insight has made it difficult to determine who exactly belongs in the category "Evangelical." Despite the theological complexity that scholars highlight, Evangelicals tend to assume an ideological unity through core

religious beliefs. In the simplest possible terms, these beliefs include the inherent sinfulness of humanity, the power of God to intercede in human affairs, salvation through Jesus Christ, and the obligation to share this information with others. The Bible is understood to be the infallible word of God that can exercise power over people's hearts and minds. My use of the term "Evangelical" refers to these core beliefs as well as to the political history of Christian institutions that prioritize gospel outreach. See Robert Wuthnow, *The Restructuring of American Religion: Society and Faith Since World War II* (Princeton: Princeton University Press, 1988); Randall Balmer, *The Making of Evangelicalism: From Revivalism to Politics and Beyond* (Baylor, Tex.: Baylor University Press, 2010); and Christian Smith, *American Evangelicalism: Embattled and Thriving* (Chicago: University of Chicago Press, 1998).

2. Christian Smith explores distinction and moral superiority as facets of Evangelicalism at length in his work, *American Evangelicalism*.

3. Nontheistic vegetarian or vegan proponents often focus on the social ethics of food consumption. See Michael Allen Fox, *Deep Vegetarianism (America in Transition)* (Philadelphia: Temple University Press, 1999); and Kerry Walters and Lisa Portmess, *Ethical Vegetarianism* (New York: State University of New York Press, 1999).

4. George Malkmus, *You Don't Have To Be Sick!: A Christian Health Primer* (Shelby, N.C.: Hallelujah Acres, 1999), 9. It is interesting to note that because Hallelujah Acres views its diet as inherently healing and as God's true intention for human eating, the group believes the diet can heal atheists, because even an atheist following the diet is following God's will.

5. George Malkmus, *Why Christians Get Sick* (Shippensburg, Penn.: Destiny Image, 1989).

6. Hallelujah Acres, "Vegetarian Recipes, Health Eating, Hallelujah Diet: Hallelujah Acres," http://www.hacres.com.

7. To protect the privacy of organizers and participants, all names have been changed.

8. These DVDs included *The Miraculous Self-Healing Body* (Hallelujah Acres, 2007); Michael Klaper, *A Diet for All Reasons* (Feel Good Again, 1992); Mike Anderson, *Eating* (Ravediet.com, 2008); Mike Anderson, *Healing Cancer from the Inside Out* (Ravediet.com, 2008); Neal Barnard, *Breaking the Food Seduction* (Modern Manna, 2003); and Lee Fulkerson, *Forks Over Knives* (Monica Beach Media, 2011).

9. On Evangelicalism's relationship with American culture, see D. Michael Lindsay, *Faith in the Halls of Power: How Evangelicals Joined the American Elite*

(New York: Oxford University Press, 2008); Michael P. Young, *Bearing Witness Against Sin: The Evangelical Birth of the American Social Movement* (Chicago: University of Chicago Press, 2007); and Jason C. Bivins, *The Fracture of Good Order: Christian Antiliberalism and the Challenge to American Politics* (Chapel Hill: University of North Carolina Press, 2002).

10. On Evangelical marriage, see John Bartkowski, *Remaking the Godly Marriage: Gender Negotiation in Evangelical Families* (New Brunswick, N.J.: Rutgers University Press, 2001); and Sally Gallagher, *Evangelical Identity and Gendered Family Life* (New Brunswick, N.J.: Rutgers University Press, 2003).

11. Scholars of Evangelicals and popular culture have noted that the tools of media engagement helped shape Evangelical self-understandings by positioning Evangelical spokespeople as broadcasting to an audience of nonbelievers. While the consumers of Christian media remained largely Christian, the ability to imagine this media as an Evangelical tool informed production sensibilities and consumption practices. See, for example, Tona J. Hangen, *Redeeming the Dial: Radio, Religion, and Popular Culture in America* (Chapel Hill: University of North Carolina Press, 2001); Crawford Gribben, *Writing the Rapture: Prophecy Fiction in Evangelical America* (New York: Oxford University Press, 2009); and David W. Stowe, *No Sympathy for the Devil: Christian Pop Music and the Transformation of American Evangelicalism* (Chapel Hill: University of North Carolina Press, 2011).

12. For an extended analysis of the use of the rhetoric of "something missing" in conservative Christian politics, see Susan Harding, *The Book of Jerry Falwell: Fundamentalist Language and Politics* (Princeton: Princeton University Press, 2000), 183–209.

13. Field notes by author, May 16, 2011, Lake Lure, N.C.

14. George Malkmus, "Welcome to the Villages!" *The Villages of Hallelujah Acres: A Guide to Garden Home Plans* (Shelby, N.C.: Hallelujah Acres, n.d.).

15. Field notes by author, May 16, 2011, Lake Lure, N.C.

16. Ibid., May 19, 2011.

17. Anderson, *Healing Cancer*; field notes by author, May 18, 2011, Lake Lure, N.C.

18. Field notes by author, May 19, 2011, Lake Lure, N.C.

19. This ambivalent relationship parallels Evangelical use of science in defense of creationism. See Jeffrey P. Moran, *American Genesis: The Evolution Controversies from Scopes to Creation Science* (New York: Oxford University Press, 2012); and Barbara Forrest and Paul R. Gross, *Creationism's Trojan Horse: The Wedge of Intelligent Design* (New York: Oxford University Press, 2007).

20. Field notes by author, May 16, 2011, Lake Lure, N.C.

21. Ibid., May 10, 2011.

22. R. Marie Griffith, *Born Again Bodies: Flesh and Spirit in American Christianity* (Berkeley: University of California Press, 2004).

23. Norman Vincent Peale, *The Power of Positive Thinking* (New York: Simon and Schuster, 1952).

24. Field notes by author, May 17, 2011, Lake Lure, N.C.

25. Ibid.

26. E-mail interview by author, August 30, 2011.

27. Telephone interview by author, September 28, 2011.

28. Ibid., September 26, 2011.

29. Ibid., September 30, 2011.

30. Malkmus, *You Don't Have to Be Sick!*, 15.

RECOMMENDED READING

Griffith, R. Marie. *Born Again Bodies: Flesh and Spirit in American Christianity.* Berkeley: University of California Press, 2004.

Sack, Daniel. *Whitebread Protestants: Food and Religion in American Culture.* New York: Palgrave Macmillan, 2001.

Smith, Christian. *American Evangelicalism: Embattled and Thriving.* Chicago: University of Chicago Press, 1998.

Part Two

IDENTITY FOODWAYS

Five

DRAYDEL SALAD

THE SERIOUS BUSINESS OF JEWISH
FOOD AND FUN IN THE 1950s

RACHEL GROSS

I N THE 1950s the Jewish publishing house KTAV embarked on a quest to capture the hearts, minds, and stomachs of American Jewish children. Educators feared that unless they made Jewish children's education more entertaining, the young baby boomers would rapidly lose interest in their cultural and religious heritage. Against the force of what one Jewish journalist called children's "ordinary (and, as a matter of fact, entirely absorbing) American life," traditional Jewish forms of accultura- tion at home would not suffice and, worse still, were no longer reliable, while classroom instruction seemed of no avail.[1] A critique of the conven- tions of formal Jewish education had been part of the American Jewish communal conversation for some time; as early as 1920 one veteran of Hebrew school declared that he held Jewish afterschool religious instruc- tion responsible "for the larger part of dislike for all things Jewish," and it was generally acknowledged that there were far more interesting ways for Jewish children to spend their time in the increasingly commoditized world of American children's entertainment.[2] Jewish children in America had, it seemed, fully assimilated to the mainstream culture of American youth and lacked knowledge of and interest in Jewish culture and religious practices. American Jews needed a new, more fun way to impart religious knowledge and culture to the next generation.

Highlighting postwar Jews' anxieties about the future of their religious practices and culture, KTAV's 1956 publication of the *Junior Jewish Cook Book by Aunt Fanny* taught children to enact social identities that vacillated uneasily between the markedly Jewish, the modern American, and a self-consciously diverting blend of the two. While cookbooks designed for Jewish American children abound today, the *Junior Jewish Cook Book* is the earliest example of this genre.[3] Published by KTAV, one of the first distributors of American Jewish children's educational material, and pseudonymously authored by Sol Scharfstein, its enterprising president, the slim, sixty-four-page volume aimed to synthesize children's bifurcated American and Jewish identities through the palpable and playful medium of food.

At a glance the style of the cookbook's text and illustrations mimics popular mainstream counterparts such as *Betty Crocker's Cook Book for Boys and Girls* (1957) and *Mary Alden's Cookbook for Children* (1956). Its recipes range from traditional Jewish dishes with eastern European origins such as potato kugel (a baked pudding or casserole) to 1950s staples like hamburgers and creative concoctions designed to entertain young cooks, such as Noah's Ark cookies. The book's wide spectrum of recipes, from fried fish to baked bananas, was intended to strengthen its young readers' Jewish home lives. American Jews had moved out of ethnic urban neighborhoods into suburbs, where they were eager to assimilate into mainstream America. Definitely Jewish but not "too Jewish" in appearance so as not to repel Jewish suburbanites eager to shed idiosyncratic religious and ethnic identifiers, the *Junior Jewish Cook Book* encouraged its young readers to participate in normative American culinary practices by purchasing canned and packaged goods, using modern kitchen implements, and arranging food in fanciful forms according to current mainstream tastes, but to do so in service of Jewish practices. Using a children's cookbook format, a popular and distinctly American form of entertainment, KTAV linked Jewish practices to American foodways and recreation. Through the presentation of a series of seemingly light-hearted holiday-themed recipes, the cookbook encouraged children to take Jewish culture into their own hands, fostering excitement about their heritage through play.

The need for an altered approach to children's instruction arose as American Jews reorganized their communities in the postwar suburbs.

In contrast to urban Jewish neighborhoods of an earlier generation in which Jewish identity developed organically, Jewish life in this new environment required self-conscious choices and activities, leading to a perceived distinction between the practice of "Judaism" the religion and a sense of participation in "Jewishness," a culture.[4] Religious precepts and practices could be taught, but how did one teach a social identity? In a 1949 review of Jewish children's books in *Commentary*, Isa Kapp addressed the challenge of not only teaching children religious practices but also passing on a culture:

> A tone (and it seems to me that the Jewish tradition consists in large part of tone . . .) can only be absorbed haphazardly and to a large extent unconsciously, in the gradual, thoughtless way that a child comes to know that he is an American, that his home is in the city, that he is more interested in science than in music. There is a difference between overhearing a family joke and memorizing a sugared jingle, the difference between spontaneity and artifice.[5]

But Jewish leaders feared that many children would not come by this vaguely identified "tone" of Jewish culture naturally, through parental guidance. To acculturate children in the most natural and attractive way possible, KTAV and other Jewish publishers launched onto the market a blitz of "alphabet blocks, spelling games, coloring books, flip charts, film strips, fun books, cassettes, workbooks, and notebooks along with graduated texts" in order to interest children in Jewish living and education.[6] Through their appealing, up-to-date products for children, publishers rebranded Judaism as fun and playful, giving games a not-so-hidden objective. Jewishness would reach children through the guise of recreation.

Using a cookbook to acculturate Jewish children made sense for American Jews: as historian Hasia Diner identifies, Judaism's traditional ritual requirements "put food in the foreground," so teaching children to link Jewish identity and eating followed cultural norms.[7] At the same time, Jews, along with other Americans, were adapting to the rapidly changing food mores of postwar America. Notions of domesticity and child's play were changing too. Burdened by Cold War concerns about atomic weapons, still reeling from World War II, and shaped by the legacy of the Depression, Americans enthusiastically and assiduously created a family-centered culture that historian Elaine Tyler May identifies as a "psychological fortress" against perceived social and political threats. Pediatrician Benjamin's Spock's description of play as "serious business" in his 1946 bestseller, *Baby and Child Care*, epitomized this trend.[8] As Dr. Spock and others urged the professionalization of child rearing, KTAV marketed professional aids for raising Jewish children, working to normalize American Judaism within mainstream culture by equating Jewish and American identities through food and fun.

"AN ATMOSPHERE OF ANXIOUS CONCERN"

The *Junior Jewish Cook Book* spoke to a generation of Jewish children whose experience of Judaism differed dramatically from that of their parents, themselves largely the children of European immigrants who arrived at the turn of the twentieth century. In his influential work *Protestant-Catholic-Jew*, the eminent Jewish sociologist Will Herberg identified the plight of Jewish baby boomers who "became American in the sense that had been, by and large, impossible for the immigrants and their children." Nonetheless, issues of belonging and identification remained unresolved. "They were Americans," worried Herberg, "but what *kind* of Americans?"[9]

Herberg might have done well to question what kind of Jews they were as well. In the years following World War II, middle-class migration to the suburbs had an indelible impact on the communal structures of American Judaism. Though Jews suburbanized more rapidly and in larger numbers than other Americans and tended to live in neighborhoods surrounded by other Jews, they viewed their move from the ethnic neighborhoods of the city as a demonstration of their participation in mainstream American culture. In its new suburban context, the Jewish community had more organizations, especially denominationally affiliated synagogues and Jewish community centers, but despite the numbers, many Jews saw their suburban communities as "diluted and pallid" and "less Jewish" than the urban Jewish life of an earlier era.[10]

Having largely rejected the Orthodoxy of their elders, the second generation now relied heavily on Jewish organizations to educate their children while leading home lives undifferentiated from those of their non-Jewish suburban counterparts. As a result, synagogue services, religious education, and other Jewish activities seemed divorced from their children's everyday, secular American lives. In the 1954 pamphlet "Perplexities of Suburban Jewish Education," Dr. L. H. Grunebaum wrote:

> Children . . . suffer from a kind of mild schizophrenia. *Here* are the rabbi, director, cantor and teachers; *there* are the parents. . . . *Here* is supernaturalism, prayer, the Ten Commandments, Jewish customs and ceremonies. *There* is science, atomic facts, sex and Mickey Spillane, American ways and values. . . . So it comes about that the attempt to make children more secure as members of the Jewish community has in many cases the opposite result.[11]

Without the dynamic, continual ethnic reinforcement of Jewish neighborhoods in the city, the maintenance of the Jewish identity of the next generation seemed imperiled. To counter this, Jewish authors and educators sought fresh ways to interest American Jewish youth in their heritage, attempting to fill the perceived Jewish gap at home. Recognizing the limited value of formal education, too easily dismissed as stiflingly boring, they turned their attention to playtime.[12] New Jewish storybooks, biographies, and activity books were intended to foster a culture of Jewish childhood that might not arise organically.

In this context, the cheerful, seemingly innocuous genre of Jewish children's books bore heavy communal expectations. The editors of *Commentary* summed up the prevailing attitude of American Jews in an introduction to Kapp's 1949 review of Jewish children's books: "An atmosphere of anxious concern surrounds the production of children's books for Jewish children. Can they be counted on to make our youngsters conscious, self-respecting Jews? Or—others ask—do they stress Jewish uniqueness (or Israeli prowess) so much as to separate and estrange Jewish children from the common American life?"[13]

By the 1950s KTAV Publishing House had expanded from a small Jewish bookstore to a major business, just beginning to have a significant influence on Jewish education; today it is a major Jewish publishing house. The brothers Sol and Bernie Scharfstein built up the business, which they named KTAV, Hebrew for "writing." In 1951 Sol Scharfstein wrote KTAV's first book, a popular "Dick and Jane" style Hebrew reader called *Chaveri*, "my friend."[14] He continued to write and publish texts designed for Jewish classrooms and homes over the next six decades. "Anything that improves

Jewish education, even a little toy, has some value," Scharfstein later explained.[15]

Expanding their efforts to interest children in Judaism and Jewish culture, KTAV and other Jewish publishers began to publish books of Jewish-themed activities, in addition to storybooks. Children needed to take a more active role in their acculturation, to "play the games, paste the pictures, solve the riddles and enjoy reading the stories."[16] Interactive books made being Jewish a fun activity, not a lesson or a story to be passively absorbed.[17] The *Junior Jewish Cook Book* took this educational technique a step further, as an activity book with palatable results, quite literally providing a taste of Judaism.

"COOKLESS COOKERY" AND CREATIVITY

Even as it entered the changing world of the Jewish marketplace, the *Junior Jewish Cook Book* appeared amidst the burgeoning cookbook industry of the 1950s, a decade that would become infamous for the ubiquity of its packaged foods. In linking Judaism with cooking, KTAV did not tie the former to a stable social entity. The kitchen prompted at least as much communal anxiety among Americans at large as Jewish home life did among Jews. As marriage and birthrates soared after World War II among Jews and non-Jews alike, and couples raised families in newly developed suburbs, postwar America saw an unprecedented expansion of cookbook production. Although cooking served as the quintessential expression of middle-class femininity, 1950s cookbook authors assumed that young wives of the postwar marriage boom had little or no experience in the kitchen.[18] In this "era of the expert," suburban women required formal instruction to fulfill their social function and nourish their growing families.[19]

Not only did American home cooks appear less experienced and more open to professional advisement than did their mothers, but the contents of their kitchens had also undergone a dramatic transformation. Following World War II, myriads of astonishing timesaving household appliances became affordable for the middle class for the first time. Refrigerators and freezers brought new food products into the home, and electric stoves and ovens, blenders, dishwashers, and other appliances reshaped housewives' work. Encouraged by the development of rations for the army and the home front during the war, enthusiastic scientists and manufacturers put an array of canned, frozen, and packaged foods on the market.[20]

Embracing these symbols of idealized suburban ease, cookbook authors provided bewildered housewives with instructions on how to use the new culinary devices properly and how to serve prepared foods. Aided by new marketing techniques, the food industry promoted a new way to think about cooking, emphasizing creativity over labor. Manufacturers and cookbook authors (sometimes one and the same) taught modern housewives how to save time and energy by using prepared foods and modern culinary appliances, while maintaining a personal involvement and ownership over their creations by "doctoring up" or "glamorizing" the food they served. The modern housewife "may spend less time in the kitchen and she may buy canned food," wrote Ernest Dichter, the psychologist who pioneered the new fields of advertising and consumer behavior studies, "but *she makes up for it by greater creativeness*."[21] What popular cookbook author Poppy Cannon termed the "social art" of "cookless cookery" combined the moral responsibility of the housewife with the modernity and ease of manufactured goods.[22] The 1950s food culture made creative rearrangement the highest accolade in a world of manufactured uniformity, strikingly exemplified by Beth McLean's New Pineapple Look in the *Modern Homemaker's Cookbook*, a "good-tasting fake" consisting of liver sausage molded to look like a pineapple, covered by sliced olives serving as pineapple skin and topped by a real green pineapple top.[23] Whatever their final shape, the inclusion of canned and packaged ingredients in postwar recipes made manifest the modern American refinement and ingenuity of both cookbook author and home cook.

Strangely enough, even as cookbooks emphasized manufactured goods, they became more inclusive of recipes from other cultures—or at least American adaptations of them. In the late nineteenth century, proponents of scientific cooking and cooking school experts had urged immigrant families to give up the dishes of their homelands for a more uniformly "American" diet consisting of bland New England fare.[24] Accordingly, most American Jewish cookbooks published before World War II neither included distinctively Jewish dishes nor followed kashrut (the Jewish dietary laws), attempting to moderate what were seen as outlandish ethnic identifiers. But by the 1950s American culinary trends broadened to accept adaptations of immigrants' foodways. *The Complete American Cookbook* (1957), for example, included recipes for chow mein,

Javanese rice, tamale pie, egg foo young, and Italian sausage in cabbage leaves. Denominational cookbooks, like Catholic Florence Berger's *Cooking for Christ: The Liturgical Year in the Kitchen* (1949), now explicitly linked ethnic foodways with religious practices. "Most American families threw their spiritual and social traditions into the sea when they left Europe," Berger lamented. "They no longer wished to appear Dutch or French or Swedish—so they left you and me without a background"—a situation she fought by sharing recipes for German "Easter sweet bread," Italian "St Joseph sfinge (cream puffs)," and Greek spice cake.[25] Amid a torrent of increasingly specialized recipe books, Jewish cookbooks came into their own, reconfiguring the traditional fare of Eastern European Jews as American food and an increasingly diverse vision of "American" food as Jewish: *The Complete American-Jewish Cookbook* (1952) adapted "an amazing collection of American, Continental, and even international recipes" to accommodate Jewish dietary laws, including, as its advance publicity heralded, egg foo young and boo loo gai.[26]

"PITY THE POOR YOUNG PALATES"

Just as the cookbook industry was expanding, children's entertainment underwent rapid growth, accommodating the unprecedented size of the postwar baby boom generation. Cookbooks, like other modern, adult instruments, were adapted as novelties for children's play, and a surge of children's cookbooks entered the market in the postwar years.[27] With playful and simplified culinary trends in vogue, it was no great stretch for food manufacturers and cookbook authors to turn women's work into child's play in juvenile cookbooks. Like their counterparts for adults, children's cookbooks in this period tended to emphasize combining or reheating canned, processed, or frozen ingredients, often promoting the products of manufacturers such as General Mills and Quaker Oats. In these recipes, preparation of premade food served as an easy method for girls to learn to imitate their mothers in the kitchen and introduced them to the modern market at an early age.

Aimed primarily at girls, juvenile cookbooks echoed the culinary habits and gendered social roles of cookbooks aimed at adults. While cookbook authors encouraged the boomers' mothers to take ownership of new packaged goods by "doctoring up" their dishes, arranging them in trendy, creative shapes, children's cookbooks encouraged children to engage in "food fun," a child-sized version of the same fad. Cookbook authors seemed convinced that children loved to make and eat food shaped like animals or disguised as other food.[28] Symptomatic of this trend, *Good Housekeeping*'s June 1950 issue commended an editor on her practice of shaping her nieces' and nephews' dinners into storybook images. The magazine carefully documented her transformation of mashed potatoes, cottage cheese, or scrambled eggs into an edible Humpty Dumpty with pea eyes and nose and carrot mouth, sitting on a chopped-spinach wall.[29] Feeding children deserved careful consideration and advice from experts, from *Good Housekeeping* to Dr. Spock, and a lighthearted playfulness belied the serious issues at stake.

Such whimsical food arrangements had trickled down from the creative preoccupation of modern suburban housewives to their children's playtime. In 1954 *Saturday Review* bemoaned the reappearance of the once-fashionable candlestick salad in a children's cookbook: "it was rather disheartening to see that bridge-club pest of yesteryear turning up again—a fantasy consisting of lettuce leaf, one slice of canned pineapple with a half banana standing upright at its center, the whole thing dripping with mayonnaise. But perhaps—pity the poor young palates!—it has found its niche, a birthday party attended by befrilled small girls."[30] Despite reviewers' exhortations, food arrangement moved from the business of homemakers to child's play, instructing children in modern attitudes toward food, with all their fanciful trends and serious implications.

SHABBAT CANDLESTICK SALAD

In the *Junior Jewish Cook Book*, KTAV Publishing House applied this modern fad to Jewish communal purposes. They were not the first to do so: a 1953 *Commentary* review chided the authors of *The American-Jewish Cookbook* for including "a horror titled 'Menorah Salad'—a representation of a candle-stick done in fruit and vegetables."[31] Similarly, with a simple name change, the classic candlestick salad became the *Junior Jewish Cook Book*'s "Shabbat Candlestick Salad." Children could transform "just plain food" into "a social art" while celebrating Shabbat, the Jewish Sabbath. By tying familiar foodways to a Jewish practice, the *Junior Jewish Cook Book* employed American culture in the service of Judaism, merging children's

American and Jewish identities. At the same time, it made Jewish education fun: children could play with their food while learning about the ritual of lighting candles on Friday nights, the eve of Shabbat. The activity demonstrated that American and Jewish values were in accord and even enhanced each other, as did biblically inspired recipes such as Noah's Ark Cookies and Queen Esther Salad.

Playfulness also served to sugarcoat the cookbook's pedagogy. A recipe for draydel salad called for children to place raisins on top of the pear halves in the shape of the Hebrew letters on the dreidel, bounded by banana wedges arranged in the shape of the Chanukah top. Jewish children could learn Hebrew letters and Jewish customs through tactile and edible means. If they did not replace the oft-bemoaned Jewish Sunday school, such practices could serve as a delightful supplement. Preparing typical 1950s fare in celebration of a Jewish holiday, children played with their food just like their non-Jewish neighbors, guided by sources like *Good Housekeeping*, while forging a stronger connection to Jewish culture.

Despite, or because of, its Jewish theme, the book's appearance and layout carefully echoed those of non-Jewish juvenile cookbooks of the 1950s, with straightforward, easy-to-follow recipes accompanied by simple, attractive illustrations of the ingredients, the necessary culinary equipment, and the finished dish. It diverged from mainstream children's cookbooks, however, in its organization, instead following Jewish cookbook convention by dividing recipes according to their association with Jewish holidays rather than by the type of food or method of preparation. Its appearance and layout managed a comfortable and practical compromise between the two genres, actually performing the synthesis of Jewish and juvenile American identities that its intended audience should achieve.

"TO BECOME A JEW BY FREE ASSOCIATION"

Before the market grew larger and more specialized, midcentury Jewish children's books appealed to a wide audience, across denominational lines. Like other Jewish children's activity books, the *Junior Jewish Cook Book* promoted Jewish-themed play without presuming any level of Jewish observance or foreknowledge by the reader, following KTAV's goal of promoting "Jewish education and generational continuity" across the board.[32]

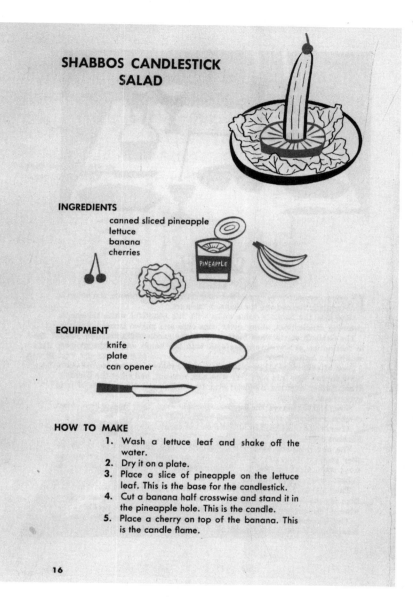

SHABBOS CANDLESTICK SALAD

INGREDIENTS

canned sliced pineapple
lettuce
banana
cherries

EQUIPMENT

knife
plate
can opener

HOW TO MAKE

1. Wash a lettuce leaf and shake off the water.
2. Dry it on a plate.
3. Place a slice of pineapple on the lettuce leaf. This is the base for the candlestick.
4. Cut a banana half crosswise and stand it in the pineapple hole. This is the candle.
5. Place a cherry on top of the banana. This is the candle flame.

16

FIGURE 5.1 *Junior Jewish Cook Book* adapted a cocktail party dish, candlestick salad, to teach children about the Jewish Sabbath. Author's collection; used with permission of KTAV Publishers.

DRAYDEL SALAD

Here is an easy Chanukah surprise to make.

INGREDIENTS
canned pear halves
raisins
banana

EQUIPMENT
knife
can opener

HOW TO MAKE

1. Place one-half pear on plate, flat side down.
2. Use raisins to make a draydel letter.
3. Cut banana into long slices.
4. Use one slice for the handle of the draydel.
5. Use a short slice for the tip of the draydel.

FIGURE 5.2 Draydel Salad made learning about Chanukah traditions and Hebrew letters a tactile and edible experience. *Junior Jewish Cook Book.* Author's collection; used with permission of KTAV Publishers.

The book was marketed to emerging gift shops of suburban Conservative and Reform synagogues, just beginning to appear as a resource for instructing parents and children in creating a Jewish home life.[33] Attempting to avoid alienating Jews who did not follow kashrut, the *Junior Jewish Cook Book* downplayed the role of ritual dietary laws, in contrast to Jewish cookbooks for adults, frequently marketed with the subtitle "in accordance with the Jewish dietary laws." Although the *Junior Jewish Cook Book* also contained a note assuring readers who cared that its recipes followed kashrut, it appeared in small font on the third page, not on the book's cover. Jewish children might easily follow KTAV's recipes without keeping kosher, even without an awareness of kashrut, since the book provided no explanation of that practice. Recipes were not labeled *milchig* (dairy) or *fleishig* (meat) to facilitate the user's practice of kashrut, as is common in later Jewish children's cookbooks. By minimizing mention of kashrut, the cookbook refrained from imposing ideology or ritual practices upon its young readers, leaving such formal instruction to the discretion of their parents. Instead, it encouraged Jewish unity through the tangible, sensory experience of making food and eating in celebration of Jewish holidays.

Extraneous commentary in *Junior Jewish Cook Book* underscores the communal anxiety underlying the cookbook's educational aims. A small note, for example, introduces the recipe for the once popular Jewish dish of fried fish: "Fish has always played an important part in all holiday and Sabbath meals. Serve cold fried fish at your Saturday and holiday afternoon meals. Serve fish with potato salad and pickles."[34] Such explanations were intended to subtly acculturate children to Jewish domestic practices; rather than detailing the correct ritual practice of Shabbat, the cookbook encouraged eating potato salad and pickles—familiar, Americanized versions of Eastern European Jewish foodways. More than providing religious instruction, KTAV aimed to acculturate children to cultural signifiers that it feared might disappear in the American melting pot.

KTAV's effort to speak to a readership with varying degrees of familiarity with Jewish culture provides a glimpse into American Jews' practices in the 1950s. The cookbook includes a summary of Jewish holiday customs, placing a holiday story and a description of its observances before each group of recipes. After describing Friday night home rituals, the Shabbat section narrates, "The next morning everyone is up bright and early, and off to temple they go. The youngsters hold their own service. Some of them act as cantors; some of them read the Torah; and all of them join in singing the Sabbath prayers just as the grownups do."[35] Here children act independently but mimic the ritual and liturgical activities of the adult community. Aiding children in leading services and cooking for holidays on their own, KTAV hoped that children would come to explore Judaism independently, learning by doing and gaining an attachment to Jewish practices through their performances. In her review of Jewish children's books, Kapp explained that for children, "the real fun is to be left to one's own devices, to stare unnoticed at busy adults, to discover unexpected gestures and voice intonations, to become a Jew by free association."[36] KTAV did not trust that Jewish children would acquire Jewish knowledge and identity if left entirely to their own devices, but it did its best to foster their Jewish sensibilities, providing the resources for Jewish child-only activities.

"EVERYONE'S FAVORITE"

Associating Jewishness with the fashionable ease of "cookless cookery," the ingredients of the *Junior Jewish Cook Book*'s recipes often feature cans and boxes. Queen Esther Salad, an edible arrangement of a simple face adorned with a crown in celebration of the holiday of Purim, consists exclusively of packaged food, emphasized by illustrations of a can of almonds, a bag of raisins, a can of pineapple, and a container of cottage cheese; one placed raisins on a round ball of cottage cheese to form the face, while almonds served as jewels in a pineapple crown. Pancakes, associated with Chanukah, are made from a mix, while the more challenging fried fish is made with a staple of the modern American Jewish kitchen, packaged matzo meal.[37] To the 1950s reader, the inclusion and creative arrangement of these ingredients proclaimed that Jewish cooking could be modernized. American Jews had enthusiastically embraced the growing market of packaged foods; kosher packaged food items, certified as ritually permissible, demonstrated the synchronicity of modernity and religious practice.[38] As kosher items appeared with increasing frequency on the shelves of mainstream grocery stores, one no longer needed to live in an ethnic enclave to participate in Jewish culinary culture. Jewishness could be bought prepackaged and rearranged to suit one's tastes.

KTAV boldly appropriated not only canned food but also quintessentially American dishes by associating them with specific holidays. Eating popular American food became a key element of holiday fun. A note accompanying a recipe for patties of ground meat prepared with store-bought breadcrumbs and canned tomatoes declared, "Meatburgers are everyone's favorite. Try these as a main dish for one of your Sukkos meals," seemingly arbitrarily connecting burgers to the practice of eating outside in a sukkah, a small, temporary booth for the fall harvest holiday.[39] While another note in the book described kugel as "everyone's favorite," implicitly referring exclusively to American Jews, here "everyone" refers to a general American public.[40] This declaration is prescriptive; as a true American, the Jewish reader should enjoy this quintessentially American dish. With this phrase, the *Junior Jewish Cook Book* normalizes seemingly exotic Jewish practices, making them fun for a juvenile audience with American sensibilities. In neatly planned suburbs, Jews' practice of eating in a sukkah would stick out as exceedingly strange. But with the inclusion of hamburgers, a family's celebration of the holiday might be mistaken for a barbecue, a recognizable suburban practice. Through the cookbook's manipulation of food culture, the holiday becomes a characteristically American party associated with the supposed ease of suburban living.

PLAYING GROWN-UP

Scharfstein's inclusion of the character Aunt Fanny as the author of his cookbook also spoke to mainstream culinary trends. As food companies taught children and adults new ways to cook and eat, many created fictional female characters to serve as the public face of the company and provide advice to women on modern home economics. The most successful of these characters, General Mills's Betty Crocker, was often mistaken for a real home economist, with her signed responses to women's letters and appearances on radio and television.[41] The character guided baby boomers as well as their mothers in *Betty Crocker's Cookbook for Boys and Girls*.[42] She and her brand-name compatriots taught postwar children not only how to cook, but how to shop and to which brands they should be loyal. Even more so, they coached young cooks in the complexities of gender dynamics in the kitchen.

The link between children's play and women's work in the *Junior Jewish Cook Book* was not incidental. Since at least the 1920s, girls' toys have centered on the home, epitomized by dollhouses and kitchen sets.[43] Postwar children's cookbooks took gendered play a step further, turning the kitchen into the playroom and foreshadowing the popular 1960s Suzy Homemaker toys, a line of real, working household appliances for girls. Such works encouraged girls to play make-believe within conservative, gender-specific roles, even as women were challenging traditional gender divisions at home and in the workplace.

While mainstream juvenile cookbooks made cursory and uneven overtures to boys as well as girls, the *Junior Jewish Cook Book* directed itself to both genders, featuring both a girl and a boy wearing toques on its cover. Nonetheless, it maintained contemporary gender norms in the fictional culinary authority of Aunt Fanny, whom Scharfstein named after his mother, and by acknowledging readers' mothers' jurisdiction over the kitchen. Still, the Jewish cookbook's underemphasis on readers' gender is exceptional among juvenile cookbooks. Lacking reference to the users' gender through language or illustration beyond the cover, the book primarily aims to acculturate children of both sexes to Jewish practices rather than to delineate gender roles.

"RECIPES FOR LIVING"

KTAV's method of acculturating children to Jewish norms and folkways rather than offering straightforward instruction on theology or religious observance can best be highlighted by comparison with a Christian analogue. The Evangelical Moody Bible Institute published Frances Youngren's *Let's Have Fun Cooking: The Children's Cook Book* in 1953, just three years before the publication of the *Junior Jewish Cook Book*. *Let's Have Fun Cooking* contains an assortment of clearly written recipes accompanied by Bible verses, stories, graces, and prayers.[44] The two cookbooks correspond visually, drawing from the same set of simple clip-art images of ingredients, culinary equipment, and figures of children and chefs. Their recipes, too, included a similar range of hot dinner entrées to simple snack foods, with an emphasis on snack foods prepared from packaged goods. Jews and Evangelicals, both outside the mainstream of American Protestantism and each with a stake in proving their truly American character, worked to tie religious identities to mainstream American culture in the form of modern children's cookbooks.

But unlike the Jewish book, which organizes its recipes by holiday and links children's Jewish identity with foodways, *Let's Have Fun Cooking* provides no connection between the food and its religious context beyond the use of weak metaphors. Its table of contents divides the material into "recipes" and "recipes for living," and an introductory letter explains that the book contains instruction about "two kinds of food . . . food for you to cook and Bread for you to feed on. For just as your bodies need good food to grow and develop, so does your soul need to be fed."[45] While the Jewish book includes notes to the reader linking the recipes to religious practices, the Christian cookbook juxtaposes theological material with food without explanation; one set of facing pages places biblical verses about creation opposite a recipe for Frankfurter quails.[46] With the exception of communion, Christian food, unlike Jewish food, derived its denominational significance from the religious setting in which it was prepared or eaten, not from components of the dishes themselves.[47]

While the Jewish children's cookbook included descriptions of holidays, *Let's Have Fun Cooking* interspersed short, explicitly theological stories among the recipes, concluding heartwarming stories by questioning young readers, such as "Have you been cleansed by the precious blood of the Lord Jesus Christ?"[48] In contrast, the Jewish cookbook rarely mentions God but uses cooking and eating as a Jewish practice through which children could construct their Jewish identities. In keeping with differences between Christian and Jewish practices, while Christian children were taught the fundamentals of their faith, Jewish children were taught how to participate in the Jewish community by preparing and sharing food in order to celebrate Jewish holidays in a distinctly American style.

PRAYING GENTEELLY

Both the Christian and Jewish children's cookbooks taught children how to mimic their elders in behavior as well as religious practices, evinced by their inclusion of etiquette rules. As Jews and Evangelicals made a conscious effort to be respectable Americans, adherence to social conventions was not insignificant. But while the Christian book includes an etiquette section as an afterthought on its final page, several pages of "Rules of Etiquette" precede the recipes in the Jewish book. KTAV instructed children to "always wash your hands before starting to eat," "eat quietly without making any undue noise," and "don't be afraid to try a new food" because "all food is good." This blanket categorization of *all* food as "good" has a highly ambiguous tone that might be interpreted as a subtle move away from kashrut, which defines food as ritually acceptable or unacceptable for consumption. In the effort to integrate American and Jewish sensibilities, not only what one ate but also how one ate was significant.

The final etiquette rule in the *Junior Jewish Cook Book* suggests that children say the following grace before meals:

> Thank you God,
> For bread and meat,
> We pray that others too,
> May have enough to eat.[49]

This rhyme makes it clear that KTAV did not have an Orthodox or ritually observant audience in mind. Though the book recommends the Jewish tradition of praying before and after eating, in contrast to the Christian grace said only before a meal, it offers a generic premeal prayer that might have easily appeared in the Christian *Let's Have Fun Cooking*. Moreover, the inclusion of this prayer among etiquette rules rather than alongside descriptions of holiday customs reveals a seam in the still-uneasy joining of American and Jewish practices. Reciting this brief prayer—the only mention of God in the cookbook—imitated Christian practices without explicitly contradicting traditional Jewish practices. Ultimately the *Junior Jewish Cook Book* left the final decisions about Jewish observance in the hands of the young readers' parents while endorsing American culinary sensibilities. Extremely equivocal, it attempted to appeal to Jewish families across the spectrum of religious observance and Jewish knowledge while avoiding a strong endorsement of practices that would set Jewish diners apart from their non-Jewish neighbors.

Burdened by communal concerns over the identity of young American Jews, the *Junior Jewish Cook Book* vacillates uneasily between leaving children space to synthesize their bifurcated identities on their own and providing prescriptive instructions on how to enact American and Jewish identities. At times, the book insists on an increasingly rare religious reality. The sweeping inclusiveness of statements such as "In every Jewish home, Friday is a busy day. Before sundown, the house is thoroughly cleaned and the Sabbath table set" gestures toward a normative Jewish home life that KTAV wanted to encourage rather than conveying the actual state of affairs in 1956.[50] By publishing the *Junior Jewish Cook Book* and other hands-on activity books, KTAV aimed to fill a perceived void in Jewish homes, where children might not otherwise naturally acquire a "Jewish tone." In this endeavor American culture was both threatening and desirable. Jewish communal leaders feared that Jewish children would be seduced by American entertainment, but they also wanted them to identify as fully American.

Participating in the mainstream "domestic revival" of the 1950s, the *Junior Jewish Cook Book* aimed to create a distinctly Jewish home life using forms and images created by non-Jewish culture. Following the cookbook's instructions, Jewish children not only read stories, dressed dolls, and pasted pictures in the service of their multiple identities but enacted and reinforced both their Jewish and American identities by playing in the kitchen, chopping vegetables, boiling noodles, mixing cake batter, and, finally, eating the fruits of their labors according to carefully constructed recipes. Unlike the Christian *Let's Have Fun Cooking*, the *Junior Jewish Cook Book* made no attempt to dictate belief and gestured only minimally toward ritual practices. It reached for something less defined and perhaps more difficult to achieve: the development of children's enthusiastic attachment to Judaism through domestic practices, in concert with their normative American identities and as enjoyable as their mainstream games. Jewish foodways should appear as American as canned pineapple and as fun as playing with dolls, though the book's didacticism belies the naturalness its publishers wished to convey. The cookbook vehemently insisted that American Jewish children could happily incorporate both cultures into their lives and play, at least in the kitchen, where they could create burgers and kugel and serve hamantaschen and marshmallow pops side by side.

DISCUSSION QUESTIONS

1. What kind of American Jewish identity did the *Junior Jewish Cook Book* teach to children?
2. How did creative food preparation demonstrate home cooks' modern sensibilities?
3. In what ways did the *Junior Jewish Cook Book* use mainstream food culture for Jewish communal purposes? How did it subvert them?

4. How was the *Junior Jewish Cook Book* different from or similar to the Christian *Let's Have Fun Cooking*? What does the comparison suggest about American Jewish culture in the 1950s?

5. What kind of cookbook, recipes, and ingredients are indicative of American society today?

NOTES

1. Isa Kapp, "Books for Jewish Children: The Limits of the Didactic Approach," *Commentary* 8 (December 1949): 547.

2. Quoted in Jenna Weissman Joselit, *New York's Jewish Jews: The Orthodox Community in the Interwar Years* (Bloomington: Indiana University Press, 1990), 35.

3. Sol Scharfstein, *Junior Jewish Cook Book by Aunt Fanny* (New York: KTAV, 1956); and Bernard Scharfstein, president of KTAV, telephone conversation with author, November 11, 2010.

4. Riv-Ellen Prell, "Community and the Discourse of Elegy: The Postwar Suburban Debate," in *Imagining the American Jewish Community*, ed. Jack Wertheimer (Waltham, Mass.: Brandeis University Press, 2007), 71.

5. Kapp, "Books for Jewish Children," 548.

6. Howard P. Chudacoff, *Children at Play: An American History* (New York: New York University Press, 2007), 164; and Charles A. Madison, *Jewish Publishing in America: The Impact of Jewish Writing on American Culture* (New York: Sanhedrin, 1976), 88–89.

7. Hasia R. Diner, *Hungering for America: Italian, Irish, and Jewish Foodways in the Age of Migration* (Cambridge: Harvard University Press, 2001), 178.

8. Elaine Tyler May, *Homeward Bound: American Families in the Cold War Era* (New York: Basic Books, 1988), 11, 164.

9. Will Herberg, *Protestant-Catholic-Jew: An Essay in American Religious Sociology* (Garden City, N.Y.: Doubleday, 1956), 43–44; emphasis in original.

10. Prell, "Community and the Discourse of Elegy," 68–69.

11. Quoted in Theodore Frankel, "Suburban Jewish Sunday School: A Report," *Commentary* 25 (June 1958): 490; emphasis in original.

12. For the changes in formal Jewish education, see Joselit, *New York's Jewish Jews*.

13. Introduction, "Books for Jewish Children: The Limits of the Didactic Approach," by Isa Kapp, *Commentary* 8 (December 1949): 547.

14. Johanna Ginsberg, "Publisher, 86, Still Thrills at Chance to Inspire," *New Jersey Jewish News*, August 7, 2008, http://www.njjewishnews.com/njjn .com/080708/mwPublisher86StillThrills.html. *Chaveri* is still in print and has sold over one million copies.

15. Andy Newman, "Where the Elves Wear Yarmulkes," *New York Times*, December 20, 1992, http://www.nytimes.com/1992/12/20/nyregion/where-the -elves-wear-yarmulkes.html.

16. Edythe Scharfstein and Sol Scharfstein, *Paste and Play Bible.* (New York: KTAV, 1957).

17. B. Scharfstein, telephone conversation.

18. Jessamyn Neuhaus, *Manly Meals and Mom's Home Cooking: Cookbooks and Gender in Modern America* (Baltimore: Johns Hopkins University Press, 2003), 174–76.

19. May, *Homeward Bound*, 26.

20. Laura Shapiro, *Something from the Oven: Reinventing Dinner in 1950s America* (New York: Viking, 2004), 8–9.

21. Ibid., 64, italics in original.

22. Ibid., 268, 253–56.

23. Neuhaus, *Manly Meals and Mom's Home Cooking*, 173.

24. Ibid., 19–22.

25. Florence S. Berger, *Cooking for Christ: The Liturgical Year in the Kitchen* (Des Moines: National Catholic Rural Life Conference, 1949), 7.

26. Ruth Glazer, "Where's the Pyetroushka?" review of *The Complete American-Jewish Cookbook*, by Anne London and Bertha Kahn Bishov, *Commentary* 15 (January 1953): 106.

27. Gary Cross, *Kids' Stuff: Toys and the Changing World of American Childhood* (Cambridge: Harvard University Press, 1997), 147.

28. Neuhaus, *Manly Meals and Mom's Home Cooking*, 173–74.

29. Alice Carroll, "Who's Who Cooks," *Good Housekeeping* (June 1950), 10–11.

30. A.I.M.S. Street, "The Gastronomical Year," *Saturday Review* 37, no. 7 (February 13, 1954): 35.

31. Glazer, "Where's the Pyetroushka?" 106.

32. Jonathan Krasner, "A Recipe for American Jewish Integration: *The Adventures of K'tonton* and *Hillel's Happy Holidays*," *The Lion and the Unicorn* 27 (2003): 351–52; and "Scharfstein Family Saga," http://www.KTAV.com/aboutus.php.

33. B. Scharfstein, telephone conversation; Joellyn Wallen Zollman, "The Gifts of the Jews: Ideology and Material Culture in the American Synagogue Gift Shop," *American Jewish Archives Journal* 58, no. 1/2 (2006): 57–77.

34. Scharfstein, *Junior Jewish Cook Book*, 18.

35. Ibid., 15.

36. Kapp, "Books for Jewish Children," 548.

37. Scharfstein, *Junior Jewish Cook Book*, 47, 38, 18.

38. Joselit, *The Wonders of America*, 187

39. Scharfstein, *Junior Jewish Cook Book*, 33. *Sukkos* is the Yiddish or Ashkenazic Hebrew pronunciation of Sukkot. Out of KTAV's desire to appeal to the entire spectrum of the Jewish community or as a result of careless editing, the *Junior Jewish Cook Book* followed an inconsistent pattern of Hebrew pronunciation. The cookbook alternated between the Sephardi pronunciation adopted in the Reform and Conservative movements and the Ashkenazi pronunciation used by eastern European Jews and retained by the Orthodox. While Sephardi pronunciation generally appears in the chapter titles (e.g., Sukkot), notes on the recipe pages frequently employ the Ashkenazi pronunciation (e.g., Sukkos).

40. Ibid., 21.

41. See Susan Marks, *Finding Betty Crocker: The Secret Life of America's First Lady of Food* (New York: Simon and Schuster, 2005).

42. Shapiro, *Something from the Oven*, 171–96.

43. Ellen Seiter, *Sold Separately: Children and Parents in Consumer Culture* (New Brunswick, N.J.: Rutgers University Press, 1993), 74.

44. Street, "The Gastronomical Year," 35.

45. Elizabeth Tilden Hildebrandt, introduction to *Let's Have Fun Cooking: The Children's Cook Book*, ed. Frances Youngren (Chicago: Moody Press, 1953), 3.

46. Frances Youngren, ed., *Let's Have Fun Cooking: The Children's Cook Book* (Chicago: Moody Press, 1953), 28–29.

47. Daniel Sack, *Whitebread Protestants: Food and Religion in American Culture* (New York: St. Martin's, 2000).

48. Youngren, *Let's Have Fun Cooking*, 61.

49. Scharfstein, *Junior Jewish Cook Book*, 11.

50. Ibid., 15.

RECOMMENDED READING

Diner, Hasia R. *Hungering for America: Italian, Irish, and Jewish Foodways in the Age of Migration*. Cambridge: Harvard University Press, 2001.

Joselit, Jenna Weissman. *The Wonders of America: Reinventing Jewish Culture, 1880–1950*. New York: Hill and Wang, 1994.

May, Elaine Tyler. *Homeward Bound: American Families in the Cold War Era*. New York: Basic Books, 1988.

Neuhaus, Jessamyn. *Manly Meals and Mom's Home Cooking: Cookbooks and Gender in Modern America*. Baltimore: Johns Hopkins University Press, 2003.

Shapiro, Laura. *Something from the Oven: Reinventing Dinner in 1950s America*. New York: Viking, 2004.

Six

SALMON AS SACRAMENT

FIRST SALMON CEREMONIES
IN THE PACIFIC NORTHWEST

SUZANNE CRAWFORD O'BRIEN

AUGUST 1, 2011

It is a warm August day, under a clear blue sky. Four hundred people have gathered at the Arcadia Boat Launch near the Squaxin Island Indian Reservation. The tide is out, and children scatter across the beach, searching for shells and critters exposed by the tide. A path leading from the water to a table above the tidemark has been marked out with cedar branches and sword ferns. A canoe approaches the beach, crewed by five young women, five young men, and an older captain. A drum calls the people on the beach to attention, and children are gathered together. An elder from the Indian Shaker Church steps forward to pray, her white dress bright in the sunshine. She is flanked by other church members, who ring bells to accompany her singing and prayers of blessing. The speaker steps forward then, welcoming the crowd and explaining the purpose of this ceremonial gathering. He thanks those who have helped to make the day possible. Pendleton blankets are given to the young man who caught the ceremonial salmon, to the man who filleted the fish for the day's feast, and to another man responsible for maintaining the community's oral traditions. A young woman in the canoe stands to sing a song, announcing the arrival of their honored guest. The drum group on the beach sings welcoming songs in return, as several women perform a traditional welcome dance beside them. Four men walk down the path to the water, each holding a pole supporting a carved cedar platter, covered in cedar branches. Amid song and drumming, they bring the salmon from the canoe.

The fish is filleted, and the head, tail, and backbone are returned to the young woman in the canoe, who receives the remains. As the canoe paddles far out into Puget Sound, songs and drumming continue. The gathered crowd on the beach stands silent. Even children seem to know that this is a solemn moment, aware that the remains of Chief Salmon are being returned to his village under the sea where he will gain new life, ensuring that salmon will return in years to come. We stand on the beach, watching the canoe as it moves toward Squaxin Island, Mt. Rainier looming snow-capped above.

The sight reminds me of John Slocum's resurrection: the founder of the Indian Shaker Church is said to have been in his burial canoe when he awoke and called the Squaxin people to begin a new religion. It is evocative as well of the Coast Salish spirit canoe ceremony—in which medicine men undertook a spiritual canoe journey to the land of the dead to recover lost souls. In Coast Salish

FIGURE 6.1   Neighbors and members of the Squaxin Island Tribal Nation gather on Puget Sound to commemorate the First Salmon ceremony, August 2011. Photo by Suzanne J. Crawford O'Brien, used with permission.

cultures canoes and water are one place where spirit worlds meet, places of pas-
sage and movement between this world and the world of the salmon people, the
world of the dead, the world of the spirits.

The canoe turns back, its task completed. The remains have been returned
to the sea. At this, the drumming concludes, and the speaker steps forward. He
encourages the gathered crowd to remain until the ceremonial First Salmon has
been cooked, so that everyone can receive a bite of this special fish. It will bring
you good luck for the coming year, he says. With that, he invites the elders to
lead the line toward the buffet. The Squaxin are impressively displaying the
honored Salish value of generosity today, providing everyone with a complimen-
tary feast of salmon, clams, clam chowder, and fry bread.

SALMON AS SACRAMENT

It is not possible to make a simple statement defining how food and faith
intersect with "the" Native American culture, for there is no single Native
American culture.[1] Instead, one finds over eight hundred distinct Native
nations in North America alone, each with their own culture and history,
sharing in hundreds of different languages and dialects, and dwelling
within ecosystems ranging from arctic tundra to high desert. But within
this vastly varying cultural and ecological landscape, common themes
do emerge. One of these is the importance of first foods ceremonies: the
honoring and celebrating of seasonal foods. Such ceremonies are practiced throughout Native North America and are not merely gestures of
gratitude but the honoring and reaffirming of ancient relationships between human communities and the plant and animal people on whom
they depend. While all such resources are important and honored, some
carry particularly important spiritual and symbolic significance. For the
Coast Salish of western Washington and southwest British Columbia, one
of these resources is salmon.[2]

In the 1850s Catholic missionary Father Eugene Casimir Chirouse undertook a translation of the Lord's Prayer into Coast Salish Lushootseed.
Nearly a century and a half later, Christopher Vecsey and Coast Salish
elder and culture bearer Taqʷšəblu (Vi Hilbert) provided an analysis of
his translation.[3] Taqʷšəblu explained that Chirouse's Lushootseed phrase
for the first sentence of the prayer literally translates as "establish the

nobility of Our Father because He gives us that which is our food each day." Chirouse's choice of language was good, she said, because it reflected Coast Salish ethics wherein the nobility of people is demonstrated through their ability and willingness to provide food for others. She paused, however, at the generic Salish term for "food" that Chirouse had chosen to use for bread. Taqʷšəblu was "surprised that Chirouse had chosen not to use a word for salmon, which might carry for the Lushootseed all the sacramental qualities of bread as food for the early Christians."[4] While the term "sacramental" is complex and can be interpreted in many different ways, in this instance it would appear that Taqʷšəblu is referring to the sacrament of the Eucharist. Like the bread of the Eucharist, salmon is both mundane and holy. It is the most daily of foods, and also the most sacred. Like the Eucharist, salmon represents fundamental spiritual relationships, manifest in food. Through a shared meal, one communes with those within one's human community, and through eating the sacrament, one communes with the sacred (the plant and animal people) as well. Through the collective ceremonial experience of eating, one affirms and literally embodies that relationship. One ought not push this parallel too far, however, for we are talking about fundamentally different worldviews and value systems. For Native people the spiritual world is not transcendent, separate from the material and natural world, but intrinsically within it.

American religious historian Albert Raboteau has defined a "sacramental vision of the world" as one in which "another world, a spiritual world, coinheres with this one." Within a sacramental perspective, "material objects of ritual not only symbolize spiritual realities, but make them present."[5] Such a definition raises the questions: When portions of an honored First Salmon are ritually distributed to a gathered assembly, what spiritual world is being made present? What spiritual realities are in that moment being embodied? In this essay I argue that salmon—particularly when brought into the "sacramental" ritual of a First Salmon ceremony—make real the spiritual relationship of kinship that exists between Coast Salish people and Salmon people. Salmon are not only resources but *relatives* to the indigenous people of this region, and as such they exist within a relationship of reciprocity and respect. The sacred is tangibly manifest within the First Salmon ceremony, an expression of kinship grounded in a common spirit.

SALMON AND THE COAST SALISH

The symbolic importance of salmon is best understood by considering its location within a broader cultural geography. Traditionally, Coast Salish communities identified themselves by the location of their winter villages along particular watersheds. Extended families dwelt together in (sometimes enormous) longhouses, separating into small groups from spring to fall to fish, hunt, and gather. Villages along the same watershed shared similar dialects, and a regular exchange of goods and resources. Watersheds were the main means of communication and travel (the precolonial highways), uniting communities through trade, common languages, and intermarriage. Because of this close affinity between people and place, the names of many Coast Salish nations can be translated as "the people of X watershed."[6] The term "natal waters" can thus be applied to both salmon and Coast Salish people: these waters are the place of their birth, to which they return every year. The Stó:lo, a Coast Salish people in British Columbia, make a similar point, arguing that they are the "People of the River"—not the People by the River or the People near the River, but the People of the River.[7]

This identification with particular waterways is expressed by fishing rights advocates who argue that fishing is "a remaining avenue of close relationship with the natural world."[8] Fishing remains "the center, in a sense the soul . . . of the feeling of relationship to the environment." Nisqually fishing rights activist Billy Frank Jr. put it this way:

> That river was my life. You understood it right from when you were a little boy. The winter floods, the spring floods, the low summer water. We lived right on the bank, right near the edge of tidewater. At Frank's Landing you know exactly when the tide comes and when it goes out. And there was a relationship between your life as a little boy and the salmon. You knew that every year the salmon came back. Spring salmon, summer salmon, fall salmon, then the winter run of chum salmon up to Muck Creek. Then the cycle would start over again. [9]

Salmon runs were traditionally a primary food source of the region, providing sustenance that maintained communities throughout the year, and were honored with the First Salmon ceremony. Many early explorers, including Lewis and Clark, observed these ceremonies, noting that Native people insisted on careful ritual treatment of these first fish, restricting non-Native people's access to them, lest the sacred first salmon be mistreated and so fail to return in future years.[10] While First Salmon ceremonies varied by family and village, several features have remained consistent throughout the region: A fisherman is chosen to harvest the first salmon, a great honor that requires prayer and ritual purification. Once caught, the salmon is ceremonially brought to shore, carefully prepared and cooked, and ritually distributed to the people. Ideally everyone present will have at least a single bite of this Chief or Mother Salmon. Finally, every bone is carefully collected and returned to the river, so that the fish will be restored to life and able to return in future years.[11] These traditions are based on the belief that there are "five races of salmon people, of human form, living to the west in 'homes beyond the ocean.'" During spawning season the salmon people put on their salmon cloaks, leave their villages, and travel to their natal waters. Each species is led by a chief who is the stu'yičad, or "boss of the salmon." As Elmendorf noted regarding the historic ceremony, "Each ordinary salmon killed during the year was a salmon person whose soul returned to the salmon country and came back as a fish with the following year's run."[12] If the fish are treated respectfully and ethically, and their bones returned to the river so that they can find their way back home, the salmon will return every year, giving their lives so that human beings might live.

The reverence that Coast Salish people have for salmon is also shaped by their experience with a colonial history that has taken a heavy toll on salmon and on Native people's right to fish. As early as the 1840s, missionaries in the Northwest hoped to shift Native peoples' subsistence patterns away from the semimigratory nature of seasonal fishing, hunting, and gathering and toward a more settled agricultural lifestyle. The introduction of the reservation system further challenged Native peoples' access to traditional fishing and gathering locations. When Native peoples ceded sixty-four million acres in return for six million acres of reservation land, they insisted on treaty language that reserved their right to fish "in usual and accustomed places."[13] Despite this, access to traditional fishing locations was quickly compromised by the rapid settlement of the region during the late nineteenth century. Within a single generation, many traditional fishing sites were lost.[14] Native salmon runs throughout the region would face precipitous declines during the twentieth century because of dams, overfishing, habitat destruction, and polluted waterways. In 1804 an estimated thirty million salmon annually migrated up the Columbia and Snake Rivers.[15] By the 1970s the annual migration was estimated between three and four million, and overall salmon runs were reduced to perhaps one-sixth of their original numbers.[16] Of those that remain, 80 percent are hatchery fish, not wild salmon.

Where Native people still had access to traditional fishing sites, they continued to fish, though doing so became increasingly difficult and dangerous. State regulations on fishing became increasingly onerous as salmon runs declined and officials disproportionately targeted Native fishermen. Beginning as early as the 1950s, Native people protested, holding "fish ins" that gained national notoriety and support. The protests would serve as inspiration for other American Indians working toward political and cultural revitalization in the 1960s and 1970s.[17] Two court decisions in Oregon (*SoHappy v. Smith*, 1969) and Washington (*United States v. Washington*, 1974) restored the treaty right to fish, and tribal communities responded by forming intertribal fish commissions to establish hatcheries, undertake habitat restoration, and regulate tribal fishing industries. An essential part of these efforts has been the revival of First Salmon ceremonies.

In her 1987 study of this revival, anthropologist Pamela Amoss described the ceremony as primarily political and economic, an attempt "to justify the new economic order" by portraying Native people's ancient association with and responsibility to care for salmon. The inclusion of non-Natives in the ceremony, she argued, marked a shift in political sensibilities, away from the confrontational nature of the 1950s, 1960s, and 1970s and toward "complementary relations."[18] Amoss's emphasis on economics and politics, while insightful, obscures the vital religious and spiritual implications of the ceremony. In particular, her argument misses the sacramental way the ceremony makes present the spiritual reality of Coast Salish people's kinship relationship with salmon.

SALMON AND KINSHIP

But what is meant by "kinship"? The Coast Salish notion of *shxwelí* can help to shed light on this notion of salmon as ancestors and kin. When viewed from a perspective of *shxwelí*, places, animals, and plants not only are food resources but are considered "like an ancestor." As Naxaxalhts'i (Albert McHalsie) explains, in the Sto:lo tradition "there's a connection there, and that connection is known as shxwelí. Shxwelí is what's referred to as the spirit or the life force, and everything has that spirit and everything's connected through that."[19] Placing her hand on her chest, Sto:lo elder Rosaleen George explains it this way: "'Shxwelí is inside us here.' And she put her hand in front of her and she said, 'shxwelí is in your parents.' She raised her hand higher and said, 'then your grandparents, your great-grandparents, it's in your great-great-grandparents. It's in the rocks, it's in the trees, it's in the grass, it's in the ground. Shxwelí is every-where. . . . What ties us? . . . It's the shxwelí.'"[20] Oral traditions describe a landscape filled with plants, animals, and rock formations that had once been human ancestors but were changed to their present form by the mythic hero known in English as the "Transformer." Though changed, they retain their shxweli. "So, our resources are more than just resources, they are our extended family. They are our ancestors, our shxweli. . . . Our Elders tell us everything has a spirit. So when we use a resource we have to thank our ancestors who were transformed into these things."[21] When honoring salmon, then, one recognizes it as more than a natural resource. One acknowledges it as an ancestor.[22] In her study of the Coast Salish, Crisca Bierwert also observed this view of the landscape, explaining that natural resources and places "have agency, intelligence and will. . . . The river rocks, the mountains, the salmon runs, the flow of the river itself" all serve as sentient beings to be reckoned with.[23]

Salmon hold a central place in this sentient landscape, both because of their primary importance as a food resource and because many oral traditions describe communities as directly descended from salmon. The Tuwaduq on the Skokomish Indian Reservation on Hood Canal, for instance, are the descendants of a young woman who married Chum Salmon when her community was destroyed by fire. Her salmon children were returned to human form when Sequalal (Grandmother Cedar) gifted them with a song, transforming them into the ancestors of the present-day community.[24] The Katzie on Pitt River in British Columbia share a similar story, wherein their first ancestor married a sockeye salmon. As a result, spawning sockeye salmon return to Pitt River each year and are welcomed as "relatives, returning to give themselves to their kin."[25] Among the Snohomish, humpback salmon are referred as "old grandmother," or ki'kaya.[26] First Salmon ceremonies are thus moments when the "spiritual world coinheres with this one" because they are spaces where the kinship relationship between Coast Salish people and salmon people is renewed.

KINSHIP REQUIRES RECIPROCITY

Describing salmon as "ancestor" is no small matter if one considers the importance of kinship relations within Coast Salish communities. Here one does not necessarily distinguish between close and distant relations. In Lushootseed Coast Salish, the same words can be used for siblings as for cousins, for grandparents as for great-aunts or great-uncles, for grandchildren as for grandnieces and grandnephews, even to several degrees removed. The relative proximity of relationships is less important than the maintenance of that relationship through reciprocal exchange. Members of one's kinship network can be counted on to provide emotional and material support through a lifelong exchange of mutual care and reciprocal obligations. Having a kinship relationship with someone in foreign territories was particularly valuable because a traveler could then be assured of safe passage. In this case, a kinship relationship between people and salmon means that salmon should be guaranteed safe passage into the human world. In return for honoring their kinship obligations to human communities (offering their bodies as food), their human relatives respond by caring for salmon habitats, regulating their take, and treating the remains with the necessary care and respect to ensure their rebirth and return. The Lummi story "Bear and the Steelhead" helps make this clear: "Now, each year, with the arrival of the First Salmon Children, the people remember that the death of the Salmon Children is a spiritual matter, and if we want them to come back every year then we have to be respectful . . . they are, after all, spiritual sacrifices for the benefit of the human children."[27]

Ideal Salish kinship relations are defined by generosity and the free exchange of resources. And indeed, it may be difficult to find a greater symbol of generosity than a flourishing salmon run, as millions of fish offer themselves as food for their human kin. This is an abundant region, but resources tend to come in sudden bursts: enormous quantities of berries, roots, salmon, or game may be available at one time in one place and not in another.[28] Because of this, families and villages depended on a free exchange of food within their extended kinship network in order to survive. Importantly, food was not categorized as a gift of wealth (which would place the receiver in the giver's debt) but was considered a gift from the Creator or other spiritual beings. It was xEʔxE sʔíłən, "holy food," according to a Semiahmoo elder, and as such was to be shared freely. Within the network of kinship, one should never hesitate to offer food or to receive it.[29]

Notably, salmon are both givers of holy food *and* the food itself. The annual return of salmon is the fulfillment of an ancient agreement between the salmon people and the human people: the salmon have generously agreed to offer their lives so the people might live. In return, the people agree to treat the salmon with care, respect, and gratitude.[30]

Today that reciprocity also means restoring the rivers. The Lower Elwha Klallam First Salmon ceremony, for instance, is held at the three locations along the Elwha River where the tribe release salmon fry raised in the tribal hatchery. As fishery manager Rachel Hagaman explains, salmon

remains are placed in front of the minister and all participants, and an opening prayer is said to thank the Creator for helping the salmon return to the river to complete their lifecycle. There is also a prayer put forward on behalf of the people and the river for help when removal of the Elwha River dams begins, that the salmon will return once again. After the blessing ceremony is completed, the first set of salmon remains is released into the river. After this has occurred, then the other remains are brought to the other two locations and prayers of thanks are again completed. The salmon meat is distributed to the elders of the community.[31]

KINSHIP REQUIRES RESPECT

Subsistence practices for Coast Salish peoples have never been simply about finding something to eat: they are part of a complex religio-ethical system built on respectful reciprocity with a sentient world. Nineteenth-century ethnologists working in this area agreed that food was never something acquired by personal skill, but rather "something which has been voluntarily and compassionately placed in his hands by the goodwill and consent of the spirit of the object itself." Such a view demands that one show reverence, care, and respect when harvesting food and disposing of waste, taking care so that the plant or animal in question will be able to renew its life, providing food for future generations.[32]

And indeed the first salmon is treated as an honored guest, and its arrival is heralded like that of a visiting dignitary who should be welcomed with ceremony.[33] As Squaxin tribal member Joe Peters has said,

> It's important to us culturally . . . our ancestors were out here fishing, harvesting salmon. And we're out here to honor the first salmon that came to us, and show it respect, and treat it well, and hope that the spirit of the first salmon goes back and returns to its people, and tells them that we treated it well. And in return, hopefully bringing a good run of salmon back to us to feed our people. That's what's important about today. Honoring the fish and the people. We are the people of the water, so we are respecting what's coming from the water.[34]

As Peters makes clear, the purpose of the ceremony is "bringing the spirit back to the water, to send a message back to the salmon people, that it was treated respectfully, and it's ok to come back home."[35]

Ceremonies are where these values of respect, reciprocity, and generosity are transmitted from one generation to another. This is particularly clear in the case of the Lummi Nation First Salmon ceremony that is held in the Lummi Nation school gymnasium. Carefully integrated into the school's curriculum, the ceremony includes an important role for young people, who spend weeks preparing artwork for the event, including placemats, table decorations, and pictures to cover the walls of the gymnasium. Elders lead the salmon into the gymnasium, with students from the Lummi Nation school carrying the salmon itself. Students proceed in after the salmon, with the youngest preschool students bringing up the rear. They carry the salmon around all the tables and then back to the front of room, where it is distributed into small cups, enough for everyone to have a single bite.[36]

A central part of the Lummi ceremony is sharing the Legend of Mother Salmon with the gathered guests.

> They say that Salmon Woman was hurt by the [poor] treatment she and her children were receiving. . . . She decided to take her children and leave. She stood by the water's edge and sang a new song. She sang this song and as

she did all the Salmon Children came back to life. The dried, the smoked, the boiled, all of it came back and rolled to the water. As each neared the water they turned back into whole salmon and leaped into the water, swimming toward the bay, and waiting for their mother-Salmon Woman. When she finished her song, and all the children had transformed, then she walked into the water and transformed back into a salmon, just like her children. She swam away, singing a song, while all her children followed her. They went in the direction that they originally came. . . . Soon they were out of sight, gone forever. She vowed to never bring her children to a place that they are not wanted or appreciated. She would not tolerate the disrespect of herself or her children's great sacrifice.[37]

When the story is concluded, Lummi Nation students offer a song and dance to honor Mother Salmon, and assembled guests are asked to carefully save every bone, returning them to the servers so they can be carried back to the sea.

The story of Salmon Mother is one of many oral traditions from throughout the region that present beings like salmon as both natural resources and persons that must be treated with care and respect. Melville Jacobs recorded a Coos narrative, for instance, wherein young boys brought about a lethal tidal wave as a result of playing disrespectfully with salmon. As the storyteller concluded: "That is why it is not a good thing when children do all sorts of tricky things. You are not to do such things. You should not belittle food, because the people die (from that)."[38]

KINSHIP MEANS INTERDEPENDENCE

The kinship relationship between people and salmon is reflected in other oral traditions wherein the health and well-being of human and salmon communities are inextricably linked.[39] Consider for instance a saga told among the Coast Salish of British Columbia in 1897 by a Squamish elder, which describes four periods in the people's history, each marked by destruction and rebirth. The story begins with an account of the creation of Kalama ("first man") by the Transformer. The Transformer gave Kalama the essential elements of life: a wife, a chisel, and a salmon trap. The pair had many children, and the people prospered in their lush environment, until a great flood killed everyone except Kalama's first son and his wife.

The first sign of returning life after the flood were salmon. Coming up the river, the salmon gave their lives, and the couple regained their strength, going on to have many children. The community recovered, and "many salmon came upon the Squamish every season, and there was food for everybody and to spare." However, one winter a snowstorm struck the community, with tiny flakes that "penetrated everywhere, freezing everything. . . . Soon the children and old people began to die in scores and hundreds. But still the snow came down and the misery of those that were left increased. Dead bodies lay around everywhere, dead and dying lying together." The starving people waited for the salmon to return, "but when this long-looked-for relief came it was found that the salmon were so thin that there was nothing on them but the skin and bones." Again, only two people survived this time of starvation. And again the community revived. But the people were to face extinction once again: "One salmon season the fish were found to be covered with running sores and blotches, which rendered them unfit for food. They put off eating them till no other food was available, and then began a terrible time of sickness and distress. A dreadful skin disease, loathsome to look upon, broke out upon all-alike. None were spared. Men, women and children sickened, took the disease and died in agony by hundreds, so that when spring arrived, and fresh food was procurable, there was scarcely a person left of all their numbers to get it." But "little by little the remnant left by the disease grew into a nation once more, and when the first white men sailed up the Squamish in their big boats, the tribe was strong and numerous again."[40] The story provides a powerful illustration of the interdependence of Coast Salish people and salmon: when the people starve, salmon starve; when salmon have smallpox-like symptoms, the people share them as well. The survival of each depends on the other.

In a similar fashion, Coast Salish and salmon both need intact ecosystems: salmon have not only been "the mainstay of their diet, but the foundation of their culture as well."[41] Salmon are not merely food but kin, ancestors, symbolic of the people themselves and the relationships they have built and maintain with their ancestral homeland. And as such, their fates are intertwined. Human communities are responsible for providing safe and healthy habitat, and for treating salmon with respect and gratitude. And in return, salmon provide both sustenance and a spiritual foundation for their cultures and communities. Lummi natural resources director Merle Jefferson recalled that, "When I was a young boy, I heard my grandfather say, when he was eating a salmon, 'This is good medicine.' "[42]

The late spiritual leader of the Skokomish Nation, subiyay (Gerald Bruce Miller), argued passionately that "protecting the environment is essential" because Native cultures focus "not on events but on relationships with entities like the earth, water, air, animals, and plant people. Maintaining this symbolic connection is important to the survival of our traditional culture, because a spiritual relationship with other life forms pervades all aspects of our life."[43] Protecting and restoring salmon habitat has become sacred work for many Coast Salish people, work that is inseparably linked to the maintenance of their kinship relationship with salmon and the revival of Native cultures, communities, and traditions.

CONCLUSION:
SALMON AND CULTURAL RENEWAL

As the narratives above reflect, many Native communities would argue that they are *relatives* of these resources, and that their fates are intricately interwoven. Salmon fishing is central to Coast Salish economies and spiritual traditions, powerfully and tangibly making present the spiritual reality of the interdependence of salmon and human populations and cultures.[44] Each year salmon give their lives to the people, and each year they return to the sea, are reborn, and return with new life. As both a central food source and symbol of culture and community, salmon convey an identity that emphasizes rebirth and renewal.

Salmon resonate so deeply with Coast Salish spiritual traditions because they reflect a central narrative within Coast Salish healing and spiritual traditions, where prophets and healers journeyed to the spirit world, returning with wisdom and spiritual power for their people. Likewise, salmon leave their home villages and undertake a dangerous journey to another world where they encounter powerful beings, suffer, and struggle before returning to their salmon-villages where they will be reborn. The story of salmon reflects healing traditions in the region as well, where medicine men and women must at times undertake dangerous journeys to the land of the dead to retrieve lost souls and return them to their ailing patients, lest they die.[45] In a similar fashion, salmon journey away from their village homes to another world. The journey is treacherous and their return is not guaranteed, but if proper behavior and ritual restrictions are observed, the salmon will be able to return, gaining new life. In many ways, First Salmon ceremonies affirm the belief that contemporary communities can likewise find their way home and be restored to a new strength. Like human communities, salmon populations can "fluctuate markedly over time" and can "experience failures from such cataclysms as landslides, flooding, drought, and the like," yet can also "recover in a few cycles. They are resilient populations."[46]

Within Native North America, a great deal of religious life focuses on subsistence activities and the cultivation of relationships with spiritual beings that dwell in the natural world. Food is at the heart of much of faith and practice, the link that seamlessly blends the metaphysical and the extremely practical, the individual and the community, the human and the more-than-human worlds. When Taqʷšəblu called attention to the sacramental nature of salmon, it was this meeting, this kinship, this mutual survival and *revival* to which she referred. Such themes are powerfully illustrated in the work of Interior Salish poet Sherman Alexie. I close this essay with his poem "The Powwow at the End of the World."

I am told by many of you that I must forgive and so I shall
after an Indian woman puts her shoulder to the Grand Coulee Dam
and topples it. I am told by many of you that I must forgive
and so I shall after the floodwaters burst each successive dam
downriver from the Grand Coulee. I am told by many of you
that I must forgive and so I shall after the floodwaters find
their way to the mouth of the Columbia River as it enters the Pacific
and causes all of it to rise. I am told by many of you that I must forgive
and so I shall after the first drop of floodwater is swallowed by that salmon
waiting in the Pacific. I am told by many of you that I must forgive and so
  I shall
after that salmon swims upstream, through the mouth of the Columbia
and then past the flooded cities, broken dams and abandoned reactors
of Hanford. I am told by many of you that I must forgive and so I shall
after that salmon swims through the mouth of the Spokane River

as it meets the Columbia, then upstream, until it arrives
in the shallows of a secret bay on the reservation where I wait alone.
I am told by many of you that I must forgive and so I shall after
that salmon leaps into the night air above the water, throws
a lightning bolt at the brush near my feet, and starts the fire
which will lead all of the lost Indians home. I am told
by many of you that I must forgive and so I shall
after we Indians have gathered around the fire with that salmon
who has three stories it must tell before sunrise: one story will teach us
how to pray; another story will make us laugh for hours;
the third story will give us reason to dance. I am told by many
of you that I must forgive and so I shall when I am dancing
with my tribe during the powwow at the end of the world.[47]

DISCUSSION QUESTIONS

1. How does thinking about food as sacrament help illuminate the importance of salmon for Coast Salish people? Does this idea help you think about the role of food in ritual more broadly?
2. How might first foods ceremonies help people develop a relationship with place? What do these ceremonies accomplish socially? Economically? Spiritually?
3. If you were to take the time, individually or collectively, to ritually honor and reflect on your connection with food, would it change the way you eat? Live? Interact with the natural world?

NOTES

1. I use the terms "Native American," "Native," and "American Indian" interchangeably. "First Nations" refers to Canadian aboriginal people.
2. The Coast Salish are the indigenous people that for millennia inhabited a territory ranging from the Oregon coast through the Puget Sound to southwestern British Columbia. While they comprise seventy distinct tribal nations and communities, the Coast Salish are linked geographically, linguistically, culturally, and through a complex network of kinship relations.

3. Christopher Vecsey in Janet Yoder, ed., *Writings About Vi Hilbert, by Her Friends* (Seattle: Lushootseed Research, 1992), 50.

4. Ibid., 51.

5. Albert Raboteau, *A Fire in the Bones: Reflections on African American Religious History* (Boston: Beacon Press, 1986), 189. A similar definition is provided by Tillich, who argues that "any object or event is sacramental in which the transcendent is perceived to be present." Paul Tillich, *The Protestant Era* (N.p.: Nabu Press, 2011), 108.

6. American Friends Service Committee, *Uncommon Controversy: Fishing Rights of the Muckleshoot, Puyallup and Nisqually Indians* (Seattle: University of Washington Press, 1970), 6.

7. Bruce Granville Miller, *Be of Good Mind: Essays on the Coast* Salish (Vancouver: University of British Columbia Press, 2007), 255.

8. American Friends Service Committee, *Uncommon Controversy*, 71.

9. Charles Wilkinson, *Messages from Frank's Landing: A Story of Salmon, Treaties, and the Indian Way* (Seattle: University of Washington Press, 2000), 29.

10. See Gary Moulton, ed., *The Definitive Journals of Lewis & Clark* (Lincoln: University of Nebraska Press): April 19, 1806, http://lewisandclarkjournals.unl.edu. See also Alexander Ross, *Adventures of the First Settlers on the Oregon or Columbia River* (London, 1849), 105; and Charles Wilson, ed., *Mapping the Frontier: Charles Wilson's Diary of the Survey of the 49th Parallel, 1858–1862* (Seattle: University of Washington Press, 1970), 29.

11. Charles Hill-Tout, with Ralph Maud, ed., *The Salish People: The Local Contribution of Charles Hill-Tout*. Volume 2: *The Squamish and the Lilloet* (Vancouver: Torchbooks 1978), 116.

12. William Elmendorf, *The Structure of Twana Culture* (Pullman: University of Washington Press, 1960), 531. See also William Elmendorf, *Twana Narratives: Native Historical Accounts of a Coast Salish Culture* (Seattle: University of Washington Press, 1993), 254–55.

13. American Friends Service Committee, *Uncommon Controversy*, 19.

14. Ibid., 17. See also Coll Thrush, *Native Seattle: Histories from the Crossing Over Place* (Seattle: University of Washington Press, 2007), 42, 89, 99.

15. Rhett Lawrence, "Columbia and Snake River Chinook and Sockeye Returns in 2011," *Save Our Wild Salmon*, http://www.wildsalmon.org/images/stories/sos/PDFs/Fact_Sheets/salmon.returns.2011.web2.pdf.

16. Bruce E. Johansen, "Fishing Rights," *Encyclopedia of Native American Economic History* (Westport, Conn.: Greenwood Press, 1999), 94.

17. Thrush, *Native Seattle*, 189.

18. Pamela T. Amoss, "The Fish God Gave Us: The First Salmon Ceremony Revived," *Arctic Anthropology* 24, no. 1 (1987): 56.

19. Albert McHalsie, "We Have to Take Care of Everything That Belongs to Us," in Miller, *Be of Good Mind*, 103.

20. Ibid., 104.

21. Keith Carlson, *You Are Asked to Witness: The Stó:lo in Canada's Pacific Coast History* (Chiliwack: Sto:lo Heritage Trust, 1997), 55.

22. McHalsie, "We Have to Take Care," 105.

23. Crisca Bierwert, *Brushed By Cedar, Living By the River: Coast Salish Figures of Power* (Tucson: University of Arizona Press, 1999), 69, 277.

24. Michael Pavel, Gerald Miller, and Mary Pavel, "Too Long, Too Silent: The Threat to Cedar and the Sacred Ways of the Skokomish," *American Indian Culture and Research Journal* 17, no. 3 (1993): 60.

25. Cole Harris, *The Resettlement of British Columba: Essays on Colonialism and Geographical Change* (Vancouver: University of British Columbia Press, 1997), 75.

26. Tweddell, "A Historical and Ethnological Study of the Snohomish Indian People," in *Coast Salish and Western Washington Indians*, vol. 2 (New York: Garland, 1974), 553. See also Wayne Suttles, *Coast Salish Essays* (Seattle: University of Washington Press, 1987), 104–5.

27. Jewell Praying Wolf James, "Bear and the Steelhead," Lummi Cultural Protection Committee, February 1992, http://lnnr.lummi-nsn.gov/LummiWebsite/userfiles/190_Story%20of%20Conservation%20of%20the%20Salmon(1).pdf.

28. Suttles, *Coast Salish Essays*, 46; see also Michael Kew, "Salmon Availability, Technology, and Cultural Adaptation in the Fraser River Watershed," in *A Complex Culture of the British Columbia Plateau: Traditional Stl'atl'imx Resource Use*, ed. Brian Hayden (Vancouver: University of British Columbia Press, 1992).

29. Suttles, *Coast Salish Essays*: 22.

30. Hill-Tout describes one such story of four brothers named Qais, who visit a village of salmon people. Salmon die, are eaten by brethren, ritually returned to water, and reborn. Qais request that salmon come to the human world to feed their people, and they agree, in return for ritual care, so they can return to life. Hill-Tout, *The Salish People*, 60–62.

31. http://www.elwha.org/riverrestoration/thefirstsalmonceremony.html.

32. Hill-Tout, *The Salish People*, 117.

33. Vi Hilbert and Crisca Bierwert, *Ways of the Lushootseed People: Ceremonies and Traditions of Northern Puget Sound Indians* (Seattle: United Indians of All Tribes Foundation 1980), 14.

34. Northwest Indian Fisheries Commission, http://nwifc.org/2010/08/video-squaxin-island-tribes-first-salmon-ceremony/.

35. Ibid.

36. Thanks to Ira Carterman for his thoughtful observations on the Lummi First Salmon ceremony.

37. Jewell Praying Wolf James, "Salmon Woman and Her Children," Lummi Culture Protection Committee, February 1992, http://lnnr.lummi-nsn.gov/LummiWebsite/userfiles/190_Story%20of%20Conservation%20of%20the%20Salmon(1).pdf.

38. Melville Jacobs, "Coos Narrative and Ethnologic Texts," *University of Washington Publications in Anthropology* 8, no. 1 (1939): 53.

39. Hill-Tout, *The Salish People*, 22; Robert Boyd, *The Coming of the Spirit of Pestilence* (Seattle: University of Washington Press, 1999), 55. See also Daniel Lee and Joseph Frost, *Ten Years in Oregon* (New York: J. Collard, 1844), 299–301.

40. Hill-Tout, *The Salish People*, 22.

41. Nisqually Nation. http://www.nisqually-nsn.gov/content/our-history.

42. Northwest Indian Fisheries Commission, http://nwifc.org/2009/05/lummi nation-celebrates-first-salmon/.

43. Pavel, "Too Long Too Silent," 64, 54–55, 78–79.

44. Kew, "Salmon Availability," 178.

45. June McCormick Collins, *Valley of the Spirits: The Upper Skagit Indians of Western Washington* (Seattle: University of Washington Press, 1974).

46. Kew, "Salmon Availability," 179.

47. Reprinted from *The Summer of Black Widows* © 1996 by Sherman Alexie, by permission of Hanging Loose Press.

RECOMMENDED READING

Bierwert, Crisca. *Brushed By Cedar, Living By the River: Coast Salish Figures of Power.* Tucson: University of Arizona Press, 1999.

Frey, Rodney. *Landscape Traveled by Coyote and Crane: The World of the Schitsu'umsh.* Seattle: University of Washington Press, 2003.

Harrod, Howard. *The Animals Came Dancing: Native American Sacred Ecology and Animal Kinship.* Tucson: University of Arizona Press, 2000.

Hilbert, Vi. *Haboo: Native American Stories From Puget Sound.* Seattle: University of Washington Press, 2003.

Nelson, Richard. *Make Prayers to the Raven: A Koyukon View of the Northern Forest.* Chicago: University of Chicago Press, 1986.

Salmón, Enrique. *Eating the Landscape: American Indian Stories of Food, Identity and Resilience.* Tucson: University of Arizona Press, 2012.

Seven

AN UNUSUAL FEAST

GUMBO AND THE COMPLEX BREW
OF BLACK RELIGION

DEREK S. HICKS

OBBY'S ANNUAL INQUIRY would begin before Christmas:
"When is Mama Dean gonna make her gumbo?" Robby Owens is
a childhood friend and a self-proclaimed lover of "real" gumbo.
My grandmother, "Mama Dean" as she was affectionately called by family
and neighborhood kids alike, had for years annually brewed a grand pot of
gumbo for New Year's Day. As a child the significance of this tradition was
lost on me. I could in no way understand why Robby was excited about
this odd cuisine. Back then gumbo was strange and disagreeable to my
palate. In fact, I did not have a taste for much of what is considered "soul
food"—the cuisine commonly associated with African Americans and the
southern United States. Refusing my native Louisianan grandmother's
New Year's Day gumbo and black-eyed peas, or even her sweet potato pie,
prompted many to question my blackness. I would later acquire a taste
for at least two of these traditional culinary treasures (I'm still working
on the sweet potato pie thing) and in time would perfect my own concoction of gumbo. But it was during those formative years that I would learn
by experience the magnitude of gumbo preparation and sharing as tied to
tradition, culture, and religious fellowship.

Robby, in proselytizing fashion, would strive each year to convert me to faith in this great soupy dish. His well-crafted sermon according to gumbo would be given on my grandmother's front porch even as he cracked open crab legs, sucking out the meat, and celebrated with every new piece of sausage he found in his bowl. Enduring culinary evangelism was nothing new for me. Reverberations of "you don't know what you're missing" or "how could you be raised by a southern black grandmother and not eat gumbo?" often rang in my head. Yet my recollections of Mama Dean's gumbo are powerful in that they are connected to something unexplainable, even otherworldly. From Robby's inquiry to his insistence on having the first bowl, from observing Mama Dean prepping the myriad of ingredients to the many hours it took her to "get the pot just right," gumbo took up a religious space in my home. The paradoxical smells and the communal nature of the experience reminded me of church, where fellowship, meal sharing, testimony, encouragement, song, and storytelling was custom. The gumbo party would start at my house but would ultimately be carried from house to house, where similar "congregational" exchanges would ensue, until the gumbo pot was empty. What gumbo came to represent was something more than the food itself.

Ask three people on the street familiar with gumbo what it is and you will undoubtedly get three different responses. Gumbo is a complex brew, and what it actually *is*—its correct level of thickness, its required ingredients, or even its color—remains fodder for much debate. While a fuller discussion of its composition will come later, let me state parenthetically now that gumbo is a dish of multiple meats, vegetables, and (in some instances) seafood, served in a large pot. As a dish it sits somewhere between soup and stew in consistency. As Eugene Walter simply puts it, gumbo means "everything together."[1] Gumbo is funky and urban, and simultaneously traditional and rural. It was created out of struggle, yet it is a comfort food with nostalgic and sentimental appeal. In one pot the culinary architect introduces distinct foods that coexist in peculiar ways, while simultaneously creating a wondrous single unit of gastronomic ecstasy. A spicy concoction, gumbo has for years offered unusually robust sustenance to weary souls. Authentication of one's gumbo preparation is not uncommon. In gumbo some search for something essential, even primordial to the "good old days."

Gumbo's historical origins are often debated. Does it predate the establishment of the United States, or is it a strictly African American culinary contribution to the world? If Mama Dean tells the story, gumbo was an invention of enslaved Africans and African Americans. As she told the story among those of us who gathered round the table for the feast, gumbo was born out of the foodstuffs and rationing tactics of slaveholders on southern plantations. She would explain that gumbo was created with the scraps of less desirable foods that enslaved blacks were given to eat. Those portions of meat that whites would find repugnant became staples in what would become the "gumbo pot." Making gumbo included sharing ingredients between enslaved families, making it a truly communal dish.

Clear to me as a youth was the extent to which gumbo held extrareligious significance to my community in the Watts section of Los Angeles, California. For those few days of annual gumbo sharing, I would be transported back to the Old South. Stories of places like Colfax, Louisiana, or Coffeeville, Alabama, would be told, each small town simply referred to as "home." These participants in America's Great Migration would share tall tales of the old town flirt, coalesced with grand narratives about a time when "folks really had church." Indeed, gumbo parties were in themselves religious gatherings. While slurping down a warm bowl of gumbo, African American religious life, with its messiness and contradictions, would be interwoven in the stories of struggle against long odds, of home, and of culture.

<hr />

This religio-gumbo fore story is affixed to historical antecedents of African American foodways. It demonstrates the convergence of eating and religion in the process of forging community and forming collective identity in African American life. Gumbo functions as a metaphor creating an idiom for understanding the complexity of black religious experience. En route to this conclusion, I draw attention to the historical significance of African American cooking, and the cultural implications of gumbo particularly. For example, slave cooking practices were considered peculiar by some slaveholders, who sought control of food distribution and preparation. For enslaved blacks, food was tied to fellowship, the strengthening of community, empowerment, and reaffirming the worth of bodies broken by domination.

This essay uncovers the social, cultural, and extrareligious significance of culinary space and its interconnectedness with a complex religious life. The uniqueness of this gastro-social experience, shared among disinherited people, gives rise to a distinct cuisine *and* religiosity, both aimed at mending a wounded community. Through this transformative collective experience, the gumbo theme emerges. The intricacies of gumbo preparation are linked to the untidiness of black religion in North American life. In the end, gumbo—with attention to its preparation, the roux (gumbo's thickened liquid base), its various coalescing flavors, its spiciness, the communal spirit it conjures, and the gumbo pot—is explored here as a symbol, illuminating the complexity of religion in black life while simultaneously pointing us to interplay of foodways and religion for African Americans. I am most concerned with the ways in which a shared language is available to describe African American foodways and black religious life. Offering gumbo as a unique cultural creation in the black community, this essay considers its complexity in religious terms.

ACCULTURATION IN AFRICAN AMERICAN FOODWAYS STUDIES

Foodways studies identifies social and cultural structures of eating and preparing foods within a given community. Food life is investigated for what it reveals about the nature and identity of a group. African American foodways have origins in the era of chattel slavery in the United States. Cultural food life, including gathering, sharing practices, preparation, and consumption, is a viable space to interpret African American experience in general. Some social scientists have come to see food as a source for understanding the ways in which African Americans interact with each other and with other groups. Foodways also highlights the interconnectedness of communities—even if separated by custom and tradition—that seek safer spaces to express fuller humanity. Accordingly, studying food life creates new opportunities for uncovering the ways North American blacks managed to retain certain traditions from West Africa while simultaneously adopting (and adapting to) various customs and systems of foodway culture in America.[2]

African American foodways inherently reckons with the cultural challenges of maintaining food heritage. Traditional African American cooking—that is, cooking of foods that connect the cook and those partaking of the meal to a previous time and space—values heritage. In some sense, African American foodways studies, like ethnic foodways in general, must contend with a dual cultural food formula. This formula breaks down as acculturation through cultural contact, on one hand, and the preservation of tradition to stave off enculturation, on the other. By definition, *acculturation* in this study means the meeting and assimilation of previously distinct cultures through which new cultural norms are created. Through a form of hybridity, traditions, customs, and specific ways of doing things are revised and yet include rudimentary elements of each distinct culture. For African Americans, acculturation marks the nature of cultural contact with the dominant class and with each other in colonial and antebellum America. Thus the challenge to establish a single "black" culture in the United States is immense and is always affected by social domination. Conversely, *enculturation* happens when a given group gradually (or suddenly) acquires another culture, leaving behind its own traditions and cultural distinctions.

Debate bubbles to the surface as African Americans wrestle with dueling cultural ideas and norms associated with food life. The intercultural reality of African American foodways is revealed in the ways African Americans themselves value, prepare, and eat foods. Class and income level, geographic region, social conditions, and access to certain foods all play a role in foodway acculturation. For this reason, black families will often engage in heated debates about the legitimacy of sacred culinary dishes like sweet potato pie, greens (collard or mustard), macaroni and cheese, or gumbo. Last year, for example, I was interrogated over the legitimacy of my gumbo because I left out okra, a central ingredient for some as they make the roux of the dish. Notwithstanding the reality that many "legitimate" pots of gumbo do not include okra, only on tasting it did my friend approve of *my* interpretation of the dish.

Where there exists any cultural consensus among blacks regarding experiences with food, the challenge of acculturation remains evident. One uncovers the issue when cultural contact is made with other ethnic groups' foodways. In these exchanges, stereotypes are often used as weapons to mark another group's food culture as strange or backward. The resulting equation becomes *strange food* equals *strange people*. It follows that certain ethnic groups are "othered" or considered outside of the mainstream through their foodway culture.[3] In the United States there is a long history of framing another's food culture as too exotic or repulsive. In response, some groups attempt to present their food as acceptable by connecting the cuisine to romanticized notions of the past. Formerly undesirable dishes are repackaged as "down home" to convey a sense of traditional comfort to the consumer. African American soul food is a primary example of this foodway formula. Derogatory remarks about fried chicken or comments from whites about unhealthiness of the many foods blacks enjoy disclose only part of the complex story of intercultural foodway struggles. Class also becomes a significant issue in foodway identification as certain foods, such as chitterlings in southern culture or ratatouille in French culture, are associated with the poor or provincial classes.

The labor to sustain a unique food heritage while addressing the issue of food healthiness is also apparent in black food life. Many traditional cooks of soul food, for example, attempt to serve healthier alternatives to dishes that have become staples of African American cooking. In other instances, African American foodway culture has to cope with onlookers who link their foods to a lower class status. Even with cuisine appreciation from other ethnic groups, African Americans sooner or later face challenges to their foodways. What ensues is an identity struggle related to food.

Enslavement created within the African and African American community a cohesive cooking tradition capable of taking limited resources and "making do."[4] Contemporary struggles with cultural contact in black food life are connected to foodstuff rationing practices of planters and slaveholders, who gave slaves what they considered the less desirable cuts of meat. Blacks would receive the head, intestines, fatback, neck bones, and sometimes heart, kidney, liver, or ribs of the butchered animal. If poultry was distributed, slave portions would normally include innards and gizzards.[5] Culinary creativity was therefore required of the slave cook. The cook was tasked with taking the detestable and making it desirable, even creating notable dishes that would endure for many years. Referencing the preparation of less desirable meats allowed by the slave master, a former Georgia slave recalls food that "filled you up and kept you well." Among the options made available were "lots of 'possums, coons, rabbits, and squirrels. Us cooked 'em 'bout lak us does now."[6] Creative preparation of noncustomary meats created a culture that has carried on after the period of chattel slavery.

Enslaved African Americans constructed patterns of resistance, agency, and ingenuity within their foodway activities. For example, blacks exhibited agency in keeping their own gardens on plantations. Planters would often designate a small plot for slaves to grow vegetables. According to another former Georgia slave, cultivating gardens had a twofold benefit. "In the first place he could vary his diet. In the second place he was able to earn money by selling his produce to town."[7] Proactive agency such as keeping a garden, in connection with creativity in preparing less desirable meats, increased enslaved blacks' ability to develop a complex culinary tradition. Out of this cultural milieu came unique black culinary cultural production.

African American cooking and eating draw from many parts of the world. The culture is a part of a larger ecological system, which, as anthropologist Tony Whitehead puts it, is historically created, is intergenerationally reproduced and moderated, and functions to allow humans to meet basic biological needs.[8] Several subcultures make up a single cultural unit. Within food customs are things learned and things shared.[9] Accordingly, foodway acculturation forces a fusion of foodstuffs. Enslaved blacks were often allowed to work together in a common kitchen that would serve the entire plantation community. But even with shared food preparation, each family preferred to add its own particular touches to a given dish. For every enslaved family, the concerns about food were more than a mere matter of sustenance. When it came to the timing of food rations, enslaved blacks were keen to make demands of their masters. A great majority of food was therefore distributed on the weekends in response to strong pressure from the slaves, as Sunday called for a special culinary effort for the community.[10] Even today, whether in the southern United States or in cities like Los Angeles, Chicago, or Philadelphia, black communities are knit together around a special meal.

Acculturation is also identifiable in what religious historian Wallace Best refers to as "the South in the city" aspect of postmigration black urban life. For example, beyond the Sunday meal, I recall numerous Friday night fish fries in Los Angeles where those gathered were largely from small towns in Louisiana. The scent of catfish, buffalo fish, red snapper, and gaspergou (gaspergoo) would hover over what seemed like a religious gathering of people sharing stories about life in the South. These events epitomized the religio-communal nature of gathering around a meal. Friday evenings became impromptu celebrations of life and spirit intertwined with blues and lament. Often lasting well after midnight, the Friday fish fry, as with many other meal gatherings, became much more about what happened before, between, and after eating the fish itself. In this way, different food styles have the ability to bridge broader gaps of cultural difference, even toward a celebration of difference. But what does it mean to create a distinct narrative about black food life or meal-sharing culture? Clearly, Friday night fish fries are not the sole product of African American Protestant food cultural life. Within the Catholic tradition, many consume fish on Friday in relation to the practice of abstaining from meat. For some Catholics this spiritual practice of abstaining is reserved for the Lenten season, the six weeks leading up to Easter, while for others it is carried out all year long. Yet Friday fish fries remain prevalent in the many black Protestant communities. Southern and southern migrant African American communities enjoy Friday fish fries as social family gatherings, often held outside or in grand halls. What contemporary foodway practices say about African Americans in connection to their religious life creates an untidy narrative. Inasmuch as Protestants share meals that feature various meats, including pork, members of the Nation of Islam, who also share grand meals, would shun such pork consumption. For them the eating of a pig, a filthy animal, leads to the destruction of one's sacred temple (body). In this sense, food and religion coalesce to make statements about group identity, beliefs, values, and politics.

Rooting this discussion in the African American tradition, one can say that foodway culture shares a common link with religious culture in that both originate in those spaces of coming to terms with the reality of social degradation. Through efforts to amend lives broken by oppression, food and religion gave a language for protest and offered a social space for uplifting members of the community. With both food and faith, this framing of culture becomes useful as a way of understanding African American agency in the face of the absurd.

RELIGION, FOODWAYS, AND IDENTITY IN BLACK LIFE

Through its connection to black food culture, gumbo functions metaphorically as it illumines the spiciness of African American religio-cultural life. We stop here to lay the groundwork for the intersection of foodways and religious studies generally. The role of each as an instrument of black identity formation reveals the active component within them to critically engage society, politics, and culture. Moreover, they offer spaces for cultural exchange and production and give support to creating unique languages of resistance that bind the community. Here religion is considered in terms of a striving or push toward a reconstructed identity. Historian Charles Long holds that religion in the human experience is linked to orientation in the ultimate sense—that is, how one comes to terms with the ultimate significance of one's place in the world.[11] Religion is understood less in terms of doctrine and more in terms of an activity that encourages hope and faith as social actors strive for collective change to improve the social circumstances of the community. As Long asserts, "Religion of any people is more than a structure of thought; it is experiences, expressions, motivations, intentions, behaviors, styles, and rhythms."[12] Black religion, therefore, is best understood as a conduit for the individual or collective to actively respond to domination by way of radical social inquiry and action.

Religion's role of invading the void between oppressive subjugation and providing the power to respond in affirmative ways to oppression should not be understated. Illustratively, Long presents a hypothesis of *signification*, which expresses how religion begins to work as a tool to counter maltreatment and false images about ethnic groups. Signification can be seen in three ways. First, the oppressor signifies the oppressed: in this instance the signifier constructs meaning *for* the signified. Second, the relationship between the signifier and signified is arbitrary, which instills a certain sense of terror and dread within the oppressed community, given that it may be harmed randomly and without warning.[13] And third, the signified may ultimately become a signifier—countering negative depictions of black life. Religion then manifests itself in cultural actions that deploy meanings about individuals or communities. In this way, religion has the power to forge identity.

At its core, black religion encompasses what religious studies scholar Anthony Pinn calls a quest for complex subjectivity, a desire or feeling for more life meaning. Of course, an understanding of religion on these terms does not limit it to a single tradition. Religion's impact is deeply felt among African Americans who are concerned about threats to their human dignity. Black religion's basic structure, then, entails a desire and push for "fullness." Thus complex subjectivity equals a healthy self-concept that works to reshape history. Hence religious experience entails a human response to a crisis of identity (or being signified upon), and it is the crisis of identity that constitutes the dilemma of ultimate meaning.[14] Religious life of African Americans includes a functional element of empowerment, allowing them to critically rethink the social reality. Food becomes one among other mediums through which this form of religious thought is expressed and promulgated in community.

As with religion, identity formation is certainly not a foreign topic in foodway studies. Food is a prominent marker of ethnic identity and governs a group's self-perception. Whether an ethnic group is holding on to old ways of preparing or consuming food or transitioning to new formulations of food life, identity is found within the whole pattern of what is eaten, when, how, and what a meal means.[15] Identity is not a static condition in black food and religious life. As African Americans face life as a diasporic people, whether adjusting to cultural customs from other countries or attempting to maintain traditions in northern cities after migrating from the South, they often reframe identity to adapt to new social conditions. Religion scholar Theophus Smith adds that the meaning produced in various sectors of black culture, which includes aesthetics and ritual performances, is best understood in terms of identity transvaluations. The ritual "performance" of preparing and consuming certain food or engaging in, say, a certain religious worship style reminiscent of "home" creates a feeling of belonging and community cohesion. The sense of unity created by sharing cultural life in food (and religion) is so significant that it figures centrally in many rites of inclusion.[16] In performative expressions of ethnic identity and culture, blacks disclose and exchange values, styles of communication, and meaning through religion and food. Value exchange creates a unified language of black identity even as that language perpetually evolves. Through ritual performance of African American food culture and religion, the group's ability to *re*-present customs and values to other groups works to change perceptions about black identity.

Displacement cannot easily be separated from the complex realities of black cultural life. Struggles by displaced (diasporic) black communities to keep, adapt, and shed their traditional foodways affect the repertoire of foodways succeeding generations can call on to use in symbolic displays of ethnic identity.[17] Coping with the effects of displacement on identity is highlighted by their struggles with funneling racial ethnic identity through their relationship with the larger American society. It is the struggle of both being distinct and being one of several units of

American society. W.E.B. DuBois describes this component of black life in terms of a "peculiar sensation" of being in the world. In his oft-quoted tenet, DuBois presents this peculiar existence as *double-consciousness*, as a sense of always looking at one's self through the eyes of others. For him, double-consciousness is a perpetual state of existence in a culture of sociopolitical dominance. Accordingly, blacks always feel this "two-ness—an American, a Negro; two souls, two thoughts, two unreconciled strivings, two warring ideals in one dark body."[18] Blacks striving for safe spaces in a dominant culture would create avenues for cultural production with food life and religious experience to mitigate the internal struggle with identity.

In later generations African American communities had to adjust to the ever-thinning cord of cultural foodway sharing and religious traditions to stave off their complete severance over time. African American migration patterns from the post-Reconstruction South to the North, and the post–World War II South to the West, illustrate the challenges of cultural adjustment to new life as they were confronted with the diminishing of their traditions. Often as a way to maintain a sense of black social order, migrants worked hard to cook and worship as they did back home. With respect to the black migration experience, Best advances the position that "the Great Migration stimulated new urban religious practices and traditions among black Protestant churches . . . that included aspects of both black southern religion and the exigencies of city life."[19] In such cases, blacks revised religious styles as they drew from southern folk traditions that confronted northern blacks' more sophisticated religious sensibilities. With every debate about the best sweet potato pie I have witnessed, the intercultural clash between southern and northern, even rural and urban, foodway tradition takes center stage. In the end, the effort to maintain the tastes of home takes precedence.

Food and religious identity are symbolic in nature. Allegiances and social networks are formed around church life and sharing of foods. In many traditional black Baptist churches, for example, a Sunday that does not culminate in a meal would for some be sacrilegious. The meal is seen as a primary time for fellowship, and thus a continuation of ministry and worship. Often within these spaces of fellowship around food, parishioners are affected on even greater levels by what the pastor preached from the pulpit that morning. Within these sacred spaces of food and faith, the support of the community is most apparent, bonding the group as a single unit in the face of adversity. Community adhesion becomes an important element of black migrant life as the migrants venture to new urban centers.

African Americans find in food and faith opportunities for self-preservation in the face of cultural difference. Foodway studies are a way of assessing signs and symbols communicated among cultures within their respective groups.[20] For some, food signals a code about a group. Food and religious language may also encode aspects of their communal life including thoughts, feelings, motivations, intentions, and desires. In black religious language and expression, we find modes of self-expression intended to recalibrate the sociocultural identity that African Americans find more suitable as accurate portrayals of their life experience.

Foodways' ability to communicate messages about cultural identity takes place on at least three levels. First, a group may choose to adopt a decidedly American identity through which it partially or fully rejects a diasporic or immigrant identity.[21] On this level African Americans, concerned with social and political advancement, seek to more fully identify with dominant culture in the hopes of gaining fuller access to American capitalist society. Food consumption becomes a tool for advancement, with a guiding principle that if the group consumes the food of the broader culture, external perception about blacks may change. In short: eat "their" food to gain "their" acceptance. Second, groups may instead aggressively maintain traditional foodways. In some ways, certain eating habits are used to make a political statement.[22] For instance, some African Americans make it a point to eat foods that are stereotypically black as a push back against the degradation their food culture. Reflecting on this point thrusts me back to my youth when my rejection of certain black or southern foods like collards, hot water cornbread, buffalo fish, sweet potato pie, and, yes, gumbo marked me as somehow not black enough. Third, many ethnic groups, notably African Americans, adopt blended foodway practices, fusing traditionally black styles with other American styles. In this case, what is black is complex and difficult to articulate. This is because these pluralistic foodways may include influences from West Africa or, in cities like Chicago or Los Angeles, traditions from the South. Fish and grits may be served on a table where vegan collard greens and macaroni and cheese are also served.

When passing by El Bethel Missionary Baptist Church in Los Angeles, the church of my youth, I am reminded of how food and religion contribute to black urban cultural life. For funerals, weddings, revivals, ordinations, first sermon receptions, post-Sunday services, general church gatherings, or even informal fellowships, marvelous meals were prepared and served to all who would come. In fact, I don't recall encountering any black Baptist church without an oft-used kitchen. Breaking out a cookbook would be considered poor form. Within every church kitchen were folktales about religious experience and cooking. As with the African cooking tradition, techniques related to food preparation were passed on through close sensory contact.[23] Recipes and methods of cooking were passed down by way of oral tradition. In slave systems where servants were prohibited from reading or writing, the oral tradition of sharing customs, both religious and culinary, was invaluable. To this day, most of my grandmother's recipes are in her head. Even in those instances where she has made adjustments to make a dish healthier, the magic formula of her great recipes remains an oral phenomenon. Black religion fully shares in this oral tradition. Notwithstanding efforts to gain literacy for Bible reading, owing to the mass prohibition of slave literacy, blacks benefited from an established religious oral tradition. For them, the sharing of biblical stories sewn in one's heart had as much impact as those shared through the written word. Evident, then, are the many convergences of food and religion in African American life in the creation of opportunities for agency and liberation.

GUMBO AND AFRICAN AMERICAN CULTURAL EXPRESSION

Gumbo every January; dark brown versus red gumbo; an okra roux versus a non-okra roux; New Orleans versus Northern Louisiana gumbo—these and many other topics about the preparation and origins of gumbo are deliberated. Gumbo's complexity embodies what foodways studies reveals about the multilayered expressions of black cultural life. Food and religion create new opportunities for impactful exchange. But gumbo's unique ability to both influence and reflect the black culture makes it well suited to examination in relation to religious experience. Gumbo shares characteristics with black religion, where its impact on the community is inextricably tied to its effervescence and complexity. Indicators of gumbo's complexity and its ability to metaphorically depict African American experience is highlighted in Marlon Riggs's documentary *Black Is, Black Ain't*. As Riggs puts it, "everything that you can imagine can be put into gumbo—shrimp, crawfish, sausage, crab, and chicken." As he thinks of not only the ingredients but also the required skill to combine all these flavors to get the taste right, it makes him reflect on what black life in America is. As there are many variations of gumbo, so too are there many variations of blackness. Thus Riggs challenges monolithic notions of black culture and life.

Gumbo is neither a neat dish nor a melting pot. With origins in African, African American, and Native American cultures in and around Louisiana, gumbo is an elaborate amalgam of flavors oddly coming together to form an exquisite experience of taste. The word "gumbo" is derived from a West African word for okra, which for some is also one of its referents in Louisiana.[24] The word "okra" (*okuru*) comes from the Igbo language of Nigeria, and in French it is the actual word for okra (*gombo*). Though the word has culturally transformed over time in America, it still points back to Bantu languages. As a dish it is directly connected to the many okra-based soupy stews prepared in West African regions.[25] Described by some outsiders as a thick soup of Louisiana, it is considered indescribable by my grandmother, who is from Colfax, Louisiana. The experience of gumbo is likened to what American writer Willie Morris said about the cuisine of his black friends at a dinner party, calling it "an unusual feast."[26] Referencing the unusual in reference to African American cuisine in general was not novel, and in connection to gumbo it is apropos of the dish's composition.

Let us consider gumbo's construction and components. First, good gumbo takes at least two days to prepare. One must first create the stock, which will become part of the liquid base of the cuisine. Sure, one can purchase canned stock, but it just isn't the same. The right stock helps to create the right flavor base. Then you have the roux. While debatable, the preparation of the roux is the most critical component. Roux is what brings the liquid base of the broth or stock to its thickened gumbo texture. Concocted from oil, fat, flour, and butter, roux is a tedious preparation that requires much patience to get just right. As Paige Gutierrez writes, "it is impossible to rush a roux; often a half-hour or more of the cook's constant attention is required."[27] One must also get the spices just right. The spicing of the gumbo becomes the central space where the cook's artistry is revealed. Imprecision of taste from one year of preparation to the next is not considered a fault, but rather, imprecision adds to this delicacy's magnificent nuance. Spices, and their secrets, become for the preparer a badge of honor. What results is a complex brew of flavors, not a melting pot of blended flavors.

Styles of gumbo vary. Some are seafood based—including shrimp, crab, and sometimes oysters or even crawfish. Others choose the chicken and andouille sausage version, a common formulation in southern Louisiana. Indeed, contemporary debates about gumbo's ingredients date back to southern black life during the antebellum period. Enslaved blacks in a single state may have had a different perspective on the contents or social-communal import of gumbo. Former slave Mary Scranton of Texas recalled a combination of meats as the centerpiece of gumbo: "I sho' know how t' mek gumbo. You put in d' pepper 'n' onion. . . . 'N' den you brown d' rice right brown t' mek a good gumbo. Den put w'at you wanter in it—chicken 'r' shrimp 'r' meat."[28]

Another former Texas slave lauds the merits of crawfish, stating that he would "eat plenty of crawfish" and after catching them would "jerk [us] up a crawfish, and bile (boil) him in hot water, or make de gumbo."[29] Described as a "French Negro," former Texas slave Olivier Blanchard even recollects that they "uster mek robin gumbo."[30] Whatever the meat of choice, central to gumbo's base are the "holy trinity" of vegetables: celery, onions, and bell peppers. Some gumbos use okra to thicken the roux (okra-based roux). Some use filé—dried ground sassafras leaves from Native American culture—as a base thickener or as an addition to the finished product in the bowl. These styles of gumbo are connected to non-monolithic ideas of black experience and black religion. Rice becomes the finishing component added to an already complex brew. To introduce this last element is to make whole the experience of gumbo.

On its completion, gumbo has an ethereal effect. To those who take in its bouquet of spices, it is a spiritual encounter. Yet—and this may be the most fascinating part of gumbo—it is also perpetually enhanced by its own contents. That is to say, over the life of a gumbo pot, even if it lasts only for three days, the flavors progressively, often subtly, change. The maker of the gumbo, who has tasted it along the way, is continually rewarded anew with every enjoyed bowl.

GUMBO AS A POINTER TO BLACK RELIGIOUS COMMUNITY

From the transformation of African identities in the New World, a poly-cultural African American community emerged.[31] On some level black life is observably related, and yet one can behold distinguishable features connected to tradition or geographic origin. Gumbo illumines such messiness and encourages a rethinking of religion in black life. Black religion is in touch with the complexity of acculturation through the coalescence of distinct flavors. Gumbo's hybridity of flavors works through the inherent discomfort often associated with difference, resulting in a dish drawing from multiple cultural influences that represents a multicultural community. Read this way, gumbo figuratively becomes a conduit for a way of thinking about black religion's ability to also bind a complex cultural community.

The notion of gumbo's ability to promote community is illustrated in Disney's animated film *The Princess and the Frog*. John Lasseter, the executive director of the film, stressed getting the cultural details right. He wanted to be sure the animated film captured the unique flavor of New Orleans and, to a large degree, its black cultural life. While he did make several cultural exceptions for dramatic license, the communal element of black experience in New Orleans struck a chord in me as I reflected on post-Christmas gumbo gatherings in my home. When, in the film, a young Tiana puts the final touches on her gumbo, the entire community is beckoned to come and share in the experience. As the neighbors begin to gather around Tiana's family's porch, one shouts, "I got some hush-puppies, Tiana, here they come," indicating the circular experience of sharing around food. In a pedagogical moment, Tiana's father tells her that good food "brings folks together . . . and warms them right up."

As American studies professor Psyche Williams-Forson tells us, foods are cultural products; gumbo, then, offers the world a taste of (a) community. Through gumbo, traditions and values are transmitted that give others a glimpse of cultural life. Even impromptu food events, like the gumbo sharing on Tiana's porch, have the power to define social organization as well as social and cultural identities.[32] As put forth by Bryant Alexander and H. Paul LeBlanc, the sharing of recipes and of the meal is central or core to the experience of family for a people.[33] It reflects the robustness of life; it exhibits flavorful and colorful expressions of a community. Gumbo is also linked to a general posture of sharing and encouragement. You just can't make a pot of gumbo without sharing it with other folks. Through this experience, personal stories are shared, traditions are uncovered, new traditions are formed, ideas are swapped, songs are sung, bonds are formed, and connections of heart and spirit are forged. Within food in general, and gumbo particularly, lie memory, politics, and a posture connected to identity, agency, and resistance. Thus gumbo becomes a central metaphor for black religious life, underscoring its robustness.

Food and faith have aided African Americans as they have striven to change the social and political reality of their existence. Through religious action, blacks respond to the absurd as social agents to create new identities about their self-worth. All are welcome to engage in a recalibration of harmful language that continues to give space to racism. This creative and active spirituality becomes a way of expressing all that is wonderful about gumbo. Through recalibration one changes the composition of something so that it is suitable for one's desire of taste. Gumbo is an acquired taste. It is involved, sometimes unsettling, and even peculiar. But when the flavors are brought together just right, the value of each individual ingredient becomes clear. A similar spiritual sensibility, drawing on cultural difference, marks the substance of black religion as it bolsters the community. Like gumbo, black religion draws from what may be considered good and bad aspects of life—the detestable and the delightful. The final composition is a religious life of a people whose distinct gifts are valued and shared. For this reason, African Americans are metaphorically a "gumbo people."

Gumbo is not simply a dish but a unique experience. By the same token, some scholars argue that black folks do not simply attend church, they engage in a complex expression of faith all their own. Religion's and gumbo's impact on the community cannot therefore be measured by dogma or instruction. Religion and gumbo in the black experience push back against what is normative or commonplace to find new flavors to re-create new identity. Both entail the struggle of a diverse community to create a lovable whole. They draw from the unique experiences of black life even as they feed them. Each is a complex formulation open to all those who do not fear fellowship. Diasporic elements of black life converge with new traditions to create a cuisine and religious life that includes elements of continental African, the Caribbean, and the Americas. The distinctive stories of black religious experiences are not ancillary. Every social group, race, or ethnicity has something to contribute to the grander narrative of religious life in North America. To forsake the distinct culture or context of one group is to miss an important element of American religious history. If we shun the study of those distinct communities of faith for a "melting pot" understanding of American religious life, those communities remain marginal, alien, and othered. In the end, religion and gumbo are centered on love—a love for complexity, affection for dissimilarity, a devotion to the other, and a desire to work together to create a better whole.

DISCUSSION QUESTIONS

1. What are examples of the cultural complexity of African American foodways?
2. What do African American foodway culture and religious life share in relation to community formation and identity?
3. In what way(s) does gumbo function as a metaphor for understanding African American religious life?

NOTES

1. Eugene Walter, "The Gumbo Cult," *Gourmet*, April 1962.
2. Anne L. Bower, "Watching Soul Food," in *African American Foodways: Explorations of History and Culture*, ed. Anne L. Bower (Urbana: University of Illinois Press, 2007), 8.
3. See Susan Kalcik, "Ethnic Foodways in America: Symbol and the Performance of Identity," in *Ethnic and Regional Foodways in the United States: The Performance of Group Identity*, ed. Linda Keller Brown and Kay Mussell, 37 (Knoxville: University of Tennessee Press, 1984).
4. Anne Yentsch, "Excavating African American Food History," in Bower, *African American Foodways*, 85.
5. Ibid., 66.
6. George P. Rawick, ed., *The American Slave: A Composite Autobiography*, vol. 13, Georgia Narratives, parts 3 and 4, 154.
7. Ibid., 198.

8. Tony L. Whitehead, "In Search of Soul Food and Meaning: Culture, Food and Health," in *African Americans in the South: Issues of Race, Class, and Gender*, ed. H. A. Baier and Yvonne Jones, 94 (Athens: University of Georgia Press, 1982).

9. William C. Whit, "Soul Food as Cultural Creation," in Bower, *African American Foodways*, 45.

10. Eugene D. Genovese, *Roll Jordan Roll: The World the Slaves Made* (New York: Vintage, 1972), 544.

11. Charles H. Long, *Significations: Signs, Symbols, and Images in the Interpretation of Religion* (Philadelphia: Fortress, 1986), 7.

12. Ibid.

13. Ibid., 1.

14. Anthony B. Pinn, *Terror and Triumph: The Nature of Black Religion* (Minneapolis: Fortress, 2003), 173.

15. Kalcik, "Ethnic Foodways in America," 38.

16. Theophus H. Smith, *Conjuring Culture: Biblical Formations of Black America* (New York: Oxford University Press, 1994), 125, 48.

17. Kalcik, "Ethnic Foodways in America," 41.

18. W.E.B. Dubois, *The Souls of Black Folk* (New York: Norton, 1999), 11.

19. Wallace D. Best, *Passionately Human, No Less Divine: Religion and Culture in Black Chicago, 1915-1952* (Princeton: Princeton University Press, 2005), 2.

20. Kalcik, "Ethnic Foodways in America," 46.

21. Ibid., 56.

22. Ibid., 54.

23. Whit, "Soul Food as Cultural Creation," 52.

24. C. Paige Gutierrez, *Cajun Foodways* (Jackson: University Press of Mississippi, 1992), 53.

25. Jessica B. Harris, *High on the Hog: A Culinary Journey from Africa to America* (New York: Bloomsbury, 2011), 17.

26. Willie Morris, *North Toward Home* (Boston: Houghton Mifflin, 1967).

27. Gutierrez, *Cajun Foodways*, 52.

28. Rawick, ed., *The American Slave: A Composite Autobiography*, S2, v. 9.8, *Texas Narratives*.

29. Ibid., v. 4, 253.

30. Ibid., v. 2.1, 326.

31. See Michael A. Gomez, *Exchanging Our Country Marks: The Transformation of African Identities in the Colonial and Antebellum South* (Chapel Hill: University of North Carolina Press, 1998).

32. Psyche Williams-Forson, "Chirckens and Chains: Using African American Foodways to Understand Black Identity," in Bower, *African American Foodways*, 127.

33. Bryant K. Alexander and H. Paul LeBlanc III, "Cooking Gumbo—Examining Cultural Dialogue About Family: A Black-White Narrativization of Lived Experience in Southern Louisiana," in *Communication, Race, and Family: Exploring Communication in Black, White, and Biracial Families*, ed. Thomas J. Socha and Rhunette C. Diggs, 182 (Mahwah, N.J.: Lawrence Erlbaum Associates, 1999).

RECOMMENDED READING

Boyer, Anne L., ed. *African American Foodways: Explorations of History & Culture*. Chicago: University of Illinois Press, 2007.

Covey, Herbert C., and Dwight Eisnach, eds. *What the Slaves Ate: Recollections of African American Foods and Foodways from the Slave Narratives*. Santa Barbara: ABC-CLIO, 2009.

Dodson, Jualynne E., and Cheryl Townsend Gilkes. " 'There's Nothing like Church Food': Food and the U.S. Afro-Christian Tradition: Re-Membering Community and Feeding the Embodied S/spirit(s)." *Journal of the American Academy of Religion* 63, no. 3 (1995): 519–38.

Harris, Jessica B. *High on the Hog: A Culinary Journey from Africa to America*. New York: Bloomsbury, 2011.

Eight

"I CHOSE JUDAISM BUT CHRISTMAS COOKIES CHOSE ME"

FOOD, IDENTITY, AND FAMILIAL RELIGIOUS PRACTICE IN CHRISTIAN/ JEWISH BLENDED FAMILIES

SAMIRA K. MEHTA

WHEN UPPER-CLASS, CATHOLIC television character Bridget first arrives at the home of her working-class, Jewish future in-laws, her fiancé Bernie's mother, Sophie Steinberg, cooks a meal of traditional eastern European dishes, including gefilte fish and horseradish.[1] Bridget claims to love the dishes, though the potency of the horseradish gives her a bit of a struggle. The meal is a hazing ritual of hospitality, and Bridget, who has eaten far more than her fill, clearly realizes that she is being judged. Her presence strains the conversation enough that there is a discussion about whether the Yiddish jokes will be funny in translation. The table is groaning with food, and Sophie dishes up extra helpings before dessert, when she forces the overfull Bridget to eat a prune Danish, arguing that she "got it special." Bridget takes a bite and runs to the bathroom, causing Bernie's father to exclaim, "A gentile, a Catholic, a frail stomach! That combination could ruin any marriage."

Shortly thereafter, Bridget takes Bernie home to meet her parents. He is stunned and uncomfortable at the grandeur of her parents' apartment building, and looking at it from the outside, says, "You're rich. You're stinking rich." As they walk into the dining room, Bridget's father makes it clear that he and his wife do not specifically hold Bernie's Judaism against him. "We would feel the exactly same way if you were Protestant," Walter Fitzgerald explains. The meal itself contrasts sharply with dinner at the Steinbergs': a gentleman servant serves the family in a restrained and reserved atmosphere. Mrs. Fitzgerald has chosen ham for the main course, though she has "considerately" provided salami for Bernie and suggests that they skip grace before the meal because of his presence.

The combination of class and religious difference initially causes Bernie to decide against the marriage, thinking that he and Bridget are too different. Bridget ultimately persuades Bernie to go through with the marriage, with a kiss that clearly promises more. Thus begins the popular but controversial 1973 sitcom *Bridget Loves Bernie.*[2] In the show food is emblematic of the differences and tensions that exist within interfaith families. In this example, contrasting mealtime cultures and culinary differences suggest that the couple is fundamentally too different to be happy. But Bridget and Bernie survive this test, as do many other couples.

Interfaith marriage between Protestants and Catholics and between Christians and Jews became an issue of increasing cultural concern in the years immediately following World War II, as the social factors that had previously separated the groups became less pervasive. Despite increasing concern about intermarriage in the 1950s, many studies have documented a dramatic rise in the number of interfaith marriages in the 1960s and 1970s, as the children who grew up in a postwar era that downplayed religious and ethnic differences began dating. The intermarriage rate continued to rise up to the dawn of the twenty-first century, with demographers estimating that as many as 50 percent of Jewish marriages during the 1990s were to non-Jews. While the ecumenical movements of the late 1960s resulted in decreasing conversation about intermarriage between mainline Protestants and Catholics, conversations about marriage between Christians and Jews became increasingly common and remained robust through the turn of the millennium.

This essay is primarily interested in how interfaith families create their own familial cultures. As the show demonstrates, food serves a critical role in the creation of familial religious practice and in the lives of adult children of interfaith marriage. Food is not neutral in interfaith family life. Rather, in the context of interfaith families, it provides a site where ritual and cultural meaning can become something different—and something blended. Traditionally, food has acted as an excellent conduit for the forming of intentional and unintentional blending, precisely because it is understood to be cultural rather than religious. Despite that perception, food has provided ways of carrying religious meaning from both traditions forward into the lives of children of interfaith marriages.

Proponents of keeping Judaism and Christianity alive in interfaith family life have often depicted food as a particularly fruitful avenue because they could frame it as "traditional" rather than "religious." Examining the role that food has played for interfaith families, however, demonstrates that their traditions around food do much of the work of religion, though they often do so without the problems faced by opponents of the "two religions in one home" model. Popular texts such as *Bridget Loves Bernie*, *My Two Grandmothers*, and *Chrismukkah* suggest that Christian and Jewish culture can be productively combined in family life; these sources see food as a central point of combination in part because food is traditional rather than religious. Such a neat distinction between religion and culture or tradition is problematic, however, as the personal narratives in *Half/Life* and the writings of Mary Helene Rosenbaum and Jennifer Steinhauer demonstrate by showing how food rituals perform complex religious work in the lives of family members.

To understand the tension between my argument that food has the potential to be religious and the distinctions among the terms "tradition," "culture," and "religion" in the sources, we need to think briefly about the competing notions of what it means to be religious. If my sources implicitly frame religion around affiliation with organized communities or around dedication to a specific theology, scholars of religion often take a more complicated view of what constitutes religion. First, food practice can point to ultimate concerns about right living in the world.[3] Second, Robert Orsi articulates an understanding of religion as rooted in relationships. Orsi speaks primarily of relationships between heaven and earth, writing that "religion is commonly thought of by modern people . . . as a medium, for explaining, understanding, and modeling reality." Instead he poses "religion as a network of relationships between heaven and earth involving humans of all ages and many sacred figures together. These relationships have all the complexities—all the hopes, evasions, love, fear, denial, projections, misunderstandings, and so on—of relationships between humans."[4] Food and family memories encapsulated in experiences of food demonstrate that it is a powerful means of expressing these relationships, often as they exist between the living and either the dead of their own family or of their heritage. For interfaith families, recipes and food practices offer ways to maintain sacred relationships with relatives and communities from both sides of the family, whether or not a single formal affiliation has been chosen for the household or any individual within it. Food also provides a means through which traditions can be blended rather than running in parallel, as is demonstrated in both popular depictions and memoir literature.

POPULAR DEPICTIONS OF INTERFAITH FAMILY LIFE

Popular depictions of interfaith family life often treat food as a place where cultural combination can happen unproblematically. In contrast to a body of literature suggesting that it is harmful to children to combine Christianity and Judaism in the home, Effin Older's 2000 picture book *My Two Grandmothers* and Ron Gompertz's 2006 book *Chrismukkah* use food to paint a very different possibility for the interfaith family.[5] *My Two Grandmothers* depicts food as a primary element of familial identity, passed matrilineally through the generations. The story frames food as a tradition and values the food traditions of the Christian farm family and the Jewish urban family equally, considering them both to be culturally specific. This balance acknowledges the cultural specificity of the dominant culture as well as the minority culture.

My Two Grandmothers presents a little girl named Lily who likes to visit her grandmothers: the Christian Grammy Lane on a farm in the country, and the Jewish Bubbe Silver in a tall apartment building in the city. Lily visits her grandmothers several times a year, describing the fun things she does with each of them. Each grandmother shares aspects of who she is with Lily throughout the year, and many of those aspects have to do with food. After a cold winter day of snowshoeing in the woods, Grammy Lane suggests red flannel hash to warm them up. "Flannel? Like my pajamas?" Lily asks. "Heavens, no!" Grammy Lane responds, "Flannel because it warms you up. My mother, your great-grandmother, taught me how to make it. I'll teach you someday, too. It's a Lane tradition." When Lily next sees Bubbe Silver, she tells her about red flannel hash, and Bubbe responds, "Sounds like my gefilte fish. . . . My mother, your great-grandmother, taught me how to make it. It is a Silver tradition." Like Grammy Lane, Bubbe Silver promises to pass on the tradition. Even the foods that Older chose underscore that Grammy and Bubbe are not so different—hash and gefilte fish are both recipes for using up leftovers by people who did not have the luxury of wasting anything. The word "tradition" defines the recipes, connecting Lily to her ancestors. The narrative does not address, at this moment, the idea that one grandmother is Christian, the other Jewish; Lily is simply presented as learning two sets of family recipes that ensconce her increasingly deeply in her dual identity as Lane and Silver.

As Lily works her way through her year of visits with grandmothers, she spends Hanukkah (Chanukah) with Bubbe Silver and Christmas with Grammy Lane. Lily details the Hanukkah preparations, including setting out the menorah and making latkes, "stacks of latkes." "We Silvers *love* latkes," Lily reflects before she describes the holiday celebration. "Bubbe's apartment is filled with aunts and uncles and cousins. Everyone holds hands around the menorah. Bubbe lights the Hanukkah candles, and we sing a prayer in Hebrew. After the prayer, the kids get presents. Then we all eat latkes. Sometimes I eat so many, my stomach feels like it is going to burst." Christmas at Grammy Lane's comes immediately after Hanukkah. Christmas morning comes with presents, and the cousins play games and eat chocolate fudge until dinner. "Christmas dinner looks just like a picture in a book: turkey with stuffing, mashed potatoes, cranberry sauce, and Grammy's warm homemade rolls. And for dessert? Pie. Apple, raspberry, pumpkin, and mince. We Lanes *love* pie!" After dinner, the Lane family gathers around the piano to sing Christmas carols.

In these examples, the religious differences are emphasized through the holidays. While conventional markers of religion are noted, the menorah and Hebrew prayer and Christian carol "Away in the Manger" take a back seat to the food in Lily's narrative. Hanukkah and Christmas are about latkes, a turkey dinner, and many kinds of pie. The prayer and the carol are part of each tradition but do not create the definitive statements of identity and belonging: "We Silvers love latkes" and "We Lanes love pie." For Lily, it is the participation in the holiday food culture that allows her to be comfortably part of both food traditions.

The story concludes when Lily realizes that "Grammy Lane never gets to light Hanukkah candles or sip a Donald Duck. I think about how Bubbe Silver never gets to sing Christmas carols or look for animal tracks in the snow."[6] She decides to invite both grandmothers for a party at her house.

"Please bring something traditional," she writes, and indeed, Grammy Lane brings apple pie and red flannel hash and Bubbe Silver brings geflite fish and horseradish. The grandmothers smile at each other. "She's just like a Silver," Bubbe says to Grammy, who responds, "Every inch a Lane." In the world of the children's book, Lily can be both a Lane and Silver, and since, as readers, we never learn Lily's last name, we do not know whether she is actually a Lane or a Silver. Similarly, we never see her in her own home, with the traditions forged or neglected by her parents. While it is clear that Grammy Lane is Christmas and the all-American farm and that Bubbe Silver is Hanukkah and the big city, Lily herself remains without context.

My Two Grandmothers skirts the issue of Lily's identity. It is enough that she can be a Lane *and* a Silver. In an interfaith family, food can be shared and transmitted. For Lily, it provides a family practice, referred to over and over again in the text when one grandmother or the other explains that a recipe is "traditional." Both grandmothers offer Lily treasured family recipes, telling her about the great-grandmothers who taught them and indicating that she too can be a link in both matrilineal family rituals. She can be "every inch" a Lane and a Silver, a point that Lily herself underscores when she comments that "we Silvers love latkes" and "we Lanes love pie." [7] Lily can go to their houses and sing prayers in Hebrew or Christmas carols that explicitly engage with the theme of the Christ child. The book does not concern itself with the theological incompatibilities— Lily can participate in both family traditions. When she tries to forge her own family tradition, however, the theologically oriented prayers and songs fall away. As much as Lily regrets that Bubbe Silver does not get to sing Christmas carols and Grammy Lane does not light the menorah, when the grandmothers bring something traditional, they bring the easily shareable, cultural aspects of their heritage: red flannel hash and gefilte fish. A new tradition can be born, and the sharing of traditional foods offers a safe venue for that tradition.

The narrative of the book ends with the new, safe tradition of Grandmother's Day. Though conventional Christianity and Judaism are no longer central to Lily's identity, the traditions she shares with Bubbe Silver and Grammy Lane are, nonetheless, religious traditions. The work of historian Elizabeth Pleck offers further insight into the specifically familial ways that food ritual creates a sense of identity. She argues that food rituals give Americans a sense of who they are and where they came from, serving "to define one's identity but also indicate changes in identity."[8]

Pleck suggests that women, in particular, use food to memorialize family members. During holidays, when women cook together, they commemorate a dead mother or grandmother through preparing her recipes and telling stories about her as they teach younger generations to prepare the dish. In teaching Lily the recipes that their own mothers taught them, her grandmothers are replicating this creation of family meaning—tightly tying Lily to both her Christian and Jewish family heritages. In doing so, they connect Lily to a relational network of female kin, living and dead, grandmothers and great-grandmothers, reminiscent of Orsi's relational definition of religion.

In the early twenty-first century invention of "Chrismukkah," food also served as a pivotal point of cultural combination. The term *Chrismukkah* was likely first launched on the television show *The O.C.* during its first season in 2003, though certainly some interfaith families had held dual holiday celebrations before that. The following year, Ron and Michelle Gompertz, an interfaith couple from Bozeman, Montana, launched a website, www.chrismukkah.com, and followed up with the Chrismukkah cookbook. Chrismukkah was an immediate attention-getter. In 2004 it was listed on *Time Magazine*'s list of buzzwords for the year.[9] Two years later, in 2006, Ron Gompertz published *Chrismukkah: Everything You Need to Know to Celebrate the Hybrid Holiday.* The blurbs on the back of Gompertz's book came from such elevated sources as the *New York Times*, which raved, "The double-barreled holiday offers an excuse to eat mashed potatoes and potato latkes in the same sitting, with candy canes and chocolate gelt for dessert." The *New York Times* comment picked up on one of Gompertz's central arenas of combination: food.

If, in *My Two Grandmothers*, Older does not explicitly address the distinctions among Hebrew prayers, Christmas carols about Jesus, and the recipes that each grandmother shares with Lily, Gompertz addresses the "not religious" nature of Chrismukkah head on. He articulates it as something of a joke, pointing out that "I need to admit something up front. Chrismukkah is pretend. It doesn't exist. It's made up. Wishful thinking. A holiday hoax." He points out that it would not "get you in good with God," or "bring you spiritual enlightenment." At the same time, he suggests that it allows people to retain a connection with their traditions, even if they do not consider themselves to be religious people. He explains that "like most interfaith couples," he and his wife were not religious, uninterested in converting to the other's religion, proud of their cultural heritages, and curious about the other's. While they heard the advice that to celebrate both religions would confuse their children, they want to "respect and honor" both sets of traditions and raise their daughter to be "informed, tolerant, and balanced." He also argues that, as "a multicultural family, we are part of a growing demographic trend in America that is a by-product of our country's melting pot history. From this perspective, Chrismukkah is more than just a pretend holiday about two incompatible religions."[10] Rather, it is a way to honor the two heritages, apart from their theological contexts and away from church or synagogue membership, while at the same time forging values of tolerance and balance.

Honoring heritages often comes, in Gompertz's books, in the form of recipes. These recipes are not necessarily conventional. Rather, he creates recipes for a matzo bread house and mulled Manischewitz wine called "Merryschewitz Mulled Wine." At times, his invented recipes veer into the potentially offensive, as with a Long Island iced tea called "Passion of the Iced." While the beverage merges Long Island, seen as a geographic center of American Judaism, with a central Christian story, it also trivializes both the deep religious significance of the Passion of the Christ and its justification of violence perpetrated by Christians against Jews.[11] Though the fused recipes that Gompertz suggests are largely jokes, he is serious about the idea of combining holidays. "It is a bit of a spoof, a bit of a satire, but it's something that is very, very real for those of us who are in mixed marriages and have to battle the feelings of our spouses, the feelings of our in-laws. And when things get too heavy, it's a good time to make light." Making light involves side-stepping theology, focusing instead on nostalgia and fun, a move that Gompertz repeatedly asserts is typical of what most interfaith families want and do. Food is the perfect place to make light, though Gompertz does feel that the spoof could go too far, noting in an interview with the National Public Radio program *Day to Day* that they created the new holiday food of "gefilte goose" because "gefilte ham" would be crossing over a line.[12] His delight in his merged recipes, however, suggests that food is the perfect venue both for making light and for merging traditions.

The merging of traditions, which Gompertz gleefully embraces, has served, in other contexts, as a mode for families to merge identities. In her work on American immigrant communities and their celebration of Thanksgiving, Elizabeth Pleck argues that the point of the Thanksgiving celebrations was to build national unity and that "a feast around a common table represented an acceptance of American customs and history by the newcomers."[13] At the same time that celebrating Thanksgiving provides an avenue for assimilation, immigrant families use food as a way to adapt the American Protestant holiday to their own needs, much like interfaith families.[14] Rather than copying the entire menu, families would cook the turkey, but fill and surround it with dishes from their homelands. Pleck cites examples of turkeys stuffed with Chinese rice, Armenian pomegranates, and Greek pine nuts. The food provides families with one way to reinforce an identity that blends the heritages of their former countries and the cuisines of their future home. Similarly, interfaith families blend foods and rituals from multiple heritages to meet their needs in a way that is not less authentically Christian or Jewish, simply differently so. One can easily imagine Lily growing up to teach her own daughter or granddaughter about gefilte fish and red flannel hash, telling stories about both grandmothers and emphasizing the ways in which making do were necessary on both the American frontier and the European shtetl. While Gompertz was inventing foods with as much of an eye toward humor as to taste, with, for instance, a loaf of challah decorated with red and green icing, or with recipes that are conventional but given crossover names, such as the "Yule Plotz Eggnog," his intentional combinations indicate food as a safe site for introducing cultural fusion.[15] His campaign, kitschy though it was, gave public permission to families to use food in similar ways—blending identities to create new family traditions, tying the past to the new reality.

MEALTIME MEMORIES IN INTERFAITH FAMILY LIFE

While *My Two Grandmothers* and Gompertz's articulation of Chrismukkah overtly separate food from religion, personal narratives of interfaith family life offer further support for the idea that memories of food, and food traditions, allow identities to merge and create religious, relational meaning. Sometimes that fusion is explicit, as when Laurel Snyder reflects on her formation of a Jewish yet interfaith identity in her introduction to the collection of essays *Half/Life: Jew-ish Tales from Interfaith Homes*. "And so I managed to hammer out something of an intentional religious life, a Half/Life, full of very particular choices but rooted in my haphazard beginnings. . . . I stopped eating pork and shellfish but did not claim to keep kosher," she explained as she built up an identity made out of her "muddled mishpochah."[16] To follow kashrut or keep kosher means to adhere to a set of Jewish dietary laws, including but not limited to abstaining from pork and shellfish; not combining milk and meat; and keeping separate utensils, dishes, and cookware for milk and meat.[17] While abstaining from pork and shellfish might not be enough to count as kashrut on their own, Snyder's avoidance of the term has a larger significance. She ties her refusal to name the practice kashrut to her mixed heritage, aligning it with her decision to continue to have a Christmas, to read Jewish novels, and to collect Catholic religious art. Still, food choices do play a role in her creation of a blended identity.

The centrality of food in family life and the creation of identity does not mean that food functions precisely the same way in Christian and Jewish experience. Foodways enter interfaith families with different associations and experiences. In "Bury the Knife in Yonkers," author Thisbe Nissen writes about the experience of receiving a holiday package from her grandmother. She herself was the child of an interfaith marriage and not particularly religious, but very close to her Jewish grandmother. While she was at Oberlin College, her grandmother sent her packages for Purim, the carnivalesque holiday celebrating Jews' escape from extermination at the hands of the Persians, as detailed in the book of Esther. When she opened the package of hamentashen, Nissen found herself with no explanation to offer her "blond-haired, blue eyed shiksa roommate" for the prune-filled, triangular cookies other than to sing the children's song, "My hat, it has three corners. Three corners has my hat, if it did not have three corners, it would not be my hat." The need to explain a holiday treat, Nissen notes, is in itself a mark of difference between Christian and Jewish experiences in America (outside of heavily Jewish areas). "No one went rushing out to find a priest to discuss the origins of the Easter bunny when chocolate rabbits and jelly bean eggs started arriving in the campus mailboxes. I couldn't deliver a pithy oration on the history of the Jack-o-lantern, but that did not stop me from dressing up for Halloween. I no more knew why Haman wore a three-cornered hat than I knew why Santa's sled was pulled by reindeer, and couldn't have cared less about either."[18]

The differences that Nissen highlights reflect some of the key differences between Christian and Jewish understandings of food in contemporary America. Jewish food is either easily identifiable as different, in the mode of the hamentashen, and therefore in need of explanation, or easily and broadly identifiable as Jewish. In the former case, once the explanation is given, the food becomes a marker of Jewish identity. Foodways are commonly understood to be central to the Jewish American experience. Scholarship of Jewish foodways talks about the ways in which Jews have struggled with food traditions and laws to solidify a sense of identity, while adapting them to allow themselves to feel American.[19] In scholarly discourse, Jewish food is understood to be tied to what it is to be a Jew, whether one is talking about dietary rules that may be followed closely, in the strictly kosher home; followed occasionally or partially, in the manner of students getting ham and cheese on matzo at the college dining hall grill; or gleefully violated. Of course, rules governing Jewish diets are not the only connection between Jews and food. Certain dishes are commonly understood to be Jewish, like chopped liver or matzo ball soup, be they foods to be cooked at home or nostalgically indulged in at the Second Avenue Deli.

Nissen points out that while Christian culture generates similar foods and folklore, ranging from chocolate Easter bunnies to Santa's reindeer, Christians in the United States rarely have to explain the whys behind those customs. It is commonly accepted that, for instance, there is very little connection between Cadbury creme eggs and the death and resurrection of Jesus Christ. Both, however, do represent Easter, which is a holiday of central importance in the Christian calendar. Does that make the chocolate bunny or egg inherently Christian foods, in the way that gefilte fish, for instance, is readily understood as Jewish?

In general, when food is identified with Christian holidays and life-cycle events, often participants understand the foods themselves to be associated with an ethnicity rather than with a religion, such that while doctrinal Catholic food traditions have been explored by scholars, in the popular consciousness it is not Catholic to eat corned beef and cabbage on Saint Patrick's Day; it is Irish. It is not Catholic to have large, fish-based meals on Christmas Eve until after one has returned from midnight mass; it is Italian.[20] In Protestant traditions, a Christmas pudding is English and the Easter ham is not considered to be explicitly Christian. Scholars often push against this neat division between ethnic and religious food practices, complicating the relationship between religious and ethnicity for interfaith families. While there has been less work on Protestant foodways than on Catholic and Jewish foodways, both of which are more readily understood as ethnic, Daniel Sack's *Whitebread Protestants: Food and Religion in American Culture* examines the roles that foods play in mainline American Protestantism. He considers its liturgical, social, philanthropic, and moral dimensions before concluding that "food experiences reflect the world of whitebread Protestants. . . . Food plays important symbolic roles in the church. It reveals the theological and political convictions of American Protestants, and it opens a window onto belief and practice. Church food events are full of meaning." Protestant food, "grape juice and Wonder bread, Jell-O and three-bean salad, Coke and pizza," but also the foods of the Christian home—Christmas cookies, Easter ham, hot cross buns, and mince pie—connect participants to a Christian community and identity as families pass along and replicate cultural food traditions.[21]

Sack's work underscores a key assumption for my research: while Judaism and Catholicism clearly have foodways that can be carried forward and perhaps combined with an overt identification with another religious tradition, mainline Protestantism does as well—for example, Swedish lussekatter, the saffron and currant buns served on Santa Lucia Day, and English Christmas pudding. As Nissen's example demonstrates, the ethnic traditions operate differently, based on the differences between being a majority or a minority tradition, but the culinary traditions of Protestantism can also be linked to a religious culture, rather than being simply read as American. In thinking, then, about the Christian-Jewish blended family, one must learn to see two religious cultures combining, rather than simply one "ethnic religion." In taking that step, the ethnic components of Christian cultures become associated with Christianity, and in that sense, Christianity is not dissimilar to other traditions. While it is true that chocolate bunnies have little to do with the Resurrection, it is equally true that gefilte fish is not related to the Exodus, yet for many American Christians and American Jews, neither Easter nor Passover would be the same without those foods.

As an adult, Nissen does not identify strongly as Jewish. In fact, she says that she and Judaism "pretty much play in different leagues." All she knows about Judaism, she claims, comes from her Nana Bell, "her habits and rituals and her kitchen." For her, she writes, it is not about "religion, per se," but rather "trying to live each day as best [she] can, trying to be a good person, trying to do as little harm and as much good as [she] might in this lifetime, trying to seek out some evolving meaning in this life." To Nissen, those goals are not religious because she is a person who "pray[s] and worship[s] and believe[s]."[22] If, however, as R. Marie Griffith, scholar of American religion and embodiment, points out, food practices have moral and emotional valences that connect to some of a person's most deeply held needs, then practices around food have at least the possibility of religious meaning.[23] Nissen recognizes this potential because she equates her practice with her grandmother: "I feel like I am doing right in the world by growing organic vegetables. My grandmother felt she was doing right by keeping kosher. I know one seems a lot more rational to me than the other, but that's because I believe what I believe." Nissen rests, then, on both the ethical and relational nature of religious practice. She hopes that her grandmother would approve of her, seeing her as a "religious non-religious person," because of her devotion to her garden.[24] Her interfaith family left her without formal religious affiliation, but with a way of understanding the moral meaning with which she invests her garden.

Like fictionalized depictions of interfaith family life, actual Christian/ Jewish families combine food traditions in their daily and yearly culinary practices. Those combinations result not only in hybridized family practices, but also in blended identities for the children raised in those homes. In 1995 Mary Helene Rosenbaum opened her article for the newsletter of the interfaith organization the Dovetail Institute with the following description of her family's kosher, Catholic Christmas Eve dinner.

> In our family, the night before Christmas is a highly ceremonial affair. Dinner in our kosher household is a dairy meal, reflecting the Catholic tradition of abstaining from meat on this day. It always begins with brie en croute, followed by a salmon or fresh tuna and pasta entree served on plates whose gilt snowflake design means they must be hand-washed (therefore they're only used once a year). Dessert is always a grand buche de noel not reserved for Christmas dinner itself because that's a meat meal and the buche's buttercream has to be made with real butter or there's no point to it. Everyone in the house, Christian or not, attends evening or midnight mass together. Entertainment centers around listening by candlelight to Dylan Thomas's reading of his "Child's Christmas in Wales." Not an evening to suit everyone, but it's our way and we love it.[25]

Rosenbaum and her husband Ned are committed to following both their religious practices in their home. Food is connected to many of their weekly rituals: Mary Helene cooks Shabbat dinner while Ned attends Friday night services, and when she returns from Sunday mass, he has pancakes ready for the family.[26] Christmas Eve, however, demonstrates how the family created a religious culture that fused the two traditions without arguing for their inherent sameness. Because the household is kosher, milk and meat cannot be mixed in a meal. Thus, in order to include all of the important holiday foods, Christmas Eve became an important meal. Christmas Eve is a dairy meal because of Catholic religious practices around abstaining from meat. The traditions are tightly woven together without being conflated.

Rosenbaum explains that the ritual of the special holiday dinner became so important to her daughter that, even though her daughter has chosen to be Jewish as an adult, she cherishes the ritual of her family's holiday meal. When she married and spent Christmas with her devoutly Catholic in-laws for the first time, she "secretly called [her mother] in tears."[27] In her husband's family, everyone spends Christmas Eve wrapping presents in their rooms, preparing for the main event, Christmas Day. Rather than an elaborate dinner, the family sends out for pizza. Rosenbaum's daughter was devastated and deeply homesick, despite the fact that when she had chosen a religion for herself, she chose Judaism, and that her in-laws share her mother's devout Catholicism. The food and the family celebration surrounding it were part of her ritual year. Despite her Jewish identity, the Christian calendar is marked for her by food traditions that connect her to the holiday, including Christian traditions adapted to her Jewish identity.

Food's ability to blend heritages is clear even in examples where less of an explicit attempt is made to blend heritages. In the dining section of the December 19, 2007, issue of the *New York Times*, Jennifer Steinhauer wrote, "The daughter of an interfaith marriage, I chose Judaism, but Christmas cookies chose me." In the article, "In the Kitchen Long Ago, with Grandma," Steinhauer unequivocally identifies herself as Jewish and writes of how her grandmother would begin making Christmas cookies the day after Thanksgiving, working long into the night throughout the month of December. Children and adults alike were pressed into service, painting fans with pastel-colored egg yolk wash, affixing faces to gingerbread men. In Steinhauer's family, as Orsi's explanation of relational religion suggests, the sacred relationships are not necessarily easy. "In the idealized version of a middle-aged person . . . , these marathon sessions of cookie making at Grandma's were exercises in *joie de vivre*. In truth,

Grandma was out of countenance in the face of sloppy decorating, and some family members greeted the season of midnight embellishing with a slightly heavy heart." Though decorating was not universally popular, every family member had a favorite cookie. One kind was made every year despite being so "universally hated" that it "could not even be fobbed off on the wild birds." Tins of cookies would last, growing more and more stale, until Easter, a fixture of Grandma's house. And so, as an adult, Steinhauer reflects, "even though I fashion my gingerbread into dreidels and menorahs, as I bake from her recipes, I feel close to her arms, crepe thin and marked with pronounced veins, working the dough."[28]

Steinhauer's article clearly demonstrates the possibility for some form of cultural hybridity, in that she is a Jew with a non-Jewish grandmother, and she is carrying on recipes and traditions from the non-Jewish side of her family. Why persist in calling these inclusions religious? First, it is deeply significant that Steinhauer is moved to bake her cookies in the month between Thanksgiving and Christmas. She is not simply dusting off Grandma's recipe cards and thinking about her as she bakes. She bakes during the Christmas season and in doing so brings some of the Christian calendar into her Jewish home. Of course, Jews are a minority tradition in the United States, which is largely oriented around a Christian calendar, and there are many examples of Jewish assimilation or adaptation to the norms of a Christian calendar and marketplace. "Hanukkah cookies" are an example of the kind of assimilation into a mainstream American Christian culture that many in the Jewish community deplore. Context, however, is central to interpretation of the practice. While the baking of Christmas cookies can be assimilationist, in the case of someone like Steinhauer, the baking of cookies provides a venue for connecting to her father's side of the family, particularly her Christian grandmother.

The preparation and consumption of food may take the form of a religious practice. Inherent in the idea of *practice*, however, is that the meanings of an action are shaped in part by the participants, and so the preparation of a food that seems like it should symbolize "Jew" or "Christian," "Purim" or "Christmas" also has the potential to take on the meanings and values of family or heritage, even though these are not carried forward as part of a person's dominant identity.

Indeed, food as a place of mediation is central enough to the interfaith family experience that it is a prominent theme in popular representations of interfaith families, with the nature of its depiction depending on the broader concerns about interfaith families in the given historical moment. In these representations, however, food is always portrayed as ethnic. In examples pulled from memoir and other depictions of personal experience, a much more nuanced picture emerges. Food, like other aspects of material culture, has the ability to hold persuasive and enduring emotional memories that offer an opportunity to blend traditions. This potentiality is sometimes facilitated by the fact that food can be easily read simply as ethnic and is therefore not threatening to perceived religious identities. It is precisely through the camouflage of mundanity that food offers the children of interfaith families a pathway through which religious practices can be, however imperfectly, woven together.

DISCUSSION QUESTIONS

1. Thinking about the examples in this article, do you think that familial relationships can create a form of religion? Why or why not?
2. What kinds of Christian and Jewish blending are made possible by food? What kinds of blending are not?
3. Consider the idea that Christian and Jewish cultures are treated differently in American society. Jewish food practices are commonly accepted as such. Christian food practices are less frequently considered "Christian" but are connected to ethnic identities. How might that difference shape how interfaith families understand what counts as a "Christian" or "Jewish" tradition? How does this article affect your understanding of those distinctions?

NOTES

I would like to thank my fellow members of the AAR seminar group Religion, Food, and Eating for their thoughtful comments on this essay. I would also like to thank members of the MARIAL Center at Emory University and Brian Campbell, Letitia Campbell, David King, Gary Laderman, Lerone Martin, Linda Mehta, Anthony Petro, John Senior, and Angela Tarango for offering feedback at various stages of the writing process. Their contributions have improved the essay greatly. Any errors that remain are mine alone.

1. Throughout the essay, the food referred to as Jewish food is eastern European. Jews with family backgrounds in other parts of the world—for instance, North Africa, Spain, or the Middle East—would have different familial traditions. While other Jewish food traditions are certainly part of the American Jewish culinary scene, the majority of American Jews are from an eastern European background, and therefore those foods dominated these sources.

2. *Bridget Loves Bernie*, episode 1, first broadcast September 16, 1972. Directed by Richard Kinon and written by Bernard Slade. *Bridget Loves Bernie* spent one highly controversial year, from 1972 to 1973, on CBS. Because it depicted interfaith marriage in a lighthearted manner, a variety of Jewish communal groups, pulpit rabbis, and letters from Jewish viewers encouraged the network to cancel the show. Though CBS claimed that community pressure was not a factor, it canceled *Bridget Loves Bernie*, citing a ratings dip. The show, which was the fifth most popular on television the year it was canceled, remains, at the time of this writing, the most highly rated show to be canceled by a television network.

3. Benjamin Zeller fleshes out this understanding of religion in chapter 15 of this volume.

4. Robert A. Orsi, *Between Heaven and Earth: The Religious Worlds People Make and the Scholars Who Study Them* (Princeton: Princeton University Press, 2006), 2.

5. Effin Older, *My Two Grandmothers* (New York: Harcourt Children's Books, 2000); and Ron Gompertz, *Chrismukkah: Everything You Need to Know to Celebrate the Hybrid Holiday* (New York: Stewart, Tabori and Chang, 2006).

6. A Donald Duck is a beverage that Lily enjoys at Bubbe Silver's country club. It consists of three layers of liquid—one red, one blue, and one green. Lily considers it a magic drink because the colors do not run together.

7. Ironically, while the food traditions are clearly passed from woman to woman, they are associated with the last names, "Lane" and "Silver." At no point does the book acknowledge this tension.

8. Elizabeth H. Pleck, *Celebrating the Family: Ethnicity, Consumer Culture, and Family Rituals* (Cambridge: Harvard University Press, 2000).

9. "The Year in Buzzwords," *Time Magazine*, December 20, 2004.

10. Gompertz, *Chrismukkah*, 10, 16.

11. Ibid., 90, 91.

12. "Mixed Families Set to Celebrate 'Chrismukkah': NPR," *NPR.org*, n.d., http://www.npr.org/templates/story/story.php?storyId=6630803.

13. Pleck, *Celebrating the Family*, 29.

14. For more on the history of Thanksgiving and its Protestant roots, see ibid., chap. 2; and Diana Muir, "Proclaiming Thanksgiving Throughout the Land: From Local to National Holiday" in *We Are What We Celebrate: Understanding Holidays and Rituals*, ed. Amitai Etzioni and Jared Bloom, 194–212 (New York: New York University Press, 2004).

15. Gompertz, *Chrismukkah*, 88.

16. Laurel Snyder, *Half/Life: Jew-ish Tales from Interfaith Homes* (Berkeley: Soft Skull Press, 2006), 4.

17. Many American Jews do not keep kosher, and of those who do, many follow some but not all kosher laws.

18. Thisbe Nissen, "Bury the Knife in Yonkers, or Bibbity Bobbity Jew," in Snyder, *Half/Life*, 43–52.

19. Hasia R. Diner, *Hungering for America: Italian, Irish, and Jewish Foodways in the Age of Migration* (Cambridge: Harvard University Press, 2003); Carol Harris-Shapiro, "Bloody Shankbones and Braided Bread: The Food Voice and the Fashioning of American Jewish Identities," *Food & Foodways: History & Culture of Human Nourishment* 14, no. 2 (April 2006): 67–90; Andrew R. Heinze, *Adapting to Abundance: Jewish Immigrants, Mass Consumption, and the Search for American Identity* (New York: Columbia University Press, 1992); and Jenna Weissman Joselit, *The Wonders of America: Reinventing Jewish Culture 1880–1950* (New York: Henry Holt, 2002).

20. For more information on the separation of ethnic identity from Catholicism, see Jay P. Dolan, *In Search of an American Catholicism: A History of Religion and Culture in Tension, Trade* (New York: Oxford University Press, 2003).

21. Daniel Sack, *Whitebread Protestants: Food and Religion in American Culture*, ill. ed. (New York: St. Martin's, 2001), 222.

22. Nissen, "Bury the Knife in Yonkers, or Bibbity Bobbity Jew," 50.

23. R. Marie Griffith, *Born Again Bodies: Flesh and Spirit in American Christianity*. (Berkeley: University of California Press, 2004).

24. Nissen, "Bury the Knife in Yonkers, or Bibbity Bobbity Jew," 50, 47.

25. Mary Helene Rosenbaum, "Introduction," in *The Dovetail Institute's Big Book of Christmas and Hanukkah: Celebrations for Christmas and Hanukkah* (2007), 1.

26. Mary Helene Rosenbaum and Stanley Ned Rosenbaum, *Celebrating Our Differences: Living Two Faiths in One Marriage*, rev. ed. (New York: Ragged Edge Press, 1998).

27. Rosenbaum, "Introduction," 1.

28. Jennifer Steinhauer, "In the Kitchen of Long Ago, with Grandma," *New York Times*, December 19, 2007, http://www.nytimes.com/2007/12/19/dining/19gran.html?scp=1&sq=christmas%20cookies%20interfaith&st=cse.

RECOMMENDED READING

Diner, Hasia R. *Hungering for America: Italian, Irish, and Jewish Foodways in the Age of Migration*. Cambridge: Harvard University Press, 2003.

Etzioni, Amitai, and Jared Bloom. *We Are What We Celebrate: Understanding Holidays and Rituals*. New York: New York University Press, 2004.

Pleck, Elizabeth H. *Celebrating the Family: Ethnicity, Consumer Culture, and Family Rituals*. Cambridge: Harvard University Press, 2000.

Sack, Daniel. *Whitebread Protestants: Food and Religion in American Culture*. New York: St. Martin's, 2001.

Part 3

NEGOTIATED FOODWAYS

Nine

CRYSTALLIZING SUBJECTIVITIES IN THE AFRICAN DIASPORA

SUGAR, HONEY, AND THE GODS OF AFRO-CUBAN LUCUMÍ

ELIZABETH PÉREZ

S INCE THE 1889 publication of William Robertson Smith's immensely influential *Lectures on the Religion of the Semites*, the issue of sacrifice, along with questions concerning the ethics and aesthetics of religious violence, have governed the scholarly discussion about the offerings that gods, ancestors, and other spirits are envisioned as receiving. In many religions and traditional cultures, sacrifice has been performed by men, and food preparation by women; this division of ritual labor along gendered lines, and the widespread denigration of "women's work," has reinforced academic neglect of religious offerings that do not involve the death of a victim. As a result, considerably less attention has been paid to cooking itself and to the culinary styles devised to flatter the palates of deities and ancestors. However, scholars are increasingly aware of the fact that the tremendous variety of nutritional conventions and dietary requirements observed in the feeding of supernatural entities holds out an incomparable opportunity to analyze the way human worshippers conceptualize their relationship to them.

One undertheorized ingredient of commonly ritualized foods is sugar, appearing in such diverse contexts as the candy-pellet *prasad* distributed in Hindu temples; the *amrit*, or holy sugar water, that plays a central role in Sikh ceremonies; and the sugar skulls arrayed on graves and altars on the Mexican Día de los Muertos that coincides with the Roman Catholic All Saints' and All Souls' Days. In the Afro-Cuban religion variously called *regla ocha*, Santería, or Lucumí, sugar is an important element in meals offered to the spirits of West African origin called *orishas*. Lucumí practitioners prize sugarcane and its by-products not simply for their sweetness—much less for their connection to Africa—but rather for their ability to serve as media to reinscribe and amplify highly differentiated characteristics attributed to the deities.[1] Although initiates tend to posit mythological origins for the orishas' tastes, they have been ineluctably structured with reference to the racial discourse of colonial Cuba. This discourse arranged bodies in a hierarchy according to gender, class, and color—a concept elaborated most thoroughly in the slaveholding societies of the Americas.[2]

The following essay explores the use of sugar by Lucumí practitioners and reveals the extent to which Cuban history and culture have shaped their tastes. I show that even the orishas did not escape the systemic discriminatory treatment inflicted on Afro-Cubans during the colonial period.[3] After briefly reviewing the history of sugar in Cuba, I focus on two of the major Lucumí orishas, Ogún and Ochún, understood to have food preferences deemed consistent with their respective socioeconomic statuses, and to crave different types of sugar based on them. I argue that Lucumí practitioners have traditionally sought to challenge the dominant sociopolitical and cultural order by inverting secular reality in ritual practice and transforming sugar, the commodity par excellence, into value-laden gifts for the gods.[4] As we will see, the religious meaning of sugar in Lucumí lies embedded in the soil of its cultural and historical contexts and is to be found under the fingernails of those who have labored to produce it.

SUGAR CONSUMPTION IN HISTORICAL AND CULTURAL PERSPECTIVE

Throughout the Caribbean, sugarcane has sweetened more fortunes and embittered more lives than any other commodity. Christopher Columbus introduced cane to the West Indies on his second voyage, possibly at the behest of a close relative: his first mother-in-law, the owner of a sugar estate in Madeira.[5] In Cuba, the largest of the Antilles, sugar would become the central fact of its economic life. Between 1765 and 1790 about two thousand slaves arrived in Cuba per year for the sole purpose of sugar production.[6] In 1791 a slave uprising that became the Haitian Revolution wiped the French colony of Saint-Domingue off of the economic map, paving the way for an unprecedented agricultural boom in Cuba. The prevalence of sugar plantations, often owned by absentee landlords, shaped the island's culture, politics, and society. Despite stiff competition from Brazilian cane and German beets, by 1868, fully one-third of the world's sugar came from Cuba.[7] The so-called Pearl of the Antilles was made not of nacre, but of sucrose.

During the colonial period, cane cultivation called for the unprecedented movement of accumulated capital and indentured servants from Europe and Asia; slaves entered the Americas in staggering numbers. Most West and Central African slaves arrived in Cuba between 1764 and 1868. During the middle third of the nineteenth century, many of these slaves hailed from culturally and linguistically related groups later to be called Yorùbá.[8] The Yorùbá carried with them their historical memory and a religion replete with festivals and calendrical rites; different oracular forms, including those of the Ifá and sixteen-cowries systems; food taboos acquired according to divinatory mandate; and a set of protocols for initiation into the priesthood based on personal vocation rather than heredity or ethnicity.[9] The Yorùbá also rendered tribute to a category of spirits and patrons called òrìsà (orisha), considered to be the divine patrons of practitioners and periodically summoned through music in spirit possession ceremonies that promote communal cohesion and individual well-being.[10] By the mid-twentieth century the worship of these deities would be termed Lucumí or regla ocha—"the rule of the orishas"—by practitioners, and Santería by detractors.

Slaves interpreted the imagery, narrative, and material objects they encountered for the first time in the New World in keeping with West and Central African cultural frameworks.[11] Sugar was almost entirely absent from precolonial Yorùbáland, but in the Caribbean sugar became a main ingredient in the slave diet, providing laborers with an "energy boost" to fuel them in the cane fields and boiling-houses, where they sometimes put in two eight-hour shifts a day. Sugar eventually entered the repertoire of food offerings given to the orishas and other spirits, enlarging an African-derived ritual vocabulary that had long used only honey to signify sweetness. Sugar became a node of political-economic and symbolic value creation among slaves as well as masters in Cuba; cane juice and stalks came to figure conspicuously in Lucumí cultural memory and religious worship. According to prominent orisha priest and historian Miguel "Willie" Ramos, no host of a contemporary drum ritual would consider his duties complete without first ordering dozens of pastries and special breads from a local shop. Ramos asserts, "This . . . is definitely a Cuban phenomenon, especially the addition of sweets and desserts to the orisha's food preferences, a practice [unheard of] in Yorubaland."[12]

To appreciate the significance of sugar in Lucumí, we must first become familiar with its consumption by slaves. Historical studies of Saccharum officinarum (sugarcane) tend to focus on African slaves as producers of sugar rather than consumers, and for good reason, as most of the cane processed before the twentieth century was shipped abroad to meet Europe's growing demand for this commodity as a sweetener.[13] Yet slaves also ate sugar. Many colonists approached the plantation as a laboratory, in which slaveholders and doctors could test untried techniques—including the ingestion of sugar for a variety of ills—on captive subjects. Throughout the Caribbean the leading men of science endeavored to downplay the horrors of slavery and propose that the cure for ailments from the Old World might be found in the New. Natural histories and medical manuals published prior to emancipation inadvertently paint a grim portrait of the conditions under which captives toiled on plantations. In this literature, the overall fitness of slaves despite on-the-job abuse and malnutrition is seldom viewed as cause for alarm, but instead is offered as proof of the positive attributes of sugar consumption.[14]

Drawing on a combination of oral tradition and trial and error, slaves and freed people developed their own applications for sucrose.[15] They saw the curative potential of sugarcane as well as its evils. They passed down both their ethnobotanical and culinary expertise to creole descendants, leaving an ingenious record of sugary beverages and other calorie-rich gastronomical delights.[16] But what of sugar's religious applications? For those initiated into Lucumí, Saccharum officinarum numbers among the plants, grasses, and roots belonging to the orisha Osanyin, the "lord of leaves."[17] Lydia Cabrera included sugar in the encyclopedic inventory of medicinal plants and herbs of her 1954 magnum opus, El monte: igbo finda, ewe orisha, vititi nfinda. Cabrera tells us that sugar can sweeten one's patron spirit, any adversary, and "everyone else in need of sweetening," relating a spell: "In a glass of water with two spoonfuls of sugar, place a lit candle and a piece of paper with the name of somebody you wish to sweeten to the point of . . . melting."[18] Cabrera's indications follow the principle of sympathetic magic, in which substances attract objects that have similar qualities and "an effect resembles its cause." Oils, powders, premixed cleansers, and even wands of incense laced with sugar are still sold today in the North American religious supply stores called *botánicas*, to be used in an analogous fashion by practitioners of Lucumí and other Afro-Caribbean religions.[19]

EATING TO LIVE, FEEDING FOR LIFE

Lucumí myths and divinatory verses furnish the theological basis for religious offerings, including the appropriate uses of sugar. They attempt to explain gustatory patterns, speculate on the origins of spirits' consumption practices, and stress the importance of indulging each spirit's individual tastes. For instance, Bolívar Aróstegui relates a story that features Olofi, the Yorùbá ruler of the universe.[20] Olofi sends the orishas to fight an enemy threatening his realm, and one by one they are defeated—not by arrows, but by the delectable dishes his enemy serves to them. Prepared according to the orishas' personal preferences, the meals promptly lull the eaters to sleep. Only the cemetery-dwelling Oyá, no doubt more accustomed to the odor of decay than to that of delicacies, resists the onslaught of tempting victuals! This story not only accounts for Oyá's reputation as warrior, queen, and leader of the dead; it also illustrates that the path to an orisha's heart (and to one's own desires) runs through his or her stomach. The devotee must heed the precedent established by Olofi's enemy and observe the orishas' tastes, if one would bend them to one's will.

But how is it that, in the Lucumí tradition, orishas are understood to "want," to "request," even to "eat"? The construction of spirits' subjectivity, reflected in this choice of words, merits close attention. Practitioners treat the orishas as entities similar to themselves, crediting them with agency, sensitivity to sensory stimuli, and aesthetic sensibilities. Such spirits possess something approximating the embodied "practical sense" called "habitus" by sociologist Pierre Bourdieu and defined by him as "an acquired system of preferences, of principles of vision and division (what is usually called taste), and also a system of durable cognitive structures (which are essentially the product of the internalization of objective structures) and schemes of action which orient the perception of the situation and the appropriate response."[21]

Offerings do not merely communicate an intention on the part of the devotee to build a relationship with orishas but indeed "can be held to *constitute* objects of devotion."[22] By assigning a "habitus" to orishas, practitioners manage to render impersonal forces vividly anthropomorphic, in effect creating them as subjects with whom they may enter into relationships mediated by gestures, sentiments, and material things. Through the investigation of the orishas' appetites, we can glean insights into the ways that orishas' personae have changed over time, as well as their perceived social location and occupational role vis-à-vis other spirits.

By offering food to the orishas, whether on festive occasions or somber ones, practitioners today attempt to cross the divide thought to separate divine Other from human self. Lucumí are taught that the spirits temporarily assume the characteristics of mortals—sensing hunger, thirst, and pleasure—in order to become subjects with whom communities and individuals may interact. Among Lucumí and related groups in the Afro-Atlantic world, metaphors of seeing and eating overlap, as if the taste buds of the spirits were in their eyes: neglect is "hunger," the spectacle of ritual activity, "food."[23] Although practitioners put themselves in subordinate positions relative to the orishas, they strive to attain a degree of intimacy with them that demands a firm grasp of each spirit's professed habits and proclivities. Novices soon learn that an orisha's nutritional requirements and dietary restrictions mirror his or her temperament, accomplishments, feuds, and bonds with other spirits. Favorite dishes are shorthand for personae.

Food offerings form part of elaborate displays, such as the custom-made assortment of fruits and special dishes called *plaza*, spread out for the orishas in front of altars for rites of passage and other ceremonies. In these displays sweetening agents are meant to gladden the tongues of the orishas so that they will reply generously to petitions.[24] These foods are not intended solely for the orishas' mouths, however; human guests actually consume the lion's share of food offerings after events such as drum rituals, and the ensuing feasts serve a number of interrelated purposes.[25] Guests at these communal meals are thought to incorporate the *ashé*, or sacred energy, from food consecrated through the orishas' acceptance.[26] Once infused with ashé, food becomes an extension of the orisha's per-

FIGURE 9.1   Altar constructed for drum ceremony in honor of Ochún, with Cuban sweets (including sponge cakes in rum syrup and guava-filled puff pastries) on the left and sheet cake on the right. In between the rows of fruit, cellophane wrappers hold party favors containing honey and brown sugar. August 2006. Photo by Elizabeth Pérez, used gratefully with permission from D.S.

son, and eating it acts to redistribute the ashé and seal blessings into the human body impossible to obtain without direct corporal absorption.[27] The function of communal meals thus goes far beyond the satisfaction of physical hunger, for "consumption activity is the joint production, with fellow consumers, of a universe of values."[28] To delve more deeply into this universe, we now enter the orbits of two very dissimilar, even diametrically opposed, orishas: Ogún and Ochún.

SOUL FOOD: THE ROOTS OF THE ORISHAS' SWEET TEETH

Most orishas have a sweet tooth. The elderly, imperturbable creator spirit Obatalá eats meringues and rice puddings prepared with white sugar—

all relatively soft foods that may be gummed by those without teeth.[29] Yemayá, the maternal ruler of the seven seas, savors burnt-coconut candy encrusted with brown sugar, as well as delicacies made from sweet potato.[30] Fiery masquerader Oyá devours *torrejas*, the "Spanish French toast" that dresses up day-old bread in egg, milk, and cinnamon sugar.[31] The prank-playing, joke-telling trickster Eleguá quite literally takes the cake, snacking on "the food of license, thumb-sucking, finger-licking, lip-smacking food—popcorn, jawbreakers, candy canes, cotton candy, pull-taffy, all-day suckers, stick-out-your-tongue, nonsense foods, bubble gum, lollipops, mary janes, squirrel nuts."[32] By contrast, the virile, lawgiving orisha Changó, the deity of lightning, insists on tall stems of cane with a regal demeanor reminiscent of his own; shoots cut into foot-long pieces also index his phallic potency.[33] In some communities Babalú Ayé, the orisha of illness, receives hard candies dotted with sesame seeds that recall the pox scars and lesions on his body; he is the only major orisha, besides Olokun, to accept white sugar crystals as well, no doubt because of their grainy texture and resemblance to tiny clogged pores scattered over pimpled flesh.[34]

Initiates identify most spirits as either hot or cool in temperament; the former eat strongly flavored, spicy dishes, while a few of the latter consume light-colored foods so bland they do not even contain salt. Although these terms derive from centuries-old Yorùbá categories, Lucumí practitioners now view these designations through the scratched and pitted lens of history. To wit, the "cultural hero" Ogún is the consummate hunter, warrior, and ironsmith.[35] He married Oyá, but she soon tired of his misanthropic ways and left him for his brother, Changó. A loner, Ogún lusts after women yet tends to mistreat them and counts among his only companions the forest-dwelling Eleguá, Ochósi, and Osanyin. According to myth, he lives in a hut next door to his forge and owns seven implements of labor, called *herramientas*, nestled in cauldron-shaped pots consecrated to him; these tools include an awl, a spade, and a hammer. Ogún rules the razor's edge and protects human handlers of metal, including miners, tattoo artists, butchers, surgeons, and mechanics. Ogún's solitary, arduous existence has its rewards, such as access to rare pelts and meats. He has no family to maintain and, of course, no masters—unless one counts some orishas for whom he runs errands, and others occasionally able to best him.

Ogún undoubtedly appealed most to those at the bottom of the social ladder in colonial Cuba. He lives in the woods and blazes trails, literally and figuratively; in this sense he may be interpreted as a runaway slave, marching to the beat of his own drummer. In fact, men possessed by Ogún—in rituals that employ the sacred drums called batá—frequently dance stripped to the waist, with bandannas wrapped tightly around their heads and fringes of dried palm fronds fastened around their hips.[36] When incorporated by both men and women, Ogún executes movements in dance that evoke his mythological incarnations "as warrior (brandishing his machete as a weapon), cultivator (clearing away underbrush), and smith (hammering iron)."[37] The person possessed by Ogún appears to slice repeatedly through dense foliage or deliver fatal blows, performing gestures that he or she may not remember seeing or even recognize. Nevertheless, Ogún's identity within the community condenses a collective memory of forced labor that is transmitted to every Lucumí initiate and finds routine expression at the level of the individual body.

In both Cuba and Brazil, devotees envision Ogún as the "patron deity of slave revolt."[38] To judge from his brusque behavior in possession rituals, his rejection of the house slaves' lifestyle has given him a chip on his well-muscled shoulder when dealing with more domesticated, nobler, cooler spirits. While practitioners possessed by royal orishas are dressed in crowns and vestments fit for monarchs, those seized by Ogún sometimes don "the dress attire of Spanish-Cuban military officers because of his role as a guerrero ('warrior')."[39] Even in this case, Ogún does not lose his association with slavery, for a large percentage of Afro-Cuban former slaves fought in the Wars of Independence as the freedom fighters called mambíses, rising from the status of foot soldiers to key positions within the Cuban Liberation Army.[40] Fernando Ortiz records accounts that some of the troops included runaway slaves pressed into service by the mambíses and sought Ogún's assistance by sacrificing to him in the bush, hoping to reinforce their assaults against the Spanish with magico-religious maneuvers.[41]

Ogún's consumption of sugar typifies that of field hands, no-collar laborers, and outdoorsmen.[42] Some of Ogún's recipes require red palm oil, hot in color as well as taste, along with chilies and ground pepper—two spices long used to render rancid foods palatable.[43] Initiates' familiarity with the manner in which sugarcane is eaten also contributes to Ogún's reputation as rude and untutored. To get at the soft pith of the sugar cane, one cuts away the hard, woody rind of the cane, or gnaws at it with one's teeth until the shell splits to expose the inner pulp. The juice is extracted through sheer suction, and one draws out moisture with the lips and tongue as if slurping the marrow from a bone. This image of consumption with neither dishware nor utensils fits Ogún to a tee; he does not hesitate to get his hands dirty and cannot help eating a vegetable as if it were meat. In addition to sugarcane, he also chews taffy (made from sugar, molasses, green lemon juice, and lard or oil), a compact treat easily concealed under the tongue from a fellow laborer or authority figure. Sharing is not Ogún's forte.

"Ogún has a cast-iron stomach and is said to be immune to poison," Mason writes. "His devotees concoct a peppery liquor called samba. . . . I have seen it peel the [flesh] off a devotee's hand."[44] Ogún's usual beverage of choice, *aguardiente*, an unaged rum, says volumes about not only his character as imagined by Lucumí but also the everyday life of plantation slaves. His shots of aguardiente remind one of the snorts handed out to cane-cutters at dawn, to jolt them into action as well as give them the illusion of greeting the day on full stomachs. According to David H. Brown, Ogún's use for this liquor does not end with intoxication: even his iron tools are periodically washed with aguardiente rather than water.[45] Ogún's aversion to bathing seems of a piece with his poverty and isolation, yet other orishas respect him as a formidable herbalist, aided in the hunt by weedy bundles of charms. His sideline as medicine man is registered in his consumption of *prú*, a pungent liqueur consisting of aguardiente and a tea brewed with herbs, roots, ground pepper, cinnamon, and aniseed, buried in a glass jar, and unearthed no sooner than three days later.[46]

LIQUID SUGAR

In one praise-song documented during a contemporary Nigerian festival, Yorùbá elders extolled the spirit Yemoja as "receiver of the crown of childbearing women, who has breasts of honey."[47] In Cuba, however, the orisha Ochún—goddess of wealth, intelligence, beauty, romance, and sensory pleasure—is the spirit most strongly associated with honey. She mainly receives biscuits and pastries, including the cigar-shaped *sopas borrachas* ("drunken soups"), dripping with honey and mellowed rum. She also accepts cane sugar manipulated to mimic the taste of honey, as in her vanilla egg custards, caramel flans, fruit jellies, and *yemas dobles* ("double yolks"). Some of her favorite dishes, such as boiled winter squash daubed with honey, shade toward the savory, but even the fishy dishes that Ochún craves taste sweet, as does the sparingly seasoned and easily digestible *ochinchín*, prepared with freshwater shrimp, Swiss chard, watercress eggs, and almonds.[48]

Offerings of honey and liquid sugar not only index Ochún's overwhelming sweetness of character but also bring to mind several myths in which she wields honey in the commission of a transgression, if not exactly a crime. In one story Ochún comes to "own" honey by seducing Olofi (the "owner of Heaven" himself) with the sweet substance, thus exposing his hypocrisy and vindicating Babalú Ayé, whom Olofi had excoriated for his sexual excesses.[49] According to a divinatory verse, her lawful husband Orúnmila suspects her of infidelity with Ogún; Orúnmila buys a parrot to spy on her, but she silences the bird by feeding it palm wine, honey, and aguardiente.[50] She even seduces the dead, plying the leader of the ancestors' realm with honey and rum.[51] In the most famous of her myths, however, Ochún acts as an agent of civilization. She entices Ogún out of self-imposed exile in the forest by smearing his lips with honey and luring him to town, thereby restoring the recluse to a productive place in society.[52]

Although honey usually connotes the epitome of sweetness in word and deed, Ochún's can turn bad in a heartbeat. Her honey can bring both pleasure and pain. Ochún is reputed to cause stomach ailments, dysentery, hepatitis, and diabetes, thus injuriously "'sweeten[ing]' the bloodstream of many an offender."[53] She employs her special brand of honey to capture as well as to emancipate. Castellanos points out, "'Honey' . . . can stand for her sexuality, for her suave ways of conducting business, and it also represents a means to attain freedom."[54] Indeed, Ochún cannot draw Ogún out of the woods without captivating him first, so she combines the role of bounty hunter with that of femme fatale, teasing him into submission before returning him to the life of hard labor he had fled. This aspect of Ochún does not leave a sour taste in the mouths of devotees but rather appears to substantiate the claim that she has brass balls as well as a honey-eyed tongue.

Ochún also avails herself of honey as a glue to affix prosperity and other blessings onto her devotees. For instance, in June 2008 a drum ceremony was held for Nilaja Campbell, the leader of the Chicago-based, predominantly African American Lucumí community Ilé Laroye, in her twenty-first year of initiation.[55] Ochún possessed a visiting initiate, and after she was escorted away from the drums to be dressed in a satiny sequined cap and blouse, she rejoined the crowd balancing a white plate full of honey on her head. She not only stopped to embrace practitioners en route to salute the drums without dropping the plate but also danced vigorously with it perched atop her crown. She dipped dollar bills in the honey and pressed them to the foreheads of the praise singer and a favored few. Then she coated a five-dollar-bill with honey and pasted it onto the wall above the front door of Campbell's home, where it would stay for several days. No one could have missed the symbolism, since five is Ochún's sacred number.

Many myths juxtapose the coolly cunning Ochún with the hot-tempered Ogún, and the types of sugar they each prefer render the differences between them edible as well as tangible. Ochún's sugar disguises its origins in sweat and blood through a strenuous process of purification, becoming virtually imperishable in granulated form and dissolving into other substances, leaving no discernible trace except appetite-whetting sweetness. By contrast, the sugar that Ogún receives does not permit the initiate to forget the work necessary for its cultivation.[56] Ogún stands for the untrammeled potential of primordial matter, while Ochún embodies the savoir faire necessary to convert chaos into order—or cane into sugar.[57] But the mythologies of Ochún and Ogún also record the struggle between the colonial figures they bring to life: the plantation slave and the mulatta. Just as Ogún, in myth and spirit possession, exemplifies the agricultural laborer of African descent seldom acknowledged historically, so Ochún embodies the iconic mixed-race, or mulatta, woman of leisure, graced with wavy hair, caramel-hued limbs, and indomitable coquetry.[58]

Ochún is often typecast as a "high yellow" woman capable—as a result of her relative pallor, features, and deportment—to pass as white and enter social spaces forbidden to both darker-skinned women of African descent and mulatto men. Ochún seems to toy with Ogún, never deigning to wed him (as, for example, Oyá does). The nature of their relationship bespeaks the incompatible social locations ascribed to these spirits. "By the nineteenth century," Mendieta Costa states, "[the mulatta] was part of a growing middle sector, urban and free. She was already the sensual, exotic, volatile woman, and a huntress of white men."[59] The mulatta had better prospects than did her male counterpart, since she was able to wrest some mobility from the social system by building alliances with elites, thereby improving her material status and that of her elders.[60] Conversely, men of color seldom enjoyed the luxury of moving up and across racial barriers through marriage or informal relations.[61] While in Ogún's case beggars can't be choosers, Ochún has options and eats—rice fragrant with filaments of saffron, once the costliest spice on earth; fricasseed poultry in a sauce buttery enough to convince the ascetic to become a glutton—as if she wants to do so, not out of need.

In nineteenth-century Cuba, stereotypes of mulattas gained currency in nonverbal and popular visual forms, through countless newspaper caricatures and the lithographs called *marquillas* disseminated in bundles of cigars and cigarettes.[62] A series of marquillas entitled *Samples of Sugar from My Mill* featured mulattas of varying complexions labeled with short captions that employed the blunt vocabulary of the sugar industry to indicate their desirability: *Quebrado de primera (de centrifuga)*, "First-rate (from the centrifuge)"; *Blanco de segunda (tren comun)*, "Second-grade white (common train)"; *Quebrado de segunda*, "Second-rate"; *Melaza* or *melao de caña*, "Molasses"; and *Cucurucho*, the brownest and lowest quality.[63] According to the racist discourse of the colonial period, white women presented men with well-wrought but frigid limbs, whereas women of African descent had voluptuous bodies disfigured by a combination of melanin and labor.[64] Ochún thus stood between first-rate and second-grade white: technically "impure," but elegant, polished, and toothsome nevertheless.[65]

The Lucumí tradition has addressed entrenched patterns of discrimination perpetuated by such stereotypes in a religious idiom. In the New World each orisha came to be paired with a Roman Catholic saint or apparition of the Blessed Virgin Mary, and icons continue to represent the Lucumí spirits on household altars and elsewhere. Ochún became associated with the copper-complexioned Virgin of Charity, or Caridad. Although the everyday elevation of the mulatta over other women of African descent was anything but colorblind, Caridad eventually came to personify unity among Cubans of indigenous Taíno, African, European, and Asian descent.[66] Ironically, this youthful and attractive Virgin's correspondence with Ochún in popular culture has tended to reinforce the folkloric depiction of this orisha as a one-dimensional flirt. Yet Caridad's patriotic title as the patroness of Cuba—"La Virgen Mambisa . . . fierce freedom fighter"—also suggests Ochún's extraordinary martial prowess.[67] As if in response to the usual limitations foisted on her—as on other women of African descent—divination verses and praise-songs paint a vibrant picture of Ochún as wizened medicine woman, affluent matron, talented diviner, weaver, potter, and merchant, with a vulture as her fearless, carrion-eating familiar.[68]

TOWARD THE FUTURE OF FOOD OFFERINGS

There is no idol as expensive as the stomach; it receives offerings every day.
—YORÙBÁ PROVERB[69]

African-inspired religions throughout the Americas owe much to the ingenuity of slaves faced with foreign substances and situations. Their cuisines emerged as "writing in code," replete with neologisms, double entendres, and clever turns of phrase formulated to communicate with spirits as well as other persons.[70] While practitioners of the Lucumí tradition regard aesthetic forms and styles as embodying values, it is food that lays the foundation for social relations.[71] They feed the orishas in order to preserve themselves, and to nourish a vital source of oppositional identity and community. Sacred meals become mnemonic devices, facilitating the recollection of myths shot through with the countermemory of Afro-Atlantic historical experience erased or omitted entirely from the official record.[72] It may well be that the power of sugar in Lucumí resides not so much in its sweetness as in the sweat and tears of coerced labor that sucrose crystallizes, and that devotees invite the spirits to share. As orisha worship continues to attract followers around the world, there is no guarantee that sugar will carry the same meanings delineated above, but there will undoubtedly be the need for tastes that conjure both the honeyed and bitter flavor of history.

DISCUSSION QUESTIONS

1. What role did enslaved Africans and their descendants play in the development of sugar as a modern staple?
2. Identify some characteristics of Yorùbá traditional religion to be found in Afro-Cuban Lucumí. Why might these African-derived beliefs and practices have survived in the Caribbean?
3. How does eating together and feeding the spirits ceremonially create community in Lucumí?

4. In what ways do food offerings manage to convey the personalities of different spirits?

5. How does sugar serve to indicate the gendered, racial, and class distinctions between Ochún and Ogún?

NOTES

I am sincerely grateful to Nilaja Campbell and the members of the community I call Ilé Laroye in this article for their great patience, material assistance, and tremendous generosity. I would also like to give my heartfelt thanks to D.S. for her gracious support and very kind permission to reproduce the accompanying photograph.

1. See Peter McKenzie, *Hail Orisha! A Phenomenology of a West African Religion in the Mid-Nineteenth Century* (Brill: Leiden, 1997), 12, 205, 264, 285; William Bascom, "Yoruba Food," *Africa* 11 (1951), 47; and Anthony Buckley, *Yoruba Medicine* (New York: Athelia Henrietta, 1997), 8, 79.

2. Ira Berlin, "From Creole to African: Atlantic Creoles and the Origins of African-American Society in Mainland North America," *William and Mary Quarterly* 53 (1994): 251–88.

3. Bruce Lincoln, *Theorizing Myth: Narrative, Ideology, and Scholarship* (Chicago: University of Chicago Press, 1999), 147.

4. Ibid., 150; and Michel de Certeau, *The Practice of Everyday Life* (Berkeley: University of California Press, 1984), 36–37.

5. Hugh Thomas, *Cuba, or, The Pursuit of Freedom* (New York: Da Capo, 1998 [1971]), 28 n. 8.

6. Manuel Moreno Fraginals, *The Sugarmill: the Socioeconomic Complex of Sugar in Cuba, 1760–1860*, trans. Cedric Belfrage (New York: Monthly Review, 1976). See also Fernando Ortiz, *Contrapunteo cubano del tabaco y el azúcar* (Barcelona: Editorial Ariel, 1963 [1947]).

7. Ralph Lee Woodward Jr., "The Political Economy of the Caribbean," in *The South and The Caribbean*, ed. Douglass Sullivan-González and Charles Reagan Wilson, 137, 141 (Jackson: University Press of Mississippi, 2001).

8. Jorge Castellanos and Isabel Castellanos, "The Geographic, Ethnologic, and Linguistic Roots of Cuban Blacks," *Cuban Studies* 17 (1987): 95–110.

9. Stephan Palmié, "Ethnogenetic Processes and Cultural Transfer in Caribbean Slave Populations," in *Slavery in the Americas*, ed. W. Binder (Würzburg: Königshäuser & Neumann, 1993), 346.

10. Possession in such traditions scarcely resembles its mainstream portrayal in films and on television; possessing spirits spend most of their time

ceremonially listening to problems, delivering advice, diagnosing illness, performing health-related cleansing rites, and offering blessings to their worshippers.

11. Andrew Apter, "Herskovits's Heritage: Rethinking Syncretism in the African Diaspora," *Diaspora* 1, no. 3 (1991): 235–60.

12. Miguel "Willie" Ramos, "The Empire Beats On: Oyo, Batá Drums, and Hegemony in Nineteenth-Century Cuba," M.A. thesis, Florida International University, 2000, 223–24.

13. Sidney W. Mintz, *Sweetness and Power: The Place of Sugar in Modern History* (New York: Penguin, 1985).

14. Benjamin Moseley, *A Treatise on Sugar with Miscellaneous Medical Observations*, 2nd ed. (London: John Nichols, 1800), 144. See also Robert John Thornton, *A New Family Herbal: or, Popular Account of the Natures and Properties of the Various Plants Used in Medicine, Diet and the Arts* (London: R. Phillips, 1810); William Ed Grimé, *Botany of the Black Americans* (St. Clair Shores, Mich.: Scholarly, 1976); and Mintz, *Sweetness and Power*, 175.

15. Argelio Santiesteban, *Uno y el mismo: Notas de folklore cubano, con especial atención a sus puntos de contacto con el folklore de otros pueblos* (Habana: Ediciones Unión, 1995), 44; Lydia Cabrera, *El monte: igbo finda, ewe orisha, vititi nfinda* (Miami: C&R, 1975 [1954]), 366; and José Seone Gallo, *El folclor médico de Cuba: enfermedades de la piel* (La Habana: Editorial de Ciencias Sociales, 1993).

16. Miguel Barnet, *Biography of a Runaway Slave*, trans. Nick Hill (Willimantic: Curbstone Press, 1994), 100, 141, 142; and Natalia Bolívar Aróstegui, *Afro-Cuban Cuisine: Its Myths and Legends*, trans. Carmen González Díaz de Villegas, 14–15 (La Habana: Editorial José Martí, 1998).

17. 'Wande Abimbola, *Ifá Will Mend Our Broken World: Thoughts on Yoruba Religion and Culture in Africa* (Roxbury: Aim Books, 1997), 74.

18. Cabrera, *El monte*, 366; ellipses in original.

19. James George Frazer, *The Golden Bough: A Study in Magic and Religion* (New York: Macmillan, 1922), 37. See also Carolyn Morrow Long, *Spiritual Merchants: Religion, Magic, and Commerce* (Knoxville: University of Tennessee Press, 2001).

20. Bolívar Aróstegui, *Afro-Cuban Cuisine*, 89–90.

21. Pierre Bourdieu, *Practical Reason: On the Theory of Action*, trans. Richard Nice (Stanford: Stanford University Press, 1998), 25.

22. Daniel Miller, *A Theory of Shopping* (Ithaca: Cornell University Press, 1998), 75; my italics.

23. Robert Farris Thompson, *Face of the Gods: Art and Altars of Africa and the African Americas* (New York: Prestel-Verlag, 1993), 28.

24. For more concerning ebbó, see Roberto Nodal and Miguel "Willie" Ramos, "Let the Power Flow: Ebó as a Healing Mechanism in Lukumí Orisha Worship," in *Fragments of Bone: Neo-African Religions in a New World*, ed. Patrick Bellegarde-Smith, 167–86 (Urbana: University of Illinois Press, 2005).

25. At the drum feasts I have attended, spirits have often used foods displayed in plazas to cleanse initiates ritually.

26. Brown, "Thrones of the Orichas: Afro-Cuban Altars in New Jersey, New York, and Havana," *African Arts* 26 (1993): 54.

27. Johannes Fabian, *Power and Performance: Ethnographic Explorations Through Proverbial Wisdom and Theater in Shaba, Zaire* (Madison: University of Wisconsin Press, 1990), 24.

28. Mary Douglas and Baron Isherwood, *The World of Goods: Towards an Anthropology of Consumption* (London: Routledge, 1996), 45.

29. John Mason, *Ìdáná Fún Òrìṣà: Cooking for Selected Heads* (Brooklyn: Yorùbá Theological Archministry, 1999), 121–23.

30. Ibid., 130–31; Ramos, *The Empire Beats On*, 224.

31. Ramos, *The Empire Beats On*, 224.

32. Mason, *Ìdáná Fún Òrìṣà*, 52.

33. Ibid., 104–5.

34. Ibid., 99. For more examples, see Miguel "Willie" Ramos, *Adimú: Gbogbó Tén'unjé Lukumí* (Miami: Eleda.Org, 2003).

35. Ysamur Flores-Peña, "Overflowing with Beauty: The Ochún Atlar in Lucumí Aesthetic Tradition," in *Òṣun Across the Waters: A Yoruba Goddess in Africa and the Americas*, ed. Joseph M. Murphy and Mei-Mei Sanford, 122 (Bloomington: Indiana University Press, 2001); and Julia Cuervo Hewitt, *Aché, presencia africana: tradiciones yoruba-lucumí en la narrativa cubana* (New York: Peter Lang, 1988), 80; my translation.

36. David H. Brown, "Garden in the Machine: Afro-Cuban Sacred Art and Performance in Urban New Jersey and New York," Ph.D. dissertation, Yale University, 1989, 105.

37. Morton Marks, "Havana, Cuba, ca. 1957: Rhythms and Songs for the Orishas from the Historic Recordings of Lydia Cabrera and Josefina Tarafa, Introduction" (Washington D.C.: Smithsonian Folkways Recordings, 2001), 10–11.

38. Margaret Thompson Drewal, "Dancing for Ògún in Yorubaland and Brazil," in *Africa's Ogun: Old World and New*, ed. Sandra T. Barnes (Bloomington: Indiana University Press, 1997), 225.

39. Brown, "Garden in the Machine," 105.

40. Matthias Rhrig Assuno and Michael Zeuske, "'Race,' Ethnicity and Social Structure in 19th Century Brazil and Cuba," *Ibero-Amerikanisches Archiv* 24 (1998): 412; and Aline Helg, *Our Rightful Share: The Afro-Cuban Struggle for Equality, 1886–1912* (Chapel Hill: University of North Carolina Press, 1995), 48.

41. "La secta conga de los 'matiabos' en Cuba," in *Estudios etnosociológicos* (La Habana: Editorial de Ciencias Sociales, 1991 [1956]), 107.

42. Brown, "Thrones of the Orichas," 51.

43. He consumes a variety of meats: rooster, goat, venison, turtle, and bush rat, among others.

44. John Mason, *Orin Òrìṣà: Songs for Selected Heads* (Brooklyn: Yorùbá Theological Archministry, 1992), 80.

45. Quoted in David H. Brown, "Toward an Ethnoaesthetics of Santería Ritual Arts: The Practice of Altar-Making and Gift Exchange," in *Santería Aesthetics in Contemporary Latin American Art*, ed. Arturo Lindsay (Washington, D.C.: Smithsonian Institution, 1996), 135 n.37.

46. Gabriele Volpato and Daimy Godínez, "Ethnobotany of Pru, a Traditional Cuban Refreshment," *Economic Botany* 58, no. 3 (2004): 381–95.

47. J. Lorand Matory, *Sex and the Empire That Is No More: Gender and the Politics of Metaphor in Oyo Yoruba Religion* (Minneapolis: University of Minnesota Press, 1994), 144.

48. The best places to become acquainted with Ochún's sweet tastes are the lavish parties thrown in her honor in Lucumí communities, at which devotees serve and eat foods prepared in her honor.

49. Bolívar Aróstegui, *Afro-Cuban Cuisine*, 88–89.

50. Mercedes Cros Sandoval, *La religion afrocubana* (Madrid: Playor, 1975), 198.

51. Isabel Castellanos, "A River of Many Turns: The Polysemy of Ochún in Afro-Cuban Tradition" in Murphy and Sanford, *Òṣun Across the Waters*, 39.

52. Cabrera, cited in Cuervo Hewitt, *Aché*, 167.

53. Miguel "Willie" Ramos, "Afro-Cuban Orisha Worship," in *Santería Aesthetics in Contemporary Latin American Art,* ed. Arturo Lindsay (Washington, D.C.: Smithsonian Institution, 1996), 69.

54. Castellanos, "A River of Many Turns," 44 n.13.

55. I have changed the name of the Ilé and my interlocutor for reasons of confidentiality.

56. Castellanos, "A River of Many Turns," 42.

57. Claude Lévi-Strauss observes that in the indigenous South American systems of thought on which he conducted research, neither honey nor men-

strual blood is constructed as raw, but as kindred "elaborated substances, like cooked food, but through the action of what might be called 'natural cooking.'" *From Honey to Ashes* (Chicago: University of Chicago Press, 1966), 255.

58. Brown, "Garden in the Machine," 105.
59. Raquel Mendieta Costa, "Exotic Exports: The Myth of the Mulatta," in *Corpus Delecti: Performance Art of the Americas*, ed. Coco Fusco (London: London, 2000), 45.
60. Thomas, *Cuba*, 173.
61. Assuno and Zeuske, "'Race,' Ethnicity and Social Structure in 19th Century Brazil and Cuba," 404.
62. Vera Kutzinski, *Sugar's Secrets: Race and the Erotics of Cuban Nationalism* (Charlottesville: University of Virginia Press, 1993), 165.
63. The latter conflated the mulattas depicted in the marquillas with a cloyingly sweet, inexpensive confection still made from honey, brown sugar, and coconut, served in a flimsy paper or banana-leaf cone, and sold on the street.
64. Mendieta Costa, "Exotic Exports," 45.
65. Contrast this with the appetite attributed to her sister Yemayá, seen to be of unmixed and direct African descent. See Elizabeth Pérez, "Nobody's Mammy: Yemayá as Fierce Foremother in Afro-Cuban Religions," in *Gender, Sexuality, and Creativity in the Latina/o and Afro-Atlantic Diaspora*, ed. Solimar Otero and Toyin Falola (New York: State University of New York Press, 2013), 1–20.
66. Cros Sandoval, *La religion afrocubana*, 171. Some 142,000 Chinese laborers—indentured servants and contract workers either press-ganged or deceived into accepting exploitative arrangements—arrived in Cuba in the nineteenth century, mostly from 1847 to 1874. See Lisa Yun, *The Coolie Speaks: Chinese Indentured Laborers and African Slaves in Cuba* (Philadelphia: Temple University Press, 2008).
67. Joseph M. Murphy, "Yéyé Cachita: Ochún in a Cuban Mirror," in Murphy and Sanford, *Òṣun Across the Waters*, 96.
68. Madeline Cámara Betancourt, "Between Myth and Stereotype: the Image of the Mulatta in Cuban Culture in the Nineteenth Century, a Truncated Symbol of Nationality," in *Cuba, the Elusive Nation: Interpretations of National Identity*, ed. Damián J. Fernández and Madeline Cámara Betancourt, 104 (Gainesville: University Press of Florida, 2000).
69. Isaac O. Delano, *Òwe L'Esin Oro: Yoruba Proverbs—Their Meaning and Usage* (Ibadan: Oxford University Press, 1966), 20, 106.
70. Thompson, *Face of the Gods*, 154.

71. Douglas and Isherwood, *The World of Goods*, 44.
72. Michel Foucault, *The Archaeology of Knowledge*, trans. A. M. Sheridan Smith (London: Tavistock, 1972), 81.

RECOMMENDED READING

Ayorinde, Christine. *Afro-Cuban Religiosity, Revolution and National Identity*. Tampa: University Press of Florida, 2004.

Brown, David H. *Santería Enthroned: Art, Ritual, and Innovation in an Afro-Cuban Religion* (Chicago: University of Chicago Press, 2003).

Clark, Mary Ann. *Santería: Correcting the Myths and Uncovering the Realities of a Growing Religion*. Westport, Conn.: Praeger, 2007.

Farris Thompson, Robert. *Face of the Gods: Art and Altars of Africa and the African Americas*. New York: Prestel-Verlag, 1993.

Ten

GOOD TO EAT

CULINARY PRIORITIES IN THE NATION OF ISLAM AND THE CHURCH OF JESUS CHRIST OF LATTER-DAY SAINTS

KATE HOLBROOK

W HEN IT COMES to diet, two religious groups considered outsiders by mainstream Americans have more in common than perhaps anyone imagined. Members of the Nation of Islam (Nation) have been marginalized as much for their perceived militancy and racism as for abstaining from sweet potatoes and pork, and members of the Church of Jesus Christ of Latter-day Saints (Mormons) are as infamous for a past that included plural marriage as for prohibitions against coffee and alcohol. Yet both religious groups choose what to eat by hallmarks as similar and American as apple pie: the attainment of self-sufficiency and the pursuit of good health.

As historian R. Laurence Moore has persuasively argued, religious outsiders in the United States are, in many respects, true insiders.[1] To rebel, to create one's own movement—these acts are consummately American. Through their rebellion on issues of food and drink, both the Nation and the Latter-day Saints have proved themselves to be American religious insiders. In fact, recipes for the marginalized Mormons and members of the Nation flesh out Moore's account of American religious identities. Close readings of recipes and favorite dishes show that the American values of self-sufficiency, economy, and health have influenced the cuisine of the

Nation and the Latter-day Saints at least as much as the specifics of their religious dietary codes have. What this means is that even when groups purport to reject American culture, or when popular culture rejects them, religious groups born in America are deeply influenced by American sensibilities.

WHAT THE OUTSIDERS FOUND BAD TO EAT

For Nation of Islam members, a series of articles in the official Nation newspaper, *Muhammad Speaks*, set the dietary code, which was eventually published in 1967 as two slim volumes entitled *How to Eat to Live.* Nation leader Elijah Muhammad taught that he had received these guidelines from his mentor W. D. Fard, who was also God incarnate, and thus they were revelation. Like Mormons, Nation members were instructed to abstain from alcohol and tobacco, and like Muslims and Jews they were to abstain from pork. Also forbidden were sweet potatoes, quick breads (like biscuits, cornbread, and pancakes), leafy greens, and most legumes (particularly lima beans and black-eyed peas), although Elijah Muhammad encouraged eating small pink navy beans. Those who would follow the diet were promised increased spiritual strength, freedom from disease, and longevity.

For Latter-day Saints, the dietary code is the Word of Wisdom, a short passage of just thirty-nine verses in the *Doctrine and Covenants*, a book of scripture based primarily on God's revelations to founding prophet Joseph Smith. Recorded on February 27, 1833, these verses recommended a diet of fruits, vegetables, herbs, and grains in season, with limited meat intake.[2] Prohibitions against "hot drinks," "strong drinks," and tobacco were familiar among dietary reformers of the day such as Sylvester Graham but set Mormons apart from mainstream Americans. Mormons spent the next one hundred years grappling with what it meant to obey the Word of Wisdom. (Should they be vegetarian? Were beer and wine permissible?) Church president Heber J. Grant spelled out the details in the 1920s, making obedience to the principle a firm requirement for temple attendance, hence full church membership, and defined the minimum standard of compliance as abstinence from tea, coffee, alcohol, and tobacco. Church members believed obedience to these guidelines and God's law would bring spiritual blessings, as well as physical blessings such as increased health and strength.

The uniqueness and stringency of these dietary codes set Nation members and Mormons apart from mainstream Americans. But concurrently, leaders and members justified them by making links with inherently American values of the period, particularly health and self-sufficiency.[3]

HOW DIFFERENT RELIGIOUS CREEDS LED TO COMMON RESPONSES AT THE TABLE

Bringing these two groups into apparent conversation may seem counterintuitive. There are obvious and important differences between the Church of Jesus Christ of Latter-day Saints and the Nation of Islam. Formed one hundred years apart (Mormons in 1830, the Nation of Islam in 1930), these groups were distanced by geographical roots, membership profile, and theology. Where Mormons were predominantly white in their beginning,[4] the Nation was almost exclusively African American. Where Mormonism saw itself as reforming Christianity, the Nation explicitly rejected it. Mormons defined eternal life as eternity spent in God's presence, the Nation taught that there was no afterlife.

On the other hand, each group actively set itself apart from the mainstream. The Nation read mainstream culture as racist and corrupt, citing the horrible legacy of American slavery and the bitter present of Jim Crow laws and discrimination. Mormons also saw mainstream America as corrupt, citing what they saw as Protestant heresies and persecution. Both groups, not unlike mainstream Protestants and Catholics, took to heart the Christian New Testament teaching (Romans 12:2) to be "in the world but not of the world," believing they were called to keep themselves more pure than the status quo.

As a result, both Nation members and Mormons held a common wariness about mainstream behavior and influences. Both saw peril in government financial assistance, for example. Both Mormons and Nation members believed their lives should demonstrate a spiritually higher way of living than mainstream Americans. Their pursuits of good health and self-sufficiency were not to make them *like* the mainstream, but *better* than the mainstream. Their priority, albeit practiced differently at their marginalized tables, was to please God and create their own mode of living for God's sake, not to impress their American neighbors.

As both groups worked out what this meant in everyday patterns of eating, each developed a cuisine that represented its deeply held religious priorities. Until now, the Nation's interpretation of black American racial identity has been seen as the primary influence on its cuisine, and bystanders have assumed that the Word of Wisdom most strongly influenced what Mormons ate. Yet a closer look at recipes and favorite foods of the Nation and Mormons shows that each group's cooking was deeply influenced by mainstream American values, rather than religious mandates. For the Nation, the American value of physical health was prioritized; for Mormons, the American value of self-sufficiency most strongly influenced their foodways.

THE NATION'S PURSUIT OF HEALTH

The Nation's regulations prohibited many foods that were typically identified as "southern" and that were historically prepared by enslaved African Americans, including collard greens, black-eyed peas, pork, and corn bread. As a result, most observers have viewed the Nation's food habits as a rejection of "slave food" and a deliberate embrace of foreign foods that crafted a new non-American identity. In contrast, evaluating Nation practices more broadly, historian Edward E. Curtis IV contends that rather than adopting non-American habits (African or Middle Eastern), Elijah Muhammad incorporated middle-class Protestant values into a new Islamic framework as a method of empowerment.[5] I argue that one of those middle-class values was an emphasis on cuisine as crucial to *health*; the Nation sought to make familiar dishes healthier. The changes were not necessarily healthier by today's standards of nutrition science, but Elijah Muhammad taught that they were scientifically better for health. A close reading of favorite dishes and recipes illustrates the rhetoric of health that attended the substitutions of nonslave for slave foods. For example, mashed sweet potatoes became carrot fluff, because Elijah Muhammad taught that carrots were healthier than sweet potatoes. Similarly, sweet potato pie turned into higher-protein bean pie. Barbecued ribs were made from beef instead of harmful pork. These substitutions were about keeping to the Nation's dietary code because it was healthy.

The Nation's genesis and evolution make it harder to see the connection between its new foodways and health. Nation of Islam founder Elijah Muhammad became acquainted in 1931 with a mysterious man named W. D. Fard. For three years Fard took Muhammad under his wing, teaching him truths about the black man's real identity. Fard explained that black people in the United States descended from an honorable tribe; their true nature was noble, and they were Muslim; and that he, Fard, was the incarnation of Allah himself. Fard's teachings were to be trusted as more thoroughly true than traditions that relied on less-explicit inspiration, prophecy, or centuries of scriptural interpretation.[6] Elijah Muhammad founded the Nation of Islam to help black people in America relearn and acquire their birthright. Elijah Muhammad knew that centuries of mistreatment by oppressors—slavery in the American South in particular—had left a toll on black people in America. From his perspective, they had no understanding of their worthy origins, they were largely unexposed to the correct Islamic faith of their ancestors, and whites had encouraged addiction and vice to keep blacks from realizing their splendid destiny. Worship and praxis therefore focused on the rehabilitation of and provision for the black race—in other words, the construction of a Nation of Islam. Culinary ideals, particularly proscription of particular foods, were central to realizing this goal of racial rehabilitation.

Scholars have downplayed the significance of Elijah Muhammad's rhetoric about health to reveal the "real" reason for food habits, which they have seen as the construction of non-American identity.[7] Elijah Muhammad did write in How to Eat to Live that the slave diet hurt both body and spirit, and that slaves had been forced to eat certain foods by masters with two main motives: a desire to economize (by finding a use for foods that were inexpensive and that the wealthy were not willing to eat), and the "devilish" aim to undermine slaves' well-being (through the consumption of polluted food). There were clearly strong racial themes in Muhammad's culinary directions, but he did not tell his followers to eat small navy beans in search of a new, postslave, post-American identity. He taught them to eat small navy beans because they were healthy. Muhammad's significant emphasis on health has been underinvestigated. But the health emphasis is important, not least because the attainment of good physical health was a priority of mainstream American culture.

Elijah Muhammad did not believe in life after death. There would be no blissful eternity in Heaven. "We only have one life," he taught, "and, if this life is destroyed, we would have a hard time trying to get more life; it is impossible. So try to keep this life that you have as long as possible."[8] In Elijah Muhammad's view, proper nutrition was essential, and members internalized this emphasis.[9] For example, Sister Pattie X testified: "Messenger Muhammad has taught me how to eat, when to eat, and what to eat; therefore, my life has been prolonged."[10] Those who adhered to the Nation's creeds for diet could also ameliorate already existing medical conditions, like diabetes, and be free of additional complaints. "If you eat the proper food—which I have given to you from Allah (in the Person of Master Fard Muhammad to Whom be praise forever) in this book—you will hardly ever have a headache."[11]

In Sonsyrea Tate's autobiography about growing up in the Nation during the 1960s and 1970s, she confirmed that the idea of eating well for health was deeply ingrained. She recalled eating at a Nation-run school as a child, with "wholesome smells" emanating from the cafeteria as workers prepared nutritious beef burgers and wheat doughnuts. After Elijah Muhammad's death, when Nation schools (called the University of Islam) closed, Tate transferred to a public school, where she came to dread the stench escaping cafeteria doors.[12] She said that the priority of good nutrition was so ingrained in members that even after her mother left the Nation to practice an alternate form of Islam, she continued to prioritize nutrition.[13]

Similarly, Betty Shabbaz, wife of Malcolm X, focused on the health aspects of diet both before and after her husband's martyrdom. Her daughter recalled, "My mother, as a rule, did not allow us to have much candy. Being a nurse and a Muslim she was extremely health-conscious and carefully monitored what we ate."[14]

Elijah Muhammad also stressed that healthy eating led to achieving another American value: physical beauty. He wrote: "Eating the proper food also brings about a better surface appearance. Our features are beautified by the health that the body now enjoys from the eating of proper food and also eating at the proper time."[15] For the Nation, the healthy appearance a Muslim derived from eating well was even seen as God's blessing. The Nation had held this value in common with some Evangelical Christians, who viewed slim bodies as evidence of personal righteousness, but the Nation took things a step further.[16] Elijah Muhammad taught that slenderness was more than a blessing—it was a priority.

One former member of the Nation described a penny tax implemented at temple meetings under Elijah Muhammad's leadership. Brothers had to demonstrate specific, scientifically determined standards of appropriate weight according to their height. They would weigh in at meetings, standing on a scale, and pay one penny for each pound that exceeded the standard.[17] In that odd and stern encounter stands a potent reminder of just how thoroughly the Nation of Islam had implemented, in its own distinctive way, the American emphasis on physical health and beauty as markers of success.

MODIFYING SOUL

Nation practices and mainstream American traditions began to intersect in another way too. Recipes show that popular Nation foods were derived mainly from southern tradition, instead of looking extensively to the Muslim world for culinary guidance.[18] Recipes are a reliable source for understanding praxis in the Nation because they had hierarchical support and were prescriptive. Sisters in the temple developed recipes intended to fulfill Elijah Muhammad's culinary standards, then taught them to newcomers in their own kitchens with the expectation that they would then feed their families in the same way. Thus women in the Nation learned to cook from one another, under the shaping influence of Elijah Muhammad. Tate, for example, confirmed that this is how her grandmother learned to cook according to Nation standards in the 1950s.[19] Eventually this training became more formally organized at the temples in courses called Muslim Girls Training (MGT). Women and girls attended this gender-specific training once a week, often on Saturdays, and learned how to cook as "Muslims."

The original MGT classes dissolved along with the University of Islam not long after Elijah Muhammad's death in 1975. One former student, Reda Faard Khalifah, saved her MGT recipes and published them in 1995 as *The Muslim Recipe Book: Recipes for Muslim Girls Training and General Civilization Class (MGT/GCC) of the Honorable Elijah Muhammad*—a hallmark work containing recipes used by the Nation's women throughout the movement. Because Khalifah felt she was only reporting recipes taught to her, and that they were based on Elijah Muhammad's teachings, she listed Elijah Muhammad as her coauthor.

The brief introduction to *The Muslim Recipe Book* reinforces the fact that the American value of pursuing good health was more central to the Nation's food habits than idealized racial identity. Khalifah highlights how recipes should facilitate health when she says, in the spirit of Elijah

Muhammad's priorities, that even healthier cooking options have developed since the recipes were created. For example, she explains that the old technique of browning rice to improve its nutritive value was outdated since "wholesome naturally brown rice" was now readily available. She also makes a disclaimer about the book's high proportion of meat recipes—that people are now catching up to what Elijah Muhammad already knew: "that meat is one of the major causes of sickness and disease." Her introduction calls attention to vegetable and vegetarian recipes in the book because they "build radiant health."[20]

However, the most revealing aspect of these recipes is how Nation menus incorporated what came to be known in the 1960s as "soul food." Soul food is a fluid category, overlapping with the idea of southern food. When the Black Power movement brought the phrase to popular awareness in the 1960s, restaurants began serving soul food that others deemed simply southern. For example, in an essay for the November 3, 1968, issue of the *New York Times Magazine*, Craig Claiborne reported that displaced southern devotees of soul food found the offerings in New York soul-food restaurants was "more Southern than soul. The menus mostly feature such typical Southern dishes as fried chicken, spareribs, candied yams and mustard or collard greens. One rarely finds trotters, neckbones, pigs' tails and chitterlings."[21] Others did not care to differentiate between southern and soul. And many argued that the essence of soul food was about emotion—the care that went into the food.[22] For people in the mainstream, then, soul food became a more positive term for typical slave fare of chitterlings, mustard greens, black eyed-peas, and cornbread. Soul food improved perceptions of African American identity, celebrating heritage rather than shaming through the derogatory association with slavery.

Elijah Muhammad denounced both categories—southern and soul—at once, deeming all of it "slave food." Sisters in the Nation then took familiar soul dishes and modified the recipes, substituting acceptable ingredients for forbidden ones, believing these substitutions would safeguard health. These substitutions were viewed as not just safeguards but as transformations of soul food into soul-made-wholesome food. For instance, MGT courses taught that sweet potatoes were unhealthy, full of too much starch and causing gas. So carrots were substituted for sweet potatoes in many soul food dishes. *The Muslim Recipe Book* was filled with similar ingredient swaps: barbequed meats and barbeque short ribs, similar to recipes for barbequed pork, but with beef substituted for pork.[23]

In *A Pinch of Soul*, a quintessential soul food cookbook, a recipe for barbecue sauce calls for chutney, catsup or tomato sauce, brown sugar, dry mustard, hot sauce, cayenne pepper, garlic powder, and onion to be used with pork.[24] The barbecue sauce recipe in *The Muslim Recipe Book* has a similar flavor base: vinegar (which would add the piquancy of the chutney, above), green pepper (like vinegar, often in chutney), tomato paste, dry mustard, red pepper, garlic, and onion. There is little distinction between the two sauces. The barbecue instructions are also similar, calling for the technique of cooking on top of the stove, then browning in the oven or broiler. The barbecue section of *A Pinch of Soul* instructs: "Outdoor barbecuing for simple enjoyment has not traditionally been a 'soul' thing . . . few of our grandparents indulged in a whole pig or side of beef cooked on an open fire. Soul barbecuing took place mainly in the oven of a wood-burning stove."[25] Like the *A Pinch of Soul* recipes, *The Muslim Recipe Book* calls for initial cooking on top of the stove, to be finished in the oven. Cooking time marks the main difference in technique. The soul recipe for "Mrs. Shorey's Ribs" requires thirty-five to forty minutes in the oven, while the Muslim "Barbecue Short Ribs of Beef" not only cooks in the oven for two hours, "or until the meat is well done," but specifies the meat as beef.[26] Thus the only substantive differences between the *A Pinch of Soul* recipe and the Nation sauce are abstinence from pork and cooking time, both of which were seen as by the Nation as healthy changes. Elijah Muhammad taught that, for health, meat should be cooked until very well done. In practice, many of the Nation recipes are soul-made-wholesome.[27]

Some soul food recipes contain substitutions for proper ingredients and do not include a title change. For example, *A Pinch of Soul* includes a recipe for navy bean soup, one of Elijah Muhammad's favorite dishes and a classic Nation recipe. *A Pinch of Soul*'s navy bean soup included streak 'o lean (a pork product, sometimes made into lard) and cubed salt pork, but otherwise closely resembled the MGT's recipe.[28] Because its soup is vegetarian, the Nation recipe calls for tomato paste instead of canned tomatoes and pork; tomato paste imparts a deeper flavor to compensate for the lack of meat.

Of all recipes, though, one stands out most of all: bean pie, the dish emblematic of the Nation of Islam. Often bean pie is all people know about the Nation, because they have seen well-dressed men selling individual pies on street corners in major metropolitan areas. Unlike the overlapping representative dishes of other religious groups (for example, Mormons,

Methodists, and Presbyterians might each claim green Jell-O salad), bean pie is unique to the Nation of Islam. Members of the Nation believed bean pie was healthier than sweet potato pie. Comparing the two pies was inevitable as even Nation members described bean pie as sweet potato pie made with mashed up navy beans instead of sweet potatoes (though, technically, bean pie had a custard base and sweet potato pie did not). Elijah Muhammad's son, Jabir, explained bean pie in these terms on YouTube in 2010.[29] Jabir Muhammad worked for years as Nation member and famed boxer Muhammad Ali's manager and reported that Ali's personal cook, Lana Shabazzfirst, developed bean pie to safeguard the champ's health.[30]

THE MORMON PURSUIT OF SELF-SUFFICIENCY

Mormons, too, have used American values to inform their food habits. In fact, the church's welfare program, adopted in 1936, has shaped Mormon cuisine even more than has the Word of Wisdom, which is a canonized part of scripture. Established during the height of the Great Depression, the welfare program's goal was to help Mormons be financially self-sufficient both as individuals and as a church. Its major tenets included frugality, hard work, food storage, and work on behalf of others.[31] In practice, Mormons were instructed to maintain a one- to two-year supply of emergency food. In daily life this meant rotating food storage staples into everyday cooking, and avoiding luxury items. Members made inexpensive meals from food storage staples like whole wheat and powdered milk, using inexpensive ingredients like peanut butter, canned garden produce, and seasoning mixes. It also meant working hard to cater their own parties (including weddings and funerals) instead of hiring help. In effect, then, Mormons shaped their cuisine with two of America's most intrinsic and related values: self-sufficiency and frugality.

When one woman yearned for the Mormon food of her past, she requested a dish that exemplified the welfare program's standards. Trish had not attended church for decades. Her home was big, in a fashionable section of Brookline, Massachusetts. As befits the owner of such a home, she structured her culinary calendar around traditional New England fare like Yorkshire pudding, fruitcake with hard sauce, and corned beef and cabbage. But during the final weeks of her life, these held no appeal.[32] Days before liver cancer finally took her life on August 17, 1990, she asked for a dish from her past: tuna noodle casserole. Her family called a church member, Shelley Hammond, who brought the casserole in time for dinner that night. Trish's sister recalled, "It was exactly as Trish remembered, and she ate with pleasure. . . . My mother and I took turns feeding it to her."[33] But why was tuna noodle casserole quintessentially Mormon?

Tuna noodle casserole could have been found at just about any middle American potluck. But often specific dishes distinguish a particular tradition only because they are *believed* to be distinctive, not because they actually are; tuna noodle casserole represented Mormon religious priorities, and they appropriated it as their own. It promoted the Mormon goal of self-sufficiency because it was made from items in food storage, economy because it used inexpensive ingredients, and self-sufficiency (within their religious community) because it fulfilled an ideal of food as service—easy to make in large quantities and transport. Tuna noodle casserole was a staple of the Mormon culinary lexicon.

Similarly, Mormons famously ate Jell-O and "funeral potatoes."[34] But Protestants throughout the country also brought Jell-O salads to potlucks, and funeral potatoes were simply a version of cheesy scalloped potatoes that had been assigned a particular name by Mormons. In and of themselves, these dishes were not unique to Mormons—they were, in fact, American, and Mormons helped to create that American identity by applying deeply held Mormon kitchen values that promoted the treasured American quality of self-sufficiency. As Mormons recontextualized and slightly modified these American staples, they were able to reimagine them as outside the mainstream and particular to their own religion.

Just as the Nation's cookbooks made soul food into Nation food, Latter-day Saint cookbooks interpreted middle American foods, adapting them for rotation of food storage staples and economy, and made them Mormon. A prime example is the collection in Winnifred Jardine's *Mormon Country Cooking* (1980), which called for ingredients accessible through much of the Mormon corridor (apricots, peaches, rhubarb, zucchini), and maintained the Mormon ideal of drawing upon a year's food supply.[35] Jardine's recipes actually came from multiple Mormon sources and represented a shared culinary consciousness. In 1948 Jardine became food editor of the *Deseret News,* a church-owned newspaper and one of Salt Lake City's two major dailies, and wrote food columns until her retirement in 1984. Readers submitted many of the recipes to her column and later voted on which *Deseret News* recipes to include in the cookbook. Jardine even dedicated the book "to our *Deseret News* readers who contributed many of these recipes."[36]

These recipes are not only exemplary because they were gathered from the community; Jardine herself belonged to Mormonism's inner circle. As her editor wrote: "Winnifred Cannon Jardine's food-fixing background is as Mormon as the great turtle-shaped Tabernacle on Salt Lake City's Temple Square."[37] She descended from early Mormon leaders Brigham Young and George Q. Cannon, served on the church general boards, wrote homemaking lessons for Relief Society Manuals, and sang in the Mormon Tabernacle Choir. With these qualifications, she maintained a sense of spiritual responsibility for the book, working to present an ideal Mormon cuisine; and she included recipes representative of what Mormons actually prepared and enjoyed.

Just as Khalifah made notes in *The Muslim Cookbook* when community recipes did not fully meet Elijah Muhammad's ideal for health, so Jardine tried to address similar inconsistencies in *Mormon Country Cooking* recipes. For example, when the book failed to represent the Word of Wisdom standard of limited meat intake, Jardine still looked to the ideal. The introduction to "Eggs and Cheese" reminded readers, "Eggs and cheese together make a nutritious, delicious combination that is grand for a people who have been counseled to use meat 'sparingly.'"[38] In her introductory section on "Meat, Fish and Poultry," she wrote, "Although counseled to eat meat and poultry 'sparingly,' Mormons still build many of the main meals around them. But they do not seem to eat large quantities."[39] Jardine's assessment about the quantity of meat consumption likely reflected her wishes more than actual fact, as well as her discomfort when practice failed to match ideal.

THE MORMON PURSUITS OF ECONOMY AND INDEPENDENCE

Jardine's recipes stemmed directly from Mormon practices informed by American values: using food storage staples and inexpensive ingredients to promote self-sufficiency. Mormon recipes relied greatly on wheat— more than recipes in other twentieth-century American cookbooks, which used all-purpose flour instead. Wheat was especially important to Mormons both because it was perceived as providing superior nutrition and because it was a popular component of food storage owing to its long shelf-life.[40] Jardine theorized that the penchant for bread making and baking with wheat may have come to Mormons from their pioneer ancestry. More likely the reliance on wheat came from the church's welfare program, which encouraged hundreds of pounds of wheat to be stored in the cool basements of Mormon homes. Such provision was intended to sustain families not only during natural disasters but also during personal crises like unemployment, disability, and financial reverses. Wheat was a source of security for Mormons, a convenience, and an economic advantage, since quantity buying generally meant lower prices and buying ahead slowed down the bite of inflation.[41]

Food storage practices inevitably shaped Mormon cuisine. For example, a recipe for carrot cake included no all-purpose flour and incorporated a number of items with long shelf lives: vegetable oil instead of butter, canned pineapple, preserved stock like raisins, and coconut. Mormons could store these items with staggering amounts of wheat, testifying to their commitment to self-sufficiency and economy. Other food recipes demonstrated the deliberate Mormon food choices for independence and frugality too: bread recipes from more typical middle American cookbooks called for fresh milk, whereas Mormon recipes were just as likely to use powdered or evaporated milk.

Aside from the stored foods, growing your own food was an essential element of the Welfare Program, and some recipes emphasized the use of garden produce. "Rhubarb Iced Cocktail," for instance, which involved rhubarb, sugar, and ginger ale, apparently existed solely as a means for keeping stalks of rhubarb, a fixture in Utah gardens, from going to waste. Parenthetical recipe instructions to use the extra drained rhubarb in pie or cobbler was a declaration against waste. Since drained rhubarb would not have much flavor, adding it to another dish would not improve flavor, which shows economy trumping pleasure. The "Rhubarb Iced Cocktail" recipe took a vegetable that flourished in the Utah climate and made of it a nonalcoholic party beverage. A recipe for Italian seasoning also invoked cooking with garden produce and focused on the value of frugality, since making your own Italian seasoning was supposed to save money. In her cookbook Jardine told readers in a chapter heading that this recipe, along with others for dried onion soup and French herbs, "can be made in quantity for a fraction of the supermarket price and are excellent for seasoning food storage dinners."[42]

Why not just buy Lipton onion soup mix or Italian seasoning and keep those in one's food storage? Because exercising frugality was as much a priority to Mormons as food storage, and making one's own mix or seasoning was less expensive. What is interesting here is how these values were combined with the Word of Wisdom instruction to use vegetables and herbs in season. Making one's own seasonings and mixes meant using fresh herbs from the garden but also using products like lemon pepper and garlic powder, which were obtained through the workings of a factory. Making one's own seasoning was not, therefore, about purity but about frugality. Many a well-stocked Mormon pantry prioritized self-sufficiency over other values. In some respects the Word of Wisdom was marginalized to better attain American values like economy, independence, and self-sufficiency.

Mormon eating habits did reflect Word of Wisdom standards to some extent—Mormon cookbooks contained recipes neither for tiramisu (ladyfingers soaked in cappuccino) nor boeuf bourguignon with its reliance on red wine. But whereas the Word of Wisdom text itself emphasized eating foods in season, Mormon cookbooks contained recipes for preserves and pickles, so that food could be eaten out of season.[43] The Word of Wisdom urged restrained meat eating, but cookbooks were replete with ideas for dressing viands, which fed large groups and were easily purchased when on sale and stored in the chest freezer.[44] Instead of a strict implementation of Word of Wisdom ideals, Mormon cuisine reflected practicality, frugality, and the need to assemble food stores for an ever-uncertain future.

Just as with the Nation, the Mormon diet—a complex merger of slightly modified American cuisine recontextualized within the religious community's values—served as a simultaneous emblem for a distinctive, outsider subculture and the broader American culture.

MORE AMERICAN THAN APPLE PIE

In the kitchens and dining rooms of mid-twentieth-century America, members of two outsider groups negotiated relationships with America's mainstream in creative ways. Even as they explicitly savored their outsider status, Nation of Islam Muslims and Latter-day Saints subtly bought in to mainstream American values. The ways they altered familiar American staples like sweet potato pie or tuna casseroles reflected their endorsement of broader American ideals. Two main processes were taking place in the kitchens and dining tables of these groups: the construction of difference, and a striving to be better than the mainstream according to the rules of the mainstream.

The space these outsiders created for themselves within twentieth-century America speaks to just how complex and subtle are the differences between insider and outsider groups, and how dependent they can be on the assertion that they are indeed different. Carrot fluff and funeral potatoes look and taste much the same as the American staples they are meant to replace, but in the deliberate appropriation of these and other dishes, Nation of Islam and Mormon people assert their distinctiveness. Simultaneous with their assertions of difference, Mormons and Nation members brought a fervent commitment to excellence to the mainstream. At times outsiders seem to incorporate a hypertrophied version of the insider culture. If good Americans value physical health, Nation Muslims will bring health to bear on every dish they consider at the table. If good Americans value self-sufficiency, then Mormons will build a cuisine around inexpensive, durable goods.

Watching Nation Muslims and Mormons cook and eat provides important new insights into the ways participants in American society negotiate the paradoxes of fitting in and intentionally failing to fit in, a potent reminder of the importance the perception and practice of otherness plays in the construction of American society.

DISCUSSION QUESTIONS

1. What cultural currents guide what you eat? How does food connect or disconnect you with broader American culture?
2. What kind of power do culinary differences have on relationships—even differences that might be more imagined than real?
3. How might it affect a person to begin making substitutions in the main ingredients of foods he or she had eaten and cooked since childhood?
4. What does storing a year's supply of food tell you about what Mormons value?

NOTES

1. R. Laurence Moore, *Religious Outsiders and the Making of Americans* (New York: Oxford University Press, 1986).

2. "And again, verily I say unto you, all wholesome herbs God hath ordained for the constitution, nature, and use of man—Every herb in the season thereof, and every fruit in the season thereof; all these to be used with prudence and thanksgiving. . . . All grain is good for the food of man; as also the fruit of the vine; that which yieldeth fruit, whether in the ground or above the ground." *Doctrine and Covenants*, section 89.

3. For a description of the transition in American Protestantism from a notion of physical suffering as evidence of God's love to God's love as a means to physical healing, see Heather D. Curtis, *Faith in the Great Physician: Suffering and Divine Healing in American Culture, 1860–1900* (Baltimore: Johns Hopkins University Press, 2007).

4. Newell G. Bringhurst, *Saints, Slaves, and Blacks: The Changing Place of Black People Within Mormonism* (Westport, Conn: Greenwood, 1981), appendix c.

5. Edward E. Curtis, *Black Muslim Religion in the Nation of Islam, 1960–1975* (Chapel Hill: University of North Carolina Press, 2006), 127–30.

6. Karl Evanzz, *The Messenger: The Rise and Fall of Elijah Muhammad* (New York: Pantheon, 1999).

7. Algernon Austin, *Achieving Blackness: Race, Black Nationalism, and Afrocentrism in the Twentieth Century* (New York: New York University Press, 2006), 35; Richard Brent Turner, *Islam in the African-American Experience*, 2nd ed. (Bloomington: Indiana University Press, 2003), 159; Edward E. Curtis IV, "Islamizing the Black Body: Ritual and Power in Elijah Muhammad's Nation of Islam," *Religion and American Culture* 12, no. 2 (Summer 2002): 167–96; Curtis, *Black Muslim Religion in the Nation of Islam, 1960–1975*; and C. Eric Lincoln, *The Black Muslims in America*, 3rd ed. (Grand Rapids, Mich: Eerdmans, 1994), 22, 25, 47.

8. Elijah Muhammad, *How to Eat to Live, Book No. 1* (Phoenix: Secretarius, 1997), 19. Original edition: Fard Muhammad and Elijah Muhammad, *How to Eat to Live. Book One* (Atlanta: Messenger Elijah Muhammad Propagation Society, 1967).

9. Martha Lee has argued convincingly that the Nation's fixation with this-worldly reform qualifies it as a millenarian movement: "At its core was millenarianism, the belief in an imminent, ultimate, collective, this-worldly, and total salvation." *The Nation of Islam, An American Millenarian Movement* (Lewiston: Edwin Mellen, 1988).

10. Pattie X, "Original Black Woman Is Proud of Natural Heritage," *Muhammad Speaks*, July 28, 1967.

11. Muhammad, *How to Eat to Live, Book No. 1*, 22.

12. Sonsyrea Tate [Montgomery], *Little X: Growing Up in the Nation of Islam* (San Francisco: HarperSanFrancisco, 1997), 120.

13. Interview with Sonsyrea Tate Montgomery, telephone, September 19, 2010.

14. Ilyasah Shabazz, *Growing Up X* (New York: One World/Ballantine, 2003), 44.

15. Muhammad, *How to Eat to Live, Book No. 1*, 32.

16. R. Marie Griffith, *Born Again Bodies: Flesh and Spirit in American Christianity* (Berkeley: University of California Press, 2004).

17. Interview with Sonsyrea Tate Montgomery.

18. Women in the Nation did circulate some recipes that nodded toward Muslim tradition, such as kebabs or carrot halwa. But the bulk of the recipes, including the most popular dishes, closely resembled the foods their female ancestors had prepared.

19. Interview with Sonsyrea Tate Montgomery; Tate, *Little X*, 15–21.

20. Reda Faard Khalifah, *The Muslim Recipe Book: Recipes for Muslim Girls Training & General Civilization Class (MGT/GCC) of the Honorable Elijah Muhammad* (Charlotte: United Brothers Communication Systems, 1995), 6–7.

21. Craig Claiborne, "Cooking with Soul," *New York Times Magazine*, November 3, 1968, 109; Doris Witt, *Black Hunger: Food and the Politics of U.S. Identity* (New York: Oxford University Press, 1999), 80–82.

22. Frederick Douglass Opie, *Hog & Hominy: Soul Food from Africa to America* (New York: Columbia University Press, 2008), 130–31.

23. Khalifah, *The Muslim Recipe Book*, 31, 34.

24. Pearl Bowser and Joan Eckstein, *A Pinch of Soul* (New York: Avon, 1970), 201.

25. Ibid., 197–98.

26. Khalifah, *The Muslim Recipe Book*, 30.

27. Muhammad, *How to Eat to Live, Book No. 1*, 64–65.

28. Bowser and Eckstein, *A Pinch of Soul*, 80; Khalifah, *The Muslim Recipe Book*, 14.

29. Katharine Shilcutt, "Bean Pie, My Brother?" December 29, 2010, http://blogs.houstonpress.com/eating/2010/12/bean_pie_my_brother.php.

30. Richard Goldstein, "Jabir Herbert Muhammad, Who Managed Muhammad Ali, Dies at 79," *New York Times*, August 27, 2008, http://www.nytimes.com/2008/08/28/sports/othersports/28muhammad.html. For recipes, see Lana Shabazz, *Cooking for the Champ* (New York: Jones-McMillon, 1979).

31. For some members, food storage was a crucial component of preparing for Armaggedon, when stores would be needed during the chaos that would

precede Christ's Second Coming. Heber J. Grant, *Gospel Standards: Selections from the Sermons and Writings of Heber J. Grant, Seventh President of the Church of Jesus Christ of Latter-Day Saints,* (Salt Lake City: Bookcraft, 1998), 111; Marion G. Romney, "Living Welfare Principles—Ensign Nov. 1981," http://lds.org/ensign/1981/11/living-welfare-principles?lang=eng; and Garth L. Mangum, *The Mormons' War on Poverty: A History of LDS Welfare, 1830–1990,* (Salt Lake City: University of Utah Press, 1993).

32. Judith Dushku, *Saints Well-Seasoned: Musings on How Food Nourishes Us—Body, Heart, and Soul* (Salt Lake City: Deseret, 1998), 72.

33. Ibid., 73–74.

34. Funeral potatoes were not known as such until the 1980s, but the recipe, calling for potatoes, cheese, sour cream, onion, and cream of mushroom soup, was in circulation before then.

35. The book's preface reinforces this fact: "Many of Winnifred's dishes start right on the Bing cherry tree, peach trees, raspberry bushes, or tomato or zucchini plants in the Jardine home garden." Winnifred C. Jardine, *Mormon Country Cooking* (Salt Lake City: Deseret, 1980), 9.

36. Ibid., 15.

37. Ibid., 7.

38. *Mormon Country Cooking,* 65.

39. Ibid., 93.

40. The Relief Society had a long tradition of storing wheat for use in emergency. Brigham Young encouraged Mormons to store wheat against famine since they first put down roots in Utah. When Young gave up on the men following his orders, he put women in charge of this task, which they pursued from 1877 to 1941. Because of this history, wheat is prominent on the Relief Society emblem. Jessie L. Embry, "Relief Society Grain Storage Program, 1876–1940," Master's thesis, Brigham Young University, 1974; and E. Cecil McGavin, "Grain Storage Among the Latter-day Saints," *The Improvement Era,* March 1941.

41. *Mormon Country Cooking,* 39.

42. Ibid., 209.

43. *Doctrine and Covenants* 89:11: "Every herb in the season thereof, and every fruit in the season thereof; all these to be used with prudence and thanksgiving."

44. *Doctrine and Covenants* 89:12 12: "Yea, flesh also of beasts and of the fowls of the air, I, the Lord, have ordained for the use of man with thanksgiving; nevertheless they are to be used sparingly."

RECOMMENDED READING

Bowman, Matthew. *The Mormon People: The Making of an American Faith*. New York: Random House, 2012.

Curtis, Edward E., IV. *Black Muslim Religion in the Nation of Islam, 1960–1975*. Chapel Hill: University of North Carolina Press, 2006.

Derr, Jill Mulvay, Janath Russell Cannon, and Maureen Ursenbach Beecher. *Women of Covenant: The Story of Relief Society*. Salt Lake City: Deseret, 1992.

Tate, Sonsyrea. *Little X: Growing Up in the Nation of Islam*. San Francisco: Harper-SanFrancisco, 1997.

Eleven

MINDFUL EATING

AMERICAN BUDDHISTS AND
WORLDLY BENEFITS

JEFF WILSON

P RACTICED IN A wide range of Asian countries and cultures, Buddhism is one of history's most successful religions and is currently
expanding into yet another area: the modern West. Moving out of
India into a wide range of different Asian regions, Buddhism penetrated
new cultures through a process of creative adaptation, especially by re-
configurations that allowed it to provide concrete benefits that each new
culture desired. For example, Buddhism's patronage in China often came
from rulers who appreciated the teaching that the buddhas and Buddhist
gods would provide supernatural support to kings who protected the
monks and made offerings for the creation of scriptures and images. In
fact, many of the scriptures that advance this teaching were themselves
written in China, not India, suggesting that this was part of an adaptive
strategy to make Buddhism fit the needs of Chinese patrons.[1] Likewise,
in the Japanese situation, Ian Reader and George Tanabe have identified
the importance of *genze riyaku* (this-worldly or practical benefits) in the
spread, domestication, and continuing patronage of Buddhism by people
at all levels of society.[2] The worldly benefits most often sought by Japanese Buddhist practitioners are faith-healing, protection from harm, love,
business success, and the bestowal of children, especially sons. While they

have undergone modifications in the modern world (Buddhist charms to prevent traffic accidents are popular today, for instance), the general patterns have remained remarkably intact from premodern times.

It should not be surprising, therefore, that as Buddhism moves into a different cultural sphere—modern industrialized America—it is being reshaped yet again to fit the desires of a new host country. For example, popular books espouse a radically modified form of Buddhism pruned of "Asian trappings" that were accumulated by "impure mixtures" of basic Buddhism with local cultural traditions and outside religions, such as Confucianism or animistic cults. This is essentially a version of the venerable Protestant critique applied to the Buddhist religion, and such modern adherents believe they are getting back to the essence of "real" Buddhism, unencumbered by Asian ideas of the divine right of kings or faith-healing, lucky charms, and love magic.

Yet, ironically, this newly pared-down Buddhism that supposedly returns to Indian roots is eminently prepared to be applied to the worldly cultural concerns of Americans, especially those in the middle-class, mainly white communities that have dominated the public conversation about what American Buddhism should be. This segment of the population has specific worldly concerns: healthy relationships in the family, balanced living that doesn't harm the environment, management of work-related stress, and individual fulfillment. Buddhism is being marshaled to assist in the achievement of all these concerns. But there is one aspect of American culture that looms even larger than the others, one that is a veritable obsession for white Buddhists and their fellow travelers: food, eating, weight, and diet. These practitioners are part of the demographic that has fueled the growth of gyms, weight-loss fads, vitamins and supplements, and even gastric bypass surgery. It should be no surprise, therefore, that they promote Buddhism as the key to solving issues related to food and body image.

This chapter argues that the recent flurry of publications around Buddhism and food represents the application of a previously unnoted "practical benefits" approach to Buddhism by American Buddhist converts and sympathizers. While this demographic believes it has done away with such "attachment-based" utilizations of Buddhism, in fact their stripped-down approach makes aspects of Buddhism available for application to new culture-specific concerns such as overeating, eating disorders, and wasteful consumption—so available, in fact, that now many of the people pioneering such applications are not even Buddhist themselves. Repeating the ancient pattern of creative reinterpretation to meet local needs and anxieties, these prominent Buddhist teachers and their non-Buddhist counterparts are domesticating Buddhism for an American culture with different—but no less worldly—concerns from those of the Asian cultures from which they received Buddhism.

METHODS AND BACKGROUND

The primary sources for this essay are a series of books, representing many of the common trends found in this movement: Jan Chozen Bays's *Mindful Eating: A Guide to Rediscovering a Healthy and Joyful Relationship to Food*; Susan Albers's *Eat, Drink, and Be Mindful: How to End Your Struggle with Mindless Eating and Start Savoring Food with Intention and Joy, Mindful Eating 101: A Guide to Healthy Eating in College and Beyond*, and *Eating Mindfully: How to End Mindless Eating & Enjoy a Balanced Relationship with Food*; Pavel Somov's *Eating the Moment: 141 Mindful Practices to Overcome Overeating One Meal at a Time*; Donald Altman's *Meal by Meal: 365 Daily Meditations for Finding Balance Through Mindful Eating*; and Ronna Kabatznick's *The Zen of Eating: Ancient Answers to Modern Weight Problems*. As the titles of these books indicate, the Buddhist practice of meditation-based mindfulness is being applied to American eating habits. This approach has been highly successful: not only have a large number of books been produced, but these authors have been variously featured in such magazines as *O: The Oprah Magazine, Newsweek, Self, Ms., Psychology Today, Healthy Weight Journal, Vegetarian Times, Tikkun*, and *Tricycle: The Buddhist Review*.

Buddhism has always had a relationship with food. For instance, monks' eating practices were minutely managed according to codes of discipline. But the teachings set forth in these volumes represent a radically new (though usually presented as if traditional) application of Buddhism. Whereas Asian Buddhist teachings about food and the body emphasize renunciation and self-denial, these American authors utilize Buddhism to help the reader "*enjoy* a balanced relationship with food" and promote "a healthy and *joyful* relationship with food." Mindfulness, it is alleged, will increase the pleasure of eating and help readers lose weight, conquer eating disorders, avoid multiple health problems, and use food for personal spiritual attainment. To understand how this represents a new adaptation, we must first examine the origin of mindfulness teachings.

Mindfulness meditation techniques developed within early Indian Buddhism and are recorded in such classic scriptures as the *Satipatthana Sutta*. In this text the Buddha teaches his monks a variety of methods for maintaining awareness of the body and mind. He describes the purpose of mindfulness practices: "Monks, this is the direct path for the purification of beings, for the surmounting of sorrow and lamentation, for the disappearance of pain and grief, for the attainment of the true way, for the realization of Nirvana—namely, the four foundations of mindfulness."[3] Here mindfulness is clearly associated with traditional transcendent monastic concerns (nirvana). But language such as getting rid of "sorrow," "pain," and "grief"—which in context suggests escape from this suffering world into nirvana—is ambiguous enough that it can be reread to suggest applications to improve and enhance ordinary lay life. It is precisely this sort of slippage that allows for creative new adaptations. In the American context, this means that mindfulness and food disciplines—both associated historically with the transcendent, renouncing side of Buddhism—are assimilated instead to an alternate but equally venerable strand of Buddhist tradition: the quest for practical, worldly benefits.

The specific method most associated with mindfulness within American Buddhism is that of simply observing changes as they occur within oneself or in one's environment. For example, if a thought arises in the mind about something, one merely notes "thinking" and tries not to react to the thought in any particular way. Similarly, if one commits an action of some sort, such as yawning, one mentally notes "feeling urge to yawn . . . . raising hand to cover mouth . . . opening mouth . . . closing mouth . . . lowering hand." Like all meditation techniques, it has not been widespread among the mass of regular lay practitioners in Buddhist countries, but—as an early technique that perhaps traces back to the historical Buddha himself—it has existed in some form in most traditions of Buddhism and thus has always been at least a dormant resource waiting to be called forth to meet new situations.

This mindfulness meditation comes to American Buddhism through several related sources. One major source is the Theravada Buddhist tradition, which includes the *Satipatthana Sutta* among its scriptures and is mainly found in Southeast Asia. Within traditional Theravada, mindfulness meditation is primarily restricted to the monks. However, reform movements in some Buddhist countries, such as Burma and Thailand, have sought in the past two centuries to emphasize meditation practice as core to Buddhist practice and to make it available to all sectors of society. Thus it is from Theravada organizations and teachers influenced by these reformist trends (such as the popular Vipassana movement) that mindfulness practice most often comes to the United States.

A second major source for mindfulness teachings in America is the Vietnamese Buddhist monk Thich Nhat Hanh. Supported by one of the most robust publishing operations in American Buddhism, Hanh is among the most popular and recognizable of all Buddhist figures in the West. The Vietnamese tradition that Hanh draws from represents a second branch of Buddhism known as Mahayana. He specifically locates himself within the Thien lineage, a close cousin of Japanese Zen, and because Zen is far better known in the West, he is often referred to as "Zen Master Thich Nhat Hanh." While deriving from the same Chinese roots and sharing many aspects with Zen, Thien is nonetheless distinctive in certain ways that makes a facile conflation of Vietnamese and Japanese traditions problematic. In fact, one of the main differences is that Vietnam, a borderland Mahayana culture also influenced by the nearby Theravada countries, includes a greater emphasis on *Satipatthana Sutta*-type mindfulness exercises. These receive major attention in Hanh's teachings, such as in his popular book *The Miracle of Mindfulness*:

> I like to walk along on country paths, rice plants and wild grasses on both sides, putting each foot down on the earth in mindfulness, knowing that I walk on the wondrous earth. In such moments, existence is a miraculous and mysterious reality. People usually consider walking on water or in thin air a miracle. But I think the real miracle is not to walk either on water or in thin air, but to walk on earth.[4]

Like the Theravada reformers, Hanh recommends meditation practice for all people, monk and lay. While he himself is a celibate monk, his positive, world-affirming message has attracted large numbers of people with little interest in full renunciation.

The third major source for mindfulness in the United States is the work of Jon Kabat-Zinn, author of *Full Catastrophe Living: Using the Wisdom of Your Body and Mind to Face Stress, Pain, and Illness*.[5] Influenced by Zen

Buddhism, Theravada mindfulness techniques, and Westernized forms of hatha yoga, Kabat-Zinn has sought to employ mindfulness as a therapeutic technique for healing and stress relief. His most famous project is the creation of Mindfulness-Based Stress Reduction (MBSR), which is taught in secular hospital, educational, and therapy settings to help patients of all religious orientations deal with pain and stress. He has also carried out or encouraged the performance of many clinical experiments designed to demonstrate the measurable medical and psychological benefits of meditation.

Kabat-Zinn seeks to make Buddhist practices available to the widest possible audience: "What I'm most interested in is the use of Buddhist meditative practices, as opposed to spreading Buddhism, if you will. There was a time that I considered myself to be a Buddhist, but I actually don't consider myself to be one now, and although I teach Buddhist meditation, it's not with the aim of people becoming Buddhist."[6]

Removing most of the Buddhist context while maintaining the Buddhist practice of mindfulness itself, Kabat-Zinn has created a sort of denatured "post-Buddhism" that is able to be performed as easily by non-Buddhists as by Buddhists themselves, and this, combined with his scientific and psychological approach, has made his work extremely popular with large numbers of psychologists, psychiatrists, counselors, doctors, and others in the helping professions, most of whom are not formally Buddhist. In this he is partially continuing the pattern set earlier by advocates of Theravada-derived mindfulness, some of whom noted a natural synergism between Buddhist techniques and modern psychology and sought to bring them into mutual influence. Kabat-Zinn's work, in turn, has been studied and furthered by many people within the Buddhist community, influencing how they understand, practice, and market Buddhism and mindfulness.

Together these three strands form the major influence on the mindfulness movement, including the emergence of mindful eating in America. Nearly all the books on mindful eating reference Theravada mindfulness teachings, quote Thich Nhat Hanh (who has his own book on mindful eating), and refer positively to Kabat-Zinn's work for validation of their claims. Along with a more diffuse background of other Buddhist teachers who included (though typically with less direct or single-minded emphasis) mindfulness practice in their teachings, these sources have helped to define Buddhism for many Americans as inherently based on mindfulness meditation. Especially in the groups influenced by these teachers, which tend toward a majority white, middle-class lay demographic who came to Buddhist practice as adults, mindfulness has come to be a near universal practice that binds different traditions together in what some have argued is an emergent general American Buddhism.[7]

Given this widespread popularity, belief in mindfulness's practical benefits, and its ability to capture the attention of both influential middle-class Buddhists and the therapy and self-help industries, it comes as little surprise that mindfulness has been applied to virtually every problem or issue imaginable. Eating, however, is an especially good example to study—not only is it an activity that all Americans engage in daily, but it is a source of considerable anxiety, desire, confusion, and stress in modern society, as evidenced by the multibillion-dollar dieting industry and the constant popular culture obsession with celebrities and their physical appearance.

Mindfulness-meditation books published prior to the rise of mindful eating as a full-fledged movement sometimes used eating-related examples in explaining Buddhist practice. For example, in *The Miracle of Mindfulness*, Thich Nhat Hanh uses the example of eating a tangerine slowly, with close attention slice by slice, as a way of learning how to develop one's powers of meditation.[8] This tangerine-meditation technique has been widely quoted by other authors as a way of introducing newcomers to simple meditation practices. However, in these earlier books food is used merely as an example of how to become mindful in general, whereas in the later books the arrow is reversed: mindfulness is specifically applied to food in order to gain the benefits derived from eating and drinking in a mindful manner. Instead of everyday activities being used as a skillful means by which to awaken to transcendental Buddhist insight into no-self and impermanence, now monastic techniques are being used to transform everyday activities so that they provide greater happiness, health, and self-control to laypeople, many of whom do not consider themselves Buddhist.

PRACTICAL BENEFITS AND WORLDLY AFFIRMATIONS

Ian Reader and George Tanabe believe that spiritual practice to obtain practical, this-worldly benefit characterizes much of Japanese Buddhism.

Indeed, they term such an approach the "common religion" of Japan because it is shared by both elites and ordinary practitioners and can be found within a variety of different types of organizations.[9] Practical benefits in this world are closely associated with new religious movements in modern Japan, and at the same time they are part of the basic stock-in-trade of traditional denominations, such as Soto Zen. They were an important part of Buddhism's initial introduction to Japan (and elsewhere), and it was the progressive development of new practical services and adaptation of such services to fit changing Japanese needs that allowed Buddhism to penetrate all levels of society. This is to say, practical worldly benefits are intrinsic to Japanese Buddhism (and other Buddhisms), and their evolution is key to the domestication of what was originally a foreign religion.

In the United States, Buddhism is once more being adapted from a foreign into a domestic religion, and practical worldly benefits are a main part of this process. But just as the story of Japan's Buddhification and Buddhism's Japanification replicates older patterns while nonetheless being a particular situation with unique local characteristics, so too the encounter of Buddhism and America is being played out with new actors and scenery while still according in many ways with ancient scripts. For example, we find mindfulness meditation being abstracted from its Buddhist context and marketed as a way of providing health, weight loss, happiness, and spiritual insight. But since Buddhism in America has been closely aligned with the Human Potential Movement, New Age, and other particular later twentieth- and early twenty-first-century phenomena, they affect the specific manifestations and trajectories that Buddhism shows as it is domesticated.

The backgrounds of the authors and their target readerships affect the process of domestication. These authors are white, from non-Buddhist family backgrounds, with middle-class professional occupations, mainly as counselors and psychologists (Bays, Albers, Somov, and Kabatznick all have doctorates). Their clients and target audience seem to share these traits: the texts always assume that readers have ready access to food, are able to afford therapy, are able to eat out, and primarily experience personal, self-critical, middle-class suffering rather than social suffering caused by poverty, discrimination, or disability. Everyone in the stories these authors use as examples has cars, televisions, desk jobs, and so on, and they are often depicted in the midst of travel for business or pleasure.

For example, Somov poses a sort of koan: "If the backseat of your Ford Taurus is good enough to make love, why is it not good enough to make love to a $250 Fritz Knipschildt dark truffle?"[10] It is taken for granted that the reader will be able to afford a Ford Taurus and spend hundreds of dollars on a bon-bon.

Another notable aspect of the authors (and especially the audiences) is the gender dynamic. Three of the five authors are female, and the great majority of the stories they tell about clients involve women. Despite protestations that "mindless eating is not just a 'girl thing,'" it is clear that the mindful eating movement is mainly directed toward women, and it is not coincidental that all the discernibly gendered persons on the covers of these books are women. This comes about in part because women experience eating disorders in far greater numbers compared to men, because women are especially well represented in the counseling professions, and because women are the main consumers of the weight loss and dieting industries. Many observers of American Buddhism have suggested that the role of women in adapting Buddhism is a particularly noteworthy phenomenon to pay attention to. Here we see this insight borne out, as Buddhism is domesticated in a manner designed specifically to provide the sort of practical benefits that women seek, especially those of the middle class.

Modern America is a realm of world-affirming culture and religion. While it is easy to caricature the instant gratification and materialistic orientations of Americans, they are undeniably a strong force in American culture. Mindful-eating proponents are aware of this and play off this dynamic as both critics and supporters. For example, they tend to be harshly critical of ordinary American culture, especially as it relates to eating practices. Altman writes, "Patience is not easily understood in our culture. If anything, our lifestyle is greatly measured by speed. Think about it: We drive on expressways. We even check out our food in 'express lanes.' TV meals are ready in minutes, and some takeout pizza restaurants promise 'thirty-minute delivery to your door or your money back.'"[11] On the very first page of her book *Eating Mindfully*, Albers paints the situation in the bleakest possible terms: "Deciding what to eat is not an easy task. It's so tricky that in the United States eating concerns and weight obsessions have reached epidemic proportions, with serious health consequences for a large part of the population."[12]

At first glance the messages attached to some forms of mindfulness might seem to contradict the general affirmative cultural trend. But these mindful eaters are not nearly as countercultural as they may appear. When certain aspects of American consumerism, distractedness, and super-sized restaurant portions are criticized in these books, it is because excessive consumption—especially of low-quality foods—is seen to be unhealthy. This is not a critique of consumption per se, but of unbalanced consumption that to some interpreters seems to denote a type of addiction (that is to say, an attachment).

When we look at the goals of mindfulness-based self-help programs, we still find that they are oriented toward delivering this-worldly benefits. Cutting down on one's eating is a strategy for achieving happiness—the problem with overeating is not that it is consumeristic, but that it fails to deliver happiness. Thus the apparent renunciation involved in mindful eating is actually a renunciation of misleading, ineffective methods for achieving benefits in favor of correct, useful methods derived from Buddhist wisdom and practice. Renunciation, in the American Buddhist world, is a world-affirming and self-fulfilling practice partially couched in the spiritual language of world-abnegation and self-denial. We can see this when we focus on some of the benefits alleged to be gained through mindful eating. For example, the process of eating and preparing to eat in a mindful way is said to produce delight:

As you become mindful of the many wonders in life, mundane tasks like fixing a bag lunch can be transformed into a cornucopia of delight. You are present enough to enjoy the graceful motion of each swipe of mustard on the bread and notice the colors of everything involved: brown bread, yellow mustard, green lettuce, purple onion, red tomato, and pale-white cheese. The variety of colors and motions is a lot more fun than wanting the dull task to be over. . . . Mindfulness helps you fall in love with the ordinary.[13]

Time and again these authors stress that eating can be a source of pleasure, not something to be detached from. Bays notes that "mindful eating is a way to reawaken our pleasure in simply eating, simply drinking. . . . What you could gain are a simple joy with food and an easy pleasure in eating that are your birthrights as a human being. . . . When we learn to eat mindfully, our eating can be transformed from a source of suffering to a source of renewal, self-understanding, and delight."[14] Here we learn that happiness is our birthright—a less renunciatory attitude could scarcely be imagined, especially when contrasted with the traditional monastic Buddhist view that life is a realm of inherent suffering that is to be shunned and escaped from. And this world-affirmation links Buddhist-derived mindfulness practices in America both within temples and meditation centers (that is, explicitly Buddhist spaces) and within the wider world of popular culture, psychology, and self-help movements that is shared by the mainstream non-Buddhist population.

Thus American Buddhism functions less as a counterculture than as a subculture, one that shares in the attitudes and concerns of the larger populace, but with particular stress on certain techniques, beliefs, and aesthetics as a way of maximizing practical and transcendent benefits. It is precisely because there are shared attitudes within and without American Buddhism that it is able to effectively market selective elements of itself to the culture at large (such as mindfulness), and conversely why it is vulnerable to fads and trends in American popular and medical/psychological culture.

Japanese religion distinguishes two categories to practical benefits: *yakuyoke* (the prevention of danger) and *kaiun* (the receipt of good fortune). Both appear in the promotion of mindful eating by Americans. For example, a partial list of the dangers caused by lack of mindful eating appears in *Eating Mindfully*: "Weakness, chronic tiredness, injuries that won't heal, cuts or bruises, inability to concentrate, headaches, palpitations, or fluttering, of the heart, stomach pain, gas, sore throat, vomiting blood, sensitive teeth, constipation, bloating, dehydration, dry skin, scar on fingers from inducing vomiting, aching muscles, easily broken bones, irregular periods, cramps, cold, lack of energy, fainting, dizzy, bowel movement problems."[15] The author of *Mindful Eating* adds: "Our struggles with food cause tremendous emotional distress, including guilt, shame, and depression. As a physician, I've also seen how our eating problems can lead to debilitating diseases and even to premature death."[16] Nearly all these authors discuss obesity, poor self-esteem, hypertension, high cholesterol, cancer, and diabetes as further risks that mindful eating can ward off. On the other hand, good fortune can also allegedly be received through mindfulness, as it provides physical attractiveness, self-confidence, pleasure in the act of eating, and enhanced self-control.

These come about through the application of mindfulness to eating because it is a useful tool:

When you pay attention to what's true in the moment (as you shop, cook, eat, or dance) that focused awareness slows you down long enough to examine your old habits. If you *know* you're reaching for a chocolate chip cookie, that moment of mindfulness can break the automatic response to mindlessly put it in your mouth. This awareness helps cut through the compulsive habit of chasing desire after desire only to experience deeper and deeper levels of hunger.[17]

Reducing such compulsions, one is able to replace them with healthy behaviors and reap their rewards. For example, "Another bonus of eating mindfully is that it improves self-esteem, while mindless eating, with the inevitable weight issues, significantly infringes upon self-confidence."[18] Indeed, for most of these authors, self-esteem (sometimes couched as "self-acceptance and body acceptance") seems to be the key factor that must be improved in order for a better relationship with food to be reached.[19]

There is an irony to such calls for acceptance of the body—and by extension one's total self—as they directly contradict traditional mindfulness teachings. The *Satipatthana Sutta* has a lot to say about bodies, and it isn't very warm or fuzzy:

A monk reviews this same body up from the soles of the feet and down from the top of the hair, bounded by skin, as full of many kinds of impurity thus: "In this body there are head-hairs, body-hairs, nails, teeth, skin, flesh, sinews, bones, bone-marrow, kidneys, heart, liver, diaphragm, spleen, lungs, large intestines, small intestines, contents of the stomach, feces, bile, phlegm, pus, blood, sweat, fat, tears, grease, spittle, snot, oil of the joints, and urine." . . . In this way he abides contemplating the body as a body internally, externally, and both internally and externally. . . . And he abides independent, not clinging to anything in the world.[20]

This traditional source for mindfulness practice advocates viewing the body as impure, full of guts and disgusting substances, and recommends detachment from—not love for and acceptance of—the body. Soon thereafter it goes into even more visceral detail, as the Buddha tells the reader to think of one's own body as a rotting, oozing corpse eaten by worms and disintegrating into its component parts. Thus not only do we see mindfulness practice recontextualized, but foundational scriptures are selectively quoted to create a new interpretation of Buddhism that can provide the sort of practical benefits Americans seek.

ENACTING DISCIPLINE

For those who market them and those who actually put them into practice, mindful eating programs are about establishing control over important aspects of one's life, reflecting an anxiety about powerlessness in a complex and fast-paced society where personal success is less than guaranteed. It seems likely that control over food is asserted when control over one's job, family, and other aspects of life is impossible: anxieties are sublimated and transferred into a realm (eating) that *is* self-manageable. Thus these authors frequently assert the need for strict personal discipline in one's approach to mindfulness. Susan Albers claims that "the key to changing the way you eat is not to develop discipline over your fork, but to master control of your mind . . . becoming aware is the first step of being in control. . . . Mindful eating requires you to consciously say to yourself, 'I choose to change my eating, and I will work through any difficulties,' every time you sit down to eat a meal."[21] Pavel Somov stresses that "control is based on presence of mind—that is, on mindfulness. . . . You can either be mindful or mindless, conscious or unconscious, in control or out of control. But you can't be both."[22] This search for discipline becomes totalistic in many of these books. Ronna Kabatznick tells readers to achieve regular mindfulness by any means necessary:

> It's impossible for me to emphasize enough the importance of daily mindfulness practice, one in which you take time to sit in silence and train your mind to attend without clinging to the present moment. Set aside a certain time and place to practice each day. Allow nothing to stand in your way of this time alone, even if it means getting up earlier or staying up later, or drastically rearranging your daily schedule."[23]

She recommends at least thirty to sixty minutes of silent meditation per day.

This emphasis on strict self-discipline is partially a trace of the monastic origins of these practices—arguably, rigorously applied mindfulness during eating and other daily activities develops into a sort of lay, fully secularized neomonasticism in the American context. These authors are convinced that you cannot expect to get something for nothing, and that mindfulness should ideally become a lens through which all of life is experienced:

> In this chapter you've learned that mindfulness is a way of being in the world. It's based on awareness and being completely present. It teaches you to look at the world through open eyes, noticing rather than judging. You can use mindfulness as a way to approach anything you do in the world, in the way you work, relate to people, or deal with painful issues in your life.[24]

PSYCHOLOGY AND THE DE-BUDDHIFICATION OF BUDDHISM

Mindful eating is arguably as much about modern psychology as it is about Buddhism proper. Much of the mainstream Buddhist worldview is downplayed or simply left out of these books on mindful eating. For example, none of the authors suggests that eating problems might be the result of karma from previous lives—a traditional explanation for problems that many Asian lineages would include as likely explanations. Instead, readers are told that "mindless eating" results from psychological attitudes acquired during one's present lifetime, the products of such things as one's childhood, assault by the media, or loneliness and poor self-esteem. Albers offers an example of the latter explanation:

> Buddhist theory identifies craving as the root of suffering. Emotional cravings can be more powerful, insatiable, and destructive than physical hunger. Your emotional desires aren't as clear-cut or predictable as your desire to eat. As you become more mindful, you will begin to realize exactly what your heart hungers for. Examples include cravings for companionship, love, power, and control. In contrast to food, these longings are not as easily fulfilled. Sometimes, people misinterpret their heart cravings, and try to feed their bodies when they actually need to take better care of their souls."[25]

In this quote Albers appears to gesture toward Buddhist understandings of suffering, since she highlights the role of desire in causing pain. Yet this description is almost exactly the opposite of traditional Buddhist advice: here the solution is to heal one's soul (Buddhism explicitly denies the existence of a soul) by giving it what it craves (rather than cultivating detachment and equanimity). Albers presents herself as a psychologist, not a Buddhist, but this approach is displayed by the overtly Buddhist authors as well, such as Zen priest Jan Bays: "Most unbalanced relationships with food are caused by being unaware of heart hunger. No food can ever satisfy this form of hunger. To satisfy it, we must learn how to nourish our hearts."[26] This demonstrates the selective adoption or dissemination of Buddhist aspects that these mindful-eating practitioners propose. They willingly appropriate Buddhist teachings about suffering and techniques such as mindfulness, but other core elements, such as no-self, impermanence, and nirvana, are often left out. Or, if included, they are recontextualized in ways that appeal to the American mindset but are generally alien to historical Buddhism: "Change is good, natural, and inevitable," Albers asserts, despite the fact that Buddhism has usually identified change as one of the primary sources of human suffering.[27]

An interesting transformation occurs in relation to Buddhist concepts of merit dedication. This is one of the few truly universal Buddhist practices, engaged in by all sects of Buddhism without exception, and shared to some extent by both monastics and the laity. In normal practice merit is generated through good actions that accord with Buddhist morality, or through quasimagical actions such as chanting mantras or scriptures, and then dedicated to other beings for their benefit. Traditionally these are almost always the deceased ancestors of the practitioner, or a more general donation on the behalf of all beings in the universe. In the mindful-eating movement, however, this practice takes on a very different form:

> Another way to give eating and the difficulties you have with food more meaning is by dedicating merit. This is the practice of offering any benefit that comes from your commitment to healthy eating to specific people or groups of people. You share any benefits that may come from your actions with others instead of holding on to them for yourself. If you know your actions might help someone in some way, you may be more motivated to do the best you can. Your actions have consequences, whether you are aware

of them or not. My friend who is a cancer survivor dedicates any merit she may receive from healthful eating to her husband and daughter. "What I put in my body is my future, and my future affects my family. It's easy for me to eat well because what I eat includes the people I love the most." . . . You can dedicate merit that comes from eating more fresh fruit and vegetables to the farmers at the outdoor market, the soil, sun and rain, to all that helped nourish you.[28]

Here the targets of merit donation are living, rather than the usual dedication to spirits. While acknowledging that merit is sometimes donated to living rather than dead beings in Asian Buddhism, we must note how here the practice has shifted entirely toward the living beings of this world, with no attention paid to the spirit world. Furthermore, the technique for generating merit has changed: eating healthy foods is not historically associated with merit production. Another example is the encouragement of readers to make self-help type phrases into mantras, such as "Eat, Drink, and Be Mindful."[29] Normal mantras are associated with specific deities or scriptural texts and can be used to generate merit, to develop one-pointed concentration, or as spells. But in this context mantras are reduced to pithy sayings that help the practitioner achieve her goal of control over food.

Of course, mindfulness itself is the practice that is being most altered. Proponents of mindful eating believe that it conveys practical benefits because by paying close attention to one's eating habits, the practitioner is able to recognize their unhealthy habits and pursue more balanced forms of consumption, and because awareness infuses the process of eating itself with fun. As Jan Bays states, "Mindfulness brings about change from within. A natural and organic process, it occurs in the manner and at the rate that fits us. It is the ultimate in natural healing."[30] All these authors talk about the "healing" nature of mindfulness, rather than its traditional context of detachment from the suffering world and escape to nirvanic consciousness beyond the slings and arrows of mortal life. Having mostly jettisoned the notions of karma, rebirth, and other realms in favor of more rationalistic and psychological modes in tune with Western science and skepticism, the authors, not surprisingly, frequently use science to justify their claims around mindful eating. Bays's assertion that "a large and growing body of scientific studies supports the claims about the surprisingly reliable healing abilities of mindfulness"[31] is echoed throughout these books.

Most authors take pains to reassure their readers that one does not have to be a Buddhist to receive the benefits of mindful eating: "It is not necessary to become a Buddhist or attend a weeklong silent retreat in order to experience the benefits of mindfulness."[32] At times Buddhism is hidden entirely, the better to market mindful eating to a mainly non-Buddhist American society. Instead mindfulness is said to derive from un-specified "ancient cultures" or vague "Eastern traditions." For example, in *Mindful Eating 101*, Albers merely says, "Ancient civilizations knew how important it is to have a clear and present mind"[33] and in *Eat, Drink, and Be Mindful* explains that "Mindfulness—or more specifically, mindful eat-ing—isn't a new concept. In fact, it is centuries old and based on the East-ern concept of mindfulness, or 'pure awareness.'"[34] These generic terms allow authors to downplay Buddhism's history as a large, premodern reli-gious tradition, transmuting it into a pared-down form of personal spiri-tuality, a rationalized form of inner philosophy, or a mere set of practices designed to provide practical benefits to the user.

It is important to note the role that non-Buddhists, as producers and consumers, play in the domestication of Buddhism in America. Bud-dhism is deliberately made "less Buddhist" in order to speak to a wider culture existing outside of Buddhism. Part of this shift involves altering the sources of authority over Buddhist practice: most of these books urge readers to seek out professional counselors to help them with mindful eating, but none recommends receiving advice from an ordained Buddhist teacher or attending a temple to further their practice. In the mindful-eating movement, Buddhist practice has been removed from the realm of religion and professionalized to become the property of psychologists and diet counselors, to be engaged in by clients rather than believers, who are not expected to take refuge, read scriptures, believe in rebirth, or become Buddhist.

To conclude, in the rise of the mindful-eating movement we can see that mindfulness has become the Buddhist equivalent of Hindu-derived yoga in modern American culture: a religious technique that has been largely stripped of its original religious context, then repackaged as a uni-versal panacea that delivers all sorts of practical benefits, especially ones relating to health issues. Because mindfulness is said to deliver practi-cal benefits—such as weight loss and better health—it is enthusiastically picked up by Buddhists and non-Buddhists alike, making a significant Buddhist contribution to American eating habits while changing what Buddhism itself is about. Thus the venerable pattern of domesticating Buddhism by using it to convey worldly benefits has been repeated once more, this time in the diet-obsessed culture of the contemporary United States.

DISCUSSION QUESTIONS

1. How are this-worldly benefits sought via eating practices by religions other than Buddhism?
2. If readers do not actually practice mindful eating but merely buy books and think about the subject, are they engaged in religious activities? Might they derive some benefits from imagining or contemplating mindful eating?
3. Is Buddhism the only religion in North America influenced by trends in modern psychology? Can you think of other examples?
4. If the techniques of a religion are applied in ways different from or even opposite to how they have been utilized in the past, is it still the same religion? Why or why not?

NOTES

1. Charles Orzech, trans., "The Scripture on Perfect Wisdom for Humane Kings Who Wish to Protect Their States" in *Chinese Religions in Practice*, ed. Donald S. Lopez Jr., 372–80 (Princeton: Princeton University Press, 1996).
2. Ian Reader and George J. Tanabe Jr., *Practically Religious: Worldly Benefits and the Common Religion of Japan* (Honolulu: University of Hawaii Press, 1998), 2.
3. Bhikkhu Nanamoli and Bhikkhu Bodhi, trans., *The Middle Length Sayings of the Buddha: A New Translation of the Majjhima Nikaya* (Somerville, Mass.: Wisdom Publications, 1995), 145.
4. Thich Nhat Hanh, *The Miracle of Mindfulness: A Manual on Meditation* (Boston: Beacon, 1987), 12.
5. Jon Kabat-Zinn, *Full Catastrophe Living: Using the Wisdom of Your Body and Mind to Face Stress, Pain, and Illness* (New York: Delacorte, 1990).
6. Jon Kabat-Zinn, "Toward the Mainstreaming of American Dharma Practice" in *Buddhism in America: Proceedings of the First Buddhism in American Conference*, ed. Al Rapaport, 479 (Boston: Tuttle, 1998).

7. James William Coleman, *The New Buddhism: The Western Transformation of an Ancient Tradition* (New York: Oxford University Press, 2001).
8. Hanh, *Miracle of Mindfulness*, 5–6.
9. Reader and Tanabe, *Practically Religious*, 29.
10. Pavel Somov, *Eating the Moment: 141 Mindful Practices to Overcome Overeating One Meal at a Time* (Oakland: New Harbinger, 2008), 124.
11. Donald Altman, *Meal by Meal: 365 Daily Meditations for Finding Balance Through Mindful Eating* (Novato, Calif.: New World Library, 2004), unpaginated entry for March 11.
12. Susan Albers, *Eating Mindfully: How to End Mindless Eating & Enjoy a Balanced Relationship with Food* (Oakland: New Harbinger, 2003), 68.
13. Ronna Kabatznick, *The Zen of Eating: Ancient Answers to Modern Weight Problems* (New York: Berkley, 1998), 32, 78.
14. Jan Chozen Bays, *Mindful Eating: A Guide to Rediscovering a Healthy and Joyful Relationship with Food* (Boston: Shambhala, 2009) 2, 5.
15. Albers, *Eating Mindfully*, 80–81.
16. Bays, *Mindful Eating*, xvii.
17. Kabatznick, *Zen of Eating*, 77.
18. Susan Albers, *Mindful Eating 101: A Guide to Eating in College and Beyond* (New York: Routledge, 2006), 8.
19. Susan Albers, *Eat, Drink, and Be Mindful: How to End Your Struggle with Mindless Eating and Start Savoring Food with Intention and Joy* (Oakland: New Harbinger, 2008), 2.
20. Nanamoli and Bodhi, *Middle Length Sayings*, 147.
21. Albers, *Eating Mindfully*, 3, 16, 45.
22. Somov, *Eating the Moment*, 127.
23. Kabatznick, *Zen of Eating*, 165.
24. Albers, *Eat, Drink, and Be Mindful*, 18.
25. Albers, *Eating Mindfully*, 115.
26. Bays, *Mindful Eating*, 58, italics in original.
27. Albers, *Eating Mindfully*, 62.
28. Kabatznick, *Zen of Eating*, 103.
29. Albers, *Eat, Drink, and Be Mindful*, 32.
30. Bays, *Mindful Eating*, 1.
31. Ibid., 3.
32. Ibid., 1.
33. Albers, *Eating Mindfully 101*, 10.
34. Albers, *Eat, Drink, and Be Mindful*, 9.

RECOMMENDED READING

Cadge, Wendy. *Heartwood: The First Generation of Theravada Buddhism in America.* Chicago: University of Chicago Press, 2004.

Prebish, Charles S., and Kenneth K. Tanaka, eds. *The Faces of Buddhism in America.* Berkeley: University of California Press, 1998.

Wilson, Jeff. *Mourning the Unborn Dead: A Buddhist Ritual Comes to America.* New York: Oxford University Press, 2009.

Twelve

THE FEAST AT THE END
OF THE FAST

THE EVOLUTION OF AN AMERICAN
JEWISH RITUAL

NORA L. RUBEL

T HERE IS A famous scene in Woody Allen's 1977 film, *Annie Hall*, where the Jewish protagonist Alvie Singer visits his girlfriend's family for Easter dinner. In a split-screen, imagined exchange between Annie's mother and Alvie's family at their respective dinner tables, the matriarch asks how the Jewish family will be spending "the holidays." Mrs. Singer immediately replies, "We fast." Mr. Singer chimes in, "Yeah, no food. You know, we have to atone for our sins." Mrs. Hall responds, "What sins? I don't understand." And Mr. Singer, still shoveling food in his mouth replies, "Tell you the truth, neither do we."[1]

Most attention to Jewish foodways involves examining the act of eating rather than that of not eating. Whether it be the ritualized foods of the Passover Seder or the conspicuous consumption at life-cycle celebrations such as bar and bat mitzvahs and weddings, scholars of foodways have an embarrassment of riches handed to them on a quasi-kosher plate. As Jenna Weissman Joselit has observed in her work on American Jews in the mid- twentieth century, "In lieu of going to *shul* or attending temple, the overwhelming majority of American Jews honed their sense of ritual not in the sanctuary but in the dining room, where they believed . . . that 'the array of traditional foods . . . is the flour that nourishes Judaism.'"[2] But the Jewish ritual year calls for abstention from food on at least six occasions, the most well-known and observed fast being that of the Day of Atonement, Yom Kippur. According to the 2000–2001 National Jewish Population Survey, 60 percent of American Jews fast on Yom Kippur, a number that is significantly higher than the percentage belonging to synagogues (47 percent).[3] The percentage of fasters rises to 79 percent if one looks only at synagogue-affiliated Jews; this percentage comes close to the 83 percent who light Chanukah candles and dwarfs the weekly lighting of Shabbat candles (48 percent). This practice of fasting is most common in communities with large Jewish populations, amusingly noted by a city study in the 1980s that concluded that "the non-Jewish spouse of a Jew in Baltimore was more likely to fast on Yom Kippur than a born Jew in San Francisco."[4]

But this essay is not about *not* eating. In many religious cultures, feasting follows a fast. The traditional Catholic fast days of Christmas Eve and the Lenten season's Ash Wednesday are followed by the feasts of Christmas Day and Easter. The monthlong daily fasts of Ramadan are followed by joyous iftars after sundown. It is, in fact, surprising that the twenty-five-hour fast of Yom Kippur is *not* directly followed by an elaborate feast. But traditionally—for a variety of economic and cultural factors—immediate postfast feasting has not been the practice of Ashkenazi (eastern European) Jews. Feasting did traditionally occur in the form of delayed gratification during the holiday of Sukkot, four days later. However, no longer content to anticlimactically sip a sweet glass of tea and nosh on a dry piece of honey cake left over from Rosh Hashanah, American Jews invented a Break Fast of their own.

In *We Are What We Celebrate*, Amitai Etzioni refers to both lightly edited and wholly engineered holidays, remarking that such "modifications . . . both reflect changes in values and power relations and help to formulate and ensconce changes in values and power."[5] The creation of the new American Break Fast likewise reflects the changing values and priorities of contemporary Jewish American culture alongside changes in American Jewish identity and practice. This essay addresses the historical and cultural evolution of the Break Fast among American Jews in the latter decades of the twentieth century as well as exploring its significance as an indicator of changing views of religious authority.

THE HIGHEST OF THE HIGH HOLY DAYS

As Orthodox rabbi Irving Greenberg has noted:

> Many American Jews who have allowed their observance of tradition to di-
> minish still observe Yom Kippur. This is a day of deprivation and denial, of
> guilt and self-flagellation. If Yom Kippur is their only contact with Judaism,
> one can only say: "O Lord, who is like your people, Israel?" What kind of
> devotion keeps people coming back year after year to a service that is long,
> exhausting, and solemn?[6]

The majority of American Jews do not attend religious services more
than a few times a year, so why do so many continue to fast on Yom Kippur?[7] This question is not new among spectators of American Jewish life.
In a 1959 study of suburban Jews, Albert Gordon suggested several motives for this observance: "Nostalgia; the feeling that parents, near or far,
would approve; the conventions of society . . . ; [and] the urging of one's
children." Almost as an afterthought he writes, "There are those, too, who
worship and pray in all sincerity and truth to a God in Whom they believe
without equivocation or uncertainty."[8] It does seem, however, at least to
Gordon, that the latter are a distinct minority, and it is clear that the in-
frequent worship patterns of American Jews are not a recent occurrence.
    In their 1967 study on Jewish identity and practice, sociologists Mar-
shall Sklare and Joseph Greenblum examined the reasons why some rituals
were retained by American Jews and why others were abandoned. Their
findings determined that rituals are most likely to be retained when the
ritual is, among other things, "capable of effective redefinition in modern terms, does not demand social isolation or the adoption of a unique
lifestyle, [and] accords with the religious culture of the larger community and provides a 'Jewish' alternative which is felt to be needed."[9] Selective observance is nothing new, particularly when the rituals that are
retained can be imbued with contemporary meaning.[10] This fast can be
broken down according to Sklare and Greenblum's findings. First, fasting on Yom Kippur can be redefined as a physical purification akin to a
contemporary cleanse detoxification diet or can be seen as spiritually pu-
rifying on a variety of other levels. While many people fast as a repentant
effort to have God hear their prayers, others may take advantage of this

day's hunger pains to think of those who have no food.[11] Second, fasting on Yom Kippur—unlike adopting a strictly kosher lifestyle—is a twenty-five-hour annual experiment; once over, there is no need to look back. And finally, and possibly most powerfully, other Jews are doing it all over the world at the same time. Fasters may feel linked to their ancestors and their community through this annual shared experience. As Martha Finch notes in her work on Puritan feasts and fasts, "suffering with others the discomforts of food deprivation . . . produced intense feelings of social bonding."[12] Likewise, the cessation of fasting with others in a shared celebration of bounty is also a bonding ritual.

BREAKING THE FAST

Historically, scant attention has been paid to the cuisine or etiquette surrounding the meal following the Yom Kippur fast in America. We can turn for evidence of this omission to Jewish cookbooks. As Barbara Kirschenblatt-Gimblett has noted, "Cookbooks, though not direct indications of what people ate, nevertheless represent Jewish cuisine and social life," and twentieth-century cookbooks, with a few noted exceptions, do not make mention of this meal with any detail until the last decades of the century.[13] The 1954 *Jewish Festival Cookbook* explains the evening following fasting thus: "All now return home to a meal as simple or elaborate as the family desires, and they while away the time before dinner is ready drinking coffee and nibbling on apples dipped in honey, and on *honey lekach* or coffee cake."[14] The authors offer a "Dinner to Break the Fast" menu, but it is a soup-to-nuts meal that includes chicken soup and roast duck or chicken, certainly not a ready-made buffet in waiting. A 1957 Ohio congregational cookbook merely comments that on "Yom Kippur night sweet and sour fish or herring is used to break the fast."[15] Jennie Grossinger's *The Art of Jewish Cooking*, a standard midcentury Jewish cookbook, gives absolutely no mention of this meal, and her book's foreword briefly describes the meal that precedes the fast, only to suggest that it be hearty but relatively bland—"to prevent undue thirst."[16] Under "Suggested Menus for the Principal Holidays," Yom Kippur does not appear. This is representative of most American Jewish cookbooks up to this point.

Elaborating a bit on the domestic practice of this festival, the popular 1964 *Guide for the Jewish Homemaker* suggests, "At home a light meal is eaten, a 'break the fast' meal." Under "Basic Holy Days Menus" the authors write: "To Break the Fast (Often this is a very light meal, almost like a breakfast): (*Suggestion*) Orange Juice, Eggs, Cheeses, Cold Fish, Salad, Cake, Coffee."[17] While these few cookbooks make brief mention of the ritual of breaking the fast, they offer no recipes and certainly do not indicate a large gathering. More common in the late 1960s was the appearance of extensive menus for the prefast dinner, complete with information on how to prepare most healthfully for the fast. The 1972 *A Taste of Tradition* offers such a menu for the prefast dinner and remarks briefly on the Break Fast: "Now, light refreshments are taken; perhaps a cup of tea and a delicate sweet. A little later, dinner that suits the personal preferences of each family is enjoyed. Some like salty foods, such as herring, to compensate for the loss of body salts; others prefer dairy dishes."[18] Again, this does not suggest more than some familial snacking to soothe the day's hunger pains.

While midcentury advice like that above describes a light family supper, later evidence from the 1980s and 1990s suggests a modern tradition of feasting, more reminiscent of those the high priests enjoyed after the Yom Kippur sacrifices at the Temple, a meal that is not "complete without a towering display of bagels, heaps of whitefish salad, ample platters of smoked salmon—and a houseful of hungry guests."[19] The 1990s and first decade of the 2000s saw magazines, cookbooks, and even supermarkets (with their enticing catering menus) give rise to new ideas regarding this feast—generally referred to as the Break Fast. The Internet, with blogs available on all elements of religious practice and dietary interests, is no exception. Conservative practitioners still tend to urge a tradition of moderation in breaking the fast, but contemporary publications frequently suggest a more satisfying—and filling—gastronomical conclusion to the day's supplications.

In the 1999 *Jewish Holiday Style*, the authors write: "This buffet is fun. Everyone is feeling wonderful, and everyone is starved, the perfect combination for a successful meal. At the conclusion of Yom Kippur, the havdalah prayer is recited over a cup of wine, and a festive meal is served."[20] They claim that it is customary to invite people over and offer an extensive menu with large numbers of servings per recipe. In 2008's *Jewish Holiday Cooking*, the author offers a story about Break Fasts before providing menus and recipes. She writes of a friend dying of pancreatic cancer who threw a Break Fast in her last year:

Phyllis had not intended her guest list to be Jewish, but this being Manhattan, as it turned out everyone who wasn't Jewish had a Jewish connection: a spouse or a parent, a loved one who was. And though only some of us had fasted, the delicious festive meal—catered smoked fish and salads from Russ and Daughters on the Lower East Side and home-baked desserts—tasted sacred to us all.[21]

Of course, through the contemporary availability of Jewish cookbooks that highlight the exotic cultures of Jews outside of eastern Europe, one is no longer restricted to the traditional blintzes and bagels of Ashkenazi cuisine.[22] One could break the fast with almond milk as the Iraqi or Indian Jews do, or with a spiced anise bread as Algerian Jews do, or with the delicious hearty bean soup known as *harira* that the Moroccan Jews adopted from their Ramadan-observant Muslim neighbors.[23] The popular culinary website Epicurious.com has even offered a "Mix-and-match Yom Kippur menu-maker for the Break Fast."[24] The menu suggestions for this meal found in these contemporary cookbooks, magazines, and websites again reflect the shift from a traditionally modest Break Fast to a far more lavish, brunch-style event. Despite what appears to be a rather high-class problem of deciding what to serve, the significance of participation in this new ritual should not be underappreciated.

Cookbooks are not the only evidence of the growing popularity of this ritualized gathering. A 2003 essay in the Jewish weekly *Forward* found an author declaring: "[W]hen a dish is not only delicious but also happens to be among those traditionally eaten at the close of Yom Kippur—when you join yourself with other Jews not just in the fasting, but in the eating as well—it becomes greater still, by satisfying more than one kind of hunger."[25]

What are these foods that are "traditionally eaten"? The assumption is that it is "Jewish" food—a subject too broad for the scope of this essay, as this category can include both bagels and lo mein.[26] Given a survey of Jewish cookbooks, both commercial and communal, that describe this meal, the most popular foods are dairy foods that can be served cold—essentially a brunch-style meal.[27] This eating of agreed upon Jewish food at the close of Yom Kippur reflects what Herbert Gans described in his 1979 essay on "symbolic ethnicity," which he defined as "a nostalgic allegiance . . . a love for and pride in a tradition that can be felt without having to be incorporated in everyday behavior."[28] However, the *Forward* writer suggests that by eating foods one identifies as Jewish, and by eating with other Jews, this ritualized Jewish experience can be more than just symbolic; it can be transformative.

In an essay in the Jewish journal *ZEEK*, Marilyn Sneiderman, executive director of AVODAH: The Jewish Service Corps, describes her annual Break Fast practice:

> Every year, . . . my family hosts a Yom Kippur Breakfast for 200 or so of our Jewish and non-Jewish friends. It is a time we reflect on what is going on in the world, ask ourselves what role we've played in challenging injustice, and recommit ourselves as a group to work for justice. I will never forget when we gathered after 9/11. Three of us led prayers, mine in Hebrew, a Christian friend in English, and a Muslim friend in Arabic. At a moment of such despair, it was incredibly powerful for our community, made up of people of different races and faiths, to join together on Yom Kippur to rededicate ourselves to rising above hate.[29]

Unlike Jewish holidays like Passover, Chanukah, or even Tu B'Shvat, which can be celebrated for their universalist themes and home-based practice, Yom Kippur is a different holiday entirely—one that speaks specifically to the relationship between Jews and their God and takes place primarily in the synagogue. But in the way that Sneiderman has crafted her Break Fast, she has been able to redefine Yom Kippur as potentially universal—a holiday that can be shared with non-Jews. Notably, she also redefines her community.

The solemnity of Yom Kippur traditionally is set apart from the more familiar food-centered Jewish calendar year, but with this increased popularity of the Break Fast party, the holiday becomes a bit more palatable to those Jews who enjoy the time with family and friends but may be less likely to spend the day in organized prayer. Cookbook author Joan Nathan, in her comprehensive *Jewish Cooking in America*, makes note of a "famous break-the-fast with every notable in Cincinnati attending. [According to one of the attendees:] 'Fifty percent of the people were gentiles who came and half of the Jews who came had not been to synagogue. This break-the-fast kept them within the periphery of Jewry.' "[30] According to another observer of Jewish cultural trends, "Many Jews—from articulate atheists to those for whom God 'isn't really an issue'—can now attend religious ceremonies tailored to appeal to their secularized tastes and values."[31]

Most of the comments about the Break Fast praised the emphasis on inclusivity, which extended to both the guest list and the observance level of the guests who attended. This might be partially due to the inevitable presence of those who are prohibited from fasting owing to age or medical necessity.[32] According to a Virginia woman interviewed for a 2011 *New York Times* story on the Break Fast, "It's a big break-fast, . . . but it's very inclusive, in that they make an effort to invite people like us, who are new in town. And nobody ever asks whether I have fasted or not. Sometimes I bring it up, like, 'You should eat first, I didn't fast.'" When she chose to host a Break Fast of her own, she made a point of inviting her Muslim neighbors who were ending their Ramadan fast for the day. In the same article, Alana Newhouse, editor of the online magazine *Tablet*, admits a longstanding antipathy toward Yom Kippur. But, she claims that "ever since deciding to make a big deal out of the break-fast, the fast itself has become much more meaningful to me. There is something to look forward to, in the interaction with other Jews, and non-Jews."[33] Anthropologist Carole Counihan remarks that "sharing food ensures the survival of the group both socially and materially," and this Break Fast—which as we have seen can be defined in a myriad of ways—therefore serves as a recommitment ritual for the family and the community.[34] And unlike other such recommitment rituals, this event is more about the "good parts" of religion, without the convention and hierarchy many American Jews eschew. Parallels can be seen here to the observance of Shabbat dinners by Jews who have no intention of observing the restrictions of Shabbat or attending services on the following morning.

Amitai Etzioni's work on the modification of holidays explores the difference between edited holidays—those that are altered "on a relatively small scale"—and engineered holidays—ones that are newly created.[35] An example of an edited Jewish holiday would be Chanukah, a relatively minor holiday in the Jewish calendar year that has come to be one of the more widely celebrated holidays by American Jews, mainly for reasons that have to do with the American consumer calendar. The twentieth-century creation of the bat mitzvah celebration can be seen either as a new life-cycle event or as an egalitarian editing of the bar mitzvah.[36]

But what of the Break Fast? The fasting itself is not edited—even though its meaning may be redefined—but the subsequent feasting is newly engineered. Jenna Weissman Joselit has suggested that the Break Fast might be called a "Judaized Thanksgiving," one that "seems to have grown steadily in popularity over the years, eclipsing even the fast itself."[37] But this Judaized Thanksgiving may have come at a cost, and that cost may have been the observance of the eight-day-long Thanksgiving feast of Sukkot.

JEWISH THANKSGIVINGS

Sukkot, also known as the Festival of Booths, is celebrated as both an agricultural harvest holiday and a reminder of the Exodus. It is observed by the constructing of temporary shelters, and the commandment of "dwelling in booths" is primarily satisfied by eating in these booths. In the Jewish ritual year, the fast on Yom Kippur serves to purify the Jewish community before the subsequent Thanksgiving feasting of Sukkot, which occurs several days later. Celebration of Sukkot by Jewish immigrants in America was well-documented at the turn of the twentieth century.[38] However, the observance of Sukkot has decreased (only 28 percent of American Jews claim to observe it in some way), and it appears that the Break Fast has stepped in to take its place.[39]

There are several reasons that Sukkot did not find resonance among twentieth-century Jewry. It is in some ways more helpful to first see what holidays have succeeded. Chanukah, as mentioned before, has become widely celebrated as a Jewish alternative during the Christmas season. It was adapted for children as a result of an active campaign in the mid-twentieth century. One can "build Jewish memory through latkes," declared one Chanukah activist.[40] Through food, gifts, and games, Chanukah becomes a holiday that can be celebrated with various meanings, including secular ones. Likewise, Passover (which was always a major holiday) is constantly being redefined through the publication of countless themed haggadot (some calling for the freedom for various oppressed peoples, or even promoting veganism as the *Haggadah for the Liberated Lamb* does).[41] Passover also, not unlike Christmas, has become a commercial success because of the promotion of packaged food created specifically for that holiday. Twentieth-century Jewish leaders attempted to combat Jewish assimilation by any means necessary. One stealth weapon in the arsenal was *Jewish Home Beautiful*, a publication that attempted to increase religious ritual through aesthetic domesticity. Similarly, synagogue gift shops encouraged the purchase of Judaica items to beautify the commandments performed in the home. Ritual items such as Chanukah candelabras and

Passover Seder plates made perfect wedding gifts and, in addition to beautifying the home, could also be used during the associated holiday.

In contrast, while the etrog and lulav (a citron and a bundle of branches from four stipulated trees) are traditional ritual objects for Sukkot, they are both expensive and perishable. In urban Jewish neighborhoods in the early twentieth century, it was not uncommon for congregations to share these items.[42] However, like Sabbath observance, this tradition has faded with suburbanization.[43] Additionally, the sukkah—the booth—involves some willingness to annually construct a temporary structure in one's yard or on a balcony for all to see. While Reform and Conservative synagogues continued to build them onsite for their congregations, congregants themselves became less likely to build individual sukkot at home. Restriction of immigration in the first half of the century also did away with the odder rituals in favor of those that are more in keeping with Gentile America. As Philip Roth writes of this precariously amicable relationship in his fictional midcentury town of Woodenton in "Eli the Fanatic," "For this adjustment to be made, both Jews and Gentiles alike have had to give up some of their more extreme practices in order not to threaten or offend the other."[44] Samuel G. Freedman, more than forty years later, writes of a neighborhood dispute where one Jewish couple was incensed by the erection of a sukkah in their next-door neighbors' front yard. "'Flaunting it' [and] 'In your face,'" complained the neighbors.[45]

Nostalgia, particularly in the form of foodways, plays a big part in the retention of holidays. Unlike Passover and Chanukah, Sukkot has no notable symbolic foods. It is the *where* one eats, not the *what* that matters. Unlike Thanksgiving, a holiday menu carefully designed to reflect New England harvest traditions (even when observed in sunny California or the deserts of Utah), the best one can say is that it is good to eat "stuffed" foods on Sukkot in order to symbolize abundance. Chanukah and Passover, while filled with religious symbols, can be celebrated in a secular way that embraces American ideals of freedom. Sukkot remains purely religious. And what of its celebration of the harvest? Couldn't that be a secular entrance into this observance? In fact, Americans have a secular thanksgiving already, one that began as a religious holiday and now is happily embraced by most Americans regardless of creed.

Finally, Sukkot suffers—intentionally—from bad chronological placement. If it is too close on one end for American Jews to Thanksgiving, it is also too close on the other end to Rosh Hashanah and Yom Kippur.

Even in his 1959 *Jews in Suburbia*, Albert Gordon noted that "people have grown 'weary' of the Holy Day season," and many of the moderately affiliated Jews surveyed by sociologists Steven Cohen and Arnold Eisen in the 1990s complained of a High Holiday overload by the time Sukkot arrived.[46] So, sadly, the holiday of Sukkot, one of the three biblical pilgrimage holidays—a holiday so important it was known in the Talmudic period as *Ha Chag, The* Holiday—has been reduced to the butt of a sitcom joke. In a contract negotiation on the television sitcom *30 Rock*, an employee requests time off for every Jewish holiday, "no matter how ridiculous." In response, his employer says that he can only have one: "What's the one where they go into the little huts?"[47] In the context of the scene, this barb suggests that Sukkot is the most ridiculous holiday of all, and not a valued holiday worthy of time off from work. With the decrease in the observance of Sukkot, the feasting season that follows the self-denial of Yom Kippur, came the dramatically edited—if not wholly invented—Break Fast ritual among American Jews.

RITUAL INNOVATION AND ITS DETRACTORS

This new American Break Fast is certainly not without its more conservative critics, particularly the Orthodox. When Jenna Weissman Joselit suggested in a *Forward* column a few years ago that we might see the Break Fast "as a testament to the creative power of the grass roots and its appetite for new forms of ritual engagement. Or better yet, as an exercise in fellowship and community," an online commenter responded to her column, "My wife and I ended the Taanit on Kippur with a modest meal and juice. I've found that most of the participants in the elaborate "Breakfasts" the author described, don't even fast on Yom Ha-Kippurim to begin with!"[48] The derision shown by this disgruntled commenter is not an unusual response to new ritual—particularly in the case of those who fancy themselves the keepers of tradition. Ritually observant Jews are less likely to observe an elaborate Break Fast than their more acculturated coreligionists. In an article on the High Holidays, Steven Katz of Boston University described the Break Fast as follows: "There are no special customs for breaking the fast. Rituals for this meal are a new thing. You can eat whatever you want, and usually it's only the nonreligious people who make a big deal about it. The religious Jews finish their meal, go back out, and start building the sukkah, the temporary hut used during the weeklong autumn festival of Sukkoth."⁴⁹ This attitude is true on the whole for the Orthodox community—and somewhat understandable given the subsequent feasting that occurs only a few days later during Sukkot.

It is rare to find a mention of the Break Fast in Jewish cookbooks published under Orthodox commercial or community auspices. In what is arguably the most popular kosher cookbook in the first decade of the twenty-first century, the 2003 *Kosher By Design*, Susie Fishbein (the Orthodox Martha Stewart) writes: "Yom Kippur is not about food. However, eating before the fasting begins is as much of a *mitzvah* as the fast itself. It should be a full holiday meal."⁵⁰ There is no reference to a Break Fast at all. In the aforementioned *New York Times* article, she was asked about this omission and responded that she "felt it inappropriate to set up a Yom Kippur break-fast 'party.' It doesn't fit the mood of what we've done all day." Fishbein is right that Yom Kippur is not about food. Additionally, the fast that is called for requires more than just abstention from food. Other prohibited activities include bathing, sexual relations, and the wearing of leather shoes. But the emphasis on eating at the end of the day demonstrated by the Break Fast appears to suggest that the day is about food. After all, nobody's in a rush to hop in the shower or put their shoes back on. Fishbein does admit—albeit reluctantly— that "it's definitely somewhat of a happy occasion. When the fast is over, the hope is that your prayers were answered, and you were written in the Book of Life and it will be a good year. So in those emotions you want to be surrounded by friends and family."⁵¹

Yet the Orthodox, despite their reputation as the standard bearers of Judaism, are a true minority among American Jews. And this new Break Fast ritual may very well have legs, as it is already showing signs of moving from a purely domestic celebration to one with institutional sponsorship. The bat mitzvah, which seemed nonsensical to many traditionalists eighty years ago, is now observed by even the strictest of Torah observers. And it is rather unlikely that Chanukah will ever again be a minor holiday in the United States. Some of these edited or engineered holidays have become so familiar that many are unaware of their novelty. In Vanessa Ochs's *Inventing Jewish Ritual*, she writes of a "minhag America." Minhag refers to a religious custom which has become so ingrained as to have the power of law. "The [Jewish] authenticity of a ritual was a feeling cultivated over time, through repeated practice, and sustained by enough cherished memories to guarantee predictability and when necessary, flexibility."[52]

Yom Kippur is in many ways a recommitment holiday, one that employs "narratives, drama and ceremonies to directly enforce commitment to shared beliefs."[53] The rituals that enforce this commitment are no longer limited to the fast and traditional liturgy. The new American Break Fast feast as it is now observed fills a need not just for those who are hungry after twenty-five hours of self-denial, but also for those American Jews who have been able to engage with the Jewish ritual calendar mainly through the embrace of secular symbols such as dreidels, potato pancakes, and even Chinese food. The Break Fast therefore embraces a symbolic ethnicity of bagels and lox in order to offer a sincerely Jewish thanksgiving (in lieu of or in addition to Sukkot) for the ability to share food with loved ones and community.

DISCUSSION QUESTIONS

1. In what ways does the contemporary Yom Kippur Break Fast reflect American Jewish values?
2. What does resistance to the Break Fast suggest about the concerns of its critics?
3. What makes a religious ritual endure?
4. How much influence do newspaper lifestyle articles and cookbooks have on religious practice?

NOTES

1. Woody Allen, *Annie Hall* (USA: United Artists, 1977).
2. Jenna Weissman Joselit, *The Wonders of America: Reinventing Jewish Culture 1880–1950* (New York: Hill and Wang, 1994), 219.
3. United Jewish Communities, "The National Jewish Population Survey 2000–01" (New York, 2003).
4. Sylvia Barack Fishman, *Jewish Life and American Culture* (Albany: State University of New York, 2000), 129.
5. Amitai Etzioni and Jared Bloom, *We Are What We Celebrate: Understanding Holidays and Rituals* (New York: New York University Press, 2004), 30.

6. Irving Greenberg, *The Jewish Way: Living the Holidays* (Northvale, N.J.: J. Aronson, 1998), 118.

7. Pew Forum on Religion & Public Life, "U.S. Religious Landscape Survey," ed. Pew Research Center (Washington, D.C.: Pew Research Center, 2008).

8. Albert Isaac Gordon, *Jews in Suburbia* (Boston: Beacon Press, 1959), 136.

9. Marshall Sklare and Joseph Greenblum, *Jewish Identity on the Suburban Frontier: S Study of Group Survival in the Open Society*, Lakeville Studies, vol. 1 (New York: Basic Books, 1967), 50–55.

10. See the discussion of "Sheilaism" in Robert Neelly Bellah, *Habits of the Heart: Individualism and Commitment in American Life* (Berkeley: University of California Press, 1985), 221.

11. For more on fasting. see Caroline Walker Bynum, *Holy Feast and Holy Fast: The Religious Significance of Food to Medieval Women* (Berkeley: University of California Press, 1987); R. Marie Griffith, *Born Again Bodies: Flesh and Spirit in American Christianity* (Berkeley: University of California Press, 2004).

12. Martha L. Finch, "Pinched with Hunger, Partaking of Plenty; Fasts and Thanksgivings in Early New England," in *Eating in Eden: Food and American Utopias*, ed. Etta M. and Martha L. Finch Madden (Lincoln: University of Nebraska, 2006), 38.

13. Barbara Kirshenblatt-Gimblett, "Kitchen Judaism," in *Getting Comfortable in New York: The American Jewish Home, 1880-1950*, ed. Susan L. and Jenna Weissman Joselit Braunstein (New York: Jewish Museum, 1990).

14. Fannie Engle and Gertrude Blair, *The Jewish Festival Cookbook, According to the Dietary Laws* (New York: McKay, 1954), 54.

15. Anshe Chesed Congregation Sisterhood and Irene Rousuck, *The Fairmount Cookbook* (Cleveland, 1957), 7.

16. Jennie Grossinger, *The Art of Jewish Cooking* (New York: Random House, 1958), xii.

17. Shonie B. Levi and Sylvia R. Kaplan, *Guide for the Jewish Homemaker*, 2nd rev. ed. (National Women's League of the United Synagogue of America, 1964), 90, 93.

18. Ruth Sirkis, *A Taste of Tradition: The How and Why of Jewish Gourmet Holiday Cooking* (Los Angeles: W. Ritchie, 1972), 17.

19. Jenna Weissman Joselit, "Breaking Down the Break Fast," *Forward* (2007), http://www.forward.com/articles/11731/.

20. Rita Milos Brownstein and Donna Wolf Koplowitz, *Jewish Holiday Style* (New York: Simon and Schuster, 1999), 24. Havdalah is the brief ceremony marking the end of the holiday.

21. Jayne Cohen, *Jewish Holiday Cooking: A Food Lover's Treasury of Classics and Improvisations* (Hoboken, N.J.: Wiley, 2008), 186.

22. Joyce Esersky Goldstein, *Sephardic Flavors: Jewish Cooking of the Mediterranean* (San Francisco: Chronicle Books, 2000); and Joyce Esersky Goldstein, *Saffron Shores: Jewish Cooking of the Southern Mediterranean* (San Francisco: Chronicle Books, 2002).

23. The restriction of immigration in the first half of the twentieth century led to an ignorance of break fast rituals of the international community.

24. "Break the Fast: A Mix-and-Match Yom Kippur Menu-Maker," http://www .epicurious.com/articlesguides/holidays/highholydays/yomkippur_recipes.

25. Food Maven, "Breaking the Fast: Feeding the Body After Feeding the Soul," *Forward* (2003), http://www.forward.com/articles/8231%3E/.

26. For a discussion of Jewish affinity for Chinese food in early twentieth-century New York, see Gaye and Harry Levine Tuchman, "New York Jews and Chinese Food: The Social Construction of an Ethnic Pattern," *Journal of Contemporary Ethnography* 22 (1993).

27. In August 2011 I spent a week at the Radcliffe Institute's Culinary Collection in the Schlesinger Library. I examined ninety-eight English-language Jewish cookbooks published over the last century.

28. Herbert J. Gans, "Symbolic Ethnicity: The Future of Ethnic Groups and Cultures in America," *Ethnic and Racial Studies* 2 (1979): 9.

29. Marilyn Sneiderman, "Home and Work, Community and Advocacy," *ZEEK: A Jewish Journal of Thought and Culture* (2010), http://zeek.forward.com/articles/117056/.

30. Joan Nathan, *Jewish Cooking in America*, expanded ed. (New York: Knopf, 1998), 147.

31. Sara Bershtel and Allen Graubard, *Saving Remnants: Feeling Jewish in America* (New York: Free Press, 1992), 158.

32. Jews are not obligated to fast until they have come of age (boys at age thirteen and girls at age twelve). Also, pregnant women, nursing mothers, and those with medical concerns are urged to refrain from fasting.

33. Mark Oppenheimer, "Traditional Meal Ending Holy Days Becomes an Event," *New York Times*, October 1, 2011.

34. Carole Counihan and Penny Van Esterik, *Food and Culture: A Reader* (New York: Routledge, 1997), 13.

35. Etzioni and Bloom, *We Are What We Celebrate*, 30.

36. Elizabeth Hafkin Pleck, *Celebrating the Family: Ethnicity, Consumer Culture, and Family Rituals* (Cambridge: Harvard University Press, 2000), 173.

37. Joselit, "Breaking Down the Break Fast."

38. Andrew R. Heinze, *Adapting to Abundance: Jewish Immigrants, Mass Consumption, and the Search for American Identity* (New York: Columbia University Press, 1990), 69.

39. Steven Martin Cohen and Arnold M. Eisen, *The Jew Within: Self, Family, and Community in America* (Bloomington: Indiana University Press, 2000), 90.

40. Joselit, "Merry Chanuka" 315.

41. Haggadot is plural for haggadah, the book that forms the basis of the Passover Seder ritual.

42. Myrna Frommer and Harvey Frommer, *Growing up Jewish in America: An Oral History* (New York: Harcourt Brace, 1995), 174.

43. Fishman, *Jewish Life and American Culture*, 131.

44. Philip Roth, "Eli the Fanatic," in *Goodbye, Columbus, and Five Short Stories*, ed. Philip Roth (Boston: Houghton Mifflin, 1959), 262.

45. Samuel G. Freedman, *Jew vs. Jew: The Struggle for the Soul of American Jewry* (New York: Simon and Schuster, 2000), 15.

46. Gordon, *Jews in Suburbia*, 138; Cohen and Eisen, *The Jew Within*.

47. "Hardball," *30 Rock*, season 1.

48. Joselit, "Breaking Down the Break Fast." Comment made by Sephardiman, October 9, 2007.

49. Susan Seligson, "In Days of Awe, Rituals Sweet and Somber: Steven Katz Walks Us Through High Holy Days," *BU Today* (2010), http://www.bu.edu/today/node/11462.

50. Susie Fishbein, *Kosher by Design: Picture-Perfect Food for the Holidays & Every Day* (Brooklyn: Artscroll, 2003), 70.

51. Oppenheimer, "Traditional Meal Ending Holy Days Becomes an Event."

52. Vanessa L. Ochs, *Inventing Jewish Ritual* (Philadelphia: Jewish Publication Society, 2007), 34, 28–29.

53. Etzioni and Bloom, *We Are What We Celebrate*, 11.

RECOMMENDED READING

Cohen, Steven Martin, and Arnold M. Eisen. *The Jew Within: Self, Family, and Community in America*. Bloomington: Indiana University Press, 2000.

Counihan, Carole, and Penny Van Esterik. *Food and Culture: A Reader*. New York: Routledge, 1997.

Etzioni, Amitai, and Jared Bloom. *We Are What We Celebrate: Understanding Holidays and Rituals*. New York: New York University Press, 2004.

Finch, Martha L. "Pinched with Hunger, Partaking of Plenty; Fasts and Thanks-givings in Early New England." In *Eating in Eden: Food and American Utopias.* Edited by Etta M. and Martha L. Finch Madden, 35–53. Lincoln: University of Nebraska Press, 2006.

Gans, Herbert J. "Symbolic Ethnicity: The Future of Ethnic Groups and Cultures in America." *Ethnic and Racial Studies* 2 (1979): 1–20.

Ochs, Vanessa L. *Inventing Jewish Ritual.* Philadelphia: Jewish Publication Society, 2007.

Pleck, Elizabeth Hafkin. *Celebrating the Family: Ethnicity, Consumer Culture, and Family Rituals.* Cambridge: Harvard University Press, 2000.

Part Four

ACTIVIST FOODWAYS

Thirteen

KOINONIA PARTNERS

A DEMONSTRATION PLOT FOR FOOD, FELLOWSHIP, AND SUSTAINABILITY

TODD LEVASSEUR

*[M]an has lost his identity with God [and] with his fellow man. . . . As a
result, the poor are being driven from rural areas; hungry, frustrated, angry
masses are huddled in cities . . . the chasm between blacks and whites grows
wider and deeper; war hysteria invades every nook and cranny of the earth.
We must have a new spirit—a spirit of partnership with one another.
But how can these things become flesh and blood?*
—CLARENCE JORDAN, 1968

THE PAST SIXTY years have seen a tremendous growth in environmental consciousness in American society. This is due to insights from the science of ecology and the development of more sophisticated technologies that can measure human impact on the environment. Such increased consciousness has resulted in humans deliberating about the perceived ills of industrial agriculture, bemoaning the rapid loss of species diversity, and debating the reality of human-induced climate change, to name only three of many environmental issues. Such consciousness is also entering into the doctrines, ethics, and institutional governance of a wide variety of religious groups, leading

FIGURE 13.1   Sign at entrance to the main campus of Koinonia Farm. Photo by Todd LeVasseur, used with permission.

to an ongoing "Ecological Reformation" within certain segments of the world's religions.[1]

This chapter explores this growing Ecological Reformation and does so by focusing on a particular North American Christian group: Koinonia Farm. Koinonia (which is Greek for "fellowship" or "community") is an intentional, ecumenical Christian community located outside of the rural town of Americus, Georgia, itself one and a half hours southwest of Macon, Georgia. For those living at Koinonia, food—and especially the growing and sharing of food—provides an entryway that allows residents and visitors alike to engage in practices and discussions that pertain to the central concerns that guide the community. These concerns include focusing on racial and gender equality, immigration acceptance, providing opportunities for the poor and the uneducated, care for the environment, finding alternatives to materialism and militarism, and Koinonia's unique history of Christian hospitality.

Because of its care for the environment, Koinonia is involved in the larger Ecological Reformation, placing it at the forefront of North American communities of faith that are grappling with issues of sustainability, and especially sustainable food production. However, Koinonia's own storied history makes it a unique example of how food is a marker of race, of environmental practice and stewardship, and is a key ingredient in the gathering and sharing of fellowship. The chapter argues that food is important to Koinonia for the group's identity, theology, farming practices, and corporate vision. Furthermore, the central importance of food for Koinonia ranges across the community's history, from its early conception to its role in today's Ecological Reformation. Koinonia is thus an exemplar of how food is a marker of religious identity for certain segments of North American religions, and, for the purposes of this case study, this identity is premised on mutually reinforcing poles of Christian fellowship and Christian environmental concern.

"A DEMONSTRATION PLOT FOR GOD"

During the first half of the 1900s in the American South, some things were as certain as the changing of the seasons. In no particular order, these included—but were not limited to—hot, humid summers of toil in agricultural fields; religion (which for most southerners meant church); poverty; volunteering for and serving in two world wars; and racism. Dominant concepts of masculinity permeated white society, while wealth and family connections went a long way in deciding a person's social status in the top tier of this society. Excluded from the top tier were the rest of white people, who ran shops and worked on farms and whose views, dreams, and social conditioning were in large part shaped by a southern aristocracy. Equally running through the gamut of residents who constituted this half of the South's color line were white supremacist groups, annual and regional celebrations of the Southern Army and Confederacy, and churches, with very fluid lines between the three.[2]

In opposition to this was black society, located on the other half of the early 1900s color line. Suffering under the abuses of Jim Crow racism, crippled by high rates of illiteracy and poverty, and largely living lives of indentured servitude under the guise of sharecropping, southern blacks were largely united by church, fraternal lodges, diet, and poverty. They were further united by the collective need to navigate the myriad dangers to their bodies and fortunes from white southern culture and the power of its legal, economic, and political machinations.[3] Although there were regional differences, nuances, and complexities in wealth, religion, society, and happenstance for blacks (and, to be sure, for whites), the specter of race and poverty nonetheless meant that some things were unavoidable in the South during these years; these included long days of toil in agricultural fields and segregated Sundays spent in church.

One person born into this environment made a concerted effort, along with his wife, to challenge the entrenched power hierarchies of the time. These challenges were levied at the status quo of church, field, and table. The person's name was Clarence Jordan.

Jordan was born on July 29, 1912, to well-off, white Baptist parents. A precocious child, Jordan was devout in his beliefs about Jesus and active in church. However, biographies reveal that he recognized something was amiss as he memorized and sang various hymns that praised God and taught that God loved all of creation equally.[4] According to these biographies, Jordan's young mind and conscience struggled with trying to find answers to various questions, among them, if God loved all equally, then how come blacks and whites did not go to church together? How come wealthier whites kept poorer whites and blacks in a form of bondage and servitude via the institution of sharecropping? How come both the aboveground and underground workings of southern law and "justice" did not echo the design of God's kingdom, which according to the Bible was based on equality and compassion for the poor and broken of society? These questions took root in Jordan's young mind and slowly sunk deeper and deeper into his being so that by the time he was thirty years old and married to his life partner, Florence, these concerns became the inspiration behind creating Koinonia.

In the interlude Jordan matriculated at the Georgia State College of Agriculture at the University of Georgia under the stated intent of learning how to make agriculture accessible, affordable, and successful for poor, illiterate farmers—both white *and* black.[5] He was heavily influenced by the Sermon of the Mount found in the Gospel of Matthew.[6] The ethical mandate of Jesus' teachings as shared in this gospel crystallized for Jordan in two ways: first, he became a pacifist and walked away from his ROTC duties and a career in the U.S. Cavalry. Second, he entered into the ministry and also became a New Testament scholar at the Southern Baptist Theological Seminary. In effect, Jordan's upbringing in a farming community and in church shaped his adult path; yet his own interpretation of the

Gospels and his experience of the poverty of Georgia's farming communities influenced the direction of this path.

Furthermore, while enrolled in the seminary, Jordan was equally influenced by the image of the early church found in the book of Acts. This New Testament book shares that the early, primitive church that existed right after the death and resurrection of Jesus held all in common and was a fellowship open to all people—men, women, Jews, and Gentiles—because Christ's substitutionary atonement and God's love applied equally to all people, regardless of class or race. The rich compost of Christ's teachings and example of this early church helped Jordan's seed vision of challenging southern power structures take root; the fruit was a run-down 440-acre farm in rural Americus, Georgia, that the Jordans, along with friends Martin and Mabel England, purchased and called Koinonia.

"Koinonia" is a Greek word that translates into fellowship and community, and the goal of Koinonia from day one has been to create an inclusive church, open to all members of God's creation. The term is found in Paul's first letter to Corinthians (1 Cor. 10:16) and implies fellowship in both the body of Christ and the sharing of one's purse and worldly possessions (equally implied in the Book of Acts 2:42–47). In Jordan's eyes and words, Koinonia was to become the "demonstration plot" where blacks and whites were to live, work, eat, and worship together, side by side, showing that even in the heart of the South, reconciliation and fellowship were possible.[7]

In essence, Koinonia was to model living and creating God's kingdom in the here and now, in both word and deed, as shared in the Book of Acts. Given that Americus was a rural farming region fractured by the dual realities of racism and poverty, Jordan specifically made the interracial growing and sharing of food the center point of the Christian community. Jordan further believed that good farming, with the labor shared equally by both races and the sharing of the products of that labor, whether this be profit from sales or at a lunch table under a tree, all undertaken within a structure of shared daily prayer, was a modern re-creation of the early church described in Acts. Thus the uplift of both race and finance via shared farming and devotion to God was the guiding Christian vision of Jordan's life until his death in 1969.

During his life Jordan labored to put into practice the description of God's love found in Paul's Epistle to the Galatians, where Paul writes that all are one in Christ Jesus—black and white alike in Jordan's reading. It is this commitment to racial equality that separated Koinonia from other Christian agrarian communities of the era, such as the much more insular Brüderhof and Amish.[8] This vision of racial, spiritual, and economic equality is still present at Koinonia today, and it is this unbroken lineage and theologically grounded beginning in interracial fellowship that makes Koinonia unique in today's Ecological Reformation.

FELLOWSHIP AND FOOD

Koinonia has been many things and has seen many people over its seventy years. In its earliest days it became a place where Jordan shared his agricultural training with poor sharecroppers in the region, black and white alike. It was a place where progressive (for the time) methods of agriculture were attempted, such as utilizing different methods of composting the soil. It also became a place where blacks and whites shared labor and the fruits of that labor.

For a majority of Christians, food has always played a central part in the mystery surrounding the death and resurrection of Jesus. In many ways what is today called the Last Supper captures the central teachings of Jesus. According to the New Testament and those who believe its historical accuracy and subsequent theological meanings, "For [Jesus], eating socially with others in Israel was a parable of the feast in the kingdom which was to come. . . . Eating was a way of enacting the kingdom of God, of practicing the generous rule of the divine king. As a result, Jesus avoided exclusive practices, which divided the people of God from one another in his view."[9] Thus the ministry of Jesus—his parables, his miracles, his healings, and especially his feeding of the masses, coupled with his words during the Last Supper that became the basis of the Eucharist/Communion—was about opening the kingdom of God to all, regardless of social class, gender, race, or national provenance. Therefore, in the mind of Clarence Jordan and his own exegesis of the New Testament, sharing a meal that has been blessed by prayer and a spoken-aloud grace was one of the supreme acts of Christ-centered fellowship, and even more so in a racially segregated South. For Jordan, a shared meal at the dining table at Koinonia was the way to make "flesh and blood" Christ's atoning love.

However, Jordan's forthright and blatant attacks against the entrenched systems—systems backed by both black and white churches—of race and power found in the rural South were not met without resistance. Indeed, for Jordan, "life in the body of Christ from the perspective of Sumter County, Georgia [where Koinonia is located], involved three interconnected passions: the practice of nonviolence as the moral disposition of the Gospel; the preservation, cultivation, and protection of the soil, 'God's holy earth'; and the proclamation and provision of hope to 'those who suffer and are oppressed.'"[10] Tragically, the response, precipitated by powerful local whites, to these three passions was violent and thorough: boycotts of Koinonia products; pressure to not sell seed stock and other farming tools and agricultural necessities to members of Koinonia; and at its worse, drive-by shootings. Nonetheless, Jordan and his supporters remained steadfast in his vision throughout, and he continued to preach and enact his message of embodying God's kingdom in the here and now at Koinonia.

Over time, tensions eased and the civil rights movement brought a renewed sense of mission and urgency to the community after the boycotts of the 1950s. Koinonia became instrumental in helping host and house leaders in the civil rights movement during these tumultuous years, providing a base of operation for Freedom Riders to move further into the South.[11] This era was followed by the back-to-the-land movement of the 1960s and 1970s, when many Jesus "hippies" found the farm, worked in its fields, and helped construct new buildings on the campus. These include the current cafeteria where the community gathers Monday through Friday for shared noonday lunch.

One other key event occurred in the 1960s: Millard Fuller and his wife joined the community and worked with Jordan to build homes on community property that were then sold to poor blacks at no interest. Jordan called this the "Fund for Humanity," and it laid the foundation for Fuller's now world-famous Habitat for Humanity, which is based in Americus.

By the beginning of the 1980s, the community turned its attention to campaigning for solidarity with war-torn countries in Central America, adding to the community's institutional concern for immigration, peace, and justice work that in large part still defines Koinonia today. Also in the late 1980s and early 1990s, Bob Burns joined the community and proceeded to transform a small section of the farm into a certified organic market garden, selling produce to Atlanta to help the community meet its financial budget. Burns had spent time in the tropics of Asia as a Mennonite volunteer, where his botanical knowledge fused with indigenous agroecology practices. Upon returning to the United States and joining Koinonia, Burns put into practice his own approach to sustainable farming. This approach included both organic certification and the development of permaculture practices (explained below), with the latter becoming the key agricultural approach Koinonia uses today as the community attempts to grow its food sustainably.

KOINONIA TODAY

In many respects Koinonia today resembles the original version, teachings, and practices birthed by Clarence Jordan. It is still an inclusive community that is home to permanent residents who have all accepted a Christ-centered life of voluntary poverty, prayer, contemplation, and hospitality. Some are married, some are not but have children, while all take a vow of voluntary poverty, and most would be considered liberal Protestants, although there are Catholics and nondenominational members. Here liberal means a progressive reading of the Bible, as well as an ecumenical Christianity that includes participation in interfaith coalitions. It also means a biblically and Christ-inspired support for environmental and social justice issues, including issues of sustainable agriculture and ecological food production.

Residents who have pledged their lives to residing on the campus are called stewards, whereas novices are residents who have lived at Koinonia for three months to a year, at which point they become provisional members and begin the process of becoming full stewards. There are also interns who reside at Koinonia for three to six months—if they feel called to stay, they may begin the process of becoming a full-time novice resident and eventually a steward.

Koinonia makes most of its income from selling seasonal pecan products. The pecans come from acres of monoculture pecan groves, and some of the trees Jordan himself planted. The pecans become value-added products at an on-site bakery and processing center and are then sold via mail and online catalogs. Products include granolas, pastries, and chocolate pecan bars and chocolate/pecan/coffee bars made with fair-trade chocolates and coffee beans.

The latter product reflects the continuing commitment of the community to support ethically traded and grown food products, and the

FIGURE 13.2 Rotational grazing cattle under monoculture pecan orchard, with Clarence Jordan's writing shack to the right behind the trees. Photo by Todd LeVasseur, used with permission.

long-term goal of the community is to become a certified fair-trade processor. Overall this reflects the community's continued commitment to justice, paying a living wage (to both suppliers and community workers via a shared purse), and providing earth-friendly products—the same principles that motivated Jordan to begin Koinonia.

Koinonia is currently guided by both vision and mission statements, and also by eight Partner Covenant ideas that guide the lives of stewards. These statements are held up and enacted via the community's current corporate structure, which includes an executive director and various department heads who oversee an aspect of campus and community life to which the community is committed. For example, there is a farm crew director, a hospitality director, and a marketing director, all of whom oversee and manage employees, interns, community members, and volunteers in their area of responsibility. The covenants, vision, and mission statements help guide the community and keep its identity intact amid the thousands of annual visitors, continual flux of interns, departure of novices, and inevitable turnover in paid staff.

The need for paid staff is a result of the campus being too big (over 400 acres, with a welcome center and museum, library, chapel, residence halls, and various buildings associated with pecan production) and the jobs too many to be met by just interns, provisional members, and stewards. Therefore, the community hires local residents to work in the kitchen and to help around the campus; many of these are black residents whose parents were active in the community when Jordan was alive or shortly thereafter and who bought houses through the Fund for Humanity.[12]

Koinonia has adopted a mission statement to guide and manage all these activities and personnel. The community's current mission statement dates to 2007 and states, "We are Christians called to live together in intentional community sharing a life of prayer, work, study, service and fellowship. We seek to embody peacemaking, sustainability, and radical sharing. While honoring people of all backgrounds and faiths, we strive to demonstrate the way of Jesus as an alternative to materialism, militarism and racism." Many of Jordan's original motivations for creating Koinonia are still present in this current mission statement; these include pacifism, discipleship, reconciliation between races, and a sharing of fellowship (and economic livelihood) in community life. Explicitly added to the statement is a modern, vibrant concern for sustainability that is both institutional and individual. Taken together, Koinonia's concerns and activities make the community an exemplar of "prophetic activism," which is a faith-based, progressive activism that seeks to redress social inequalities and that "envisions an altered future in which human relationships to one another and the natural world are repaired."[13]

These prophetic concerns are also found in the vision statement created by a group of community stewards and members to help guide Koinonia through its next fifty years, as well as in the Partner Covenant enacted in 2002. The seventh Partner Covenant asks stewards to be "a steward of the earth, recognizing the beauty and wonder of the earth as God's creation," while the sixth covenant asks stewards to "participate in Jesus' ministry of reconciliation, recognizing that we are one family regardless of race, creed, gender, nationality, sexual orientation, economic status, or any other difference."[14] Meanwhile, Koinonia's vision statement reads:

Love through service to others
Peace through reconciliation
Joy through generous hospitality

This statement is enacted through concrete measures and actions that are influenced by the further results of a "visioning weekend" held in 2003. During this weekend fifty members and friends of the community jointly agreed on five challenges that the community needed to face and address in the coming fifty years of Koinonia's existence. The fifth challenge to be met is a "demonstration of new community based and environmentally responsible ways of farming." As a result of this vision, a "Friends of the Earth" focus group has been developed. This group meets to discuss issues of sustainability and to first brainstorm and then come up with concrete actions about how the community can grow healthier, more sustainable food.

Given the vision of joy through hospitality, peace through reconciliation and sharing, love through service to others (and for many community residents, this includes nonhuman others), and the mission and covenant of sustainability and stewardship, food has once again become the de facto center of Koinonia's identity. Whether it is through selling pecan and fair-trade products to meet financial needs, developing sustainable farming techniques, or sharing meals as a form of fellowship and hospitality, food at Koinonia is a central marker of life for residents and visitors alike.

FOOD—SHARED AND SUSTAINABLE—IS EVERYWHERE

The heading for this section is as much a truism as it is a rhetorical use of language. This is because at Koinonia, all someone has to do is look outside any window of campus, or take a walk fifty yards in any direction, to see and come across pecan orchards, chickens, cows, goats, and a wide variety of other plant and animal life that will one day become food for a human body. As a living, breathing farm, the evolutionary and ecological realities of birth and death, growth and decay, and quotidian caloric needs are inescapable and impossible to miss. For Koinonia, these realities are embraced and incorporated into values of hospitality, love, and sustainability; for members of Koinonia, they are incorporated into the living body of Christ, present through the mysterious and wondrous workings of Creation, whether in the field or at the table. And at Koinonia, how this food is grown and shared is a marker of both institutional mores and a quest for environmental stewardship.

The concept of stewardship is found in the first chapter of the Hebrew Bible, specifically in Genesis 1:26–28. In the cosmology story related therein, Yahweh/Elohim grants humans dominion over creation. The Hebrew used in this passage, how it is translated, and the ethical and environmental implications thereof have become an issue of much debate by religion and nature scholars, ecotheologians, and those in Abrahamic subtraditions involved in the Ecological Reformation. For many Christians, especially Protestants, and even more so, Evangelicals, the concept of stewardship has morphed into the concept of "Creation Care." While Koinonia is not an Evangelical community (although some members are Evangelical), it has adopted similar language, and community members see themselves as being called to steward the campus in sustainable ways. This calling is reflected in the community's mission statement, Partner Covenants, and the results of its visioning weekend. What this means in practice is that Koinonia, largely through the efforts of the farm crew, is putting into practice permaculture farming techniques throughout the fields and campus of the community's four hundred–plus acres.

Permaculture is a system of sustainable farming created in the 1970s by the Australians Bill Mollison and David Holmgren at their ecovillage, Crystal Waters. The two began to host permaculture trainings and workshop so that now there is an international network of permaculture practitioners, teachers, and publications. Owing to the influence and groundwork (both literal and figurative) of Bob Burns, quite a few members of Koinonia's farm team as well as stewards and members of the overall community have received permaculture training. The community actively hosts ten-day permaculture trainings that are open to the public for a fee, with instruction provided by community members and outside permaculture teachers. Some members see this as Koinonia's next gift to the culture-at-large, and especially to fellow Christians. According to some at Koinonia, the first gift of the community was interracial fellowship, followed by the gift of Habitat for Humanity, and next it is hoped it will be sustainable ways of growing food, with Koinonia providing practical example, method of instruction, and inspiration.

In a nutshell, permaculture is a mix of systems theory, holistic ecology, and sustainable agriculture practices whose goal is to create permanent agriculture systems, and thus permanent human cultural systems that are embedded in local landscapes. Therefore the ideal of permaculture is to create a self-enclosed, regenerative, sustainable feedback system of agriculture that requires minimal off-farm/site inputs. This ideal is embodied in "edible forests" of perennial stone fruit trees, as these require the least amount of human management and provide annual, nutrient-dense fruits. The trees also provide shade and fodder for grazing animals such as chickens, pigs, and goats, who in turn help fertilize the trees; leaves for making compost to be used elsewhere on site; wood for building houses; seeds that can be pressed for oils; and habitat for indigenous species of flora and fauna.[15]

Furthermore, many within various permaculture circles, both in the United States and internationally, criticize the current industrial model of agriculture that has flourished since the onset of the Green Revolution. The Green Revolution is a term used to describe the large-scale industrial agriculture model that has gained adherents around the world beginning in the 1940s and which depends on mechanization of work and the use of petroleum-based chemicals and fertilizers. Critics of the Green Revolution claim that this method of farming requires intensive inputs of petroleum-based insecticides, herbicides, fungicides, and artificial fertilizers, all of which are seen to be unhealthy and toxic for the environment and especially agricultural soils and farm ecosystems. They also argue that the industrial model of farming displaces humans to urban environments, and that it is based on a model of monoculture (meaning one crop is grown at large scales of hundreds to thousands of acres) crops for export markets, so that taken together it is harmful to both society and food supplies.

Permaculture advocates hold their own model of farming up as the ideal corrective, as permaculture is about designing polyculture (the opposite of monoculture) systems of food production that use nature's own patterns and "energy" to create healthy, safe, bountiful, seasonal, petroleum-free (ideally) food items for human consumption. As this is an ideal, the reality is that it takes many years to approach edible forests and self-regeneration, but it is this ideal toward which Koinonia is aiming. And this aim of self-sufficient, eco-friendly food production is highly motivated by the community's Christian identity, at both institutional and individual levels.

For example, one community member stated that "sustainability is one of our areas . . . because of the sacredness of the land and of creation. . . . None of this 'God gave us this land and we can do whatever we want to.' It's 'God gave us this land and we better take [care] of it.' "[16] This member traces this view back to the original agricultural vision for Koinonia as articulated by Clarence Jordan himself. Another past member and current employee who works on the farm crew expresses similar sentiments. This employee's duties include caring for the community's milking cows and goats and culling rabbits, turkeys, and chickens to be eaten by those community members who are omnivores. He claims, "I mean I just think it's an obvious fit: that care for creation ought to be part of Christian consciousness." He goes on to explain that he is motivated to practice sustainable food production because of

> the health factor . . . you know, eating foods that are more nutritious, that don't have the negative aspects of chemicals being ingested into the body. . . . We all feel safer eating foods that are naturally grown without chemicals. I think that lines up with a Christian view of stewardship of creation, caring for the soil, supplementing the soil. . . . So I think that all of these things ought to be a part of a Christian consciousness.[17]

Such a belief leads to one of the current tensions in the community: how to transition the pecan orchards, which are needed for the community to remain economically viable, to sustainable, organic, permaculture groves. The current groves require chemical fungicides and insecticides, as pecan trees suffer from blight and pest infestation. Yet there are currently almost no organic pecan orchards anywhere in the South, so Koinonia sees itself as once again blazing trails as it slowly begins to diversify its varieties of pecan trees and attempts to begin new groves that are organic and sustainable. Moreover, this approach to growing and marketing food (in this case, pecan products) is one that is thoroughly influenced by Christian concepts of justice, fair trade and labor practices, and sustainable stewardship.

These sentiments are also shared by the community's current executive director, who has been instrumental in advocating that sustainability become part of the community's future, and who is equally supportive of this occurring in the fields and groves on campus. For this director, "I think that, well, getting right to the heart of it, I think we as humans are called to be in partnership with the Creator to re-create the garden. And we have done the opposite." Therefore, for this community steward, sustainable farming methods become a tool for re-creating the garden. As she explains, "The land, the animals, the buildings, the people . . . to me, it's all holistic. That's the reason why we started looking for a philosophy . . . some holistic way of nurturing all of this back to health. That's why we came upon permaculture."[18]

The practical results of these beliefs are that Koinonia now has blueberries and muscadine grapes that are grown organically; a one-acre garden that supplies the cafeteria with seasonal organic greens and summer fruits like tomatoes, squash, and strawberries, and a variety of other vegetables; a three-acre permaculture field with built-in swales that provides corn, squash, and beans; and a variety of animals that provide meat and milk. These include bees for honey and pollination, chickens, turkeys, geese, rabbits, goats, and cows. The community is also actively seeking out regional domestic varieties of many of these animals to help build on-farm diversity and to find breeds that are able to withstand the hot summers and cool winters of the region. Last is the slow process of transitioning to permaculture-designed pecan orchards that will also contain a wider variety of stone-fruit trees that will be intermixed with the pecans, all fertilized and "mowed" by rotational grazing of the cows and goats. All this work with food and farming connects Koinonia with a slow but growing North American Christian movement that sees caring for God's creation via sustainable food production to be a Christian duty.[19]

SHARING FOOD: FELLOWSHIP AND HOSPITALITY

The attempt to sustainably grow as much produce and meat as possible on-site is one aspect of Koinonia's relationship to food; the other key aspect is how this food is prepared and shared. And it is in the preparation and sharing that Koinonia gives truth to the claim of Gary Fick, Protestant agronomist and advocate for sustainable farming, that "what we eat and how we eat is full of meaning about what we believe and what we value."[20] Throughout the history of Koinonia, the values most associated with food have been fellowship, reconciliation, health, and sharing. These values are present at every step of each noon lunch prepared in the community's kitchen, which is located adjacent to the community's cafeteria.

This common dining hall and hospitality center is the heartbeat of Koinonia's campus, and it is metabolically connected to, serves, and is served by the fields, the chapel, the visitor's center, and the residential halls.

Everyone who is on the campus of Koinonia at noon between Monday and Friday is invited to the cafeteria to share in the noonday lunch that is prepared by a mix of employees, community members, and interns.

There is a standard format for these shared meals, including dining options for vegetarians and vegans; the placement of all the food along a twelve-foot table, with silverware and plates first, then food, and then cups for drinks; and the ringing of a large bell that hangs outside the cafeteria's door, alerting the community that lunch is about to begin. After the bell rings, those on campus who are participating in the meal (participation is expected of stewards, interns, and volunteers and encouraged for everyone else, especially including visitors) gather around the table and share in a grace/benediction/blessing. (Logistically this can create a problem, for if there is a tour of fifty people on campus that day the cafeteria can rapidly fill to capacity.) This benediction is either read or given by a community member, or by someone invited by a community member, while a peace candle is lit. The grace is often Christian based but can be interfaith. After the meal, everyone who is visiting the campus is encouraged to stand up and introduce themselves.

The cafeteria consists of six long tables with space for eight to twelve people to fit around, and two smaller tables that seat four to six people. There are also couches and chairs and, if the weather permits, picnic tables outside. Community members and interns are encouraged to visit with and get to know visitors, so that the community's vision statement of love, peace, and joy in service and sharing can be put into practice during these noon meals. No one is turned away from this meal due to dietary restrictions, race, age, nationality, or place of residency. This shared noonday meal is the same shared meal instituted by Clarence Jordan at the beginning of the community's history, and today it features food items sustainably grown on site.

Koinonia is able to communicate its storied history via this institutional practice of sharing meals with visitors; however, the meals also become a vehicle for community members to put the vision of Christ's sharing of food with all people into practice. This is because the "table fellowship of Jesus [points] to the community as the standard venue for thinking about [Christianity]."[21] Many visitors report that they are genuinely moved by the communal sharing of food in the dining hall, and for some this experience is heightened when remembering the revolutionary act that such sharing meant in rural 1940s Georgia. As the community's hospitality director and permaculture teacher explains, "I just have this idea that we are a place for . . . drawing people together. . . . So if we have [a visitor] who's a Buddhist and they want to meditate and that's what they're comfortable with and they want to share with us about that, that's great. And we can all sit down and have a meal together and talk about it."[22] We see here that Jordan's original vision of acceptance, hospitality, and fellowship over a shared meal is present in this current member's approach to the various people who spend time in the community, even if that person is not Christian.

Another visitor who was vacillating on becoming an intern and eventually married a community member had this to say about their experience of sharing food at Koinonia's noonday lunch:

I believe that Koinonia is part of God's plan: people need to see this and then go out and be like, "Whoa. There's a different place to live." Like just the other day there was a guest here and she was from Atlanta and she's always wanted to come out to Koinonia. . . . She came with a couple of her good friends and her husband and she had never experienced radical Christianity or community or permaculture. She had never heard of any of this stuff [and] she got a tour right before lunch. And then at lunch we were talking about . . . the earth and loving the earth and loving each other and . . . she introduced herself after lunch like everyone always does, and she was like "I'm so happy to be here." And the [community member in charge of lunch that day asked if] one of our guests [could] lead us in prayer, and the woman stood up and she was sobbing. She was . . . so moved by lunch, by the way [we] were doing lunch . . . this person . . . was so moved by lunch that she was crying so hard that she couldn't even say a prayer! And she finally choked out something and [she was so moved] by the way the people were eating lunch together! And I've seen that again and again since I've been here.[23]

Similar stories about such moments of transformation that take place in the dining hall and fields are not uncommon and are frequently shared among community members and by members with visitors. Such moments of transformation around food have been present at Koinonia throughout the years, beginning with Jordan, his family, subsequent black and white members, and continuing through today's vision of earth and human stewardship and hospitality.

I believe that God's action of creating, sustaining, redeeming, and
saving . . . converge in the mundane, pedestrian events of . . . daily
life . . . and probably the most mundane event of all—eating food. . . .
These everyday events are pervaded by sacredness, meaning, and
value, and they constitute the arena in which God bestows grace. . . .
When placed in this context, food consumption assumes an en-
tirely new meaning. . . . Like it or not, eating food is a moral and
theological activity whereby we define ourselves; construct politi-
cal, social, and economic institutions; and respond to God.
—MARK GRAHAM, *SUSTAINABLE AGRICULTURE*, 2005

From harvesting pecans to pasturing sheep and cows, Christians at Koinonia are responding to their conception of God and to Clarence Jordan's
original vision for the community with joy, love, fellowship, reconciliation, radical sharing, and peacemaking. They are also responding to God's
creation by implementing permaculture practices, thus demonstrating a
way to grow food that they believe is holistic and sustainable. Although
eating food is indeed one of the most mundane events of life, it is an event
that is fraught with meaning, whether acknowledged or not. At Koinonia, this event is imbued with several layers of meaning, all grounded
in an understanding of Christianity influenced by the early church, yet
that is equally influenced by an ecological view of the world afforded by
the environmental sciences of today. It is this unique combination that
places Koinonia at the forefront of North America's Ecological Reformation, where the community's own unique approach to growing and sharing food is a practice of both sustainability and Christian reconciliation
and fellowship.

DISCUSSION QUESTIONS

1. How did the history of segregation and sharecropping influence
   the formation of Koinonia, and especially shape how food became
   a central focus of the community? Are such issues still found in
   America today, especially in farming communities where there are
   migrant workers?

2. How is food central to Koinonia? Discuss its importance in terms of how it is grown, its economic role, and how it is shared.
3. Does the human relationship with food change when it is shared communally, especially in a religious setting? Why or why not? How is this reflected at Koinonia? Furthermore, who and what counts as a member of a "community"?

NOTES

1. Martin Palmer and Victoria Finlay, *Faith in Conservation: New Approaches to Religions and the Environment* (Washington, D.C.: World Bank, 2003); Mallory McDuff, *Natural Saints: How People of Faith Are Working to Save God's Earth* (New York: Oxford University Press, 2010); Bron Taylor, "A Green Future for Religion?" *Futures* 36 (2004); and Mary Evelyn Tucker and John Grim, "Introduction: The Emerging Alliance of World Religions and Ecology," *Daedelus: Journal of the American Academy of Arts and Sciences* 130 (2001).
2. Christine Leigh Heyrman, *Southern Cross: The Beginnings of the Bible Belt* (Chapel Hill: University of North Carolina Press, 1997); and Charles Reagan Wilson, *Baptized in Blood: The Religion of the Lost Cause, 1865–1920* (Athens: University of Georgia Press, 1980).
3. Michael Gomez, *Exchanging Our Country Marks—The Transformation of African Identities in the Colonial and Antebellum South* (Chapel Hill: University of North Carolina Press, 1998); Evelyn Brooks Higginbotham, *Righteous Discontent: The Women's Movement in the Black Baptist Church 1880–1920* (Cambridge: Harvard University Press, 1993); and Edward Jones, *The Known World* (New York: Amistad, 2004).
4. Tracy K'Myer, *Interracialism and Christian Community in the Postwar South: The Story of Koinonia Farm* (Charlottesville: University Press of Virginia, 1997); and Dallas Lee, *The Cotton Patch Evidence: The Story of Clarence Jordan and the Koinonia Farm Experiment (1942–1970)* (Americus: Koinonia Partners, 1971).
5. Lee, *The Cotton Patch Evidence*, 10, 29.
6. Jordan was also exposed to Social Gospel reformism during this time, and this liberal approach to Christianity merged with the disgust he already harbored toward southern racism. K'Meyer, *Interracialism and Christian Community in the Postwar South*, 11–30.
7. Jordan coined the term "demonstration plot" himself and used it numerous times when discussing and writing about Koinonia. It even appeared in the

community's one-time mission statement from 1992 to 2007, part of which states: "Koinonia Partners, Inc., is a Christian organization seeking to be a 'demonstration plot for the Kingdom of God.'" David Castle, "A Brief History of Koinonia: The Post-Jordan Years: 1970 to 2007," ms.

8. The Brüderhof and Amish are both intentional Protestant Christian groups with members who typically live in close-knit, agrarian-based communities.

9. Bruce Chilton, "Eucharist: Surrogate, Metaphor, Sacrament of Sacrifice," in *Sacrifice in Religious Experience*, ed. A. Baumgarten (Boston: Brill, 2002), 177.

10. Charles Marsh, *The Beloved Community: How Faith Shapes Social Justice, from the Civil Rights Movement to Today* (New York: Basic Books, 2005), 69.

11. Freedom Riders were groups of African Americans and Caucasians—some from the North, some from the South, some Jewish, most Christian—who rode together in buses to challenge with their bodies areas where racial discrimination was deeply entrenched.

12. David Castle writes that "We acknowledge that we are not going to get along perfectly all the time. In fact, community living often brings out not only the very best, but also the very worst in us" ("A Brief History of Koinonia"). To deal with the inevitable disagreements that attend to living and working with other humans, members at Koinonia try first to work things out by talking, then use a mediator, and lastly address the issue as a whole community.

13. Helene Slessarev-Jamir, *Prophetic Activism: Progressive Religious Justice Movements in Contemporary America* (New York: New York University Press, 2011), 4.

14. Castle, "A Brief History of Koinonia."

15. For permaculture design basics and the theory behind them, see Bill Mollison, *Permaculture Two: Practical Design for Town and Country in Permanent Agriculture* (Stanly: Tagari Books, 1979).

16. Interview with Anonymous "A," Koinonia, May 2009.

17. Interview with Anonymous "B," Koinonia, May 2009.

18. Interview with executive director, Koinonia, May 2009.

19. Calvin DeWitt, *Earth-Wise: A Biblical Response to Environmental Issues* (Grand Rapids: Faith Alive), 2007; and Charles Lutz, ed., *Farming the Lord's Land: Christian Perspectives on American Agriculture* (Minneapolis: Augsburg, 1980).

20. Gary Fick, *Food, Farming, and Faith* (Albany: State University of New York Press, 2008), 12.

21. Shannon Jung, *Sharing Food: Christian Practices for Enjoyment* (Minneapolis: Fortress Press, 2006), 151.

22. Interview with author at Koinonia, May 2009.
23. Interview with Anonymous "C," Koinonia, July 2009.

RECOMMENDED READING

Bauman, W., R. Bohannon II, and K. O'Brien. *Grounding Religion: A Field Guide to the Study of Religion and Ecology*. New York: Routledge, 2011.

Berry, Wendell. *The Unsettling of America: Culture and Agriculture*. New York: Avon, 1977.

Bingham, Rev. Canon Sally, ed. *Love God Heal Earth*. Pittsburgh: St. Lynn's, 2009.

Davis, Ellen. *Scripture, Culture, and Agriculture: An Agrarian Reading of the Bible*. New York: Cambridge University Press, 2009.

Fourteen

REFRESHING THE CONCEPT
OF HALAL MEAT

RESISTANCE AND RELIGIOSITY IN CHICAGO'S
TAQWA ECO-FOOD COOPERATIVE

SARAH E. ROBINSON

*Have you not seen that it is God to whom all the beings in the
earth bow themselves down—and so too the sun and the moon and
the stars and the mountains and the trees and the beasts?*
—QUR'AN 22:18

*TAQWA Eco-Food Cooperative serves four communities: consumers, food
production workers, animals, and Mother Earth. The cooperative aims
to restore Islamic ethics in the raising of livestock and poultry. It does so
by replacing inhumane farming practices with healthy and ecologically
respectful techniques, thereby improving standards of food production.*
—TAQWA ECO-FOOD COOPERATIVE

T RADITIONALLY MUSLIMS EAT *halal* meat, "permissible" meat, from particular animals that have been slaughtered using specific techniques. These food standards are defined by the Qur'an and interpreted by Muslim religious leaders.[1] Yet in 2010 founding coordinator of the Taqwa Eco-Food Cooperative Shireen Pishdadi asserted: "Halal is not just about how you slaughter the animal, right? I mean, if you are exploiting people, right, enslaving people to grow your food, how is that halal?!"[2] In the first decade of the twenty-first century, Pishdadi and other Taqwa leaders challenged norms in their local Muslim community in Chicago by broadening the view of halal standards to encompass environmental and social justice concerns. They also challenged U.S. industrial meat production, which meant resisting certain assimilation pressures in the years following September 11, 2001. Taqwa leaders applied a critical-constructive religiosity to their work, combining education with distribution of local, sustainable, and more humanely raised meat in the Chicago community, and they did it in a historical moment fraught with particular challenges for Muslim Americans.

In the 2004 book *Globalized Islam*, political scientist Olivier Roy describes an increase in religiosity among Muslims living in non-Muslim majority countries, which here applies to Taqwa leaders. Roy defines religiosity as "self-formulation and self-expression of a personal faith" in contrast with religion, "a coherent corpus of beliefs and dogmas collectively managed by a body of legitimate holders of knowledge."[3] As laypeople rather than formal religious leaders, Taqwa coordinators critiqued the U.S. industrial food system for its mistreatment of farmers, land, and the animals themselves.[4] They held a vision of Muslim food practice emphasizing the spirit of Islamic law and its multilayered justice, rather than the letter of Islamic law as expressed in contemporary halal standards and still framed within the industrial system of food production. Taqwa meats kept consistent with the letter of the law, however, ensuring *zabiha* meat from halal animals, slaughtered by a Muslim in a prescribed ritual manner.[5] These terms are described further below.

Taqwa encouraged the community to express religious commitments through daily food practices, promoting a wider interpretation of Islam's environmental and social relevance. It focused on eating only local, sustainably farmed animals, a perspective not widely shared in the larger Midwestern or American culture, nor in the local Muslim community in the early 2000s. At that time, local, sustainable, and more humanely raised meat options were absent in the urban Chicago landscape. Taqwa's meat choices sharply contrasted with readily available, lower-priced meats from the industrial farming norm, including those industrially produced meats labeled halal. Thus, as an organization, Taqwa faced a double challenge, critiquing mainstream U.S. industrial food systems and inviting local Muslim families to do the same at an awkward moment in history. Post-9/11 the local Muslim community was subject to discrimination and targeting. In this climate, according to Pishdadi, many Muslims preferred to assimilate than to challenge American norms. As anti-Muslim sentiment increased and pressures to assimilate were extraordinarily high, Taqwa's critique of industrial halal standards and conventional food production practices proved controversial.

In addition to the challenges in doing practical and educational work on behalf of Taqwa, Pishdadi faced controversy by opposing certain aspects of the local community's focus on halal certification and branding. Although she attributed this division to the community's preference for assimilation, with the changing tides of U.S. popular culture, "green" living has shifted from an alternative practice to a quasi-mainstream one since the early 2000s. Thus, a private business named Whole Earth Meats, Taqwa's next of kin, may benefit from the increasingly positive valence of green living and local, sustainable meats, as well as from the groundwork Taqwa laid in the realm of community education.[6]

HALAL AND ZABIHA: DEFINITIONS AND AMBIGUITIES

In Islamic law, *halal* is a general legal term meaning "lawful or permissible." Avoiding alcohol and pork are very basic interpretations of halal practice among diasporic Muslims. For authoritative explanation of foods and eating, religious leaders refer to passages from the Qur'an, including this one:

> People, eat what is good and lawful from the earth . . . [God] has only forbidden you carrion, blood, pig's meat, and animals over which any name other than God's has been invoked. (Qur'an 2:168, 173)

The Qur'an defines halal foods and names an extreme case—starving to death—when breaking the law is allowed (Qur'an 2:173, 5:3, 6:145, 16:115). In industrial food systems, halal certification indicates food acceptability for Muslims. For meat to be considered halal, Qur'anic law requires that the animal be killed in a specific way: God must be invoked and, to avoid prolonged suffering, a carotid artery and the trachea must be cut with a sharp knife. In this case there is a particular way of naming God that is invoked in animal slaughter, first stating intent (*niyya*) to begin the ritual act of slaughter, followed by naming God according to this formula: "In the Name of God, God is most Great," spoken in Arabic: "*Bismillah, Allahu' akbar.*" An additional instruction involves turning the animal in the direction of Mecca before slaughter, which is required only in Shi'i contexts.

Various organizations provide halal certification in the United States and globally. For example, another Chicago nonprofit organization, the Islamic Food and Nutrition Council of America (IFANCA), provides halal certification and education on a global scale, assessing food, pharmaceuticals, skin products, and packaging. Organizations like IFANCA use both business people and religious leaders to interpret the meaning of halal within contemporary food systems. Its halal definition excludes pork and its by-products, improperly killed animals, alcohol and intoxicants, carnivorous animals and birds of prey, and foods tainted with any of these ingredients.[7] Though other Chicago Muslims worked toward establishing halal standards for Illinois state and for the world, Taqwa leaders were less concerned with the global business of industrially produced foods that received the stamp of halal approval. Products like Starbucks mocha Frappuccinos and Pringles potato chips are halal simply because they contain no pork byproducts or alcohol-based flavorings, but these products remain industrially produced and thus ethically suspect.[8] Instead, Taqwa leaders focused on humane local meat-sourcing options.

Halal foods depend not on visibly discernible qualities but on consumer trust in purveyors accurately representing the conditions of food production, packaging, distribution, and sales. In this way, halal certification somewhat parallels organic certification, marking otherwise invisible aspects of food. Unfortunately, the term halal can be subject to variable interpretation and misuse. For this reason, further terms like zabiha become useful. Following migrations of Muslims to the West in general and to the United States in particular, a distinction has arisen between the more general moniker halal and the more specific zabiha (also *dhabiha*) meat.[9] Zabiha is a helpful marker in diasporic communities of Muslim immigrants owing to the use of the term halal to refer also to animals slaughtered by Christians and Jews, fellow "people of the book" or *Ahl al-Kitab*.[10] Some Sunni Muslims argue that the Prophet Muhammad ate meat slaughtered by Jews and Christians.[11] Without assessing historical accuracy, this notion functions socially to permit the same behavior, since the Prophet Muhammad is considered the exemplar of good practices. Although Sunni laws allow for eating meats prepared by *Ahl al-Kitab*, Shi'i law is less lenient.[12] Some Islamic legal scholars have concluded that meat slaughtered by Christians and Jews is permissible if, before eating this meat, the Muslim eater prayerfully names God.

Despite halal certification agencies, and thus certain degrees of consensus, varying interpretations provide inconsistent meanings for the terms halal and zabiha. Some writers use the term halal instead of zabiha to refer only to animals killed in accordance with Qur'anic laws on slaughter, excluding animals slaughtered by adherents of other Abrahamic religions, such as Jewish kosher meats. Thus the terms are sometimes, but not always, used interchangeably in reference to meat. Zabiha slaughter is halal or lawful, so combining terms can be somewhat redundant. In addition, the Muslim Consumer Group defines zabiha meat as halal animals hand-slaughtered by a Muslim, notably excluding the machine-slaughtered animals common in industrial-scale farming.[13]

Profound variations exist among meats labeled halal, including violations of Qur'anic laws regarding slaughter, elaborated in the following examples. In his 2010 book *Green Deen: What Islam Teaches About Protecting the Planet*, popular writer Ibrahim Abdul-Matin described research concerned with questionably halal meats produced in industrial factory farming, including surprising certification practices. Mufti Shaykh Abdullah Nana discovered the problematic "drive-by" halal certification whereby a shaykh reads a blessing while he drives past a slaughterhouse, which is far from slaughtering by hand with the name of God on one's lips. In another case, Shaykh Abdullah found the same machine and blade used to kill pigs and halal animals, potentially rendering the halal-certified meat *haram* (not permissible) if the knife was not properly cleaned.[14] He concluded that half of American Muslims eat questionable meat even when they buy halal-certified meat.[15]

These kinds of questionable practices were among the things Taqwa sought to avoid. Taqwa's website included meat slaughter standards consistent with Qur'anic zabiha specifications: naming God, using a presharpened blade, avoiding needless suffering and excess fear in the animal, and attending to the animal's hunger and thirst and offering soothing before slaughter. Qaid Hassan was a slaughterer for Taqwa and its last coordinator, as well as becoming the initiating director of Whole Earth Meats, the private business that continued with the work and legacy of Taqwa. Hassan described Whole Earth Meats products as zabiha-halal, fusing terms to perhaps doubly indicate their legal permissibility and acceptability. In sharp contrast with the drive-by slaughter blessing, Hassan described witnessing a traditional zabiha slaughter while visiting Mauritania, West

Africa, in 2002, two years before he began with Taqwa. The cattle herd walked near his tent during his entire two-month stay. His Mauritanian friend performed the ritual slaughter technique, which Hassan witnessed: "[Y]ou wouldn't even have known that an animal was being slaughtered. It was so much finesse there, just so much compassion and so much ease and method."[16] Hassan's experience made a deep impression about the potential for a prayerful relationship with the act of slaughter and with the sacrificed animal. Hassan brought this encounter to his work with Taqwa, as well as to Whole Earth Meats.

Efforts to refresh traditional and accepted notions of halal are complicated by the Qur'anic injunction against new declarations on permissibility, a problem that Taqwa faced. The Qur'an specifically prohibits new claims to define permissible or non-permissible things:

> So we eat of the good and lawful things God has provided for you and be thankful for His blessings. . . . Do not say falsely, "This is lawful and that is forbidden," inventing a lie about God: those who invent lies about God will not prosper—they may have a little enjoyment but painful punishment awaits them. (Qur'an 16:114, 116)

All foods are halal unless specifically named in the Qur'an or in a reliably sourced *hadith* (narrative detailing actions and sayings attributed to the Prophet Muhammad and his close companions). Because of this injunction against erecting false laws, Islam does not, for example, encourage vegetarianism generally. Nevertheless, certain poets, historical figures, and some contemporary Muslims prefer a vegetarian diet. Similarly, Taqwa's work proved periodically controversial because it depended on alternative notions of food practice beyond more common interpretations of halal laws. Although Taqwa leaders found their project consistent with Islamic principles, they also differed in approach and interpretation from others in both the local Muslim community and beyond.

TAQWA ECO-FOOD COOPERATIVE: ENACTING JUSTICE THROUGH FOOD PRACTICE

Taqwa was originally envisioned, organized, and funded by a Chicago interreligious and environmental nonprofit organization, Faith in Place. Shortly after September 11, 2001, Director Rev. Dr. Clare Butterfield witnessed increasing vilification of local Muslim Americans and endeavored to strengthen interfaith connections. Butterfield hired Shireen Pishdadi, who became Taqwa's founding coordinator, and they defined the potential needs that an environmental project could fill in the local Muslim community. Their agricultural project showed the potential to both address the existing concern of sourcing healthy halal meat and counteract the ethical challenges—environmental and social—of industrially produced meat.

The Arabic term *taqwa* has multilayered meaning, translated as "fear of God" or more specifically "being mindful of God." This ethical concept encourages Muslims to live with reverence for and awareness of God in daily living, making choices knowing that God will judge each person accordingly. Pishdadi explained that Islam is a way of life, a worldview of perpetual spiritual attentiveness, lacking separation between religious and mundane practice. In the context of abuses present in U.S. industrial agriculture, Pishdadi led the organization to define project goals, making central the practice of taqwa. To Pishdadi, the term taqwa reflected a Muslim sense of constant attentiveness to God's presence and judgment, a directive to live justly. The organization strove to do this through community education about agriculture and a program of meat distribution. Coordinators from the local Muslim community shaped Taqwa's scope and direction, in consultation and collaboration with their religious communities, volunteers, Faith in Place staff, board directors, and all cooperative participants who bought meat.

Interviews with Taqwa's first and last coordinators, Shireen Pishdadi and Qaid Hassan, showed that both brought enthusiasm, idealism, and critical-constructive religiosity to the project, expressed through a strong commitment to the health and well-being of every person and animal they encountered. They paid particular attention to farmers, reaching out to people who may never have met a Muslim, developing business partnerships and friendships, and strengthening respectful relations through paying a living wage. Taqwa coordinators did not represent Islam as official religious leaders such as imams and shaykhs. As laypeople, they did not engage in formal legal inquiry with the intention of establishing Islamic juridical precedent, thus rendering their voices more marginal within the tradition. Nevertheless, Pishdadi and Hassan genuinely sought to engage their religious tradition concerning food, including its quality, reflected by relationships with people, animals, and land as expressions of religious commitment. They provided critical attention to problems while working to provide constructive solutions, and they spoke poetically and with inspiring vision.

Pishdadi emphasized a preference for local sustainable farms over organic ones because, as popular demand increased, industrially produced organic options arose. *Sustainable* refers to environmental, if not also economic and human community, sustainability. The word *sustainable* denotes practices that do not deplete soil, water, or communities beyond that which can be replenished in the natural cycles of renewal. Exploitation of workers and farmers by distributors, financiers, landowners, other farmers, chemical and seed companies, or other entities are examples of unsustainable practices. *Local* food is region-specific and seasonal, reducing or eliminating many environmental costs. Local food contrasts with industrial agriculture, which can transport foods literally across the planet (e.g., Chilean summer fruits during Northern Hemisphere winters) and require agricultural inputs like petrochemical fertilizers and pesticides, plus packaging, transportation, refrigeration, storage, and other energy-intensive steps. The rise of large-scale, industrial organic farms changed the playing field for organic agriculture, reducing fossil fuel-based pesticide and chemical fertilizer use. Even so, Pishdadi warned that industrial organic farms can exploit animals, land, and workers, consistent with conventional industrial agriculture.

Illinois's local, sustainable food producers provided the solution of ethically raised animals, which could be hand-slaughtered by Taqwa volunteers with local distribution to interested families. Visiting the farms and farmers, Pishdadi and Hassan verified that the animals' living conditions were natural and healthy, and the farmers were good stewards of the land without depleting soil and water resources on the unsustainable scale that industrial agriculture can. To Pishdadi and Hassan, these factors exemplified a broader Islamic perspective on justice for land, animals, and the farmers whose high standards exemplified a natural, traditional animal husbandry, which might be more like practices in the Prophet Muhammad's era (c. 570–632 C.E.). The perpetual challenge was to educate consumers and generate a willingness to pay higher prices for meat, in order for farmers to be paid a living wage for their more humane work raising local, sustainable livestock.

Taqwa leaders emphasized the integration of all agricultural issues into the worldview of belief in God and relationship with God as the fundamental marker of Muslim identity. This religious perspective translated into action in the following ways in the Taqwa project:

- Questioning industrial farming methods and their exploitative destructiveness to land, water, animals, farmers, and farm workers
- Supporting smaller-scale, local farms that raise animals with kindness and nourish the land's regenerative capacity
- Paying small farmers a living wage
- Living faithfully by acting wisely within God's creation in accordance with divine law

These goals expressed a desire not only to respect Islamic law regarding slaughter, but also to ensure that the meat they offered the community was *tayyib*, or wholesome. In his description of Taqwa's next-of-kin project, Whole Earth Meats, Hassan showed his commitments as inclusive of people's physical and spiritual health, the end goals of the emphasis on wholesomeness, quality, and care for the animals and people at all levels of the process. These goals are explained further below.

Near industrial meat operations, the water supply can often be polluted. The quantity of animal waste produced can exceed that of a city. Even so, regulations do not adequately address the factory's responsibility to safely process the waste before dumping it in local waters or creating ponds of animal waste. Pishdadi integrated her understanding of water pollution from factory-farmed animal waste with her understanding of Islam's injunction against polluting water: "It's not halal, it is haram to pollute water, it is explicitly haram to pollute water, so if the food we're eating was raised in a way that pollutes water, is it halal? And nobody wants to answer that question, nobody would have that conversation in the community."[17] Pishdadi offered wide-vision interpretations that contrasted with common perceptions, highlighting responsibilities of Muslims and the potential role of the local Muslim community in finding and advocating alternatives to industrial farming's excessive water pollution.

A hadith reported by Abu-Dawud asserts, "The Apostle of Allah [God] prohibited eating the animal which feeds on filth and drinking its milk."[18] Some Islamic scholars interpret this to mean that animals who eat a nonvegetarian diet that deviates from natural feeding norms are haram, or impermissible.[19] One could argue that the industrial factory-farming system does both by feeding cows corn (unnatural because ruminants like cows eat grass) and animal by-products (nonvegetarian feed, which led to mad cow disease). Since the occurrence of mad cow disease, or bovine spongiform encephalopathy (BSE), in the 1990s, U.S. Food and Drug Administration (FDA) regulations disallow "most" mammal protein in feed for cattle and other ruminants.[20] In 2001 FDA inspections showed that a quarter of ruminant feed tested did not meet the guideline. Industrial animal production facilities can use "protein supplements" in feed, which may include pork, rendering the animal nonhalal, which is not necessarily communicated to purveyors and customers.[21]

These assessments confirm the claims of Taqwa leaders that factory-farmed meat at the very least appears questionable for Muslims to eat and certainly is not *tayyib*, or wholesome, the basis for any law regulating halal food. This position is shared with some, though not all, Muslims beyond Taqwa: "The underlying principle for halal is that food has to be . . . permissible [*halal*] and wholesome, or good [*tayyib*]."[22] The term *tayyib* appeared on the Taqwa website: "Wholesome foods, *Tayyib*, are those that are conducive to goodness and well being and free of harmful effects."[23] Pishdadi used this principle to explain the need to ensure safe, wholesome, and healthful meat, focusing on a Muslim's responsibility to God to follow wider Islamic principles to avoid questionable, industrially produced halal meats.

In addition to concerns for animals, water, feed, and pollution, Taqwa leaders found that many social justice issues hinge around agriculture, increasing their commitment to work with small, sustainable farmers. Pishdadi and Hassan expressed concern about the nationwide reduction in small, family-owned farms as bigger agricultural players priced them out, and the subsequent detrimental effects on quality of life and quality of products. They were uneasy about increasing corporate control of large-scale food distribution systems, again reducing the playing field for smaller farmers. In larger-scale food production, Hassan and Pishdadi found ethically problematic the exploitation of farmworkers and meat-packing workers, who sometimes work in slavelike conditions. Pishdadi spoke about the inspiration she found in the Coalition of Immokalee Workers, a movement opposing the little-known slave conditions for U.S. farm workers on Florida tomato farms.[24] Faced with the challenge to change exploitative food systems that served cheaper food with side orders of environmental and social injustices, Taqwa worked directly with small, local, sustainable farmers and returned to the Qur'an's teachings about balance, slavery, and justice.

The Qur'an, Pishdadi said, depicts an abundant earth and the universe in balance. She argued that if humanity would use the "God-given gifts of intellect," then people would live in harmony and the earth would reflect God's balance. This statement implies that there is human-made imbalance inherent in scarcity that can be righted by engaging human reason toward the goal of balance, or *mizan*. Nature's balance is most apparent in small, local farms; thus Taqwa worked with these exclusively.

To explore Islamic values and ethics for sustainable agriculture, Pishdadi cited a narrative from the Qur'an regarding Moses and the Tribe of Israel. She described the people growing tired of eating manna from heaven, complaining that they preferred the "lentils, cucumbers, and onions" they ate as slaves in Egypt. Moses replied that they should return in shame, since they disliked the "pure food" of their freedom, given directly from God (Qur'an 2:47–61). Pishdadi inferred from this Qur'anic narrative that people can refuse God's gifts, preferring familiar foods available only through bondage, rather than pure, divinely given, yet still unfamiliar foods. Pishdadi cited this story without a detailed explanation of how it related to her work. This story may reflect the challenge of educating the Muslim community (or any U.S. community more familiar with lower-priced, industrially produced meats) about problems with common meat-production practices, which reflects a larger U.S. cultural myopia regarding relations with workers, animals, and land in contemporary industrial farming.

Hassan also reflected on social justice in the Qur'an. He cited a narrative with people witnessing injustice and asking, "Where is God?" Hassan explained that God responds by turning the question around: "No, the question is where are you?" Hassan asked: If you see a problem, what will you do to address that problem? Hassan spoke of the human capacity to honor God through action. As people recognize social and environmental problems—such as inhumane treatment of animals, water pollution, food contamination, and exploitative labor practices—they need not wait for a divine panacea but can work toward solutions as a religious practice. This is the heart of Taqwa Eco-Food Cooperative's community work, which successfully educated many local Muslim families about both industrial and local, sustainable farming. In the early 2000s Taqwa met challenges against its efforts to generate widespread appeal in the local Muslim American community, as pressures to assimilate weighed heavily on many in this often misunderstood minority.

CONTROVERSY CLOSE TO HOME, ASSIMILATION, AND THE CHANGING GREEN LANDSCAPE

Pishdadi objected to the ways in which the local Muslim community employed the term halal within an exploitative model of industrial factory farming. Through Taqwa she encouraged the Muslim community to challenge industrial food production and indiscriminate halal labeling, to encompass social justice emphasized in other aspects of Islam beyond food laws. Pishdadi explained that the Muslim community kept its primary focus on halal slaughter, but Taqwa's concerns were more far-reaching:

> Islam is about principles, and applying just principles, justice, it's not about blindly following the letter of the law. Even in the Qur'an it says, don't eat pork but if you're starving and you're going to die then eat it. . . . It's not black and white like that. Yeah, so the halal thing in the community I think is really misguided.[25]

Pishdadi questioned people's motives related to business and politics as they differed from her sense of Islamic principles reflecting a justice-based vision central to Taqwa's environmental-religious commitments, both practical and educational.

Pishdadi disliked the way the term halal—or lawful—became co-opted for marketable ends in the food industry without adequate attention to other aspects of Muslim religious integrity. Pishdadi saw the potential for grave misuse in an ambiguously hybrid culture of industrial meats receiving halal certification. She opposed the overuse of the term halal in the service of profit seeking. She saw the profit motive as distinct from a more prayerful Muslim identity, judging the basis of U.S. economics as neither the pinnacle model of human economic potential nor the best means of practicing daily religious commitments. Her critique concurs with a more general critique made by scholar of Islam and the environment Seyyed Hossein Nasr: "It is the secularized worldview that reduces nature to a purely material domain cut off from the world of the Spirit to be plundered at will for what is usually called human welfare, but which really means the illusory satisfaction of a never-ending greed without which consumer society would not exist."[26]

Nasr and Pishdadi might agree that the modern, Western perspective is infused with a hazardously materialist secularism. Pishdadi added a layer of critique toward the acceptance and acculturation of her local religious community into this problematically exploitative worldview, whereas Nasr implied that the onus remains with Western influence, even when found among Muslims. Industrially produced, factory-farmed meats and other foods labeled halal represented another means of assimilation into problematic aspects of American culture (secularism, consumerism, exploitation). Pishdadi noted the absence of more widespread Muslim ethical critique of U.S. industrially produced food and instead a strong focus on establishing legislation for halal foods.

Pishdadi described the Muslim community organizing around a proposed halal act for the state of Illinois.[27] She compared the process to establishing Jewish kosher standards, explaining that the Jewish community had bureaucratic entities empowered to certify not only products but also organizations seeking the capacity to do kosher certification. She pointed out that Muslims did not have the same infrastructure to grant authority to a certifying agency. Thus, because of laws separating church and state in the United States, Pishdadi argued that anyone could apply to the state to become a certifying agent, but "the state has no protocol for what makes a certifying agent or what makes halal."[28] Thus, at a public hearing on the subject, Pishdadi pointed out the weaknesses of legislation creating certifying agents to declare certain foods halal:

> Anybody could become a Muslim certifying agent and they can certify pork as halal and the USDA admitted. . . . "Yeah that's kind of a loophole." What do you mean it's kind of a loophole?! . . . It's just crazy so, yeah, that's what the [Muslim] community is doing. And then they would be like, "Well, we should just be happy that we're getting a law." You know? I'm like, this is the wrong attitude! It's an immigrant community . . . they're just trying to assimilate into the system.[29]

Pishdadi expressed disbelief and critique about the focus on institutionalizing the halal brand, which showed priority for assimilation but also potential for dramatic misuse. Passed by the Illinois General Assembly in 2002, the Halal Food Act also classified deceptive practices as misdemeanor offenses, reducing the loophole to a less gaping size.

About Illinois's proposed halal legislation, Pishdadi said, "Forget the halal act and all this stuff, kosher or whatever. We don't need that stuff. We're working with the local food people."[30] To Pishdadi, attempts at legislating halal standards were distractions owing to their limited scope within the industrial model of agriculture that did not fit a model of Muslim prayerful practice and justice building found within the small-farming, local-food model.

Pishdadi emphasized that she did not blame people in the community for prioritizing assimilation because of the negative attention local families, neighborhoods, and mosques faced in the years after the 2001 terrorist attacks that firmly tied extremist terrorism to Islam in myriad U.S. media narratives. These narratives too often lacked subtlety to differentiate between peaceable, faithful families and violent extremists whose attacks affect other Muslims more than any other group worldwide. With a cultural backdrop of all too common misunderstanding and discrimination, many American Muslims have chosen to avoid conflict and controversy. This can mean avoiding public critique of U.S. norms like industrial food. In the case of industrial halal foods, a major marker of Muslim identity becomes infused with aspects of assimilation.

Pishdadi displayed a self-defined religiosity—as in Olivier Roy's definition above—by taking the initiative to interpret religious tenets for herself and her work in the community, willing to stand by a different interpretation from those of local leadership to remain true to her "self-formulation and self-expression of a personal faith." She offered interpretations of Muslim text and heritage relevant to contemporary food issues. Pishdadi likened her divergence from the local community to a test from God, that rather than focusing on her political position and benefit, she acted on behalf of justice. Despite her moments of conflict within the Muslim community, she believed that she served God as a sincere, devoted Muslim. Again, her religiosity took precedence over the opinions of people shaping the halal certification discussion. Pishdadi explained that only God knows a person's sincerity and judges her or his actions.

Despite periodic challenges, Taqwa widened appreciation for environmental and social aspects of meat and agriculture in the local Muslim community through education and logistics coordination. Taqwa's community education worked slowly, particularly as Taqwa asked the community to pay higher prices for their meats than people were accustomed to paying. Taqwa leaders agreed that the project was successful in meeting its goals of community education and outreach among various families and individuals in the local Muslim community, interfaith community building with the umbrella nonprofit organization Faith in Place, plus building respectful relations with local, sustainable farmers. Pishdadi's work against the halal brand did bring some controversy, as she worked on local and national levels with leaders who differed from her broader approach to food, religion, and halal. Nevertheless, many local families responded positively, participated in, and benefited from Taqwa's vision and practice. One local family established a small family farm, naming Pishdadi's work with Taqwa as a strong influence.

Despite successes in education and partnership building, Taqwa did not reach the goal of financial sustainability. The board agreed with Taqwa's last coordinator, Qaid Hassan, when he proposed to transform Taqwa into a private business. After Taqwa's end in 2009 and with the support of Faith in Place, Hassan founded a meat-distribution business, Whole Earth Meats, based on the Taqwa model of social justice and environmental stewardship and built on Taqwa's farm contacts, but widening the potential market to include both Taqwa's preexisting meat purchasers and a larger constituency. A journalist described Whole Earth Meats as employing "humane halal" in its inclusive practice, and Hassan used the term *zabiha-halal*.[31]

Even with challenges encountered by Pishdadi from some in the local Muslim community, the environmentally minded green movement has become increasingly fashionable since Taqwa's early days, and possibly more attractive to Muslim Americans working with American cultural trends. This transformation is exemplified by Ibrahim Abdul-Matin and his popular book, *Green Deen*, featured in the 2010 Green Festival in San Francisco, which integrated a green Muslim into the mainstream of environmental discourse.[32] Whole Earth Meats, which continues the work of Taqwa in a new form, may benefit from the heightened popularity of "going green" as Qaid Hassan sells more humanely raised, local, sustainable, zabiha-halal meat in the wider Chicago community. Hassan is not alone; other Muslim American environmental projects include D.C. Green Muslims and Muslim family farms like Norwich Meadows Farm in the Northeast.[33]

In a post-9/11, twenty-first-century urban U.S. context, Taqwa leaders found most relevant to their daily Muslim food practice not the industrial halal food industry, but the wholesome, small-scale work of local, sustainable farmers. Committed religiosity fueled Taqwa's goals of education and community outreach, plus coordination of sustainable, local, more humane meat distribution. Taqwa's meat provided an ethical alternative to the problems of industrial meat, ensuring a healthier life for livestock animals, fair wages for small farmers, and environmentally sustainable land stewardship. Thus Taqwa refreshed the concept of halal meat, resisting definitions of halal within the industrial food system, providing the most environmentally and socially ethical zabiha-halal meat available in Chicago at the time.

The leaders in Taqwa were not religious leaders or Islamic scholars, but rather community members expressing religiosity, applying their religious understandings to address contemporary issues in food and agriculture. Its leaders cited Qur'anic passages that inspired and supported Taqwa's work. Islam's principle of justice infused Taqwa's commitment to respectful relationships with animals, land, and the local, sustainable farmers that cared for them. The religiosity of Taqwa leaders existed in dynamic tension with heightened pressures for Muslim Americans to assimilate into U.S. cultural norms after 9/11, as Taqwa resisted both U.S. industrial foods and halal standards within the industrial food model. Pishdadi's internal critique proved particularly uncommon as the community faced anti-Muslim sentiment. Taqwa's work in the local Muslim American community in Chicago showed the diversity within a particularly misunderstood minority group. The tides of U.S. cultural norms have brought green living to a more mainstream audience, which may assist both Qaid's Hassan's Whole Earth Meats business and other green Muslim projects in their broader appeal.

Despite myriad challenges, Pishdadi and Hassan mindfully considered their work with Taqwa as an extension of their commitments to Islamic principles and a fuller expression of Muslim religious conscience. With Taqwa, consumers, farmers, land, and animals received respect and care within a critical-constructive religious worldview. As expressed in many environmental circles, Pishdadi and Hassan both described their work with Taqwa in relation to their care and commitment as parents for their children's future.

DISCUSSION QUESTIONS

1. Taqwa Eco-Food Cooperative's name uses the Muslim concept of taqwa to represent an intention to practice "constant attentiveness to God's presence and judgment." How does this concept apply to Taqwa's work with food? Does the taqwa concept resemble other religious ideas you have studied?

2. Taqwa leaders integrated insights from Islam with contemporary issues in environmental and social justice. How did they accomplish this fusion? Name one example, and explain how it relates to justice, both environmental and social.

3. What are three complicating factors in defining halal?

4. If you were given the opportunity to start a food-justice project in your community (religious or otherwise), what specific issue would be most relevant for fostering further education and outreach? Why? What could be the first steps toward beginning this new project?

NOTES

1. The Qur'an is written in Arabic. Qur'an translations that appear here are generally from M.A.S. Abdel Haleem, trans., *The Qur'an* (New York: Oxford University Press, 2004/2008). In certain cases, I have offered translational interpretation, which reflect consideration of multiple translations, including Muhammed Asad, trans., *The Message of the Qur'an* (Bristol, England: Book Foundation, 2003).

2. The quotation about Taqwa is from Taqwa Eco-Food Cooperative, "About Us," http://taqwaecofood.org/moved. Taqwa was a Chicago-based, nonprofit project from 2002 to 2009. In October and November 2010 I conducted interviews with key people regarding Taqwa Eco-Food Cooperative. Coordinators Qaid Hassan and Shireen Pishdadi spoke from within a Muslim worldview and practice, and their voices receive focus in this essay. The third interviewee, Rev. Dr. Clare Butterfield, was director of the interreligious nonprofit organization Faith in Place, which launched and funded Taqwa. Clare Butterfield, interview by author, digital recording, Chicago, October 21, 2010; Shireen Pishdadi, interview by author, digital recording, Chicago, October 21, 2010, parts 1, 2, and 3; Qaid Hassan, interview by author, digital recording, Chicago, October 22, by phone November 14, and by phone November 16, 2010. Pishdadi interview 3, lines 837–39.

3. Olivier Roy, *Globalized Islam: A Search for a New Ummah* (New York: Columbia University Press, 2004), 5–6.

4. Agricultural environmental thought has a complex history, from Rachel Carson to Raj Patel and beyond. Rachel Carson, *Silent Spring* (Boston: Houghton Mifflin, 1962); Raj Patel, *Stuffed and Starved: The Hidden Battle for the World Food System* (Brooklyn: Melville House, 2007).

5. The word *zabiha* derives from the verb to slaughter, *dhabaha* or *zabaha*. Single Arabic terms consistently have multiple spellings in transliterations for the Roman alphabet, such as *dhabiha*, *zabiha*, and *zabeeha*. These alternate spellings are due to variants based on how local languages shape pronunciation in Arabic. For example, the accurate transcription from Arabic is *dh*, but in the Urdu and Farsi languages, the *dh* is pronounced *z*, hence the alternate transcription. The spelling *zabiha* appears here owing to its use by Taqwa.

6. This chapter reports on and reflects the perspectives of Taqwa's coordinators, Shireen Pishdadi and Qaid Hassan. For this reason I do not deal directly with meat eating as a consumer choice or a moral question. Likewise, I remain in keeping with an anthropocentric (human-centered) view of nature's abundance that arises in various, though not all, Muslim and Islamic contexts. Terminologically, Muslim refers to the nearly one billion adherents of Islam, and Islamic refers to official religious representatives and doctrine.

7. In my interviews, Taqwa leaders named no organizations or individuals involved in halal certification. The geographic proximity prompted my inclusion of IFANCA. The IFANCA halal certification symbol is a crescent circling a letter M. According to IFANCA, all Muslim countries and halal importing areas accept their certification standard. Islamic Food and Nutrition Council of America (IFANCA) website, http://www.ifanca.org/media/#prof.

8. Taqwa leaders did not mention these products, which are exmples of consumer goods listed as halal in the following book. Syed Rasheeduddin Ahmed, *A Comprehensive List of Halal Food Products in U.S. Supermarkets* (Huntley, Ill.: Muslim Consumer Group for Food Products, 2005), 20, 28.

9. Zabiha slaughtering techniques represent one example of halal or permissible acts. M. G. Fareed describes the differentiation between halal and zabiha as rooted in geography and migration, with Muslims living as minority communities in various Western countries. Muneer Goolam Fareed, "Dietary Laws," in *The Encyclopedia of Islam and the Muslim World*, ed. Richard C. Martin (New York: Macmillan Reference USA, 2004), 180–81.

10. A. H. Sakr, "Dietary Regulations and Food Habits of Muslims," *Journal of the American Dietetic Association* 58 (1971): 123–26; and M. M. Hussaini, *Islamic Dietary Concepts and Practices* (Bedford Park, Ill.: Islamic Food and Nutrition

Council of America, 1993), cited in Kaijn Bonne and Wim Verbeke, "Religious Values Informing Halal Meat Production and the Control and Delivery of Halal Credence Quality," *Agriculture and Human Values* 25 (2008): 41.

11. Sakr, "Dietary Regulations," and Hussaini, *Islamic Dietary Concepts and Practices.*

12. Princeton University professor of Islamic Studies Mark Cohen appears without specific citation in Howard Blas, "One Man's Meat . . . ," *Jerusalem Report*, December 31, 2001, 38.

13. Muslim Consumer Group website, http://www.muslimconsumergroup.com/halal_selection_criteria.html.

14. Although the practice is considered distasteful, a properly cleaned knife may legally be used on halal and nonhalal animals. Washing with water is key to rendering the knife ritually pure.

15. Ibrahim Abdul-Matin, *Green Deen: What Islam Teaches About Protecting the Planet* (San Francisco: Barrett-Koehler, 2010), 146–49.

16. Hassan interview 1, lines 431–36, 476–80.

17. Pishdadi interview 1, lines 806–9.

18. Abu-Dawud, Book 27, 3776, in Bonne and Verbeke, "Religious Values," 35–47, 40.

19. Bonne and Verbeke, "Religious Values," 40.

20. "Title 21 Part 589.2000 of the Code of Federal Regulations, Became Effective on August 4, 1997," in Mian N. Riaz and Muhammad M. Chaudry, *Halal Food Production* (New York: CRC Press, 2004), 140–41.

21. Ibid., 141.

22. The full quotation reads: "The underlying principle for halal is that food has to be halalun tayyaban, meaning permissible and wholesome, or good." *Halalun* and *tayyaban* are derivations of the words *halal* and *tayyib*. Ibid., 136.

23. Taqwa Eco-Food Cooperative website, http://taqwaecofood.org/faqs/faqs_islamtwo.html.

24. Coalition of Immokolee Workers website, http://www.ciw-online.org/.

25. Pishdadi interview 1, lines 809–21.

26. Seyyed Hossein Nasr, *Religion and the Order of Nature: The 1994 Cadbury Lectures at the University of Birmingham* (New York: Oxford University Press, 1996), 271.

27. From her description and the timeline, the following Halal Food Act in Illinois is likely to be the one to which Shireen Pishdadi referred. Illinois General Assembly, "PUBLIC HEALTH (410 ILCS 637/) Halal Food Act," January 1, 2002,

http://www.ilga.gov/legislation/ilcs/ilcs3.asp?ActID=1581&ChapterID=35; Pishdadi interview 3, lines 801–84.

28. Pishdadi interview 3, line 854.

29. Ibid., lines 851–53, 855–58, 863–69.

30. Pishdadi interview 1, lines 1167–68.

31. Michael Gebert, "Whole Earth Meats Aims for Humane Halal," *Grub Street Chicago*, New York Media LLC, August 10, 2010, http://chicago.grubstreet .com/2010/08/whole_earth_meats_aims_for_hum.html.

32. Green Festival website, http://www.greenfestivals.org/speakers/ibrahim -abdul-matin.

33. Leah Koenig, "Reaping the Faith," *Gastronomica: The Journal of Food and Culture* 8, no. 1 (2008): 80–84; Norwich Meadows Farm website, http://www .norwichmeadowsfarm.com/press.htm; DC Green Muslims website, http:// dcgreenmuslims.blogspot.com/2011/06/green-muslims-has-moved.html.

RECOMMENDED READING

Abdul-Matin, Ibrahim. *Green Deen: What Islam Teaches About Protecting the Planet.* San Francisco: Berrett-Koehler, 2010.

Foltz, Richard C., Frederick M. Denny, and Azizan Baharuddin, eds. *Islam and Ecology: A Bestowed Trust.* Cambridge: Harvard University Press, 2003.

Waldau, Paul, and Kimberley Patton, eds. *A Communion of Subjects: Animals in Religion, Science, and Ethics.* New York: Columbia University Press, 2006.

Fifteen

QUASI-RELIGIOUS
AMERICAN FOODWAYS

THE CASES OF VEGETARIANISM
AND LOCAVORISM

BENJAMIN E. ZELLER

"FOOD IS MY religion." So declares a participant in Shannon Hayes's study of "radical homemakers," women who defy consumer culture through intentionally and playfully subverting traditional gender roles.[1] Variants of this statement abound in food magazines, cooking shows, and food blogs, not to mention everyday conversations. People have declared chocolate, beer, and cheese their religions. So too with various types or approaches to food, such as vegetarianism or locavorism (eating food that one identifies as produced locally). The question is not whether people consider food and eating as something akin to religion. They do. Rather, what does this reveal, and what value is offered to us by thinking about food as something akin to religion?

There are several parallels between religion and eating, many of which have been developed throughout this book. But this essay looks to something somewhat different: food and eating *as* a religion, and the process of conversion that people undergo when they change foodways. Scholars have identified many cultural pursuits as things akin to religion, or what I call "quasi religions," since they do not involve Gods, supernatural forces, teachings about the soul or life after death, institutions or churches, or many other elements of what people normally call religion.[2] Yet quasi religions are religious, since they share some of the qualities as other religions, notably rituals, conversions, central texts, and ideas about saving the individual and the world. There are many examples. Scholar of religion David Chidester has written of the religion of Coca-Cola, which he characterizes as a "global religious mission" and "supreme icon of modernity."[3] More recently, historian Gary Laderman has authored an entire book on American quasi religions such as film, music, and sports. Laderman explains that rather than envisioning religion as isolated in institutionalized forms such as Christianity, Judaism, and Islam, "religion is instead a ubiquitous feature of cultural life, assuming many expressions though tied to and inspired by basic, universal facts of life and fundamental biological phenomena in human experience: suffering and ecstasy, reproduction and aging, family and conflict, health and death."[4] I add eating to Laderman's list.

This essay focuses on two foodways as quasi religions: vegetarianism—encompassing its more rigid variant of veganism—and locavorism. I have based my research on a series of twenty oral histories of vegetarians and locavores that I collected in 2009. During these oral histories, vegetarians and locavores discussed what they eat (and do not eat), why they eat it, and how they came to make these decisions and follow these quasi-religious food practices.

What does it mean to call these foodways quasi religions, and why does it matter? Certainly it replicates what practitioners of these foodways say about their practices, in both the oral histories and popular culture. Perhaps, similar to the theory of religion proposed by theologian Paul Tillich, vegetarians or locavores invest these practices with ultimate concerns and values. Therefore, calling these foodways quasi religions does justice to how their practitioners self-understand and describe their practices. But studying these foodways as quasi religions offers more than merely descriptive value; it offers real analytic traction. If we treat these foodways like religions, we can use the scholarship of religion to understand what happens when people adopt and practice these foodways. Later this essay considers how and why people become vegetarians or locavores, using the sociology of religious conversion to understand these processes. By looking at these foodways as quasi religions, we can begin to understand why vegetarianism and locavorism represent far more than simple food choices for their practitioners; they are ways of life, systems of values, and symbols of meaning.

VEGETARIANISM AS QUASI RELIGION

Vegetarianism is one of the most commonly practiced alternative food-ways in North America and the contemporary West. A survey commissioned by *Vegetarian Times* in 2009 showed that 3 percent of the American population—over nine million people—identified themselves as vegetarian.[5] Vegetarianism possesses strong analogs to religious practice, with its focus on control and purity. Mary Douglas has called attention to the intersection of food, religion, purity, and control in her analysis of pollution and taboos in world religions, explaining that "rituals of purity and impurity create unity in experience."[6] Keeping polluting impurities at bay removes sources of danger and allows groups and cultures to instill order. Vegetarianism, as a practice of excluding polluting foods, functions analogously. Vegetarians establish control over their eating, and therefore their bodies and social situations, by excluding foods deemed impure or inappropriate. This is especially true among vegetarians who oppose the eating of meat on health, aesthetic, or visceral grounds.

Yet vegetarianism functions on multiple levels, and not all vegetarians understand their food practices with reference to the ideas of control, purity, or pollution. Nor do all vegetarians adopt this diet for health reasons. In many cases, a quasi-religious sense of holism characterizes much vegetarian discourse, often combined with an ethics of animal rights or concern for the wellbeing of the earth. Such holistic vegetarianism is equally religious. For example, vegetarianism advocates Sharon Yntema and Christine Beard extol the holism of vegetarian family living, arguing that families that follow a vegetarian foodway innately possess superior ethical characteristics. "Feelings of love, trust, and honesty lie at the very heart of vegetarian families: love of life, and love of each other; trust in the ability of the planet to sustain and feed us, and trust in our ability to feed ourselves; and honesty about the damage we have done to that planet and the other animals and how the solution lies with us and the choices we make every day." While Yntema and Beard do not explicitly denigrate omnivore foodways, their implication is clear: vegetarianism leads to a holistic morality emphasizing love, trust, and honesty. They explicitly link this to what they call a "healthy soul," which they argue vegetarianism instills.[7] The health of the soul and the development of holistic moralities certainly look like what scholars identify as religion, at least in the West.[8]

Other researchers have noted further connections between vegetarianism and religion. Food and nutrition sociologist Alan Beardsworth identifies the root of this in what he calls the life/death paradox of food, namely, "the fact that while eating is an absolute and unavoidable necessity for the maintenance of life, it frequently involves the dissolution of some other organism in the process of being consumed."[9] This gives rise to anxiety, a state that he has found in his study of vegetarianism. Vegetarians, Beardsworth discovered through the interview process, are particularly sensitive to anxiety and perceive the anxiety more acutely. He has also noted that the traditional means by which societies regulate such anxieties—notably mythological, religious, and ritual means—have declined in the modern era. Some people choose to adopt vegetarian foodways as a solution to such anxiety.

Journalist, writer, and ex-vegetarian Alissa Herbaly Coons invokes such a sense of paradox and anxiety in retelling her childhood memory of realizing the nature of meat. "I have carried a deep ambivalence about my place in the food chain since the summer I raised a flock of chickens at age thirteen," she writes. Having named her chicks, Coons experiences a shock when her mother emerges from the freezer with a bag of frozen chicken. She frames this shock in explicitly religious terms: "I underwent a crisis of faith." Coons became vegetarian in response to this crisis of faith. Yet she eventually spurned her youthful adoption of vegetarianism. Coons also describes the reversal of her vegetarian conversion process as cementing itself through cooking chicken stock, inverting the original moment of shock that catalyzed her crisis of faith. "For hours, I boiled the last nutrients out of the chicken, claiming the goodness of its skeleton for myself and for the soups of my future, a small act of faith in my slow reconversion."[10] Religious language predominates in Coon's essay on "converting" to and then "reconverting" back from vegetarianism. Clearly numerous authors, journalists, and individuals refer to their vegetarian practice as something akin to religion. That is because it is in fact akin to religion.

LOCAVORISM AS QUASI RELIGION

Locavorism is a newer foodway than vegetarianism, at least if one judges by the propensity of people to explicitly claim it as a practice. Of course individuals and groups have eaten local food for eons, and local food eating long precedes consuming food that is not produced locally. But intentional locavorism as a phenomenon is quite recent, and only exists within and against the context of the globalized corporate food market. Scholars and participants disagree on the precise origin of the term, but they concur that it arose during the first decade of the twenty-first century as a way to describe a foodway predicated on eating local, sustainably produced foods. Sociologists Jeffrey Haydu and David Kadanoff argue that locavorism is rooted in what Marx would call an alienation from the production of food and the search for what they call "idealized community of face-to-face relations and tradition."[11] Locavorism centers on authenticity and the quest to reestablish authentic eating and social relations in a globalized world. It is primarily a middle- and upper-class attempt to reconnect to the land, a connection that has been severed as a result of the Industrial Revolution and twenty-first-century late capitalism. An effort to root identity, society, and meaning, locavorism possesses obvious religious parallels.

Based on the oral histories I recorded, nearly all its practitioners first encountered the phenomenon through two best-selling books promoting locavorism, Michael Pollan's *The Omnivore's Dilemma* (2006) and Barbara Kingsolver's *Animal, Vegetable, Miracle* (2007). Since those books are the primary means of propagating locavorism, they merit extended consideration.

Pollan frames his subject—what he calls the omnivore's dilemma—as a state of anxiety produced by the human ability, propensity, and need to eat a variety of foods without clear biological guidance. Pollan writes that we mentally construct what scholars of religious studies would call a Manichean or dualistic view of food, or in Pollan's words, "The Good Things to Eat, and The Bad." Our foodways help us decide what belongs where and how we relate to them. For Pollan, the omnivore's dilemma becomes a fundamental cause of anxiety, tension, and bewilderment. Our foodways help us respond to this anxiety. Yet in the United States, with its admixture of immigrant foodways and postindustrial food production scheme, "the lack of a steadying culture of food leaves us especially vulnerable" to a crushing anxiety best met by leaping into a variety of competing food choices. Such examples include vegetarianism, locavorism, organic eating, low-carbohydrate diets, and raw foods.[12]

For Pollan, the solution to such anxiety lies in locavorism. Pollan leads his readers on a literary field trip to a sustainable farm at the center of the locavore movement in central Virginia, Polyface Farm. He uses explicitly religious language to describe this farm, calling it a form of "reformation" akin to the Protestant Reformation, a challenge to the corruption of American industrial foodways. Of the farm's founder Joel Salatin, Pollan declares that "farming is his ministry, and certainly his four hundred or so regular customers hear plenty of preaching." Pollan describes the customers as parishioners and the newsletter as a "jeremiad," a strongly worded critique named for the prophet Jeremiah and usually associated with religious discourse.[13] The religious language is clear, all the more so because the farm's operator uses such religious language as well. Salatin considers his farming a form of ministry, and he invokes Evangelical Christian language as well as rhetoric drawn from political libertarianism and alternative foodway subcultures, creating a bricolage of quasi-religious locavore discourse.[14]

Pollan concludes his book with an explicit description of eating as religion. Having personally collected mushrooms, hunted boar, and grown vegetables in his garden, he creates a meal comprised of foods evocative of specific events, symbols, and teachings. He calls the meal "a wordless way of saying grace . . . a ceremony . . . a thanksgiving or a secular seder, for every item on our plate pointed somewhere else, almost sacramentally, telling a little story about nature or community or even the sacred." In an explicitly Christian turn, Pollan (a nominally secular Jew) calls his meal a sacrament comprised of eating "the body of the world."[15] In identifying it as a seder, he also invokes religious imagery. A Jewish seder utilizes food to symbolize the story of the Passover, just as Pollan's seder uses food to tell the story of his locavorism.

The religious parallels of Pollan's project are obvious. In describing the omnivore's dilemma as a root cause of anxiety and locavorism as a response to such anxiety, Pollan reproduces one of the fundamental approaches to understanding religion. As early as Sigmund Freud, scholars of religion have defined their subject as a response to anxiety and an attempt to overcome the anomie of human life. For Freud, religion allows humanity "to deal by psychical means with our senseless anxiety," offering some sense of relief from overwhelming paralysis.[16] Such psychological theories of religion emphasize religion's role in offering solutions to basic human anxieties, often in the form of divine reassurance. More recently the rational choice school of sociology of religion has taken the same approach, envisioning religion as an exchange that offers "compensators" to assuage the various psychological needs of religious consumers.[17]

Yet Pollan roots his ultimate solution to the anxiety of the omnivore's dilemma not so much in a theology of food but in actual practice; in his case a ritualized meal that he describes as akin to a thanksgiving or seder, two explicit examples of religious food practices. As the foundation of a religious practice, Pollan's locavorism resembles what sociologist and theorist Pierre Bourdieu calls *religious habitus*, "a lasting, generalized and transposable disposition to act and think in conformity with the principles of a (quasi-) systemic view of the world and human existence."[18] Locavorism offers its practitioners a systemic view, in Bourdieu's words, of how one can act and think in relation to the world around them. For Bourdieu, such a habitus hinges on the relation of individuals to capital, which includes social capital, monetary capital, and resource capital. Food, land, agricultural subsidies, grocery stores, and factory farms are all part of this network of capital that locavorism encompasses. As a quasi religion, locavorism offers its practitioners a means to navigate the field through quasi-religious practices.[19]

The second book that most locavores mention as bringing them into the fold is Barbara Kingsolver's *Animal, Vegetable, Miracle*. Despite its title, the book has little to do with religion and invokes the spirituality of eating and quasi-religious practices of eating less than does Pollan's book. Yet the locavorism of Kingsolver's book—a term she uses explicitly— nevertheless represents a quasi-religious relationship with food. In her book, Kingsolver sets out to record a memoir of and commentary on a year of eating locally and sustainably produced food alongside her family and friends. For Kingsolver, this attempt was an exercise in "one good year of food life."[20] The nature and purpose of life, living beings, and the relational networks of life served as central themes in her recounting of the experience, and the creation and destruction of life as part of the food and eating processes represent the "miracle" of the book's title. Food offers communion with the living and dead, and a means of forging connections with the natural world. Kingsolver muses on cooking as a form of remembrance, and the slaughter of food animals as an occasion for serious reflection on the nature of life and death and the morality of killing in order to eat. The religious relevance is clear: locavorism is a way to come to grips with the nature of life and death.

Kingsolver laments that the unsustainable nature of the industrial food project has become a "spiritual error" that steals from future generations in order to provide conspicuous consumption to the current ones. Her use of the rhetoric of spirituality must be read as intentional and situational. She notes that "our culture is not unacquainted with the idea of food as a spiritually loaded commodity," and that it is generally seen as culturally acceptable and legitimate to accept choices by Jews, Muslims, and Buddhists on religious grounds. "Is it such a stretch," she asks, "to make more choices about food based on global consequences of its production and transport?"[21] Here Kingsolver treats eating in a quasi-religious manner in order to harness the legitimacy of religious difference and religious practice, in effect arguing that if one permits Jews to keep kosher or Muslims to follow halal requirements, then one ought to at least take seriously the claims of locavorism.

Kingsolver's locavore project can be subsumed under the notion of fighting what she calls "alimentary alienation." Here Kingsolver tips her hat to Karl Marx, whose idea of alienation undergirds not only economic and social theory but also many approaches to religion as well. Americans have become alienated from our means of food production, and Kingsolver envisions locavorism as a means to alleviate this alienation and restore a cohesive social bond among people, community, animals, and the land. Fostering this web of relationships will create, in Kingsolver's approach, a more sustainable, healthy, and moral world for current and future generations. Such an approach is implicitly religious, and Kingsolver recognizes it. "I feel like a Wiccan," she admits, as she cuts and drains the curds of her homemade cheese.[22]

Like vegetarianism, there are certain resonances between locavorism and religion. Since locavorism is a newer phenomenon—at least in its contemporary formulation—less scholarly work exists on it. Yet whatever else locavorism represents, it certainly functions as a means of investing one's space with sacred meaning, since it ties together ideas of life, death, meaning, and practice with reference to space. Political scientist and food theorist Chad Lavin roots the locavore movement in space as well, specifically spatial anxieties. "In other words," Lavin writes, "local foods is but one symptom of a broader concern with political space, when traditional notions of space would seem to be collapsing." The decline of local autonomy and the nation-state in an age of corporate and imperial growth drives people to seek solace in what Lavin calls the "utopian fantasy of postpolitical reconciliation with neighbors and food."[23] Lavin dismisses locavorism as a retreat from the political and real into fantasy and nostalgia, yet in doing so he misses the profound spiritual meaning that locavorism offers its adherents. Locavorism roots its practitioners in space.

Scholars have long looked to religion as rooting individuals and societies in space. Mircea Eliade and Emile Durkheim wrote of this phenomenon, and Eliade made it central in his work on sacred space.[24] More recently, theorist of religion Thomas A. Tweed calls this property of religion *dwelling* and considers it one of the two fundamental properties of religion (along with crossing). "Dwelling, as I use the term," Tweed writes, "involves three overlapping processes: mapping, building, and inhabiting. . . . In other words, as clusters of dwelling practices, religions orient individuals and groups in time and space, transform the natural world, and allow devotees to inhabit the worlds they construct."[25] This property of religion, that of homemaking, reveals why locavorism functions as such an apt quasi religion. (Tweed would discount it as a true religion, since it lacks supernaturalism.) Locavores invest space and time with meaning and construct understandings of the world that allow them to inhabit meaningful and relational space. Locavores mark some space and spatial practices as good—growing food oneself, buying food from nearby farmers, visiting restaurants that serve local food—and other spaces and spatial practices as bad—convenience stores, the central aisles of grocery stores, buying and eating processed foods—thereby orienting practitioners within a web of meaning. In a Tweedian sense, locavorism is certainly a quasi religion.

FOODWAY CONVERSIONS

Having considered how the practitioners of two contemporary foodways use the language of religion, and how these foodways function in quasi-religious manners, one is left with an obvious question. So what? It is all very interesting that eating looks like religion, and that people describe their food practices as religions, but what is the relevance of this phenomenon? The answer lies in the utility of the tools of religious studies to understand religion as practiced. If food and eating look like religion, then we can study them using the tools of religion. One particular manner in which we can do so is to ask how the idea of *conversion* helps us understand the processes by which people adopt new foodways.

Scholars do not agree on any one theory of religious conversion. In fact, there are several competing theories. Putting aside those that assume particular historical or political contexts (e.g., mass conversions) or extremely unusual psychological conditions (e.g., coercion), scholars still debate why and how people covert. Yet there are two basic approaches to conversion, as sociologist James T. Richardson has argued: passive and active.[26] Passive conversions "happen to you," occurring outside the convert's control. By contrast, active conversions are processes by which the convert seeks and affirms a new identity. These are best understood as two ideal types of theoretical conversions, often combined to one extent or another in actual life. But both help explain how and why people become vegetarians and locavores.

Sociologists John Lofland and Rodney Stark set out the earliest and most classic form of what Richardson calls the passive model of conversion, the "world-saver model." Theorized in their 1965 article, "Becoming a World-Saver: A Theory of Conversion to a Deviant Perspective," Lofland and Stark's model understands conversion as a multistep process beginning with a feeling of "relative deprivation"—anxiety, anomie, or discomfort—followed by an encounter with an outside force (person, book, advertisement, etc.) that results in a new religious affiliation and culminates in a completely motivated convert willing to proselytize on behalf of his or her new beliefs.[27] Key to Lofland and Stark's approach, potential converts not only experience some sense of deprivation, but understand this deprivation in a religious sense and subsequently accept the religious solutions to their perceived problems offered by the outside force.[28] Converts generally describe the process as an inexorable draw toward their new faith.

Something analogous happens among foodway converts who recognize some sense of discomfort present in their lives, understand this discomfort as rooted in their food and eating patterns, and finally encounter people, texts, or movements that inspire them to reject their current foodways and follow new ones. Among the locavores who provided the oral histories, one of the more striking examples of such people is Madeline. Madeline explained that her parents had been overweight all their lives, and before they died, both her mother and father had "lost their digestive systems" from surgeries. Madeline had to feed her parents on a special diet during that time, and as a result she "became really interested in food." Her sister had already adopted a macrobiotic diet, a health diet predicated on Japanese medical and spiritual teachings, and Madeline followed suit. She decided "not to end up like [her] parents, without digestive systems when they died." After experimenting with macrobiotics, Madeline eventually went to culinary school and became a proponent of local healthy food.[29]

Many vegetarians described experiences akin to Madeline's. Among the vegetarians whose oral histories I recorded, Gillian told an equally striking story. "Vegetarianism chose me," she explained. "One night, I ate some fish or pork—I don't remember which one—and for some reason I suddenly felt very ill. I nearly became ill and threw up. And then I gave up meat. I never questioned it." Gillian's conversion is reminiscent of the radical conversion account of Paul (né Saul) in the New Testament, who describes being struck down by the power of God and the Truth of Christianity. For Gillian, the Truth of vegetarianism literally made her ill when she ate meat. When I asked her about any experiences that may have prepared her for this radical disjuncture, she said that she had already read about the horrors of factory farming and the need for responsible eating. Immediately after this incident, Gillian's partner suggested that they become vegetarians. Following her conversion to vegetarianism, Gillian became increasingly involved in the animal rights movement and eventually became a vegan. She described it as "an enlightenment, a waking up."[30] Importantly, she noted that the conversion occurred not because she wanted it to happen but because it happened to her.

Madeline's and Gillian's stories are representative of many other conversion accounts included in the oral histories of locavores and vegetarians. In all such accounts, the person experienced a sense of anxiety and discomfort, what Lofland and Stark call relative deprivation, which culminated in a particular moment of distress. Such turning-point moments are keys to this model of conversion since it is at those points that the perceived anomie leads a person to reexamine his or her religious assumptions (or quasi-religious, in the case of food). The sources of anomie differed—for Madeline, her parents' declining health and deaths, and for Gillian, her discomfort with factory farming that culminated in her nausea-inducing meal—but both experiences instilled in each of them a sense of anxiety and anomie. Both women understood this anomie as rooted in their food choices and framed the discomfort in those terms. Such a distinction is important since had Madeline understood her parents' declining health in some other way, such as bad luck or genetics, or had Gillian framed her illness as the result of a virus or just random chance, neither would have looked to food-based solutions. But having done so, both Madeline and Gillian reexamined their food practices and decided to make changes. Both had already encountered an external authority that offered a foodway solution, namely, Madeline's sister's macrobiotics and Gillian's books about the horrors of factory farming. Finally, both Madeline and Gillian adopted new foodways and became proponents of their newfound approaches.

Several commonalities stretch across these and other similar conversion narratives. Often a moment of crisis preceded the conversion, again akin to the classic Pauline conversion narrative. One vegetarian described a visit to a sausage factory and the vision of dead animals hanging on hooks as directly causing her conversion.[31] A locavore described reading Michael Pollan's *Omnivore's Dilemma* as "an epiphany moment" that drove him to reject mass-produced corporate food.[32] Such converts to locavorism and vegetarianism generally found friends and associates who shared their new foodways and could support them in their endeavors, but not always. One vegetarian described a lifetime of repeated conversions as he became vegetarian when around other vegetarians but then backslid into an omnivore's diet when not supported by others.[33] Another vegetarian, Isabelle, explained that she "would have become vegetarian anyway" but joined a vegetarian eating group because it gave her "significant support" and "sped up" the process.[34]

When I asked these foodway converts if the idea of conversion made sense to them as a means of understanding their trajectories into vegetarianism and locavorism, nearly all of them said that it did. Given the commonalities between their experiences and the typical Pauline view of conversion—based on the description of Paul's conversion in the New Testament—that suffuses Western Christian culture, this is not surprising. After I mentioned the idea of looking at their experiences as conversions, the individuals I spoke with used terms like "born again," "backsliding," "fundamentalist dietary choices," and "self-reflection." While nodding her head, Harriet explained, "That comparison makes sense. It was definitely a conversion moment."[35] Gillian and Madeline also made broader connections to food as a quasi religion, with Madeline explaining that "the spirit comes back into people who start to eat right . . . food and spirit and everything are connected through energy."[36]

How and why is it that people become vegetarians or locavores? For those whose conversions align with what Richardson calls passive conversions, the process occurs because these individuals perceive some degree of tension or cognitive dissonance between their current eating habits and what they think is the correct, better, or true way to eat. They generally experience some sort of turning point, and through an encounter with a person, text, or group come to reexamine their foodway choices. In the most extreme of such examples, the process might be entirely passive. "It happened to me," Gillian told me, in reference to her conversion.[37] In others, a combination of factors lead to the eventual shift from one foodway to another. Yet the theoretical approaches to conversion—approaches that we can use since food can be studied as a quasi religion—nevertheless help explain the process.

ANOTHER MODEL OF FOODWAY CONVERSIONS

By contrast to the world-saver model and its variants, a number of social scientists have developed what Richardson calls active models of conversion, all of which understand conversion as a religious practice that a person undertakes, rather than happening to them. Sociologists of religion Robert W. Balch, James Taylor, David Bromley, and Anson Shupe have all offered various forms of active conversion models. Balch and Taylor's approach highlights seekerhood, or "conversion careers" during which individuals try out different religious approaches.[38] Bromley and Shupe have generally focused on people who make a decision to convert within the context of community.[39] All of them understand individuals as driving their own conversions. They see conversion as an active process during which a person converts himself or herself within a social setting. As such, they look to conversion as a long process that entails give-and-take from both convert and the group into which he or she converts.

One of the best examples of the active model of foodway conversion to locavorism is Jessica. Jessica described her food trajectory as "a long process" beginning with "typical Midwestern" eating practices and culminating several decades later in a locavore practice. After college Jessica sought a job at a living history farm and learned about historical cooking practices, which led her to take another job in museum education teaching about foodways and cooking. Several years after that, she moved to an eclectic southern college town, where she discovered farmers markets and "learned all about local food." Later that decade she relocated to New England, joined a gardening community, and learned about the heirloom-vegetable and seed-saver movements. There Jessica again worked on a living history farm and taught children how to do eighteenth-century hearth cooking. Eventually she moved to North Carolina, where she became interested in rare local breeds of rice, traditional southern foodways, and biodiversity. She also joined the Slow Food movement—an international group focused on local and intentional eating—and attended conferences sponsored by that group. "It just evolved," Jessica explained of her foodway choices. "It is a many layered social side, shared, slow, and [based on] community." In telling her oral history Jessica repeatedly used words like "process," "experiment," and "learning."[40]

Among vegetarians the active model is also strong. Larry described his process as "a philosophical investigation, not an immediate change." Larry became involved in vegetarianism in college, the same time that he also began questioning his religious and political upbringing. He initially considered becoming vegetarian after reading Peter Singer's *Animal Liberation*, which led him to "look more into it, read more and more." Six months later he bought a package of vegetable burgers and "decided that [he] would either become vegetarian if they were good, or live as a hypocrite [if they were bad.]" At first Larry continued to eat fish, but eventually he decided that he should avoid that as well for ethical reasons. More recently Larry had become vegan after reading about "ethical, health, and environmental reasons [to do so]." He explained that "intellectual honesty is important to [him]" and that he "couldn't deal with the unresolved cognitive dissonance" between his readings and practices. Unlike Jessica, Larry avoided food-based groups or communities. "They're too New Age," he explained. "Rationalism is the most important. I would change my mind if presented with a convincing argument."[41]

Both Jessica and Larry exemplify active conversions to these quasi-religious foodways. Both saw their experiences as processes rather than moments and understood themselves as active agents choosing between different options. Larry had obviously analyzed his own experience, offering psychological and intellectual insights about the nature of his choices. His reference to the psychological theory of cognitive dissonance was not unusual. Several locavores and vegetarians also mentioned their experiences as predicated on exploring and resolving their cognitive dissonance, a remarkably self-reflective observation that is less surprising when one notes that all the individuals with whom I talked were college educated, and many had graduate degrees. Both of these quasi religions are most predominant among middle- and upper-class Americans, so awareness of psychological theories is not surprising.

Balch and Taylor emphasized the idea of "seekerhood" in their study of religious conversion, and this description seems apt when applied to the quasi-religious conversions of locavores and vegetarians. One locavore described his experience as "a journey."[42] Another called it "an evolution" spurred on by reading, experimentation with living in an intentional community, and her evolving sociopolitical views.[43] A vegetarian noted that her own ten-year experimentation with veganism and then vegetarianism resulted from her "obsession with purity" that she constantly balanced with "pragmatism and exceptions."[44] The reasons for these converts' seekerhoods varied, but all undertook intentional paths of experimentation, reading, study, cooking, or alternative living arrangements in order to discover what they considered the best foodway for them.

Like the foodway converts who underwent more passive processes, the active converts recognized religious conversion as apropos of their own experiences. (The one exception was a woman who hated religion and anything smacking of religion.) One locavore who had actually converted religions as well as foodways had an "a-ha moment" when I asked her about this possibility. "Oh yeah, it is parallel to my religious conversion! I am a pathfinder in both. . . . It took a long time. I had to experience it. Both conversions took a long time. But you really mean it that way," she explained.[45] A vegan who ran a vegan cooking school even added her own evidence to the idea: "I've seen it happen. People have had conversion moments [in my classes]."[46] Particularly when I explained the theoretical approaches of active conversion processes, these locavores and vegetarians agreed that this was precisely what they had experienced.

Such conversations often elicited broader thoughts on the quasi-religious nature of food. The vegan cooking instructor noted that many of her new converts were "zealots and fundamentalists," but that "faith does not equal facts."[47] A locavore explained that growing and eating local food provided a sense of "ritual" that he imagined "primitive people" found in religion but that "modern primitives" such as himself found in food.[48] Patricia, who had also converted religions, explained that cooking and eating had "become a form of meditation and wisdom."[49] Larry, who frowned on anything nonrational, nevertheless understood food as somewhat religious, since both centered on "strong commitment."[50] Finally, Betsy, a longtime vegetarian, used the idea of food as quasi religion as a way for her to understand her treatment of other people. "This definitely parallels my religious history," she explained. "I'm a [religious] liberal. Don't judge others. Do what you think is right. And I'm a foodway liberal too!"[51]

EXPLAINING FOODWAY CONVERSION

Looking at food as a quasi religion is helpful not only to Betsy and the other people with whom I spoke; it provides real analytic traction to explain how and why people adopt new foodways. Without the theoretical insights provided by the study of religious conversion it is difficult to study how and why people become vegetarians and locavores, but with the help of such approaches, scholars can begin to understand the processes. Becoming a vegetarian or locavore is very much akin to a religious conversion, and this is because vegetarianism and locavorism are very much akin to religion.

This essay began by noting examples of people who call food, foodways, and eating choices their religions. I then asked why this is important, and what it shows. Food as quasi religion demonstrates the way in which eating choices and alternative foodways offer practitioners new ways to root their identities, practices, and choices in systems that appeal to something greater than mere personal choices. Contemporary eaters in the West have become alienated from food, and many experience anxiety because of that alienation. Like religious beliefs, practices, and membership in religious communities, beliefs, practices, and communities based on food help assuage such anxiety and root people in space and society.

DISCUSSION QUESTIONS

1. Do you think that foodways like vegetarianism or locavorism are similar to religions? Why or why not?
2. How do different ways of defining or understanding religion affect our way of looking at food practices as akin to religion?

3. What sort of other food rituals and practices are comparable to religious practices? Why is this so?

4. What other ways are there of understanding conversion, and how might they help you understand people changing between foodways?

NOTES

The author wishes to thank the Wabash Center for Teaching and Learning in Theology and Religion, which provided him with a research fellowship that made this project possible.

1. Shannon Hayes, *Radical Homemakers: Reclaiming Domesticity from a Consumer Culture* (Richmondville, N.Y.: Left to Write Press, 2010), 267.

2. Academics have many ways of defining religion, and by some definitions what I call quasi religions would be real religions. Here I use the terms in the sense of their common everyday usage, the way that people outside of colleges and universities talk about them.

3. David Chidester, *Authentic Fakes: Religion and American Popular Culture* (Berkeley: University of California Press, 2005), 136.

4. Gary Laderman, *Sacred Matters: Celebrity Worship, Sexual Ecstasies, the Living Dead, and Other Signs of Religious Life in the United States* (New York: New Press, 2010), xiv.

5. Vegetarian Resource Group, "How Many Vegetarians Are There?" http://www.vrg.org/press/2009poll.htm.

6. Mary Douglas, *Purity and Danger: An Analysis of Concepts of Pollution and Taboo*, Collected Works ed. (London: Routledge, 1996), 2.

7. Sharon K. Yntema and Christine H. Beard, *New Vegetarian Baby* (Ithaca: McBooks, 2000), 244.

8. There are of course other ways of defining religion. See the conclusion of this chapter for a consideration of how studies such as this one actually challenge our definitions and assumptions about the nature of religion.

9. Alan Beardsworth, "The Management of Food Ambivalence: Erosion and Reconstruction?" in *Eating Agendas: Food and Nutrition as Social Problems*, ed. Donna Maurer and Jeffrey Sobal (New York: Aldine de Gruyter, 1995), 120.

10. Alissa Herbaly Coons, "Tasting the (Animal) Kingdom," in *The Spirit of Food: Thirty-Four Writers on Feasting and Fasting toward God*, ed. Leslie Leyland Fields (Eugene: Wipf & Stock, 2010), 89, 90, 95.

11. Jeffrey Haydu and David Kadanoff, "Political Consumerism, New and Old," paper presented at the American Sociology Association Comparative and

Historical Sociology Section Mini-Conference: Comparing Past and Present, Berkeley, 2009, 21.

12. Michael Pollan, *The Omnivore's Dilemma: A Natural History of Four Meals* (New York: Penguin, 2006), 4–9; also 295–96.

13. Ibid., 240–42.

14. Todd S. Purdum, "High Priest of the Pasture," *New York Times*, May 1, 2005.

15. Pollan, *Omnivore's Dilemma*, 407–8, 411.

16. Sigmund Freud, *Future of an Illusion*, trans. James Strachey (New York: Norton, 1961), 20.

17. Rodney Stark and Rodger Finke, *Acts of Faith: Explaining the Human Side of Religion* (Berkeley: University of California Press, 2000).

18. Pierre Bourdieu, "Legitimation and Structured Interests in Weber's Sociology of Religion," in *Max Weber, Rationality, and Modernity*, ed. Scott Lash and Sam Whimster (London: Allen and Unwin, 1987), 126.

19. "Field" is a technical term for Bourdieu. For more on Bourdieu's approach to religion, see Terry Rey, *Bourdieu on Religion: Imposing Faith and Legitimacy* (London: Equinox, 2007).

20. Barbara Kingsolver, Steven L. Hopp, and Camille Kingsolver, *Animal, Vegetable, Miracle: A Year of Food Life* (New York: HarperCollins, 2007), 347.

21. Ibid., 67–68.

22. Ibid., 131.

23. Chad Lavin, "The Year of Eating Politically," *Theory & Event* 12, no. 2 (2009): 4, 6.

24. Mircea Eliade, *The Sacred and the Profane: The Nature of Religion*, trans. William R. Trask (San Diego: Harcourt Brace, 1959) 20–67; and Emile Durkheim, *The Elementary Forms of Religious Life*, trans. Karen E. Fields (New York: Free Press, 1995), 141–66.

25. Thomas A. Tweed, *Crossing and Dwelling: A Theory of Religion* (Cambridge: Harvard University Press, 2006), 82.

26. James T. Richardson, "The Active vs. Passive Convert: Paradigm Conflict in Conversion/Recruitment Research," *Journal for the Scientific Study of Religion* 24, no. 2 (1985).

27. John Lofland and Rodney Stark, "Becoming a World-Saver: A Theory of Conversion to a Deviant Perspective," *American Sociological Review* 30, no. 6 (1965).

28. John Lofland, ""Becoming a World Saver" Revisited," in *Conversion Careers: In and out of New Religions*, ed. James T. Richardson (Beverly Hills: Sage, 1978), 874.

29. Madeline (pseud.), oral history interview with author, July 20, 2009.

30. Gillian (pseud.), oral history interview with author, July 3, 2009.

31. Harriet (pseud.), oral history interview with author, July 10, 2009.

32. Ronald (pseud.), oral history interview with author, July 25, 2009.

33. Charley (pseud.), oral history interview with author, June 24, 2009.

34. Isabelle (pseud.), oral history interview with author, July 10, 2009.

35. Harriet (pseud.).

36. Madeline (pseud.), Gillian (pseud.).

37. Gillian (pseud.).

38. Robert W. Balch and David Taylor, "Salvation in a UFO," *Psychology Today* 10, no. 5 (1976); and Robert W. Balch and David Taylor, "Seekers and Saucers: The Role of the Cultic Milieu in Joining a UFO Cult," *American Behavioral Scientist* 20, no. 6 (1977).

39. David G. Bromley and Anson D. Shupe, Jr., " 'Just a Few Years Seem Like a Lifetime': A Role Theory Approach to Participation in Religious Movements," in *Research in Social Movements, Conflicts, and Change*, ed. Louis Kriesberg (Greenwich, Conn.: Jai, 1979).

40. Jessica (pseud.), oral history interview with author, July 11, 2009.

41. Larry (pseud.), oral history interview with author, July 20, 2009.

42. Ronald (pseud.).

43. Olivia (pseud.), oral history interview with author, July 23, 2009.

44. Emily (pseud.), oral history interview with author, June 29, 2009.

45. Patricia (pseud.), oral history interview with author, July 23, 2009.

46. Fran (pseud.), oral history interview with author, July 2, 2009.

47. Ibid.

48. Ken (pseud.), oral history interview with author, July 17, 2009.

49. Patricia (pseud.).

50. Larry (pseud.).

51. Betsy (pseud.), oral history interview with author, June 14, 2009.

RECOMMENDED READING

Beardsworth, Alan. *Sociology on the Menu: An Invitation to the Study of Food and Society*. New York: Routledge, 1997.

Grumett, David, and Rachel Muers. *Theology on the Menu: Asceticism, Meat and the Christian Diet*. New York: Routledge, 2010.

Kingsolver, Barbara, Steven L. Hopp, and Camille Kingsolver. *Animal, Vegetable, Miracle: A Year of Food Life*. New York: HarperCollins, 2007.

Pollan, Michael. *The Omnivore's Dilemma: A Natural History of Four Meals*. New York: Penguin, 2006.

SELECTED BIBLIOGRAPHY ON RELIGION AND FOOD

Albala, Kenneth, and Trudy Eden, eds. *Food & Faith in Christian Culture.* New York: Columbia University Press, 2011.

Anderson, Eugene N. *Everyone Eats: Understanding Food and Culture.* New York: New York University Press, 2005.

Avakian, Arlene Voski, and Barbara Haber, eds. *From Betty Crocker to Feminist Food Studies: Critical Perspectives on Women and Food.* Amherst: University of Massachusetts Press, 2005.

Beardsworth, Alan. "The Management of Food Ambivalence: Erosion and Reconstruction?" In *Eating Agendas: Food and Nutrition as Social Problems.* Edited by Donna Maurer and Jeffrey Sobal. New York: Aldine de Gruyter, 1995.

Bell, Rudolph M. *Holy Anorexia.* Chicago: University of Chicago Press, 1985.

Berry, Ryan. *Food for the Gods: Vegetarianism and the World's Religions.* New York: Pythagorean, 1998.

Bierwert, Crisca. *Brushed By Cedar, Living By the River: Coast Salish Figures of Power.* Tucson: University of Arizona Press, 1999.

Bolívar Aróstegui, Natalia. *Afro-Cuban Cuisine: Its Myths and Legends.* Translated by Carmen González Díaz de Villegas. La Habana: Editorial José Martí, 1998.

Bourdieu, Pierre. *Practical Reason: On the Theory of Action.* Translated by Richard Nice. Stanford: Stanford University Press, 1998.

Bower, Anne, ed. *African American Foodways: Explorations of History and Culture*. Urbana: University of Illinois Press, 2007.

——. *Recipes for Reading: Community Cookbooks, Stories, Histories*. Amherst: University of Massachusetts Press, 1997.

Bryan, David. *Cosmos, Chaos, and the Kosher Mentality*. Sheffield, UK: Sheffield Academic Press, 1995.

Bynum, Caroline Walker. *Holy Feast and Holy Fast: The Religious Significance of Food to Medieval Women*. Berkeley: University of California Press, 1987.

Carson, Gerald. *Cornflake Crusade*. London: Gollancz, 1959.

Certeau, Michel de. *The Practice of Everyday Life*. Berkeley: University of California Press, 1984.

Chilton, Bruce. "Eucharist: Surrogate, Metaphor, Sacrament of Sacrifice." In *Sacrifice in Religious Experience*. Edited by A. Baumgarten, 175–88. Boston: Brill, 2002.

Cooper, John. *Eat and Be Satisfied: A Social History of Jewish Food*. Northdale, N.J.: Jason Aronson, 1993.

Counihan, Carole M., ed. *Food in the USA: A Reader*. New York: Routledge, 2002.

Counihan, Carole, and Penny Van Esterik, eds. *Food and Culture: A Reader*. 2nd ed. New York: Routledge, 2008.

Diner, Hasia. *Hungering for America: Italian, Irish, and Jewish Foodways in the Age of Migration*. Cambridge: Harvard University Press, 2001.

Douglas, Mary. "Deciphering a Meal." *Daedalus* 101.1 (Winter 1972): 61–81.

——, ed. *Food in the Social Order: Studies of Food and Festivities in Three American Communities*. New York: Russell Sage Foundation, 1984.

——. *Purity and Danger: An Analysis of the Concepts of Pollution and Taboo*. London: Routledge, 1966.

Douglas, Mary, and Baron Isherwood. *The World of Goods: Towards an Anthropology of Consumption*. London: Routledge, 1996.

Etzioni, Amitai, and Jared Bloom. *We Are What We Celebrate: Understanding Holidays and Rituals*. New York: New York University Press, 2004.

Fick, Gary W. *Food, Farming, and Faith*. Albany: State University of New York Press, 2008.

Finch, Martha. "Food, Taste, and American Religions." *Religion Compass* 4 (2010): 39–50.

Forster, Robert, and Orest A. Ranum, eds. *Food and Drink in History: Selections from the Annales, Économies, Sociétes, Civilisations*, Volume 5. Baltimore: Johns Hopkins University Press, 1979.

Freidenreich, David M. *Foreigners and Their Food: Constructing Otherness in Jewish, Christian, and Islamic Law*. Berkeley: University of California Press, 2011.

Fuller, Robert C. *Religion and Wine: A Cultural History of Wine Drinking in the United States.* Knoxville: University of Tennessee Press, 1996.

Greenspoon, Leonard J., Ronald A. Simkins, and Gerald Shapiro, eds. *Food and Judaism.* Studies in Jewish Civilization. Omaha: Creighton University Press, 2005.

Griffith, R. Marie. "Body Salvation: New Thought, Father Divine, and the Feast of Material Pleasures." *Religion and American Culture* 11 (2001): 119–53.

——. *Born Again Bodies: Flesh and Spirit in American Christianity.* Berkeley: University of California Press, 2004.

——. "Fasting, Dieting, and the Body in American Christianity." In *Perspectives on American Religion and Culture.* Edited by Peter W. Williams, 216–27. Oxford: Blackwell, 1999.

Grumett, David, Luke Bretherton, and Stephen R. Holmes. "Fast Food: A Critical Theological Perspective." *Food, Culture & Society* 14, no. 3 (2011): 375–92.

Grumett, David, and Rachel Muers. *Theology on the Menu: Asceticism, Meat, and the Christian Diet.* London: Routledge, 2010.

Hamilton, Malcolm. "Eating Ethically: 'Spiritual' and 'Quasi-Religious' Aspects of Vegetarianism." *Journal of Contemporary Religion* 15, no. 1 (2000): 65–83.

Hardy, III, Clarence E. "'No Mystery God': Black Religions of the Flesh in Pre-War Urban America." *Church History* 77, no. 1 (2008): 128–50.

Harris, Marvin. *The Sacred Cow and the Abominable Pig: Riddles of Food and Culture.* 2nd ed. New York: Simon and Schuster, 1987.

Harris-Shapiro, Carol. "Bloody Shankbones and Braided Bread: The Food Voice and the Fashioning of American Jewish Identities." *Food & Foodways: History & Culture of Human Nourishment* 14, no. 2 (April 2006): 67–90.

Harrod, Howard. *The Animals Came Dancing: Native American Sacred Ecology and Animal Kinship.* Tucson: University of Arizona Press, 2000.

Heinze, Andrew R., *Adapting to Abundance: Jewish Immigrants, Mass Consumption, and the Search for American Identity.* New York: Columbia University Press, 1990.

Hilbert, Vi. *Haboo: Native American Stories From Puget Sound.* Seattle: University of Washington Press, 2003.

Jha, D. N. *The Myth of the Holy Cow.* London: Verso, 2002.

Jolles, Carol Zane. *Food, Faith, and Family in a Yupik Whaling Community.* Seattle: University of Washington Press, 2002.

Joselit, Jenna Weissman. *The Wonders of America: Reinventing Jewish Culture, 1880–1950.* New York: Hill and Wang, 1994.

Journal of the American Academy of Religion 63 no. 3 (Fall 1995).

Khare, R. S., ed. *The Eternal Food: Gastronomic Ideas and Experiences of Hindus and Buddhists.* Albany: State University of New York Press, 1992.

Khare, R. S., and M. S. A. Rao, eds. *Food, Society, and Culture: Aspects in South Asian Food Systems.* Durham: Carolina Academic Press, 1986.

Kimball, Linda Hoffman, ed. *Saints Well Seasoned: Musings on How Food Nourishes Us: Body, Heart, and Soul.* Salt Lake City: Deseret, 1998.

Kirshenblatt-Gimblett, Barbara. "Kitchen Judaism." In *Getting Comfortable in New York: The American Jewish Home, 1880–1950.* Edited by Susan L. and Jenna Weissman Joselit Braunstein. New York: Jewish Museum, 1990.

Koenig, Leah. "Reaping the Faith." In *Gastronomica: The Journal of Food and Culture* 8, no. 1 (2008): 80–84.

Kraemer, David C. *Jewish Eating and Identity Throughout the Ages.* New York: Routledge, 2008.

Lelwica, Michelle M. *Starving for Salvation: The Spiritual Dimensions of Eating Problems Among American Girls and Women.* New York: Oxford University Press, 1999.

Madden, Etta M., and Martha L. Finch, eds. *Eating in Eden: Food and American Utopias.* Lincoln: University of Nebraska Press, 2006.

Masquelier, Adeline. "Consumption, Prostitution, and Reproduction: The Poetics of Sweetness in Bori." *American Ethnologist* 22, no. 4 (1995): 883–906.

Mintz, Sidney W. *Sweetness and Power: The Place of Sugar in Modern History.* New York: Penguin, 1985.

Muers, Rachel, and David Grumett, eds. *Eating and Believing: Interdisciplinary Perspectives on Vegetarianism and Theology.* London: T&T Clark, 2008.

Murphy, Joseph M., and Mei-Mei Sanford, eds. *Òsun Across the Waters: A Yoruba Goddess in Africa and the Americas.* Bloomington: Indiana University Press, 2001.

Murrell, Nathaniel Samuel. *Afro-Caribbean Religions: An Introduction to Their Historical, Cultural & Sacred Traditions.* Philadelphia: Temple University Press, 2010.

Nelson, Richard. *Make Prayers to the Raven: A Koyukon View of the Northern Forest.* Chicago: University of Chicago Press, 1986.

Nissenbaum, Stephen. *Sex, Diet, and Debility in Jacksonian America: Sylvester Graham and Health Reform.* Westport, Conn.: Greenwood, 1980.

Numbers, Ronald L. *Prophetess of Health: Ellen G. White and the Origins and Seventh-day Adventist Health Reform.* Knoxville: University of Tennessee Press, 1992.

Opie, Frederick Douglass. *Hog & Hominy: Soul Food from Africa to America.* New York: Columbia University Press, 2008.

Pleck, Elizabeth H., *Celebrating the Family: Ethnicity, Consumer Culture, and Family Rituals.* Cambridge: Harvard University Press, 2000.

Powell, Horace B. *The Original Has This Signature—W. K. Kellogg.* Englewood Cliffs, N.J.: Prentice Hall, 1956.

Primiano, Leonard Norman. "Manifestations of the Religious Vernacular: Ambiguity, Power, and Creativity." In *Vernacular Religion in Everyday Life: Expressions of Belief.* Edited by Marion Bowman and Ülo Valk, 382–394. Sheffield, U.K.: Equinox, 2012.

——. "Vernacular Religion and the Search for Method in Religious Folklife." *Western Folklore* 54 (January 1995): 37–56.

Puskar-Pasewicz, Margaret. *Cultural Encyclopedia of Vegetarianism.* Santa Barbara: Greenwood, 2010.

Rapport, Jeremy. "Eating for Unity: Vegetarianism in the Early Unity School of Christianity." *Gastronomica: The Journal of Food and Culture* 9, no. 2 (Spring 2009): 35–44.

"Religious Values Informing Halal Meat Production and the Control and Delivery of Halal Credence Quality." *Agriculture and Human Values* 25 (2008): 41.

Roof, Wade Clark. "Blood in the Barbecue? Food and Faith in the American South." In *God in the Details: American Religion in Popular Culture.* Edited by Eric Michael Mazur and Kate McCarthy, 109–21. New York: Routledge, 2001.

Sack, Daniel. "Food and Eating in American Religious Cultures." In *Perspectives on American Religion and Culture.* Edited by Peter W. Williams, 203–15. Malden, Mass.: Blackwell, 1999.

——. *Whitebread Protestants: Food and Religion in American Culture.* New York: St. Martin's, 2000.

Sakr, A. H. "Dietary Regulations and Food Habits of Muslims." *Journal of the American Dietetic Association* 58 (1971): 123–26.

Salmón, Enrique. *Eating the Landscape: American Indian Stories of Food, Identity and Resilience.* Tucson: University of Arizona Press, 2012.

Shapiro, Dolores J. "Blood, Oil, Honey, and Water: Symbolism in Spirit Possession Sects in Northeastern Brazil." *American Ethnologist* 22, no. 4 (1995): 828–47.

Spivey, Diane M. *The Peppers, Cracklings, and Knots of Wool Cookbook: The Global Migration of African Cuisine.* Albany: State University of New York Press, 1999.

Thursby, Jacqueline S. *Foodways and Folklore: A Handbook.* Westport, Conn.: Greenwood, 2008.

Tinker, George. "Jesus, Corn Mother, and Conquest: Christology and Colonialism." In *Native American Religious Identity: Unforgotten Gods.* Edited by Jace Weaver, 134–54. Maryknoll, N.Y.: Orbis, 1998.

Warde, Alan. *Consumption, Food & Taste: Culinary Antinomies and Commodity Culture.* London: Sage, 1997.

Williams-Forson, Psyche A. *Building Houses Out of Chicken Legs: Black Women, Food, and Power.* Chapel Hill: University of North Carolina Press, 2006.

Wirzba, Norman. *Food and Faith: A Theology of Eating.* New York: Cambridge University Press, 2011.

Witt, Doris. *Black Hunger: Food and the Politics of U.S. Identity.* New York: Oxford University Press, 1999.

Wood, D. "Divine Liturgy." *Gastronomica* 4, no. 1 (2004): 19–24.

Zeller, Benjamin E. "Food & Cooking." In *The Routledge Companion to Religion & Popular Culture.* Edited by John Lyden and Eric Michael Mazur. New York: Routledge (forthcoming).

——. "Food Practices, Culture, and Social Dynamics in the Hare Krishna Movement." In *Handbook of New Religions and Cultural Production.* Edited by Carole M. Cusack and Alex Norman, 681–702. Leiden: Brill, 2012.

CONTRIBUTORS

ANNIE BLAZER is assistant professor of religious studies at the College of William and Mary in Williamsburg, Virginia. Before joining William and Mary, she spent a year on a research fellowship at Princeton University's Center for the Study of Religion where she developed the manuscript for her first book, *Faith on the Field: Sports, Gender, and Evangelicalism in America*. She finished her Ph.D. degree in religion and culture at University of North Carolina at Chapel Hill in 2009 and has taught at Millsaps College in Jackson, Mississippi, and Centenary College in Shreveport, Louisiana.

SUZANNE CRAWFORD O'BRIEN is associate professor of religion and culture at Pacific Lutheran University in Tacoma, Washington, where she teaches courses in Native American religious traditions and religious diversity in North America. Her publications include *Coming Full Circle: Spirituality and Wellness Among Native Communities in the Pacific Northwest* (University of Nebraska Press, 2013), *Religion and Healing in Native America: Pathways for Renewal* (Praeger, 2008), and *Native American Religious Traditions* (Prentice Hall, 2006). She received her B.A. degree from Willamette University, her M.A. degree from Vanderbilt University, and her Ph.D. degree from the University of California, Santa Barbara.

MARIE W. DALLAM is assistant professor of religious studies at the Honors College of the University of Oklahoma. She is the author of *Daddy Grace: A Celebrity Preacher and His House of Prayer* (New York University Press, 2007), and she is currently working on a manuscript about American cowboy churches. Her research interests include new religious movements, race and ethnicity, and the dialectical relationship of religion and American culture.

MARTHA L. FINCH is an associate professor of North American religious history at Missouri State University. She received her Ph.D. degree in religious studies from the University of California, Santa Barbara, and is the author of *Dissenting Bodies: Corporealities in Early New England* (Columbia University Press, 2010) and co-editor with Etta M. Madden of *Eating in Eden: Food and American Utopias* (University of Nebraska Press, 2006). She is currently working on a book manuscript, "Outward Adornment: Plain Dress in American Protestantism."

RACHEL GROSS is a Ph.D. candidate in religion at Princeton University and a dissertation fellow at the John C. Danforth Center on Religion and Politics at Washington University in St. Louis. Her dissertation is a material culture and ethnographic examination of nostalgia for American Jewish communal pasts, including studies of Jewish genealogists, the use of historic synagogues as museums, children's books and dolls, and American Jewish foodways. She received a B.A. degree in Jewish studies and an M.A. degree in religious studies from the University of Virginia.

DAVID GRUMETT is Chancellor's Fellow in Christian Ethics and Practical Theology in the School of Divinity, University of Edinburgh, UK. With Rachel Muers he is author of *Theology on the Menu: Asceticism, Meat and Christian Diet* (Routledge, 2010) and editor of *Eating and Believing: Interdisciplinary Perspectives on Vegetarianism and Theology* (T&T Clark, 2008). His interest in the topic of theology and food is inspired by a passion to retrieve and rearticulate Christian traditions of practice in order to address the pressing social, ecological, political, economic, and cultural questions of present-day life.

DEREK S. HICKS is assistant professor of religion and culture at Wake Forest University's School of Divinity. He is the author of *Reclaiming Spirit in* the *Black Faith Tradition* (Palgrave Macmillan, 2012). In addition, he served as assistant editor of *African American Religious Cultures* (ABC-CLIO Press, 2010) and contributed a chapter to *Blacks and Whites in Christian America: How Racial Discrimination Shapes Religious Convictions* (New York University Press, 2012) with sociologists Michael Emerson and Jason Shelton. His work examines the complexities of race, culture, and identity formation in African American religious life and thought.

KATE HOLBROOK is the Specialist in Women's History in the Church History Department, the Church of Jesus Christ of Latter-day Saints. She was the first recipient of the Eccles Fellowship in Mormon Studies at the University of Utah. She is co-editor of two forthcoming books: *This Labor of Love and Duty* (Church Historians Press) and *Women and Agency in the LDS Church* (University of Utah Press). She also co-edited *Global Values 101: A Short Course* (Beacon Press, 2006). Her dissertation, *Radical Food: Nation of Islam and Latter-day Saint Culinary Ideologies* (Boston University) and analyzes twentieth-century Nation of Islam and LDS foodways through official publications, cookbooks, homemaking manuals, and oral history interviews.

TODD LEVASSEUR is visiting assistant professor at the College of Charleston, South Carolina. He teaches in the Religious Studies Department and the Environmental Studies Program, offering courses on religion and ecology, religion and food, religion and sustainable agriculture, religion and animals, and introduction to environmental studies.

SAMIRA K. MEHTA is a candidate for a Ph.D. degree in American religious cultures in Emory University's Graduate Division of Religion, where she is completing a dissertation tracing the cultural history of Christian/Jewish blended families from 1965 to 2010. Her interests focus on familial religious practices and on religion, gender, and sexuality in the American family. She has received fellowships from Northeastern Consortium for Faculty Diversity Dissertation at Allegheny College and the Sloan Foundation's Center for Myth and Ritual in American Life at Emory University.

REID L. NEILSON is managing director of the Church History Department, The Church of Jesus Christ of Latter-day Saints. He received graduate degrees in American history and business administration at Brigham Young

University and completed his Ph.D. degree in religious studies at the University of North Carolina at Chapel Hill. He is the author of several books, including *Exhibiting Mormonism: The Latter-Day Saints and the 1893 Chicago World's Fair* (Oxford University Press, 2011) and *Early Mormon Missionary Activities in Japan, 1901–1924* (University of Utah Press, 2010). He is also the editor or coeditor of many academic books.

ELIZABETH PÉREZ is assistant professor of religion at Dartmouth College. A historian and ethnographer of Afro-Diasporic religions, she earned her Ph.D. degree at the University of Chicago Divinity School. She is currently preparing a book manuscript based on doctoral research conducted in a predominantly African American community of Afro-Cuban Lucumí, Espiritismo, and Palo Monte practitioners on the South Side of Chicago. Her most recent research project examines the challenges of transgender and transsexual people as religious actors in the contemporary United States.

LEONARD NORMAN PRIMIANO is professor and chair of the Department of Religious Studies and codirector of the Honors Program at Cabrini College, Radnor, Pennsylvania, He is the coproducer and cofounder of *The Father Divine Project* (http://scalar.usc.edu/nehvectors/luers-primiano/index), a multimedia documentary and video podcast about the Peace Mission Movement. Recent research and publications include an analysis of the musical culture of Father Divine's Peace Mission Movement, as well as a study of Roman Catholic ephemeral culture as exemplified by the "holy card." In 2011 he opened an exhibition of votive objects from his own collection at the John D. Calandra Italian American Institute in New York City. The exhibition catalog, *Graces Received: Painted and Metal Ex-Votos from Italy* (2012), contains his essay "Catholiciana Unmoored: Ex-Votos in Catholic Tradition and Their Commercialization as Religious Commodities."

JEREMY RAPPORT is visiting assistant professor of religious studies at the College of Wooster. In addition to his contribution to this volume, he has published a study of vegetarianism in the Unity School of Christianity in *Gastronomica: The Journal of Food and Culture* and the entry on the Seventh-Day Adventists for Oxford University Press's forthcoming second edition of *The Encyclopedia of Food and Drink in America*. His other research and publication focuses on American metaphysical religions, new and alternative religions, and religion and science, including "Corresponding to the Rational World," a study of use of scientific language and rationales in Christian Science and Unity in *Nova Religio: The Journal of New and Alternative Religions.* He is currently preparing a book manuscript based on his doctoral dissertation, "Becoming Unity: The Making of an American Religion."

SARAH E. ROBINSON is a Ph.D. candidate in religion with a concentration in women's studies in religion at Claremont Graduate University in Claremont, California. Her transdisciplinary dissertation combines feminist, ecological, and comparative religious studies methods to examine contemporary sustainable agriculture projects integrated into Muslim, Christian, and Buddhist contexts in the United States. She chairs the Ecology and Religion Section for the American Academy of Religion, Western Region, and previously served as chair for the Women and Religion Section. She has cocreated, cotaught, and assisted courses on globalization, peace, sustainability, transnational and women's studies at Claremont Graduate University; Pacific School of Religion in Berkeley, California; and the University of California, Berkeley. Working with the Oakland Interfaith Gospel Choir in Oakland, California, she has organized interfaith pamels of musicians and religious leaders.

NORA L. RUBEL is associate professor of religion and classics at the University of Rochester in New York, where she teaches a course on Religion and American Foodways, as well as other courses in American Religion. Her first book, *Doubting the Devout: The Ultra-Orthodox in the Jewish American Imagination* (Columbia University Press, 2009), examined the representations of ultra-Orthodox Jews in popular culture. She writes on a wide variety of topics related to religion and ethnicity, particularly in relation to food, and is currently at work on a book about *The Settlement Cook Book* and American Jewish identity.

JEFF WILSON is associate professor of religious studies and East Asian studies at Renison University College, University of Waterloo. He is the author of *Dixie Dharma: Inside a Buddhist Temple in the American South* (University of North Carolina Press, 2012) and *Mourning the Unborn Dead: A*

Buddhist Ritual Comes to America (Oxford University Press, 2009). He was the founding chair of the Buddhism in the West Group at the American Academy of Religion and a member of the 2010–2012 Young Scholars in American Religion program.

BENJAMIN E. ZELLER is assistant professor of religion at Lake Forest College, Illinois. He researches religion in America, focusing on religious currents that are new or alternative, including new religions, the religious engagement with science, and the quasi-religious relationship people have with food. He is author of *Prophets and Protons: New Religious Movements and Science in Late Twentieth-Century America* (New York University Press, 2010) and coeditor the forthcoming *Bloomsbury Companion to New Religious Movements* (Bloomsbury). He founded and served as chair of the Religion, Food, and Eating Seminar of the American Academy of Religion throughout the seminar's five-year tenure. He has also received a Fulbright Scholar Fellowship to study contemporary religion in Finland.

INDEX

abstinence: Christian basis for
vegetarianism, 8, 12; Christian
food abstinence vs. non-Christian
norms, 13, 17–19; food as regulation of sexual desire, 5, 6; as a
matter of choice: 11–13; of meat,
5, 7–9, 11; Mormon rules of, 196;
Nation of Islam's rules of, 203. *See
also* alcohol, abstention of; fasting;
vegetarianism

abundance, 43, 47, 51

acculturation, 96–99, 138, 139; of
African Americans, 137–38, 139,
140–41, 149; of Jewish Americans,
91, 94–96, 103, 106–7, 109

African Americans: and cooking,
135–136, 139, 140–41, 146–48; foodways of, 136–39, 143–45; and the
Peace Mission: 46, 61; and religion,
141, 142–43, 149–50. *See also* black
religion, gumbo; okra; slavery, soul
food

agency, 121, 139–41, 146, 150, 179, 286

alcohol, abstention of, 195, 196, 276,
277

Annie Hall (1977), 234

American culture, 91, 92, 93, 99, 105–8;
cookery and, 96; foodways and, 92

Amish, 9; and interdependence,
125–27; and reciprocity, 122–23;
and respect, 123–25

animals, treatment of, 274, 275, 276,
279, 282–83, 289; industrial factory
farming and, 275, 278, 281, 282;
standards of *halal* slaughter and,
274, 276, 282–83, 292n14

anti-assimiliationism, 14–15. *See also*
assimiliationism

"Bury the Knife in Yonkers" (Nissen), 163

Butterfield, Clare, 279–80, 290n2

candlestick salad, 99, 101

Chanukah (also Hanukkah), 245; candle-lighting in, 235, 240, 245, Chanukah cookies and, 168; and dreidels (*draydels*), 100, 102; and latkes, 104, 158, 159, 242; observance of, 240–43

children: books for, 157, 158, 159; religious education of, 92

Chrismukkah: *Chrismukkah* (cookbook), 156–57, 160–61; chrismukkah.com, 160; invention of, 160–62

Christian holidays. *See* Christmas; Christmas Eve; Easter; Lent

Christian Science, 42, 46

Christianity: dietary practices within, 4; differentiation from other religions, 17–18, 75; distinctive diet and, xxiii, 71, 82–83; distinctive food within, 164–65; environmentalism and, 255, 266–67; family food traditions within, 157–60; fasting, 13–14; food practices within, xviii, xxi, 53, 258, 268, 299; interfaith marriage and, 156–57; "mainstream," 69; progressive interpretations of, 260, 262, 269–70, 271n6; in relation to Islam, 277–78; in relation to Mormon tradition, 197; religious authority in, xxvi, 4; scholarly assessments of food within, xxii; table fellowship within, 267–70; vegetarianism, 5–8,

11–12, 75. *See also* Church of Jesus Christ of Latter-day Saints; Communion; Evangelical Christianity; Mormons; Protestantism; Seventh-day Adventism

Christmas cookies, 165, 167, 168

Christmas: Chanukah and, 242; dinner, in comparison to Communion, 43; family food traditions, 158–60, 164–65, 166–67; and gumbo, 149; practices and a blended religious identity, 163; vegetarianism and, 25

Christmas Eve: dinner, 164, 166, 167; fast, 235

Church of Jesus Christ of Latter-day Saints, 42; differences from Nation of Islam, 197; food practices of, xxviii; similarities to Nation of Islam, 197; welfare program, 204, 207. *See also* Mormons; Word of Wisdom

class. *See* social class

Coast Salish (Native American people), 115–23, 125–27, 129

cognitive dissonance, 306–7

colonialism: in Cuba 176–77, 182, 186–87; of Native Americans, 119

Commentary (magazine), 93, 95, 99

communal meals, 267–70

Communion: compared to Native American salmon practices, 117; and the Eucharist, xx, 7, 14–16; fellowship and, 258; Peace Mission Movement banquets and, 43–44, 47–48, 53–54, 59; Protestant models of, xxi, 258; variations within, xxvi conversion, religious, xxv, xxiv, 294, 295, 303–4, 308; to Buddhism, 215; to Christianity, 73–75, 79; to locavorism, 306–9; to vegetarianism, 297, 305–9

cookbooks: American, 92, 96–97, 110, 206, 207; American Jewish, 92, 97 (*see also* cookbooks, Jewish); children's, xxv, xxvii, 92, 98, 99, 100, 103, 105–9; *Chrismukkah*, 160–62; Christian, xxv, 98, 107; gender and, 96–98, 105; identity and, xxvii, 107; Jewish holidays and, 100, 103, 105, 106–8; juvenile, 98, 100, 106; Mormon, 205, 208; Nation of Islam, 201–3, 205; soul food, 203; as a tool of acculturation, 93, 105–6, 109; as a tool of enculturation, xxvii, 92, 107

cookbooks, Jewish, 97–111, 237, 239, 245; *The American Jewish Cookbook*, 99; *The Art of Jewish Cooking*, 237; *The Complete American-Jewish Cookbook*, 98–99; *Guide for the Jewish Homemaker*, 237–38; *Jewish Festival Cookbook* ,237; *Jewish Holiday Style*, 238; *Jewish Home Beautiful*, 242; *Junior Jewish Cook Book*, 104–6, 108–9; *Kosher by Design*, 245

cookless cookery, 97, 104; Jewish, 92, 94

creativity, kitchen, 98–99

culture: of food, 63, 138–39, 145, 298; and heritage, 160; of Jewish childhood, 95; production of, 144; revival of, 127

curative health treatment, 68–69, 83; and diet, 78, 83; and positive thinking, 82

diet: as curative, 78, 83; as healing atheists, 86n4

diet and health: affects of large meals on, 58; local foods and, 304; macrobiotics, 62; mindfulness, 216, 228–29; positive thinking, 31, 37, 45–48; raw foods, 70–75, 82–85; social class and, 195, 198; soul food, 139, 146; vegetarianism, 23–27, 296

dietary laws. See *halal*; *kosher*; *zabiha*

difference, religious. *See* distinction

displacement, 143–144

distinction: between religion and culture, 93, 156; boundary-making and, 72, 74–75; moral superiority and, 69, 77, 80, 84, 85; rejecting of, 138; religious, xix, xxiv, 69, 85

Divine, Father: banquets of, 43, 49, 52–54, 57–58, 66–67n38; economics of, 47–48, 55; on race, 51–52; theology of, 46–48, 52, 57–58. *See also* Divine, Mother

Divine, Mother, 43, 44, 51–52; banquets of, 52–53, 66–67n38; leadership, 45–46, 52–59; and macrobiotics, 55–59, 61–62; theology of, 44, 61, 62–63. *See also* Divine, Father

Dorrellites, 5–6

Douglas, Mary, xxii, 36–37, 296

draydel salad, 100, 102

Easter, 164, 165, 168, 234, 235

eating as religion, 294–309

eating disorders, 215, 222

Ecological Reformation, 254–255, 270

Eliade, Mircea, xxii–xxiii, 302

94; blended, 163, 166; formation, 141–44; and gumbo, 150; Jewish, 93, 95, 104, 107, 108; as protection, 94; religion and, 142–43; religious and mainstream American, 106–7; synthesis of American and Jewish, 100, 108–9

industrial agriculture, 253, 265, 274–89

industrial food, 299, 301

interfaith families, 155, 157, 159, 160, 161, 162, 166, 167, 168

interfaith marriage, 155, 163, 167

interfaith meals, 239–41

International Peace Mission Movement, 42–44, 51. *See also* Divine, Father; Divine, Mother

Islam: 199, 274–89; belief, 280; discrimination and, 275–76; identity, 281–82; Shi'ites, 277; Sunnis, 277. *See also* halal; Muhammad; Nation of Islam; Qur'an; zabiha

Jardine, Winnifred, 205–7

Jesus Christ, 73, 75, 85–86n1

Jewish children, 91, 94; children's books, 93, 95; children's cookbooks, 103, 128–44

Jewish dietary laws. *See* kosher

Jewish education, 91, 95–96, 100, 104, 109

Jewish food, 99, 164. *See also* draydel salad; kosher; latkes

Jewish holidays. *See* Chanukah; Passover; Purim; Rosh Hashanah; Sukkot; Tu B'Shvat; Yom Kippur

Jordan, Clarence, 256–60, 269–70

Judaism, 234–46; cultural assimilation of children, 92, 107–9; interfaith marriage and, 155–56, 160, 163, 167; "Jewishness" vs. "Judaism," 93; kosher dietary laws (*kashrut*), 97,103–5, 108, 163–64, 166–67, 286; Orthodox Judaism, 236, 244–45; rebranding, 93; religious education, 92; religious heritage, 91

Junior Jewish Cook Book by Aunt Fanny (Scharfstein), 92, 94, 96, 99–103, 105–9

justice, social and environmental, 275, 279–85, 286–88, 289, 290

Kabat-Zinn, Jon, 218–19

kashrut. See kosher

Kellogg, John Harvey and Will Keith, 11–12

Khalifah, Reda Faard, 201–2, 206

Kingsolver, Barbara, 298–301

kinship, 117, 120–21, 125, 128

Koinonia Farm, 254, 259–63, 267–69; founding of, 257; permaculture and, 264–67; race and, 257–9; theology of, 258, 264. *See also* Ecological Reformation; Jordon, Clarence

Koran. *See* Qur'an

kosher, 97, 103, 108, 163, 164, 166, 278, 286, 301; dairy meal, 166, 167; home, 164; meat meal, 166; and shellfish, 163

Kosher by Design (Fishbein), 245

KTAV, 91–92, 93, 99, 104, 108

Laderman, Gary, 295

latkes, 158, 242

Latter-day Saints. *See* Mormons

Lavin, Chad, 301–32

sustainability. *See* environmentalism; farming

Sweet Angel Divine. *See* Divine, Mother

sweet potato pie, 134, 138, 144, 145

sweet potatoes, 195–96, 198, 202, 204, 209

symbolism, food and, 5, 16, 144, 243–44

synagogue/*shul*, attendance of, 235, 236, 240–241

table fellowship, 267–70

taqwa, definition of, 280

Taqwa Eco-food Cooperative, background of, 279–80

Taqʷšəblu (Vi Hilbert), 116–17, 128

Tayyib, 282, 283, 292n22

Thanksgiving, 16, 25, 43, 161, 162, 167, 241–43, 299–300

Theravada Buddhism. *See* Buddhism: Theravada

Thich Nhat Hanh, 218–19

tradition, 157, 159, 160, 161; food and, 162, 164, 165, 166, 167; merged, 161

the Transformer (Coast Salish mythic hero), 121, 125

Tu B'Shvat, 240

tuna noodle casserole, 204–5

tuwaduq, 121

Tweed, Thomas A., xxiii–xiv, 302

Unity School of Christianity: International Peace Mission Movement and, 46, 61; New Thought and, 27, 31–36; origins of, 26–17; theology of, 23, 27; 31–36; vegetarianism, 24–25, 27–28, 30–32, 34–35, 37, 40n23. *See also* Fillmore, Charles; Fillmore, Myrtle

veganism, 68, 72, 79–80; nontheistic, 86, 295

vegetable-based diet, as curative, 73

vegetarianism: anxiety and, 297, 298, 299, 304; and the Bible, 32; Christian, 5–8, 11–12, 75; and Christmas, 25; control and, 296; conversion to, 304–10; holistic thinking within, 296; Islam, 279; Jesus and, 14; Nation of Islam, 202–3; Peace Mission movement, 44, 55, 61; pollution and, 296; scientific support for, 72, 75; Seventh-day Adventists, 23–26, 28–30, 34–35, 36, 38; Shakers, 10; Unity School of Christianity, 26–28, 30–34, 61. *See also* diet and heath: vegetarianism; Unity School of Christianity: vegetarianism

vernacular religion, 46, 61, 63

Vipassana. *See* mindfulness meditation

weight loss, 215, 221–22, 230

welfare program (Latter-day Saint Church program), 204, 207

West Africa, 137, 145, 147

wheat, 206–7

White, Ellen, 12, 28–29, 34, 36, 38

Whole Earth Meats, 276, 278–79, 282, 288, 289

Why Christians Get Sick (Malkmus), 71

Word of Wisdom, 196, 198, 204, 206, 208

Yom Kippur, 235, 236, 237–46

zabiha (also *dhabiha*), 277–279, 291n5, 291n9

Zen. *See* Buddhism: Zen

ARTS AND TRADITIONS OF THE TABLE: PERSPECTIVES ON CULINARY HISTORY

ALBERT SONNENFELD, SERIES EDITOR

Salt: Grain of Life, Pierre Laszlo, translated by Mary Beth Mader

Culture of the Fork, Giovanni Rebora, translated by Albert Sonnenfeld

French Gastronomy: The History and Geography of a Passion, Jean-Robert Pitte, translated by Jody Gladding

Pasta: The Story of a Universal Food, Silvano Serventi and Françoise Sabban, translated by Antony Shugar

Slow Food: The Case for Taste, Carlo Petrini, translated by William McCuaig

Italian Cuisine: A Cultural History, Alberto Capatti and Massimo Montanari, translated by Áine O'Healy

British Food: An Extraordinary Thousand Years of History, Colin Spencer

A Revolution in Eating: How the Quest for Food Shaped America, James E. McWilliams

Sacred Cow, Mad Cow: A History of Food Fears, Madeleine Ferrières, translated by Jody Gladding

Molecular Gastronomy: Exploring the Science of Flavor, Hervé This, translated by M. B. DeBevoise

Food Is Culture, Massimo Montanari, translated by Albert Sonnenfeld

Kitchen Mysteries: Revealing the Science of Cooking, Hervé This, translated by Jody Gladding

Hog and Hominy: Soul Food from Africa to America, Frederick Douglass Opie

Gastropolis: Food and New York City, edited by Annie Hauck-Lawson and Jonathan Deutsch

Building a Meal: From Molecular Gastronomy to Culinary Constructivism, Hervé This, translated by M. B. DeBevoise

Eating History: Thirty Turning Points in the Making of American Cuisine, Andrew F. Smith

The Science of the Oven, Hervé This, translated by Jody Gladding

Pomodoro! A History of the Tomato in Italy, David Gentilcore

Cheese, Pears, and History in a Proverb, Massimo Montanari, translated by Beth Archer Brombert

Food and Faith in Christian Culture, edited by Ken Albala and Trudy Eden

The Kitchen as Laboratory: Reflections on the Science of Food and Cooking, edited by César Vega, Job Ubbink, and Erik van der Linden

Creamy and Crunchy: An Informal History of Peanut Butter, the All-American Food, Jon Krampner

Let the Meatballs Rest: And Other Stories About Food and Culture, Massimo Montanari, translated by Beth Archer Brombert